For a period of thirty years in the mid-nineteenth century James Pennethorne was more intimately involved with the planning and building of London than any other major architect. A pupil of John Nash, he took over his teacher's practice and became government architect for the first half of Victoria's reign. He was responsible for the planning of new streets, the laying out of parks, and the design of important public buildings such as the Public Record Office, the west wing of Somerset House, the ballroom of Buckingham Palace and the first Senate House for the University of London (now the Museum of Mankind). It is therefore almost impossible for Londoners to avoid coming into contact with some aspect of his work.

Pennethorne was one of the leading classical architects of the period, although he has hitherto been generally neglected and undervalued. This study, one of the first in a major new series, throws fresh light on some of the main architectural issues and controversies of the time. Even more important, it contributes to an understanding of the complicated relationship between government and architects, and of the forces which created the London of the nineteenth century and of today. The book therefore makes a contribution to the history of urban planning, and to urban and architectural history in general, in addition to offering an important new assessment of Pennethorne himself.

CAMBRIDGE STUDIES IN THE HISTORY OF ARCHITECTURE

SIR JAMES PENNETHORNE AND
THE MAKING OF VICTORIAN LONDON

CAMBRIDGE STUDIES IN THE HISTORY OF ARCHITECTURE

Edited by

ROBIN MIDDLETON
Professor of Art History, Columbia University

JOSEPH RYKWERT
Paul Philippe Cret Professor of Architecture, University of Philadelphia

and DAVID WATKIN
Lecturer in the History of Art, University of Cambridge, and Fellow of Peterhouse

THIS IS A NEW series of historical studies intended to embrace a wide chronological range, from antiquity to the twentieth century, and to become a natural counterpart to Cambridge Studies in the History of Art. Volumes in the series are meant primarily for professional historians of architecture and their students, but it is also hoped to include a number of volumes for course work or of interest to the general reader.

Titles in the series

French architects and engineers in the Age of Enlightenment
ANTOINE PICON
Translated by MARTIN THOM

Sir James Pennethorne and the making of Victorian London
GEOFFREY TYACK

SIR JAMES PENNETHORNE AND THE MAKING OF VICTORIAN LONDON

GEOFFREY TYACK

Fellow of Rewley House, Oxford

CAMBRIDGE
UNIVERSITY PRESS

Published by the Press Syndicate of the University of Cambridge
The Pitt Building, Trumpington Street, Cambridge CB2 1RP
40 West 20th Street, New York, NY 10011–4211, USA
10 Stamford Road, Oakleigh, Victoria 3166, Australia

First published 1992

Printed in Great Britain at the University Press, Cambridge

A catalogue record for this book is available from the British Library

Library of Congress cataloguing in publication data
Tyack, Geoffrey.
Sir James Pennethorne and the making of Victorian London /
Geoffrey Tyack.
p.   cm. – (Cambridge studies in the history of architecture)
Includes bibliographical references and index.
ISBN 0-521-39434-1
1. Pennethorne, James, Sir, 1801–1871 – Criticism and
interpretation. 2. City planning – England – London – History – 19th
century. 3. Architecture, Victorian – England – London.
4. Architecture – England – London. 5. London (England) – Buildings,
structures, etc. I. Title. II. Series.
NA997.P395793 1992
720'.92–dc20   91–34886 CIP

ISBN 0 521 39434 1 hardback

CONTENTS

ILLUSTRATIONS

COLOUR PLATES

Between pages 178 and 179

BLACK AND WHITE ILLUSTRATIONS

PREFACE

FEW LONDONERS can have avoided coming into contact with the work of Sir James Pennethorne at some stage in their lives. In the layout of new streets and parks in the capital, and in the conception and design of public buildings, his influence is ubiquitous, and he can justly be regarded as one of the men who shaped the London of today. One of my own earliest memories is of being taken to Battersea Park, and later stages of my life have been punctuated with visits to that gloomy yet strangely compelling repository of State documents, the Public Record Office in Chancery Lane. For the mid Victorians Pennethorne was the government architect *par excellence*, the pupil and successor of John Nash and one of the leaders of the architectural profession. His career has never been fully chronicled, and this book has been written in the belief that a study of his life and work will illuminate both the history of nineteenth-century London and, more generally, that of Victorian architecture in Britain as a whole.

Pennethorne's work does not lend itself to many obvious chronological sub-divisions. Except for the first and last two chapters I have therefore treated the subject thematically for the most part, starting in the second chapter with the urban improvement schemes which preoccupied him at the beginning of his official career and proceeding to the various types of building with which he was involved later on; a chapter dealing with his chequered relationships with the politicians is placed between these two sections. A chronological summary of his executed work can be found in Appendix 1 at the end of the book.

No architectural history can be written without incurring several debts of gratitude. I am especially grateful to two of Pennethorne's descendants, Frances Few and Peter Laing, for giving me access to drawings and family papers; to Sir John Summerson for letting me see his notes on other Pennethorne family papers which appear to have vanished since he saw them in the 1930s, and for helping me elucidate Pennethorne's creative relationship with Nash; and to Professor J. Mordaunt Crook for supervising the London University doctoral thesis on which this book is based. I have received assistance from many librarians and archivists and their staffs, notably those at the Public Record Office, the Royal Library and Royal Archives at Windsor, the National Gallery and the British Geological Survey. For permission to consult and quote from the Broadlands Papers (now in the University of Southampton) I am grateful to the Trustees of the Broadlands Archives Trust. Material from the Royal Archives at Windsor Castle is quoted by gracious permission of Her Majesty the Queen. Barry Capper and Teo Reynoso have given me invaluable help with photography, and Wilbur Wright has expertly and painstakingly drawn some of the plans in the book. I am also very grateful to those who have generously taken me around buildings by Pennethorne, allowed me access to buildings or parts of buildings which are not normally seen, supplied me with information, or read parts of the manuscript. They include Sir Geoffrey de Bellaigue, Barry Booth, Graham Haslam, John Hewish, Timothy Lingard, Eileen Myhill, Hedley Pavett, Frank Salmon, Dr Elizabeth Hallam Smith, Robert Thorne, Dr Michael Turner, Christopher Walker, Ken White and Dr Selby Whittingham. My wife not only typed the original version of the manuscript; she has also provided valuable criticism throughout, and deserves the warmest thanks.

ACKNOWLEDGEMENTS FOR PHOTOGRAPHS

Private Collection: I; Crown Copyright: II; British Geological Survey: III, 69, 73; Royal Library, Windsor Castle: IV, 86, 88, 90; Royal Institute of British Architects: V, VI, 26, 57–8, 62, 75, 78–9, 92–4, 115, 121–2, 124; Christie's: 1, 81, 110; Gallery Lingard: 2, 7; Mr Peter Laing, 3, 5, 50–1, 103; Canadian Centre for Architecture/ Centre d'Architecture Canadien: 4, 6, 102, 105; Bodleian Library, Oxford: 8, 23, 36, 45–7, 55, 80, 101; Mr Barry Capper: 9, 12, 59–60, 63, 123, 125; British Museum: 10, 21, 27, 34, 38, 54, 100, 112; Public Record Office: 11, 35, 40, 49, 56, 65, 87, 96, 98, 114, 116, 120; Mr Jeremy Cooper: 14; Miss Joy White: 15; National Monuments Record: 16–18, 33, 52, 61, 66–8, 70, 76, 91, 95, 104, 106, 111, 113, 119, 127; Clarendon Gallery, Ltd: 19, 37, 117; Greater London Record Office and Photograph Library: 24, 29–30, 39, 64, 85; London Borough of Camden Libraries: 25, 28; Royal Borough of Kensington and Chelsea Libraries: 32; London Borough of Tower Hamlets: 41–4; Messrs Batsford, Ltd: 71; Victoria and Albert Museum Picture Library: 72, 83–4; National Gallery: 82; Royal Archives, Windsor Castle: 89, 97; Her Majesty's Stationery Office: 99; The Staff College: 108–9; University of London Archives: 126.

ABBREVIATIONS

BL, Add MS	British Library, Additional Manuscripts
BM	British Museum
BN	*Building News*
Commrs.	Commissioners
Hansard	Hansard's *Parliamentary Debates*
GLRO	Greater London Record Office
ILN	*The Illustrated London News*
King's Works	*History of the King's Works*
NMR	National Monuments Record
PP	*Parliamentary Papers* (House of Commons)
PRO	Public Record Office
PRO, Cres	Public Record Office, Crown Estate papers
PRO, T	Public Record Office, Treasury Papers
PRO, Work	Public Record Office, Office of Works papers
Rep.	Report
RIBA	Royal Institute of British Architects
Sel. Cttee.	Select Committee
V & A	Victoria and Albert Museum

The place of publication of works cited in the footnotes and bibliography is London unless otherwise stated.

1

THE LEGACY OF NASH

LEGENDS ABOUT his alleged royal parentage notwithstanding, James Pennethorne's origins were impeccably conventional.[1] The Pennethorne family probably originated in Wales, and branches later settled in Northamptonshire, Yorkshire, Lincolnshire and in the parish of St Giles-in-the-Fields in London, an area on which James was to leave an indelible mark. James's immediate forbears came from Lincolnshire. His great-grandfather, Thomas Pennethorne, lived in the small market town of Brigg, near the Humber. He was a Roman Catholic, and was said to have disinherited his eldest son, another Thomas (d. 1778), for marrying a Protestant, Ann Walton. She was the daughter of a Staffordshire man who was a schoolfellow of the actor David Garrick and claimed kinship with the seventeenth-century writer Isaak Walton. The couple settled in London, and it was here, in Portpool Lane, Holborn, that James's father, also called Thomas, was born in 1762. He later moved away to Staffordshire, where he married a local girl, Elizabeth Salt of Wolverhampton, before settling in Worcester, where he set up in business as a hop merchant, with a house in the Butts, just outside the line of the old city walls.[2] James, the third of their seven children, was born in 1801 and was baptised in the early eighteenth-century church of St Nicholas at the northern end of the High Street.[3]

It is unlikely that James Pennethorne would have become an architect had it not been for his family's tenuous connection with John Nash's second wife, who, like

---

1 It has often been stated, without any evidence, that he was the illegitimate son of the Prince Regent by the second wife of the architect John Nash. The subject is discussed in J. Summerson, *The Life and Works of John Nash, Architect* (1980), p. 151, and I see no reason to dissent from his conclusion that the allegations seem to have no foundation in fact.

2 Pennethorne family papers, in the possession of Mrs Few; *Universal British Directory*, 4 (1798), p. 862; *Worcester Directory* (1820), p. 56.

3 Worcester County Record Office, x.850 Worcester St Nicholas BA 3790/1b. The other children were Thomas (b. 1798), Ann (b. 1800), Sarah (b. 1803), William (b. 1804), Elizabeth (b. 1805), and John (b. 1808).

them, was descended in the female line from the Waltons of Staffordshire.[4] Nash was aged forty-six at the time of his second marriage in 1794, and had recently established himself in London as a fashionable country-house architect in partnership with the landscape gardener, Humphry Repton. The Repton connection brought him into contact with the Prince Regent (later to become George IV), and from then on he became one of the most successful members of the architectural profession. He and his wife had no children, and in about 1813, after some nineteen years of marriage, he began to take an interest in the Pennethornes with the ultimate intention of passing on to one or other of the children his large and lucrative practice. He was reaching an age when many men today would retire, and in 1821 he told the diarist Joseph Farington that 'if it were not for the King he [would] quit his profession'.[5] The dynastic principle was strongly entrenched in eighteenth- and nineteenth-century English architecture and for Nash the Pennethornes became in effect a substitute family.

For the Pennethorne parents the arrangement was equally beneficial. They were never rich, and must have been glad to be relieved of some of the responsibility of providing for their seven children. The first to benefit from Nash's generosity was their eldest son Thomas, who began visiting Nash's castellated villa at East Cowes in the Isle of Wight in 1813. Nash seems to have intended to give Thomas an architectural education, but he died in 1819 at the age of twenty-one, having shown a precocious talent for drawing (Plate 1).[6] Meanwhile Mrs Nash adopted the oldest daughter, Ann, as a companion, and was, according to Farington, proposing in 1821 to leave her £10,000.[7] Judging from her portrait by Nash's favourite artist Richard Evans, Ann was a vivacious young woman, and her entry into Nash's household must have strengthened the links with the Pennethornes.[8] The Pennethorne parents also began to move up in the world. By the 1820s they were living in a smarter part of Worcester, Foregate Street, where Mrs Pennethorne ran a 'ladies boarding academy', which was taken over by her daughters Elizabeth and Sarah when she died six years after her husband in 1849.[9]

When Thomas Pennethorne died, James took his place as Nash's architectural heir-apparent. He went to school in Worcester and visited the Isle of Wight for the first time in the spring of 1817, when Thomas was 'too unwell to be in London'. In February 1820, after Thomas's death, James became a clerk in Nash's office. Nash was now at the height of his career. His most glamorous patron, the Prince Regent,

---

4 James Pennethorne's great-aunt Mary Gregory (née Walton) was Mrs Nash's grandmother.

5 *The Farington Diary*, ed. J. Greig, VIII (1928), p. 302.

6 His sketches, in five bound volumes were sold at Christie's on 14 June 1983, and subsequently dismembered.

7 *Farington Diary*, VIII, pp. 301–2.

8 T. Davies, *John Nash, the Prince Regent's Architect* (1973), p. 58. The portrait is in the collection of James Pennethorne's great-grandson, Peter Laing.

9 Family papers; M. Billing, *Directory and Gazetteer of Worcestershire* (1855), p. 51.

1. View of Worcester *c.* 1815–18, watercolour by Thomas Pennethorne.

had just become King. He had already designed the Royal Lodge in Windsor Great Park, and had remodelled the Brighton Pavilion and some of the interiors of Carlton House in a manner whose extravagance both enthralled and repelled contemporaries and subsequent critics. Since 1815 he had been one of the three 'attached architects' in the reorganised Office of Works, the body responsible ever since the Middle Ages for public buildings and the royal palaces. Even more important, through his post as Architect in the Office of Woods, Forests and Land Revenues – the government agency which managed the Crown estates – he had become deeply involved in the remodelling of the West End of London. This undertaking dominated his later years, and work on Regent Street and Regent's Park was progressing fast when James Pennethorne entered his office, then still situated at 29, Dover Street, north of Green Park.

Pennethorne spent nearly two years as a clerk with Nash.[10] He acquired some first-hand acquaintance with the day-to-day administration of a large architectural practice, but it is unlikely that he learned very much about designing buildings. As a member of the Prince Regent's set, Nash led an active social life which often took him away from his office, and he also retired occasionally to the Isle of Wight, leaving routine affairs in the hands of his assistants and his managing clerk, William Browne. So, in order to give Pennethorne a more rigorous training, Nash arranged for him to leave his office at the end of 1821 and to learn drawing, then seen as the *sine qua non* of successful architectural design. Pennethorne's training in draughtsmanship took place under Augustus Charles Pugin, an emigré from revolutionary France who had been employed by Nash as a draughtsman and had subsequently become one of the most successful illustrators of his time.[11] While taking commissions in his own right, like that for Ackerman's *Microcosm of London* (1808), Pugin had continued to supply Nash with details of Gothic buildings for use in his country houses, and in 1821 he published some of his own drawings under the title *Specimens of Gothic Architecture*. He also established what was in effect a drawing school with a number of articled pupils, some of whom lived in his house in Bloomsbury under a regime of strict discipline described in some detail by the architect Benjamin Ferrey in his *Recollections of A. W. N. Pugin* (1861). Augustus Welby Pugin, the prophet-to-be of Victorian Gothic, was only nine years old when the 21-year-old James Pennethorne went into his father's office, and his career subsequently developed along lines which could hardly have been more different. But Pennethorne absorbed something of the elder Pugin's meticulous approach to Gothic detailing through his connection with the second volume of *Specimens of Gothic Architecture*, published in 1823.[12] Through his association with this project he visited Oxford, Cambridge and Hampton Court, and it was probably about this time that he made a meticulously detailed plaster model of Salisbury Cathedral which can still be seen in the north transept of the building. Pennethorne's early interest in Gothic architecture was further demonstrated in an atmospheric, almost Turner-esque, watercolour of the ambulatory of Westminster Abbey which was probably painted a few years later (Plate 2). While in Pugin's office, Pennethorne also did a measured drawing of Thomas Hardwick's newly built classical parish church of St Marylebone, just to the south of Regent's Park, which was published in the first volume of *Illustrations of the Public Buildings of London*, in 1825, and in 1823

10 The most reliable sources for his early career are articles in Charles Knight, *English Cyclopedia*, IV (1857), written by Edward Hall in consultation with Pennethorne himself; *RIBA Transactions* (1856–7), Appendix, 3–10; and A. Cates, 'A Biographical Notice of the late Sir James Pennethorne', *RIBA Trans.*, 22 (1871–2), 53–4.

11 Nash paid Pugin £202. 4s. 7d. from 22 Dec. 1821 to 14 Jan. 1823: RIBA, MS NAS/1, f. 49 (Nash's office ledger).

12 There are drawings by Pennethorne in the RIBA drawings collection, 'Gothic Specimens', II, f. 108; III, f. 33. See A. Wedgwood (ed.), *RIBA drawings catalogue: Pugin* (1977), pp. 18–19.

2. The south ambulatory of Westminster Abbey looking towards Henry V's chantry chapel, watercolour by James Pennethorne probably painted during the 1820s or 1830s.

3. Lower Regent Street looking south to Carlton House, watercolour by James Pennethorne. On the extreme left is the house built by Nash as his own residence. Pennethorne lived and worked here from 1823 until 1835.

he exhibited a watercolour of Nash's just-completed Regent Street Quadrant at the Royal Academy, the first evidence of his talent for perspective drawing.

Pennethorne left Pugin's office in the summer of 1823. He was still financially dependent on Nash, and now moved into his magnificent new town house, 14 Regent Street, perhaps the grandest house ever built by an English architect as his own residence (Plate 3). When the Prussian architect Karl Friedrich Schinkel paid a call in June 1826, he noted that Nash

. . . lived like a Prince in Regent Street. Even the flight of stairs was magnificent, the walls panelled with imitated beautiful green porphyry. On the landing stood the model of the Parthenon. The doors fascinated me by their perfect imitations of the most precious kinds of wood. The salon, in which I was received by Mrs Nash, was magnificently decorated in white and gold. There were several gentlemen and ladies present, among others, Mr Vernon Smith, the famous speaker of the opposition in the lower house, who, in Mr Nash's absence, guided us around. In the large hall Raphael's Loggias [painted] on the pilasters are beautifully and truly copied. In the side-niches with a lilac background stand casts of the best ancient sculptures and busts. Below is the library, in which one only sees leather bindings; the walls are panelled with red marble plates. On the tables stand plaster models. The illumination comes through round openings in the ceiling and on the sides from small lanterns. In the other rooms are copies of the best pictures; for example the Danae in Naples by Titian.[13]

It was in these glittering surroundings that Pennethorne produced his first architectural design, for a national monument (Plate 4), which was exhibited at the Royal Academy in 1824. This was one of many flights of fancy spawned by Britain's success in the Napoleonic Wars. The mood of Pennethorne's accomplished drawing is resolutely neo-classical, with Greek Doric columns flanking the entrance to the mausoleum-like structure, an ungainly turret above and a wild landscape in the background. Several European architects, including Nash, produced visionary schemes of this kind in the early nineteenth century, and Pennethorne's design gives an indication of his tastes and aspirations at the start of his career.

By 1824 Pennethorne had reached the age of twenty-three, but his training had still been limited to surveying, draughtsmanship and the lectures at the Royal Academy schools, where Sir John Soane was Professor of Architecture and J. M. W. Turner Professor of Perspective. This kind of training sufficed for many early nineteenth-century architects, as indeed it had for Nash himself, but for most ambitious young men in the years after the Napoleonic Wars it was no substitute for a foreign tour. C. R. Cockerell, thirteen years older than Pennethorne, visited Italy in 1815–17, having already been to Greece, and Charles Barry, who was six years older, broke new ground by visiting both Greece and Egypt as well as Italy. By 1824 both Barry and Cockerell had begun to receive the commissions which laid

---

13 Quoted in *A Documentary History of Art*, ed. E. G. Holt, III (1966), pp. 290–1.

the foundations of their later careers. Nash clearly hoped that Pennethorne's practice would develop on similar lines, and in the autumn of 1824 he sent him to the Continent for two years.

His first destination was Rome, which Pennethorne reached by way of Paris and Bologna on 10 December 1824. On arrival he began an intensive course of study of the chief monuments of classical antiquity. The 1820s were an exciting time for a young architect to visit Rome. Cows still grazed among the broken columns of the Forum as they had done for centuries, but systematic excavation had been begun by the French in 1808. It continued under the supervision of Giuseppe Valadier, who uncovered the hidden bases of the Temples of Vespasian and Castor and Pollux, and restored the Arch of Titus in 1821. Pennethorne's training followed the lines of that given to the young French architects sent to Italy under the Prix de Rome system. Much of the time was spent doing detailed measured drawings and conjectural reconstructions of the recognised monuments of ancient Rome:

The first thing we do is to make a picturesque sketch of a building, shewing exactly its present state and situation with regard to the other buildings, neatly finished in colours, on the spot . . . and while doing this we have time to consider and examine the general mass and proportion . . . [The] next step is to make a drawing of the remains in plain outline, to a very large scale (on the spot), shaded very slightly, but very boldly in Indian ink, to get exactly by eye the details, proportions and bas-reliefs with all the ornaments . . . and after this we shall always, as far as we can, make a restoration of the building . . . [It] must be excellent practice to endeavour to follow the ancients through the whole of their designs, and without doing this it is impossible to have any idea of their grand conceptions, or indeed the mathematical correctness of all their proportions, even to the slightest detail.[14]

Pennethorne wrote up his observations in a series of illustrated notebooks which he sent to Nash (Plate 5). Nash had not been to Rome himself, but he made great use of Roman motifs in his later, more monumental, buildings, and he may have seen Pennethorne's tour as a means of enlarging his own architectural vocabulary. In the notebooks Pennethorne attempted to break new ground by tracing chronologically the history of Roman architecture with copious examples:

When a young man first comes to Rome he is generally filled with preconceived notions that those examples of the Architecture of the Romans generally the most admired & approved of by preceding Architects . . . are the only remains to which he should direct his Studies . . . One of the greatest difficulties I have had to contend with during my stay in Rome has been to free myself of all prejudice & it is for the purpose of an Exercise & to compel myself to make use of my own observation that I have adopted the plan I have – different I believe from what others have done – and that instead of measuring minutely each *celebrated* building I have visited *all the remains*.[15]

---

14 Letter to Nash, quoted in *RIBA Trans.*, 22 (1871–2), 53–4.
15 The notebooks are in the possession of Pennethorne's great-grandson, Peter Laing.

4. Design by James Pennethorne for a national monument commemorating the battles of Trafalgar and Waterloo, exhibited at the Royal Academy in 1824.

The notebooks are valuable as an indication of Pennethorne's emerging taste. He looked at Roman architecture with eyes trained in the aesthetic climate of neo-classicism, believing that architecture had emerged from a state of rude but impressive simplicity to a state of near-perfection in the first century of the Empire, only to sink into increasing decadence and frivolity in later years before reaching its final nadir under Constantine. He admired the Ionic temple of Fortuna Virilis, erected under the Republic, for its 'great Simplicity and Strength', obtained 'by giving great boldness and decision to all the Mouldings, with but scarce any Ornament'. The portico of the Pantheon was 'the perfection of Roman Architecture', possessing 'a *grandeur* which is infinitely beyond the *pleasing*, which is a very different character'. Of the colourful interior he wrote that it must originally have been 'beautiful beyond belief . . . though nobody can be a greater Advocate for the Purity & Simplicity of Architecture than myself . . . I would defend [the use of colour] as always congenial to our feelings, every body being pleased with the appearance of riches'. The beauty of the church of Santa Maria degli Angeli – formerly part of the Baths of Diocletian – came from the fact that 'it has but few parts & those distinct & decided & of such dimensions as to strike you on first entrance with surprise'. But he deplored what he saw as the fussiness, excessive ornamentation and perverse interpretations of classical forms in Nero's 'Golden House', and the details of the vaulted Basilica of Maxentius (then known as the Temple of Peace) were 'not worth a memorandum', the cornice in itself 'a decided proof of decay', with its fascia omitted entirely, and its *cyma reversa* 'sculptured in a way to disgrace even Constantine'.

The supposed superiority of strong and vigorous early styles over what were seen as effete and debased later developments had been a commonplace of architectural thought ever since the dethronement of the Baroque and Rococo in mid-eighteenth-century Europe. This philosophy found its supreme mode of expression in the language of the Greek Revival. For all his admiration of Roman architecture, the young Pennethorne thought that it '*never* could boast of any great purity either in its proportion or details – *not even in the Augustan age* – beautiful as were some of its examples'. In view of these beliefs it is surprising that he never visited Greece. But he did see the, in many ways, better-preserved Greek temples of Paestum and Sicily in the summer of 1826, and a watercolour of the Temple of Concord at Agrigentum survives as a memento of the journey, as does an oil painting showing him saving a fellow-student from drowning in a gale off the Sicilian coast.[16]

Pennethorne's study of the architecture of the ancients implanted an architectural philosophy which remained with him for the rest of his life: a belief in simple, intelligible systems of proportion, a love of bold effects, tempered by rich but 'correct' detailing, a meticulous adherence to the language of the orders. Like many

---

16 In the possession of Peter Laing. The Agrigentum watercolour is in a private collection.

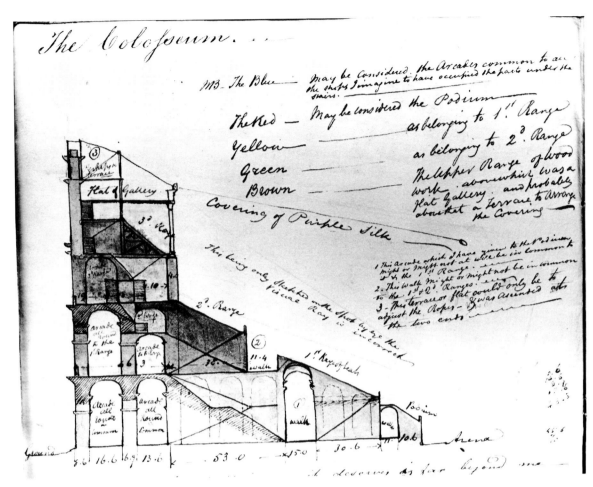

5. Cross-section of the Colosseum from one of the notebooks compiled by James Pennethorne during his stay in Rome from 1824 to 1826.

of his contemporaries, both in Britain and abroad, he believed that it was possible for the nineteenth century to improve in some respects on the architecture of the Greeks and Romans. The Roman aqueducts, for instance, could not 'in any way for one Moment, stand in Competition with our Canals', and even the Pantheon lacked 'a certain effect of greatness . . . Our custom of erecting towers and Domes . . . must be an improvement and had we *same materials* and the same purity in proportion and details our Architecture would now be superior to the Roman'. It was this optimistic, eclectic spirit which informed his own buildings.

The buildings of Renaissance Italy and eighteenth-century France showed how the principles of classical architecture could be adapted to modern needs. Before leaving for Rome Pennethorne met C. R. Cockerell, who advised him to pay 'more attention to the palaces and modern architecture of Italy than to the works of ancient art'. And only nine days after his arrival in Rome, he told Nash that 'the introduction of the Italian style of Palace into our street architecture would be quite new, and have a fine effect'.[17] Unfortunately, though he is known to have visited Florence, Venice and Genoa, few of his comments about Italian Renaissance buildings survive. Of Vignola's Sant' Andrea in the Via Flaminia in Rome he wrote approvingly: 'The architecture is very simple and all parts in good proportion . . . It may be considered a good specimen of Vignola who followed very closely the character of the Ancients & was very plain in all his works'. Santa Maria in Campitelli was 'extremely rich and finely proportioned and nearly if not quite the best of the modern churches of Rome'. But he was predictably unimpressed with the wilder excesses of the Italian Baroque, believing that 'when the detail is bad as is usual with the lavish hand of modern times . . . it is the destruction of every thing good in building and would render the best proportions detestable – and this is why [the Temple of Vespasian] which is in the worst style of the Ancients is still superior to our modern frippery'. His own preference for the architecture of the quattrocento and early cinquecento was to be shown clearly in the facades of his first important public building, the Geological Museum in Piccadilly.

Pennethorne's foreign education concluded with a six months course in draughtsmanship in Paris, starting in the autumn of 1825, from Augustus Pugin's brother-in-law Louis Lafitte, designer of the sculptural panels on Percier and Fontaine's Arc de Triomphe du Carrousel.[18] An album of drawings 'fait chez Mons. Lafitte à Paris 1825–6' provides evidence of his thorough grounding in the Greek and Roman art to be found in the Louvre as well as his continuing interest in the Gothic (Plate 6).[19] And while in Paris, he can hardly have failed to notice the great eighteenth-century buildings of Gabriel, Soufflot and Ledoux or the still uncompleted Napoleonic projects like the new Rue de Rivoli, the Arc de Triomphe and the Madeleine. These not only demonstrated how the architecture of antiquity and Renaissance Italy could be adapted and modified with new materials and technology to create a monumental yet serviceable public architecture appropriate for the modern age; in their settings they also served as contemporary examples of the unified and monumental treatment of grand urban spaces.

The most tangible result of Pennethorne's foreign tour was a conjectural restoration of the Roman Forum – a common enough exercise in the late eighteenth and early nineteenth centuries. The design first emerged in a pen and wash drawing dated 1825 (Plate 7), and was subsequently elaborated in a large watercolour (Colour Plate 1). Here Pennethorne showed himself capable of evoking the architectural 'sublime' with massive buildings dominating tiny groups of people, as in contemporary paintings by Turner and John Martin. The topography is puzzling.

---

17 RIBA, *Trans.* (1856–7), 8; letter formerly in the possession of James Pennethorne of Richmond, transcribed by Sir John Summerson in 1933, but since lost.
18 For Lafitte, see B. Ferrey, *Recollections of A. W. N. Pugin*, p. 31.
19 Canadian Centre for Architecture, Montreal, DR 1985:0024:001–026.

6. Page from an album of drawings made by James Pennethorne in France 1825–6, with two *capricci* of ruins and two drawings of unidentified French buildings.

7. 'Sketch of an idea for the Restoration of the Roman Forum'. A preliminary study, dated 1825, for the large watercolour reproduced as Colour Plate 1.

Archaeological research was beginning to show that the Forum was less spacious than Pennethorne indicated in his drawings, and that some of the buildings did not exist in the form he imagined. But the true subject is the idea of ancient Rome, not ancient Rome as it actually was. For Pennethorne the reconstruction of the Forum was an exercise in architectural experimentation and idealised civic planning. Contemporary architects were putting such ideas into effect in Edinburgh, Berlin and St Petersburg, and in his drawings of the Forum, Pennethorne showed an understanding of monumental architecture in its urban context. His design attracted enough attention in Rome for him to be elected a member of the Academy of St Luke, the oldest of Rome's artistic academies, in April 1826.[20]

At the beginning of 1826 Pennethorne was musing on Imperial Rome. At the end he was back in Nash's office and embroiled in the construction of Imperial London. London in the 1820s was probably the largest city in the world, and was certainly the richest. By 1830 the population had risen to over one and a half million – a fifty per cent increase over thirty years – and was continuing to grow rapidly through migration from the countryside. Continuous building extended from Paddington and Chelsea in the west to Limehouse in the east, and from Islington in the north to Camberwell in the south. The 'Great Wen' represented a formidable concentration of power and wealth. It housed the central Government of the United Kingdom, a state which had recently emerged from the Napoleonic Wars with enhanced international prestige. The banks and financial institutions of the City supplied capital not only for Britain's own phenomenal economic growth, but also for an expanding world-trading empire. The Port of London was the largest in Europe. The West End was the centre of fashion and 'conspicuous consumption' for the whole nation. Shops, theatres and music-halls flourished, and as the wealth of the country increased, London's importance as a resort correspondingly grew.

The end of the Napoleonic Wars brought about a relaxation of credit and led to a spate of building. The first three decades of the nineteenth century saw the construction of the docks to the east of the City – one of the great engineering achievements of the age. There were new public buildings like John Soane's remodelling of the Bank of England, a project nearing completion in the 1820s, and Robert Smirke's British Museum, where work began in 1823. Above all, there was a huge increase in speculative house building in the suburbs, a process memorably recalled by George Cruikshank's cartoon of the 'march of bricks and mortar'. London's housing stock increased by a fifth in the 1820s alone. Alongside this physical expansion came the construction of a new 'infrastructure'. Gas lighting of the streets was introduced in the 1820s, and the length of the sewers increased by a third in the same decade. Two new bridges – Waterloo (1811–17) and Southwark (1814–19) – were built to ease communication with the growing southern suburbs,

---

20 He was elected 'Accademico d'Onore' on 9 April 1826: information from Dr Frank Salmon.

and Old London Bridge was finally replaced by John Rennie's superb new bridge in 1823–31, giving rise to an important programme of street improvements in the City.

These changes were regarded as a matter for patriotic pride. Augustus, said James Elmes, the author of *Metropolitan Improvements* (1829),

. . . made it one of his proudest boasts that he found Rome of brick, and left it of marble. The reign and regency of GEORGE THE FOURTH have scarcely done less, for the vast and increasing Metropolis of the British Empire: by increasing its magnificence and comforts; by forming healthy streets and elegant buildings, instead of pestilential alleys and squalid hovels; by substituting rich and varied architecture and park-like scenery, for paltry cabins and monotonous cow-lairs . . . So rapidly indeed are these improvements taking place around us, that the absence of a few months from London produces revolutions in sites, and alterations in appearances, that are almost miraculous, and cause the denizen to feel himself a stranger in his own city.

'Metropolitan Improvements' were conceived and financed by a bewildering variety of official and private bodies. Then as now there was no single agency responsible for planning London. Within the square mile of the City, the Corporation reigned supreme. Local government elsewhere rested with the parish vestries, some of them efficient, others a byword for corruption and inefficiency. Some major works were carried out by private individuals like the sixth Duke of Bedford, who built the new Covent Garden Market in 1828–30, or by corporate landlords like the Bishops of London who laid out much of Bayswater in the 1830s. Other enterprises depended on private companies, like those which built the docks, or on *ad hoc* bodies, like the many paving commissions set up under private Acts of Parliament. Central government promoted and financed important projects like the British Museum and the General Post Office, some of which involved the clearance of old and run-down buildings and the consequent 'improvement' of an area. The London Building Acts, first passed after the Great Fire, imposed regulations for building, but they did not otherwise interfere with a landlord's right to develop a site as he wished. This lack of central direction served to accentuate the scattered, unfocused character of London, a character already created by history and topography.

The men responsible for carrying out building schemes were equally diverse in their background. Most of London's houses were designed and built by small firms with little capital and few regular employees. Builders were also responsible for the planning and development of the great residential estates of the West End, a process brought to a high pitch of refinement by Thomas Cubitt in the building of Belgravia for the Grosvenor family. Cubitt was a pioneer of the large-scale building firm contracting for all the various trades involved in a major undertaking, and eventually received a knighthood. With the growth in the scale of architectural enterprises and the development of new technology, especially that associated with iron, certain projects like bridges and dock buildings were placed in the hands of civil engineers like John Rennie or Daniel Alexander, the designer of London Docks. But the promoters of most large buildings, and of street improvement schemes with an important architectural component, still sought their designs from architects.

John Nash was more closely involved in the improvement of London than any other architect of his time. In 1811 his plan for laying out Regent's Park and its surroundings was accepted with the Prince Regent's enthusiastic support, and two years later an Act of Parliament was passed for making a new thoroughfare, Regent Street, leading from the park to the Prince's London residence, Carlton House, on the north side of St James's Park. Thus central government became, for the first time, intimately involved in the provision of new streets and open spaces in the metropolis.

When Pennethorne returned from Rome in 1826, Nash's original plans for Regent's Park and Regent Street were nearing completion. Regent Street had been largely built up and the terraces around the Park begun. These projects marked an epoch in the planning of London. A street of almost unprecedented width, lined with gleaming stuccoed buildings, now linked the West End to the rapidly expanding north-western suburbs, broadening out into the first of London's purposely created parks – a significant factor in the provision of open spaces in large cities. Overlooking the park were palatial terraces of houses evoking, through a romantic haze, the buildings of Imperial Rome. It was only at the southern end of the street that much still remained to be done. Regent Street was originally intended to end in a spacious square facing Carlton House, but, soon after becoming King, George IV decided to move his main London residence to the largely eighteenth-century house on the western side of St James's Park formerly occupied by his mother, Queen Charlotte. Nash was asked to enlarge the house, which was henceforth known as Buckingham Palace, and the task almost totally preoccupied him in the last years of his active career. Buckingham Palace made Carlton House superfluous, and under an Act of Parliament of 1826 it was demolished and its site placed in the hands of the Commissioners of Woods and Forests with a view to its being profitably developed for 'Dwelling-houses of the First Class'.[21] Nash was asked to prepare a design for these houses, and in the summer of 1826 the sites in what became known as Carlton House Terrace were being offered to would-be lessees. The houses overlooked St James's Park, which he proceeded to lay out in a fashionably Reptonian manner, with clumps of trees and an irregular lake – a landscape which still survives largely intact (Plate 8).

In 1826 Nash was also asked to finalise plans for linking the southern end of Regent Street to Whitehall and the Strand. This would ease communications

---

21 6th Rep. Commrs. of Woods, Forests, *PP* 1829, 14, p. 12.

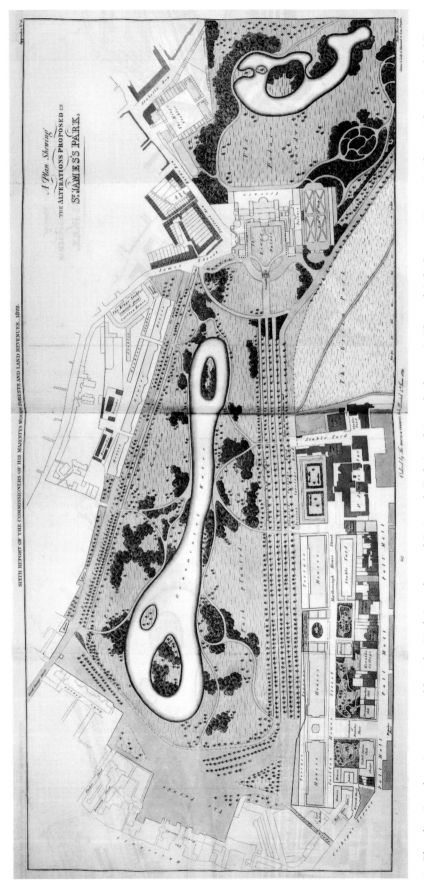

8. Plan showing alterations proposed by John Nash in and around St James's Park (north is at the bottom). The park is laid out on Reptonian lines with an irregular lake, clumps of trees and serpentine paths. To the north, beyond the Mall, lie Carlton House Terrace and another terrace (never built) on the site of Marlborough House, next to St James's Palace. Buckingham Palace stands at the western end of the park, and more terraces are indicated to the south on the site of the Wellington Barracks.

between the West End and the City, creating in the process a new open space on the site of the old King's Mews at Charing Cross.[22] So Trafalgar Square came into being. The plan also involved the redevelopment of a large triangular block of Crown property at the west end of the Strand. The development of Trafalgar Square did not work out precisely as Nash intended, but the 'West Strand Improvement' was carried out along the lines he had proposed, and he himself sketched out the design of the large block of shops and houses with their celebrated 'pepper-pot' turrets facing the Strand, work on which began in 1830.

Pennethorne was intimately involved in carrying out these plans. His training in Rome had given him a mastery of architectural draughtsmanship and an exposure to the principles of classical design. He now acquired a first-hand knowledge of the practicalities of architecture. In 1827 he was negotiating for the purchase of materials for the Marble Arch which was to stand at the entrance to the forecourt of Buckingham Palace,[23] and in the following year he became Nash's 'chief assistant', stepping into the place vacated a few years earlier by the departure of George Stanley Repton, son of the landscape gardener. This role was an important one. In his later years Nash was more the leader of a design team than a meticulous 'art architect' responsible for every detail of the buildings that bore his name. Much of the detailed work was contracted out, or placed in the hands of his office clerks who turned his inventive but often hastily conceived drawings into detailed working plans; in 1828 he spent £1,500 on preparing the drawings for Buckingham Palace alone. As chief assistant Pennethorne must have played some part in coordinating this work, his responsibilities encompassing all of Nash's work except for that on the Palace, where the older architect continued to exercise a close personal supervision.

Pennethorne was especially closely involved with the Strand improvements, the building of Carlton House Terrace and the layout of St James's Park, where he subsequently recorded that he 'set on the ground' the walks and gardens. The work involved negotiating the purchases of property, letting the ground to builders, supervising the elevations of the new buildings and drawing up their leases when completed. It is unlikely that Pennethorne had much say in matters of design. By late 1826 the main elements of the schemes had already been worked out, and in some cases published. Having sent Pennethorne to the Continent for two years at great expense, Nash would have been foolish to have made no use whatsoever of his architectural talents and discoveries. But it would be wrong to see Pennethorne as the 'ghost' behind the older man's later works. Nash was one of those artists whose talents flourished in old age, and it was not until his virtual retirement to the Isle of Wight in 1830 that Pennethorne began to emerge from his shadow.

---

22 5th Rep. Commrs. of Woods, Forests, *PP* 1826, 14 [368], 12 and Appendix 23.

23 2nd Rep. Sel. Cttee. on Windsor Castle and Buckingham Palace, *PP* 1831, 4 [329], pp. 88, 110, 319.

The most impressive of the later works managed by Pennethorne is Carlton House Terrace (Plate 9). Nash produced his final design for the main elevation to St James's Park in April 1827, just after the younger architect had returned from Rome, and in view of his recent travels it is tempting to see his influence in the facade, reminiscent of Gabriel's blocks on the north side of the Place de la Concorde in Paris, but harking back to Perrault's east facade of the Louvre and ultimately to Imperial Rome. Nash said that the Corinthian capitals were to be based on those of the Pantheon, which Pennethorne had recently seen, and it is possible that the meticulous drawings, so different from Nash's usual scrappy efforts, were by him.[24] But it was Nash, the creator of the equally spectacular Cumberland Terrace in Regent's Park, who signed the drawings, and he was still involved in the design of the plaster enrichments to the pediments as late as 1831.[25]

Work on the terrace began in mid 1827 and continued until the autumn of 1830. Internal arrangements were the responsibility of individual lessees, who could choose their own architects. Some of them turned to Nash, and one of his houses, no. 7, was nominally sub-let to Pennethorne, who seems to have introduced the heavy neo-classical chimney pieces which are similar in character to others he designed later in the 1830s. The occupier here was John Hanning, a Somerset landowner and partner in a steam carriage company whose works were in Albany Street, just to the east of Regent's Park; a few years later his son employed Pennethorne to rebuild his Somerset house at Dillington. Pennethorne was also involved with the internal design of no. 11 (later the home of William Ewart Gladstone), signing the drawings and supervising the work himself for the first occupier, Lord Monson.[26] And in October 1831 he was employed at no. 10 by the Northumberland landowner Sir Matthew White Ridley to add a bathroom, which was to be 'similar to the one in Mrs Nash's dressing room',[27] suggesting that here too he may have been responsible for the overall interior decoration, which was swept away in a lavish remodelling by one of Sir Matthew's descendants in 1906.

Pennethorne was also involved in the layout of the areas surrounding the new terraces. His first signed plan, dated 4 August 1828, shows the layout of the public gardens which it was then intended to make between the houses and Pall Mall, together with the internal plans of the houses themselves and the names of each lessee.[28] The open space was eventually appropriated by the Pall Mall clubs, starting with Nash's United Services Club of 1826, and Pennethorne's design for the

---

24 PRO, MPE 891.
25 *Ibid.*, Cres 2/235.
26 Report by Sir John Summerson on the interiors at Carlton House Terrace *c.* 1963: copy deposited in the National Monuments Record.
27 Northumberland Record Office, ZRI 33/3.
28 PRO, MPE 860.

9. The west block of Carlton House Terrace, built to Nash's designs under the supervision of James Pennethorne in 1827–33.

gardens was abandoned. But he supervised the construction of the steps from Waterloo Place to the Mall between the two main terrace blocks on either side of Benjamin Dean Wyatt's Duke of York's column in 1832, and he was also employed by some of the lessees of the houses to arrange the internal fittings in the stable block built at the eastern end of the site in 1830–2. His final involvement with the terrace came much later, in 1862–4, when he was employed by the Commissioners of Woods and Forests to complete the eastern block after the demolition of the former Riding House of Carlton House whose obstinate survival delayed the final realisation of Nash's ambitious scheme.[29]

The 78-year-old Nash finally retired to the Isle of Wight in 1830, leaving Pennethorne in charge of the London office. He took over at an unfortunate time. Public spending had become a major political issue, and concern was reaching new

29 *Ibid.*, Cres 35/1963–4.

heights against the background of social distress and vociferous demands for Parliamentary reform and an end to patronage and corruption. With the death of George IV in the same year, Nash lost the royal patronage which had been vital to his success. He was facing sharp criticism about the rising costs of Buckingham Palace, in which the new King, William IV, refused to live. He had already been questioned by a Commons Select Committee in 1828, and his speculative building schemes on Crown land came under the scrutiny of another in 1829. He emerged from these investigations relatively unscathed, but in 1830, with a new Whig government in power, he was dismissed from his post of attached architect to the Office of Works, and work on Buckingham Palace was suspended. His conduct of the works at the Palace was subjected to the scrutiny of another Select Committee in March 1831, in which Pennethorne gave evidence about the contracts and the purchase of stone. The Committee found that Nash had not used 'proper caution' in framing his estimates, that he had made 'improvident contracts with tradesmen' and that he was altogether guilty of 'inexcusable irregularities and great negligence'.[30] The completion of the Palace was placed in the hands of the safe but much less talented Edward Blore and in 1832 a further reform did away with the system of 'attached architects' altogether.

Nash's reputation did not recover from these blows. The last executed work which can be firmly attributed to him is the parish church at East Cowes in the Isle of Wight, built near his 'Castle' in 1831. But he did not lose interest in architecture, and he continued to keep a firm control over his office accounts. His diary for the year 1832 shows that he spent March, April and May in London at the height of the final Reform Bill crisis, and saw several of the occupants of the houses in Carlton House Terrace. He also inspected the progress of the remaining Metropolitan Improvements and showed a model for a proposed National Gallery in Trafalgar Square to the Prime Minister, Lord Grey, and the First Commissioner of Woods and Forests, Lord Duncannon.

The small quantity of architectural work now remaining was handled by Pennethorne. Entries in his own lost diary for 1832 show him spending a lot of time with Nash and his wife, both in London and on the Isle of Wight, and dealing with Nash's patrons and craftsmen, including Francis Bernasconi, the plasterer responsible for the decoration of the pediments at Carlton House Terrace. He also helped Nash prepare the final accounts for Buckingham Palace, made some drawings for repairing the tower at Killymoon Castle (Co. Tyrone), and was involved in Nash's project for the National Gallery, which was eventually set aside in favour of the present design by William Wilkins – a foretaste of his own long and frustrating involvement with the building. He spent most of Christmas Eve travelling by stage coach from London to Southampton, and on Christmas Day met the artist J. M. W.

---

30 2nd Rep. Sel. Cttee. on Windsor Castle, pp. 3–6, 9–16, 21–3, 37–9, 86–110, 315–19.

Turner on the quay before making a rough crossing to Cowes. The rest of the Christmas holiday was spent in wining and dining, political conversation, visits to Nash's farm at Hamstead, and amateur theatricals like those memorably recalled in a well-known painting by Turner, now in the Tate Gallery, of a candlelit interior in Nash's 'Castle'.[31]

Nash's last new commission of any size was for a 'bazaar', or set of shops, built on Crown property on the corner of St James's Street and King Street in the heart of the fashionable West End. The promoter was William Crockford, a millionaire gambling-club proprietor, 'more machine than man'.[32] His premises at 50–2 St James's Street, recently designed by Benjamin Dean Wyatt, attracted the kind of rich and flashy clientele from which Nash had derived some of his earlier work. Crockford approached Nash first, but Nash delegated the design to Pennethorne, who prepared a set of drawings in June 1830 and was describing himself in 1831 as Crockford's architect.[33] The bazaar, completed in 1832, therefore ranks as Pennethorne's first independent commission (Plate 10). The two-storied stuccoed building had its main elevation to the newly widened King Street, where a Tuscan colonnade gave access to a staircase leading upstairs to a large room 200 feet (60 metres) long – an arrangement more reminiscent of the great auction rooms, like Christie's at the other side of King Street, than of retail establishments today. Outside, the building in its original form was a competent essay in the Nash manner, and Nash may well have provided direct advice in the early stages of the design; he was certainly interested enough in the building to visit it just after its completion in April 1832. There is none of the Italianate flavour introduced by Barry in the nearby Travellers' Club in Pall Mall only two years earlier, and the bazaar – never a commercial success – does not seem to have attracted very much notice, closing after only a year. Since then the building has undergone many alterations.

In 1831 Pennethorne attempted to establish an independent reputation by entering his first competition, for a new Westminster Hospital on a site in Broad Sanctuary opposite the Abbey. In an effort to gain the commission he solicited the help of Sir Matthew White Ridley, explaining that

for the last twelve months I have through the assistance of Mr Nash been in business for myself although I manage his affairs as usual – and am building Mr Crockford's Bazaar in St James's Street & two or three minor works . . . If I can succeed in this work [the Hospital] it will be such an introduction that I shall then be more confidant [sic] of success in my profession hereafter and I am proportionably anxious to obtain it.[34]

---

31 Pennethorne's diary formerly belonged to his grandson, James Pennethorne of Richmond, and was transcribed by Sir John Summerson in 1933 or 1934. I have been unable to trace its present whereabouts.

32 F. Siltzer, *Newmarket: its Sport and Personalities* (1923), pp. 181–2.

33 PRO, Cres 2/647; *Survey of London*, 30 (1960), p. 438.

34 Northumberland Record Office, ZRI 33/3.

But his appeal did not achieve the desired effect, and the commission went to William and Henry Inwood, the architects of St Pancras church, whose Gothic building lasted until 1951. Pennethorne's design, which has been lost, was exhibited at the Royal Academy in 1832. His next attempt to secure a commission for a large public building – the new Shire Hall and assize courts at Worcester – was equally unsuccessful, despite an appeal by Nash to the Bishop in 1832. As Thomas Graham Jackson later wrote in his *Recollections* published by his son in 1950, competitions were for most young architects 'rather opportunities for practising design than openings for employment'. The crucial first commissions usually came from friends, and friends of friends. Pennethorne's early career followed precisely this pattern.

During the summer of 1832 Pennethorne was involved in the completion of Nash's last speculation on Crown property, to the north-east of Regent's Park. The 'Park Villages', with their picturesque villas dotted around a tree-studded landscape, have long been recognised as playing an important part in the development of the middle-class suburb, perhaps the most original contribution of nineteenth-century London to urban civilisation. Nash then prepared his first scheme for the area to the east of Albany Street in 1823 (Plate 11), partly for his own diversion, partly because no one else seemed likely to take the land, which at that time was on the very edge of London.[35] His original proposal showed houses 'scattered about in an irregular manner as Cottages with plantations between'. They were to be arranged along two serpentine 'village roads', one on each side of the branch waterway leading from the Regent's Canal – another Nash speculation – to a commercial basin to the east of the Park. Here a market (the Cumberland Market) grew up, and the surrounding area was gradually developed with squares and terraces of lower-middle-class and artisan housing. The first of the houses in the Park Village were built on the ground to the east of the canal (Park Village East), starting in 1825, and from the beginning they appealed to a prosperous clientele different from that originally envisaged by Nash. Some of the houses may have been designed by Nash himself, but others were delegated to his assistants, among them Charles James Matthews, one of Pennethorne's fellow-pupils at Augustus Pugin's drawing establishment, who went on to become District Surveyor for Bow and Bethnal Green and subsequently a well-known actor.[36] Many of these attractive buildings were demolished when the main line of the London and North Western Railway was widened in 1906, and despite the survival of a few Italianate houses and one large Tudor–Gothic one it is hard now to recapture the original arcadian quality.

On the other side of the canal was Park Village West – in essence no more than a loop road – and here nothing was done until July 1832, when Nash told the

---

35 PRO, Cres 2/778/ MPE 911.
36 PRO, MR 1905/4; RIBA MA NAS/1, ff. 102, 121, 203.

10. St James's Bazaar in its original state, lithograph by L. Tallis *c.* 1848. The main entrance, in King Street, led to a staircase which gave access to the large upstairs room.

Commissioners of Woods and Forests that he was about to enclose the ground.[37] In the following month Pennethorne recorded in his diary that he had 'settled with Nixon [Nash's agent] for two houses in the village', and on another occasion that he had spent an evening sketching 'cottages' there. It seems likely that these ambiguous references relate to the earliest houses in Park Village West, which were

37. MS Diary in possession of Mr Laing; PRO Cres 2/778.

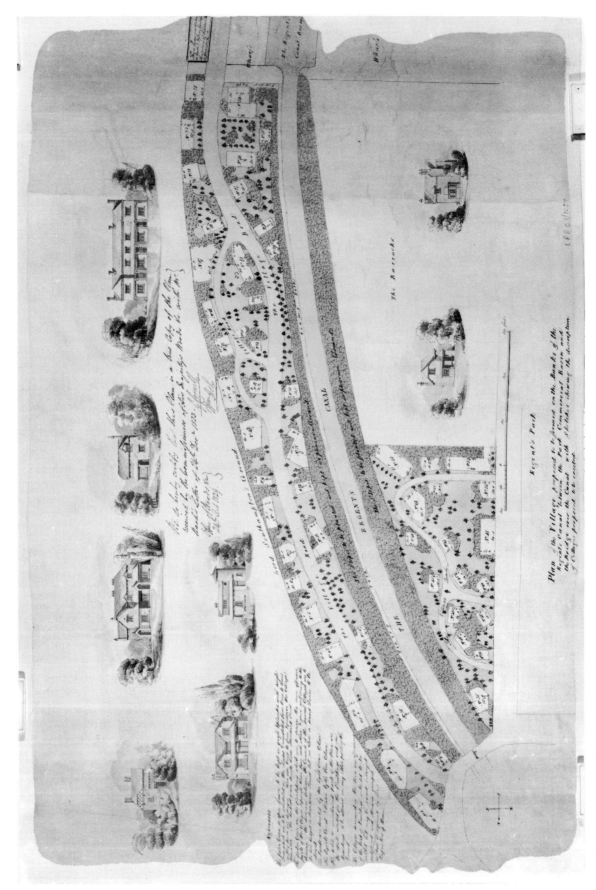

11. The original design for the Park Village by John Nash, 1823. This plan was considerably modified in execution; the alignment of the roads was changed, the 'cottages' redesigned and the open lawns shown by Nash replaced by separate gardens.

ready by September 1832.[38] They consist of a terrace of seven plain stuccoed houses with bay windows (nos. 1–7) which were purchased by a solicitor, Joseph Baxendale, and a pair of larger houses (nos. 18–19) with Tudor details. Nash took a building lease of the rest of the site in November 1833, and a tender for completing the loop road was accepted in March 1834. A fortnight later he gave up his remaining private practice to Pennethorne, although as lessee of the ground he still retained an interest in the development.[39]

The remaining houses were built between 1834 and 1837. All were in the currently popular Italian villa style pioneered by Nash at Cronkhill (Shropshire) over thirty years before. The most interesting of them, no. 12, was built for James Johnson, physician both to Nash and to King William IV, on a plot at the corner of the north side of the loop road. With its porch carried up into a low octagonal tower, it stands out from the run of speculative villas of the time (Plate 12), and it seems likely that special care was taken over its design. From what we know of Nash's methods, that could have meant that he prepared the drawings which could have been worked up by someone else, probably Pennethorne. Equally, the eighty-year-old architect could easily have turned the whole design over to the younger architect, who certainly examined the final lease after the house was finished in July 1834. But conclusive evidence of authorship is lacking, as it is for the last houses in Park Village West (nos. 8, 10–11 and 13–14), which were built on land leased to Johnson and not begun until after Nash's death in 1835. It is conceivable that these houses were built posthumously to Nash's designs, but it seems more likely that they were designed by Pennethorne or by one of Nash's other pupils, like Charles Lee, who had gone into an association with Nash's former partner James Morgan and subsequently became a well-known surveyor. Lee certainly designed no. 8 for Joseph Baxendale, and signed a plan of Park Village East in 1836.[40] In its present form, therefore, Park Village West is the joint responsibility of Nash, Pennethorne, and possibly others too.

While he was engaged on commissions which derived from the Nash office, Pennethorne also began to attract some work in his own right. Soon after Pennethorne designed the St James's Street Bazaar the promoter, William Crockford, asked him to carry out alterations to his house in Newmarket, an important part of his gambling empire. Pennethorne later said that Crockford employed him 'largely' both in London and Newmarket, and that he introduced him to other patrons, including two rather more reputable Newmarket figures, the Marquess of Exeter, 'an old fashioned sportsman of the best school', who had a house in Newmarket now called Foley House, and the Earl of Chesterfield, who 'managed to run through

---

38 PRO, Cres 6/155, pp. 310–12; MR 1905/3.
39 *Ibid.*, Cres 19/16, pp. 43; 19/17, p. 9.
40 *Ibid.*, Cres 19/16, p. 216; 19/17, p. 168; 19/18, p. 165; 19/22, p. 119; MR 1905/2; *The Builder*, 4 Sept. 1880, 301.

a princely fortune, but certainly had some fun for his money'.[41] Little of this work seems to survive. Pennethorne also did some designs for Northwood House, a stuccoed villa at Cowes in the Isle of Wight belonging to George Henry Ward, son of Nash's friend and neighbour George Ward. Pennethorne spent several days at Northwood in August 1832, and a surviving collection of unsigned designs dated September 1832 could well be by him, but work does not seem to have begun until 1835, and it is not clear whether he played any part in the design of the present much-remodelled house (now the headquarters of Medina District Council).[42] Some of the elevations for Northwood are similar to those of a house which is definitely by Pennethorne, Swithland Hall (Leicestershire), built in 1834 for George John Danvers, heir presumptive to the Earl of Lanesborough in the Irish peerage (Plate 13). Danvers wanted 'a mansion more suited to the taste of the age' than the existing gabled manor house, and Pennethorne gave him what was in effect a Palladian villa in Grecian dress, with a series of austerely decorated but well-proportioned rooms and a low three-storied tower surmounted by a pyramid roof on the garden front, like that of the almost contemporary 12 Park Village West.[43]

Pennethorne officially took over the remains of Nash's practice in March 1834. In a letter to the Commissioners of Woods and Forests Nash, now aged eighty-two, stressed that the younger man was 'acquainted with every detail' of Regent's Park, Carlton House Terrace and Buckingham Palace, and he expressed the hope that, as a 'last act of kindness', employment could be found for him in connection with future Metropolitan Improvements, as well as in surveying Crown property in London.[44] Pennethorne had already prepared some plans for continuing and extending Nash's schemes for street improvements in London, and in 1834 he proposed a scheme for building a major new east–west street linking the City with the West End which became a key feature in his later plans for remodelling the streets of central London. He was not given any formal appointment by the Commissioners for another five years, but he took over from Nash the responsibility of reporting on proposed alterations to houses in Regent Street and around Regent's Park. Such survey work formed an important part of the incomes of many nineteenth-century architects, and at the beginning of Pennethorne's independent career it must have been a useful addition to what was proving a somewhat meagre practice.

When Nash retired, Pennethorne moved out of 14 Regent Street, which was

41 Siltzer, *Newmarket*, pp. 87, 233.
42 BL, Add MSS 18157–8; Kent Record Office U.543/E7, 24 August 1835. Designs for the house by Charles Lee and George Mair, a pupil of Decimus Burton also survive.
43 R. Potter, *History and Antiquities of Charnwood Forest* (Leicester, 1842). The house was extended in 1852.
44 PRO, Cres 2/1616; Cres 19/16, pp. 81–2.

12. 12 Park Village West. This striking house, with its Italianate turret and fashionably irregular ground plan, was built in 1834, possibly to James Pennethorne's design and certainly under his supervision. Its first occupant was James Johnson, physician both to John Nash and to King William IV.

sold, and set up his own office at 26 Duke Street, St James's, subsequently moving to 30 Bury Street and then to 2 Queen Square (now Queen Anne's Gate), Westminster, where he was living in 1839.[45] Soon after establishing himself independently of Nash he married Frances, the daughter of Deane John Parker, a Canterbury banker whose elder brother Henry, a tax officer, had married Nash's sister-in-law, Grace Bradley, in 1799. The first of their eight children was born in 1835 and named Deane Parker Pennethorne after his grandfather, to whose Tory principles James Pennethorne referred approvingly[46] – the only record of his political allegiances.

Nash died in 1835, leaving his debt-encumbered property to his widow. She took up residence at the picturesque *cottage ornée* designed by Nash at Hamstead near the Newtown River on the Isle of Wight, overlooking the Solent. After her death in 1851 this house (which has since been demolished) became the home of James Pennethorne's sister Ann and his younger brother John, and the estate has remained in the family ever since. When Nash died, John Pennethorne had just returned from a spell of five years' studying architectural antiquities abroad. Like James, he had spent some time in Nash's office and subsequently visited Italy, Greece and Egypt at his expense. His route in the Levant was dogged by a succession of fevers and eye infections, and he seems to have resented James's attempts to direct him to some of the more obscure sites and monuments, writing to him from Egypt on 15 October 1833: 'What improvement is there for an architect in visiting wretched ruins of antiquity merely because they are antique – where no possible improvement can be derived it is valuable time and money thrown away . . . Almost every antiquity east of Athens excepting the Egyptian temples are [sic] bad.'[47] His real interest lay in the architecture of Ancient Greece. He had become interested in the subtle curvature of the apparently straight lines of the Parthenon in 1832, and while in Egypt made the important discovery that Grecian ornament had Egyptian origins. He visited Greece again in 1834 and 1837, and in 1844 he published a pamphlet on the 'refinements' of Grecian architecture. But by that time a German, Joseph Hoffer, had published his own conclusions on the subject, and as a result John's pamphlet, and his subsequent book on *The Geometry and Optics of Ancient Architecture* (1878), made less of an impact than they might otherwise have done. He never practised as an architect, and eventually settled down to the life of a country gentleman at Hamstead, where he 'took to agricultural pursuits'.

With Nash dead, James Pennethorne had to rely entirely on his own talents as an architect. He was in his mid thirties, but had not yet designed a really important

---

45 *Ibid.*, Cres 19/16, p. 179; PRO, Work 6/92, pp. 6, 11–12.
46 Kent Record Office U543/E7.
47 Two letters from John to James Pennethorne dated 15 and 18 October 1833 and formerly belonging to James Pennethorne of Richmond were transcribed by Sir John Summerson. The whereabouts of the originals is unknown.

13. Swithland Hall, Leicestershire (1834), Pennethorne's only classical country house. The wings were added in 1852 and since then there have been few external alterations.

building, nor evolved a characteristic personal style. The competition for a new Houses of Parliament to replace the old buildings burnt down in 1834 offered him an opportunity to do both. In November 1835 he was busy preparing his designs, though with little hope of success, since there was, in his own words, 'very good ground to believe already that promises of favor [sic] are made & the successful competitor can now be assumed – if not the two next – Barry is *sure* of a premium & expects the building – so at least I am told'.[48] These fears proved justified, and in June 1836 he seconded a resolution prepared by a group of architects convened by C. R. Cockerell, claiming that the choice of Barry's winning design had been made

---

48 Kent Record Office, U543/E7, 20 Nov. 1835.

14. James Pennethorne's design for the Houses of Parliament, made in 1835–6. The drawing shows the building as it would have looked from the river.

without 'due regard to the merits of the others'.[49] This had no effect, and it was Barry who, with the crucial assistance of Augustus Welby Pugin, designed the present magnificent building, work beginning in 1840. Pennethorne's design (Plate 14), like Barry's, was Gothic. In the description of his design, he asserted that Elizabethan – the other stipulated style – was no more than 'Romanized Gothic – a mixture of styles, picturesque, but at variance with all principle, and therefore inadmissible in a national work'. Gothic, on the other hand, was 'perfected in this Country; it is the most congenial [style] to our climate and feelings, and may be considered essentially NATIONAL; in effect it may be rendered equally grand and imposing with Grecian, and in science is perhaps almost equally correct'. His one surviving drawing, a highly accomplished elevation of the river front in pen and ink, shows a rigidly symmetrical facade with an extraordinary central tower and spire more reminiscent of Schinkel's Germanic fantasies than anything in English mediaeval architecture. The design caused little public stir, and one critic said dismissively that it 'might be mistaken for a large foreign cathedral'.[50] It certainly lacks charm, and the disproportionately tall spire, if ever built, would have dwarfed Westminster Abbey. But the drawing conveys a sense of the architectural 'sublime' which most Gothic public buildings of this period lacked, and it is this feeling of awesome power which Pennethorne later recaptured in the other great Gothic public building of early Victorian London, the Public Record Office.

Pennethorne's failure to secure the Houses of Parliament meant that he was forced back onto country-house work. His later houses were all designed in variants of the Tudor–Gothic or 'Jacobethan' styles which had been popular both with Nash's clients and with those of younger architects like Burn, Salvin and Blore. In 1836–7 he was asked by the financial expert John Charles Herries, financial secretary to the Treasury from 1823 to 1827 and chancellor of the exchequer in Lord Goderich's short-lived ministry in 1828, to carry out minor alterations to St Juliens, near Sevenoaks (Kent), a relatively small rectory-like house built in 1818–20 to the designs of John Buonarotti Papworth.[51] Herries had a London house in Carlton Gardens, to the west of Carlton House Terrace and was godfather to one of Pennethorne's children; the alterations at St Juliens involved the building of a carriage porch and a conservatory and the remodelling of the south front in the Jacobean manner. At about the same time Pennethorne also did some work at Lamorbey Park near Sidcup (Kent) for John Malcolm, and he may have been

---

49 *Catalogue of the Designs offered for the New Houses of Parliament* (1836), p. 15; M. H. Port (ed.), *The Houses of Parliament* (New Haven and London, 1976), pp. 21–5, 30–2, 50–1.
50 *Architectural Magazine*, 3 (1836), 201–2.
51 There is an illustration in C. Greenwood, *Epitome of Country History*, 1 (1838), p. 97.

responsible for giving this eighteenth-century brick house its present neo-Jacobean character.[52]

Pennethorne's largest country house was Dillington, near Ilminster (Somerset). The patron here was John Lee Lee, the son of William Hanning, whose London house, 7 Carlton House Terrace, had recently been completed. Lee inherited the Dillington estate in 1834, and in the same year he made an advantageous marriage to the daughter of John Nash's friend, neighbour and business associate, John Edwards. Her connection with the Nash circle made Pennethorne a natural choice as architect, and work began in about 1837.[53] This amounted to a 'creative restoration' of the existing early sixteenth-century building (Plate 15). Dillington had been extensively altered over the centuries, and Pennethorne gave it a homogeneous character based on the earliest work, as Nash had done at Parnham (Dorset) in 1807–11, while at the same time creating more space for reception rooms and guest bedrooms by doubling the width of the main hall range and adding a new south wing. His classical sympathies are evident in the complete symmetry of the façade and gardens, but the external detailing is correct, and the use of the local Ham Hill stone enables the house to blend in well with its surroundings.

At about the same time as these houses, Pennethorne also designed his first church, a 'chapel' built by John Malcolm of Lamorbey to serve the inhabitants of the hamlet of Halfway Street in the parish of Sidcup. A tall single-cell brick building in the conventional Tudor–Gothic style of the Commissioners' churches, it was lit by Perpendicular windows and crowned by an impressive array of crocketed pinnacles. The pre-ecclesiological interior, with its profusion of poppy-headed bench ends, did not satisfy the liturgical tastes of the next generation, and the building was demolished in 1873.[54] Late in 1835 Pennethorne was also working on the design of some churches for New South Wales, Australia, but there is no indication of whether they were ever built.[55] He had a better opportunity to develop his skills in the design of two London churches, Christ Church, Albany Street (1836–7), and Holy Trinity, Gray's Inn Road (1837–8). These were the first of his executed buildings to give any real indication of his abilities.

Christ Church (Plate 16) was built to serve the largely artisan district laid out by Nash to the south of the 'Park Village', close to the Regent's Canal basin. Its southern neighbour was Nash's Ophthalmic Hospital, a building of unusual severity for that ebullient architect. The church was sponsored by a group of lay-

---

52 None of Pennethorne's drawings for the house survive, and B. N. Nunns, the writer of some notes on the house and estate prepared by the Local Studies Libraries of the London Borough of Bexley, suggests that the remodelling might be the work of John Shaw, the architect of St Dunstan-in-the-West, Fleet Street, who is known to have worked at Lamorbey in 1812, or his son, another John Shaw.

53 A. W. Vivian-Neal, *Notes on Dillington* (n.d.).

54 There are photographs of the church in the National Monuments Record.

55 Kent Record Office, U543/E7.

15. Dillington House, Somerset (*c.* 1837). The left-hand wing and much of the main block survive from the earlier Elizabethan or Jacobean house, but Pennethorne doubled its width, tidied up the elevations, added the conservatory and designed the formal gardens which still largely survive.

men and built for only £6,000 with the help of donations from a new fund sponsored by Charles Blomfield, Bishop of London, for building churches in the poorer districts of the metropolis in order to 'reclaim hundreds and thousands of the poor from practical heathenism, and to give increased efficiency and therefore stability to the church'.[56] The first incumbent, William Dodsworth, was a Tractarian who had been the incumbent of the Margaret Chapel in Margaret Street, and later followed the well-trodden path to Rome. He was a member of the Ecclesiological Society, which held some of its meetings in the adjoining school, designed by Pennethorne. But in its original form the church bore no signs of the principles espoused by that energetic and single-minded body. It is not even correctly orientated, and the altar faces north. The interior, like Nash's All Souls, Langham Place, consists of a large, regular rectangular room divided up by blocks of pews, with galleries around three sides and no structural chancel (Plate 17) – the very antithesis of the Camdenian ideal. At first it must have been austere, but in 1845

---

56 B. F. L. Clarke, *Parish Churches of London* (1966), pp. 5, 140.

the *Ecclesiologist* remarked approvingly that 'the worthy incumbent of this church has given it a more ecclesiastical character, by removing an organ and vestry which stood behind the altar, and thereby providing a chancel of inappropriate depth indeed compared with ancient ones, but still a chancel'.[57] A succession of alterations by William Butterfield gradually made it even more appropriate for high-church worship, and in time the windows were filled with stained glass, including a panel by Dante Gabriel Rossetti, whose family worshipped there.

The main interest of Christ Church, Albany Street lies in the uncompromisingly classical exterior, an austere essay in classical abstraction drawing on Grecian sources. By the late 1830s the Church of England had largely turned away from classicism in church design, and ecclesiology was about to sound its death-knell; the church therefore stands at the very end of a tradition of Anglican building going back to Wren.[58] The need to keep costs down must have influenced the choice of material, yellow brick, and also perhaps the decision to leave out the portico found in many of the classical churches built since 1815. In his Roman notebooks Pennethorne had deplored the practice of tacking porticoes onto buildings without integrating them into the overall design; here he dispensed with a portico altogether. Visually, the building is held together by Doric pilasters or *antae*, under a heavy entablature broken up by circular roundels along the frieze. The four corners are carried up into pylons or low towers, appearing to anchor the building to the ground, and each containing a tall doorway with canted jambs in the Grecian manner. There is a similar doorway in the south or entrance front, contained within an outsize Doric frame or *aedicule*, above which the surprisingly slim tower and spire – modelled on the upper stages of Wren's St Mary-le-Bow – rise above the council flats which have replaced the original brick houses built by Nash.

Holy Trinity, Gray's Inn Road (Plate 18) was begun in 1837, the year that Christ Church was consecrated. Like Christ Church, it served part of the ancient parish of St Pancras, and cheapness was once again an important consideration. Gray's Inn Road ran through an area of early-nineteenth-century artisan and middle-class housing, some of which was developed by Thomas Cubitt as one of his first speculations. The church stood on a former burial-ground belonging to St Andrew's, Holborn and some of the money came from the Incorporated Church Building Fund.[59] Holy Trinity was smaller, though more expensive, than Christ Church, and there were no galleries inside. There was only one important facade, with a low tower surmounted by a dome, a massive pedimented aedicule containing a semi-circular tympanum within a bold relieving arch over the main doorway, and Trinitarian symbols – triangles in circles – over the side entrances. As in

---

57 *The Ecclesiologist*, 4 (1845), 54.

58 See, though, St John, Clapham Road, by T. Marsh Nelson (1840), and St Peter, North Kensington, by Thomas Allom (1855).

59 C. E. Lee, *St Pancras Church and Parish* (1955), p. 51.

16. Christ Church, Albany Street from the south-west. The corner of John Nash's Ophthalmic Hospital can be seen on the extreme right of the picture and Pennethorne's parochial school can be glimpsed to the left; these buildings, along with most of the terraced houses which lined the street, were swept away in the 1960s.

17. The interior of Christ Church, Albany Street. Pennethorne would have found it hard to recognise the church after a series of alterations which culminated in the decoration of the chancel in the early Renaissance taste in the late nineteenth century; the pulpit is by William Butterfield, the windows are filled with stained glass and there is a copy of Raphael's 'Transfiguration' over the altar. Only the ceiling, the galleries and the pilasters on either side of the chancel arch are by Pennethorne.

18. Holy Trinity, Gray's Inn Road, the west front shortly before demolition.

Hawksmoor's churches, the effect was one of solemn gravity, and the church was praised for its 'originality, as well as consistency of style and character – and so far is greatly preferable to those mawkish pseudo-Grecian structures, compounded of portico and meeting-houses stuck together'.[60]

In 1838, with Holy Trinity just completed, Pennethorne appeared before a Commons Select Committee on Metropolitan Improvements and submitted his plan for a new east–west street linking the City and the West End. In the same year the old Royal Exchange, which stood on one of the most prominent sites in the very heart of the City, burnt down. The new building was to be funded by the Government out of a tax on coal coming into the City, and the owners of the site, the Gresham Trustees, decided to hold an open competition like that for the Houses of Parliament. Pennethorne entered, and his design was placed fifth among those which the accessors thought buildable within the £150,000 cost limit.[61] His scheme (Plate 19) – an essay in the style of the early Roman Empire which he had so admired in Italy – marks his debut as a designer of monumental classical public buildings. The building was to surround a rectangular courtyard but the dominant feature, as seen from the west, would have been a deep Corinthian portico surmounted by a low pediment. The tall square tower was clearly intended to take its place among Wren's towers and spires which still at that time dominated the City's skyline. Otherwise the design is superficially not unlike that by William Tite which was eventually selected after much acrimony by the Gresham Trustees in 1840. But it shows a subtler and more scholarly mind at work. The portico is narrower and less overwhelmingly massive than Tite's, and the wall surfaces are less fussy. There is something of the sober intensity of the almost exactly contemporary St George's Hall in Liverpool, the most impressive English public building of its date. Lacking the charm of Nash's buildings and the Baroque drama of C. R. Cockerell's well-known rejected scheme, Pennethorne's design gives a clear idea of the direction in which his architectural talent was developing in the late 1830s. The appeal of Nash's buildings was essentially pictorial. Pennethorne looked below the surface of ornamental form to find an underlying order, harmony and power. Here lie the roots of his mature style.

A coloured perspective drawing of the Royal Exchange design was exhibited at the Royal Academy in 1840. It was Pennethorne's last Academy entry, and, as it turned out, his last competitive entry too. On 10 October 1839 he was appointed joint architect and surveyor for Metropolitan Improvements to the Commissioners of Woods and Forests, possibly through the influence of John Charles Herries, who

---

60 W. H. Leeds, *Illustrations of the Public Buildings of London*, supplement (1838), p. xi. There is a photograph of the interior in the National Monuments Record.
61 Guildhall Library MS 4952, ff. 1–2, 28. The four architects placed above him were William Grellier (the district surveyor of Whitechapel), Alexis de Chateauneuf (a pupil of Schinkel), Sydney Smirke and T. H. Wyatt.

19. Design for the Royal Exchange, 1838. Pennethorne's splendidly monumental scheme was placed fifth in the competition, but in the end none of the prizewinners was awarded the commission, which went to William Tite. Pennethorne's drawing was the first of several coloured perspectives he made throughout his life to record unexecuted designs; it shows his mastery of architectural draughtsmanship and his ability to enliven a drawing with dramatic effects of light and shadow and carefully placed groups of people.

was a member of the Commons Select Committee on Metropolitan Improvements. From then on he shed his remaining private practice.[62] This was the crucial event in Pennethorne's career. For the next few years he was almost exclusively preoccupied with the design of new streets and parks in London. When his career as an architect resumed, his talents had to find an outlet under the probing scrutiny of civil servants, politicians and, ultimately, of their capricious masters, the British public.

---

62 PRO, T 1/6693A/3774, pp. 40–1.

2

METROPOLITAN IMPROVEMENTS

THE IMPROVEMENT of London meant many different things: the widening of streets, the creation of open spaces, the construction of grand public buildings, the establishment of basic public services without which modern urban life would be inconceivable. Some of these objectives had been shared by statesmen and architects ever since the Renaissance. Most European cities grew as a result of countless uncoordinated decisions made by private property owners and private and public institutions, and the idea of imposing some kind of order onto the resulting chaos of individual and corporate interests could not fail to attract those who believed in towns as repositories of civilised values and as valuable human artefacts in their own right. As the urban population exploded in the nineteenth century, the need for action became more and more obvious. For all their apparent lack of planning, European cities in the eighteenth century – even monsters like London – had been manageable places. Now their uncontrolled growth seemed to threaten the very fabric of urban society, not least by imposing severe strain on the central streets which were as essential to the healthy functioning of the city as veins and arteries are to that of the human body.

The planning of London's streets first became a matter of public concern after the Great Fire had destroyed four-fifths of the area within the mediaeval city walls. Christopher Wren, John Evelyn and Robert Hooke all produced plans which, had they been implemented, might have turned the City into a model of lucid, rational street planning. But nothing happened, and the question was not taken seriously again for another century. By then London had spread well outside its original nucleus within the walls. At the time of the Great Fire most Londoners still lived within the City and its 'liberties' outside the walls; by 1800 the proportion had fallen to a tenth, and, while the City population remained stationary during the first half of the nineteenth century, that of the outer areas continued to expand at a phenomenal rate.

The first serious scheme for replanning London's streets was prepared by John

Gwynn in his *London and Westminster Improved* (1766). His proposals anticipated many of the changes by which the chaotically planned, though often picturesque, London of the eighteenth century was slowly transformed into the city we know today. New bridges were to be built over the Thames and new streets carved through the central areas. A 'Thames Quay' or embankment along the north bank of the river would provide a new route between the City and Westminster and the West End, and communications within the West End would be improved by the building of a street leading in a north-westerly direction from Charing Cross, roughly along the line of Regent Street. These ambitious projects would not only make communication easier; they would also provide opportunities for constructing imposing buildings appropriate for the capital of a country whose wealth and power were increasing daily.

Hardly any of Gwynn's proposals were carried out in his lifetime. Traffic congestion had not yet reached chronic proportions. More important, there was no public authority with the power and funds to undertake what was bound to be a very expensive operation. The government's decision to build Regent Street in 1813 transformed the situation and introduced a new standard of street architecture into the capital, with bright stucco facades replacing the plain brick of the eighteenth century. In 1825–31 the City Corporation followed suit by carrying out an ambitious programme of improvements after the building of the new London Bridge. This involved not only the construction of new streets – King William Street, Moorgate Street, Gresham Street and the southern part of Farringdon Street – but also the widening of existing streets and pavements, the provision of sewers and the rounding of corners to improve the flow of traffic. By such means the street pattern of a large part of central London was subtly changed and modernised, so that by the mid 1840s there was, in the opinion of one writer, 'no town or city in Europe where walking is more *respectable* than in London . . . Such have been the improvements of the last few years, that London, from being the dirtiest, has become the cleanest town in England.'[1]

The improvements in the City were financed by a tax on coal coming into the Port of London, a source first used after the Great Fire. Elsewhere there was no such ready source of income, nor was there a single authority like the City Corporation with sufficient power to draw up plans and carry them through. London outside the City was still governed like a series of urban villages. There were no fewer than eighty-four paving boards; and street improvements were left either to *ad hoc* commissions operating under special Acts of Parliament, or to central government. For Regent Street and the associated improvements the Commissioners of Woods and Forests acted as commissioners under an Act of Parliament, and the original intention was that the cost would be defrayed out of the improved rental value of

---

1 *Payne's Illustrated London* (1846–7), I, p. 165.

the sites along the new streets. But as costs increased, the government found itself having to foot most of the bill.[2]

The euphoria of the post-Napoleonic years enabled Nash's projects to be carried out largely unscathed, and in 1826 he recommended four new schemes. One of these was the 'West Strand' improvement, which included the formation of Trafalgar Square. The others involved making new streets from Trafalgar Square to the British Museum and from Piccadilly Circus to Holborn, and improving the existing east–west route from Oxford Street through Holborn to the City.[3] Shortages of funds prevented all but the first of these plans being implemented in Nash's lifetime, and by the time of his death the political climate had changed. George IV was now dead, Parliament reformed, and the Whigs in power. They were in constant fiscal and financial difficulties (the income tax had not yet been reimposed), and were terrified that high public spending with no immediate return would unbalance the budget and damage the economy. This attitude to Government spending on public works cast a blight over the planning of London for the rest of the nineteenth century and beyond.

But, despite the Whig government's lack of enthusiasm for public spending, a new phase of Metropolitan Improvements was set in motion at the end of the 1830s. As so often in the nineteenth century, change came about through a combination of outside pressure and growing professional expertise. Concern centred on the slums, which were seen as prime targets for the tidying-up impulse which played so large a part in shaping Victorian Britain. London's population doubled in the first forty years of the nineteenth century, largely through immigration from an increasingly overpopulated and impoverished countryside. Most of the new arrivals settled in the districts just outside the boundaries of the City, many of them in crowded 'courts' and alleys, where they found often intermittent and invariably low-paid employment in small-scale craft industries and service occupations. These conditions, common to all large cities of the time, encouraged both crime and disease. The crime rate was generally thought to be rising during the 1830s and, with fears of insurrection in the air, the idea of opening up the slums to the newly founded Metropolitan Police by building new streets came to appear more and more attractive. Typhus and consumption were also rife, and cholera had appeared in 1832, causing fears among the better-off that were later memorably recalled by Charles Dickens in *Bleak House*. The overall death-rate was rising, and distress reached a peak in 1838–42, the years of the Chartist troubles.

Epidemic disease not only created a generalised fear of premature and unpleasant death; it also forced large numbers of people to seek poor relief. The fourth and fifth reports of the Commissioners appointed to administer the new Poor Law of 1834

---

2 J. Summerson, *The Life and Work of John Nash* (1980), p. 87.
3 5th Rep. Commrs. of Woods, Forests, *PP* 1826, 14 [368], pp. 11–12.

both contained lengthy statements from Southwood Smith, physician to the London Fever Hospital, advocating unprecedented measures to cope with the problem of poverty. The most important requirements were proper sewers, effective waste disposal, and 'ventilation'. It was widely believed that many epidemic diseases were caused by 'exhalation' or 'miasmas' whose deadly effects were exacerbated by stagnant air. The opening up of wide streets through overcrowded neighbourhoods would, in the words of the architect Sydney Smirke in his *Suggestions for the Architectural Improvement of the Western Parts of London* (1834), dilute 'the noxious miasmata by the injection of a purer atmosphere'. They would also allow the building of main sewers – a *sine qua non* of the eradication of epidemic diseases. Future slums could be prevented by tightening up the London Building Acts (first inspired by the Great Fire), inserting provisions relating to the width of streets and the distance between houses, and providing for waste removal. The cost of implementing these recommendations, according to Southwood Smith, would be less than that of looking after the sick.[4]

The building of new streets through the slums could also do much to mitigate the growing traffic problems of the capital. As the slums grew, the middle classes moved out and the suburbs expanded. Suburbs led to commuting, which caused congestion in the already inadequate central streets, where carriages, hackney coaches, stage-coaches and (from 1829) horse-drawn omnibuses jostled for limited space. New streets would not only ease the flow of traffic but, according to the architect Thomas Leverton Donaldson, chairman of the Commission of Sewers for Westminster: 'Immediately a street is widened and a respectable traffic and thoroughfare is estab-lished, then a more respectable class of occupants is induced to come and live in the houses, which will also be improved by the owners to meet the improving nature of the thoroughfare'.[5] Thus new streets would play a civilising role by reclaiming the central areas of London from the dangerous and anarchic poor.

The government's first reaction to the growing call for more street improvements came in 1836, when a Commons Select Committee was asked to look at fourteen plans for street improvements outside the City boundaries. It concluded that £1,200,000 would be needed to carry them out. Pennethorne played no part in the committee's deliberations, but in 1838 he was questioned by a second Select Committee about his project for a completely new street between Piccadilly Circus and the City, to the north of the grossly overcrowded Strand and Fleet Street (Plate 20). Under his proposal eastward-moving traffic from Piccadilly and Regent Street would be taken along the north side of Leicester Square, thus avoiding Haymarket and Trafalgar Square – something still not possible today – and then through Long Acre, from which point a new street would cut through 'houses of the lowest

4 4th Rep. Poor Law Commrs., *PP* 1837–8, 28 [147], pp. 84–94; 5th Rep. Poor Law Commrs., *PP* 1839, 20 [239], p. 106.
5 Rep. Sel. Cttee. on Metropolitan Improvements, *PP* 1836, 20 [517], p. 8.

description, quite as bad as the courts near the Strand, the removal of which was one great inducement to undertake the [West Strand] improvements'. It would emerge on the southern side of Lincoln's Inn Fields, pass through the middle of Lincoln's Inn – which would be remodelled as 'one Gothic edifice' – and cross the Fleet valley by a viaduct, before joining a widened Newgate Street by St Sepulchre's church and ending in a new square close to St Paul's Cathedral.[6] From here the already widened Cheapside led past Wren's St Mary-le-Bow to the Royal Exchange, for which Pennethorne produced his impressive but unexecuted design in 1838.

It is tantalising to imagine the effect this street would have had on central London, especially if it had been built to a decent width and lined with monumental buildings. But alas the proposal received short shrift from the Select Committee, which included only the western portion, from Piccadilly Circus to Long Acre, among its immediate recommendations. These were determined by strictly utilitarian considerations; 'embellishment' was to be of a 'subordinate importance' and funding limited by what could be raised locally, while strict control over spending would be exercised by the Commissioners of Woods and Forests.

The Committee's report was followed by legislation which earmarked £200,000 left over from the coal duty funds after the building of the new Royal Exchange, and early in 1839 the Select Committee was convened again to make final recommendations. They were that work should start immediately on four streets which were urgently needed 'either for removing existing obstructions, which now impede the main lines of communication . . . or for creating new and commodious thoroughfares in poor and populous districts . . . [and] improving the health and moral habits of those districts in particular'.[7] It was hoped that they would prove the first part of a more comprehensive programme.

The decision to build the new streets led to Pennethorne's first government appointment. When Nash retired in 1835 his position as 'Architect in the Office of Woods and Forests' was allowed to lapse, and what little street-improvement work there was devolved upon the two Surveyors of Houses to the Crown estate, Thomas Chawner and Henry Rhodes. Both men had been involved in managing the Crown's property in London for many years, but neither could lay any claim to distinction as an architect, and it may have been with the aim of restoring some of the lustre of the Nash era to the office that the Commissioners appointed Pennethorne joint 'Architect and Surveyor for Metropolitan Improvements' along with the 66-year-old Chawner. Their task was to supply detailed plans and carry them through to completion.[8] The plans are jointly signed, but it was Pennethorne who answered most of the questions put by the Select Committee, and he

6 2nd Rep. Sel. Cttee. on Met. Improvements, *PP* 1837–8, 16 [418], plan 2.

7 1st Rep. Sel. Cttee. on Met. Improvements, *PP* 1839, 13 [136], pp. v–vi.

8 PRO, Work 6/92, pp. 11–12; Work 30/431, 436; MR 1082/15.

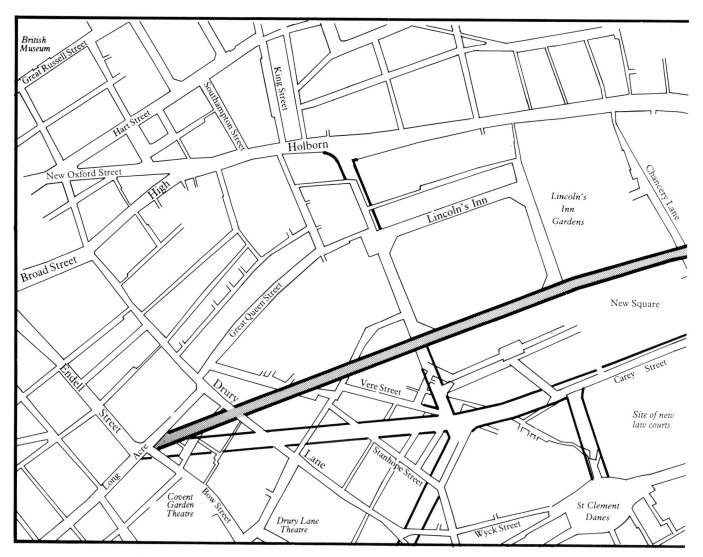

20. Pennethorne's original (1838) and revised (1847) plans for the 'Great Central Thoroughfare' linking the West End and the City' the lower line represents the revised plan, which would have passed along the northern flank of the Public Record Office.

gradually took on most of the responsibility, a process which culminated when he took over as sole surveyor after Chawner's retirement in 1845.[9] His position was strengthened in 1840 when he replaced Rhodes as joint surveyor (with Chawner) to the Crown estate. Besides the financial rewards, this appointment gave him important responsibilities in the West End, where the Crown owned more than three thousand houses within a three-mile radius of Charing Cross.[10]

9 He was given an assistant, William Smith, who left after a year to superintend the construction of the new British Embassy in Constantinople: PRO, T 1/6041A/20465.
10 PRO, T 1/6936A/20938.

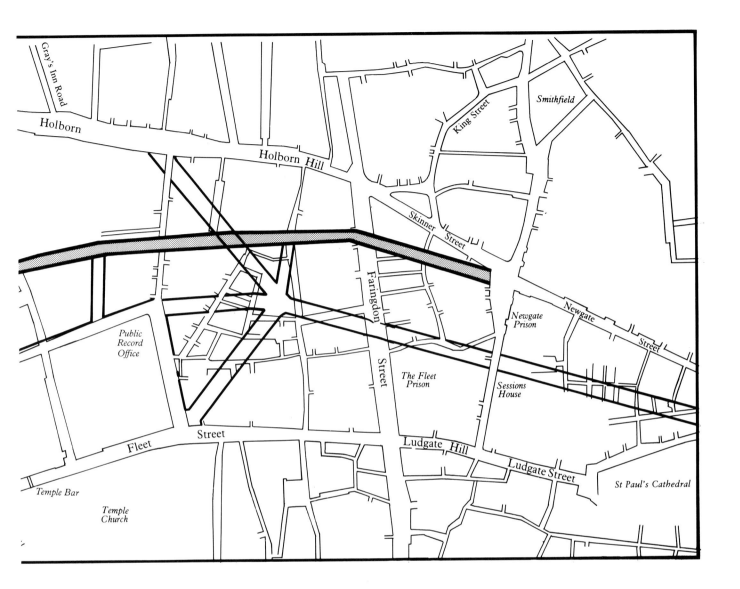

CRANBOURN STREET, NEW OXFORD STREET, ENDELL STREET AND COMMERCIAL STREET

The new streets proposed by the 1839 Select Committee were all designed purposely to pass through the poorer parts of inner London. Three of them cut through the densely packed district to the north of the Strand. This area began to grow in the late sixteenth century, as London started spreading westwards. It contained some of the first great planned developments, notably Covent Garden and Leicester Square, and some of the ground still remained in the hands of

49

aristocratic landlords, notably the Dukes of Bedford and the Marquesses of Salisbury. But with the drift of fashion to the West End it had lost its socially exclusive character, and the area now housed a largely artisan population, interspersed with pockets of great poverty. Carriages for the Covent Garden and Drury Lane theatres and carts for the rebuilt Covent Garden market struggled to find their way through its narrow and dingy streets, and through-traffic from the West End to the City was regularly caught in notorious bottlenecks like the 'Middle Row' which blocked Broad St, St Giles.

By far the most ambitious and important of the new streets was New Oxford Street. This was designed to run through what was universally agreed to be one of London's worst slums. Contemporary writers and social reformers were by turns fascinated and appalled by the area known as the 'Rookery' which lay just to the south of the solidly respectable Bedford estate in Bloomsbury (Plate 21). From an early stage the area attracted large numbers of Irish immigrants, and in the early nineteenth century overcrowding increased, with disastrous effects on public health. It was 'one dense mass of houses, through which curved narrow tortuous lanes, from which again diverged close courts – one great maze, as if the houses had originally been one block of stone, eaten by slugs into numberless small chambers and connecting passages'.[11] The courts, according to Pennethorne, were 'very small and very narrow, the access to them being only under gateways; in many cases they have been larger courts originally, and afterwards built in again with houses back to back, without any outlet behind, and only consisting of two rooms and almost a ladder for a staircase'. The larger houses, without drains or sewers, were subdivided and sublet. In 1841 Church Lane had an average of twenty-four people per house, amongst whom there was a disproportionate number of street dealers, crossing-sweepers and prostitutes.[12] Privies were often choked up and pigs roamed the streets, which played host to a colourful and wild sub-culture; on one occasion Pennethorne was shocked to hear from a resident 'that frequently, on a Sunday morning, he sees a dozen women, perfectly naked, without the least dress at all, dancing to a fiddler'.[13] The land was in multiple ownership, and the owners had neither the power nor the inclination to improve the area as a whole. The new street (Plate 22) would cut through the middle of the slum, bypassing St Giles High Street and sending traffic in a direct line from Oxford Street to Holborn, the City and the north-eastern suburbs. It would be lined with 'good houses of handsome elevations', four stories high with shops underneath. Traffic management would thus go hand in hand with social engineering.

Halfway along New Oxford Street there was to be a square, where it would be

11 J. Timbs, *Curiosities of London* (1855), p. 329.
12 *Journal of the Statistical Society of London*, 9 (1848), 16, 19.
13 Rep. Sel. Cttee. on Health of Towns, *PP* 1840, 11 [384], p. 171.

21. Church Lane, St Giles, in 1840. The street – one of the most notorious in the Rookery – housed a large population mostly made up of Irish immigrants. The western part was demolished to make way for New Oxford Street, but the rest survived for some years because of the cutting back of Pennethorne's original plans for the street.

met by the second of the new streets, Endell Street. This was intended as part of a route leading north from the recently constructed Waterloo Bridge, part of which – the Wellington Street extension – had already been built by the Commissioners of Woods and Forests to the designs of Chawner and Rhodes in 1833–5.[14] Endell Street would be formed by widening Belton Street, a shabby thoroughfare of small eighteenth-century houses, thus making it possible for traffic to pass easily from the southern suburbs over Waterloo Bridge and through Wellington Street and Bow Street to Bloomsbury. The third of the streets, Cranbourn Street, was also to follow the line of an existing street for some of its way. Here the main aim was to take traffic eastwards to Piccadilly Circus by extending Coventry Street to Leicester Square and then driving a new route through an area inhabited by makers and sellers of straw hats and 'fancy goods' to Upper St Martin's Lane, which would be widened. From here Bloomsbury, Holborn and Covent Garden could be reached. By linking Piccadilly to Long Acre the new street could be seen as the first instalment of Pennethorne's proposed 'Great Central Thoroughfare' between the West End and the City.

The last of the four routes, Commercial Street, was designed to pass through a district no less poor, overcrowded and unhealthy than the Rookery. Whitechapel and Spitalfields first grew as a result of the huge expansion of London in the sixteenth and seventeenth centuries, and the coming of the docks further south in the early nineteenth century led to another massive increase in population. The influx of immigrants led inevitably to poverty and overcrowding, and the collapse of the once flourishing local silk industry made matters worse. Spitalfields contained some of the finest early eighteenth-century houses in London, but the courts and alleys leading off Essex Street and Wentworth Street, north of the Whitechapel Road, were 'without any drainage and extremely filthy and close'.[15] The area was notorious for crime, harbouring 'an exceedingly immoral population; women of the lowest character, receivers of stolen goods, thieves and the most atrocious offenders'.[16] Stephen Lushington, MP for the Tower Hamlets, thought that a new street was 'of the last moment to the happiness, comfort, health, and morality of that district . . . The expense of these improvements would be more than repaid by the moral advantage the public would derive from them'.[17] Commercial Street was designed to run south through the worst of the slums from Hawksmoor's Christ Church, Spitalfields to Whitechapel High Street, from which point the existing streets leading to the Docks would be widened. It would subsequently be extended north to the proposed Eastern Counties Railway terminus in Shoreditch, thus keeping heavy carts out of the City and forming the first part of an 'inner ring road'

14 *Survey of London*, 36 (1970), pp. 226–8.
15 4th Rep. Poor Law Commrs. (1837–8), p. 9.
16 2nd Rep. Sel. Cttee. on Met. Improvements (1837–8), p. 103.
17 *Hansard*, 49 (17 July 1839), 726–7.

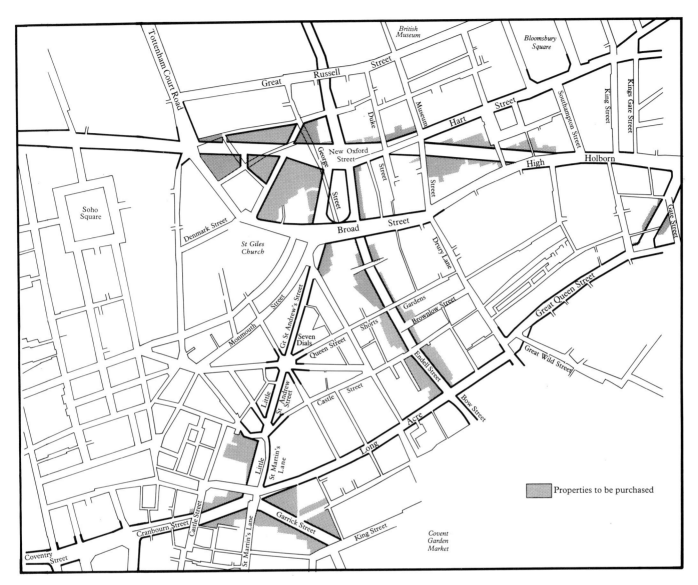

22. The first plan for Cranbourn Street, New Oxford Street, and Endell Street 1839–40. The scheme envisaged the demolition of many acres of slum property, including the whole of the Rookery, and the opening up of east–west and north–south routes which were to converge in a new open space between Broad Street and New Oxford Street. The shading represents proposed demolitions.

designed to lead eventually via Old Street to New Oxford Street: an idea for which Pennethorne claimed the credit.[18] Together with the 'Great Central Thoroughfare' and a new street on the South Bank, these projects at least held out the hope of

18 E. Hall, 'Pennethorne and Public Improvements – a Retrospect', *Mechanics' Magazine*, 21 (1871), 273. The station (later known as Bishopsgate) was subsequently replaced as a passenger terminus by Liverpool Street, and has since been demolished.

imposing a rational street pattern on central London as useful, if rather less splendid, than those associated with Haussmann in Paris.

Financial difficulties arose immediately. The estimated cost of all four streets (£638,000), was three times the sum set aside from the coal tax, and the Government refused to raid the Consolidated Fund as it had done when the costs of Regent Street had escalated.[19] The idea of funding new streets out of local rates had been discussed in 1837, but was rejected on the grounds that the coal tax bore less heavily on the poor; and no consideration was given to the idea of raising loans directly from the public, as Napoleon III and Haussmann were later to do in Paris.[20] Financial institutions did not want to lend the money either, because new streets did not bring in any immediate income and it took some time, especially in poor areas, for ground rents to increase to a point where a return could be made on the investment. The middle classes, unlike their counterparts in nineteenth-century Paris, preferred living in the suburbs to city-centre flats. Ruthless cuts were therefore inevitable. The Select Committee was reconvened, and, at the suggestion of the Second Commissioner of Woods and Forests, Alexander Milne, the plans supplied by Chawner and Pennethorne submitted for revision to James White Higgins, a well-known surveyor, and Richard Lambert Jones, 'a person of great influence in the City, and one who was alive to the chance of diverting money to his quarter of the metropolis'.[21]

From the point of view both of aesthetics and traffic management this was a disastrous decision. Jones had played a large part in the City's programme of street improvements, and he now recommended that the width of the new streets should be reduced by fifteen feet to that of King William Street in the City. At the same time purchases of property on either side of the streets should be kept to a minimum. The result, as Pennethorne told the Select Committee, was that run-down old buildings would be retained and awkwardly shaped plots of land created which would be difficult to let. But given the government's determination to cut costs, the architects could do little more than protest ineffectively. They had a series of meetings with Higgins and Jones, and in June 1840 they submitted a new series of plans incorporating most of their proposed amendments.[22]

Under the new plans the estimated cost of the work was reduced from £638,000 to £399,000. New Oxford Street was to be narrowed, the proposed square at the junction with Endell Street left out and about half the Rookery left standing. Savings were made in Endell Street by forming an irregular junction with Bow Street, so that traffic coming north had to turn first into Long Acre. And the

19 1st Rep. Sel. Cttee. on Met. Improvements, *PP* 1840, 12 [410], p. 39; T. H. Rickman, 'On Metropolitan Improvements', *RIBA Transactions*, 1st series, 60 (1859), pp. 71–2.

20 Rep. Sel. Cttee. on Met. Communications, *PP* 1854–5, 10 [415], p. 169.

21 *The Builder*, 1 Dec. 1866, 877; *Mechanics' Magazine*, 21 (1871), 272.

22 1st Rep. Sel. Cttee. on Met. Improvements (1840), pp. 36–64 and plans 1–4.

narrowing of Cranbourn Street made it more difficult to envisage that thoroughfare as the grand opening of Pennethorne's proposed new route from the West End to the City.

The decision to revise the plans was bitterly attacked in the *Westminster Review*, one of the organs of radicalism. It was pointed out that an extension of the coal tax for only two extra years would have brought in enough money to carry out the original plans in full: 'We lose our temper with vexation when we see how by the *crooked* policy which has been pursued, public convenience, architectural effect, and the improvement to a very great extent of the pecuniary value of property along the whole line, have been sacrificed'.[23] These fulminations were in vain, and an Act allowing work to start in Commercial Street, Endell Street and New Oxford Street was passed in the summer of 1840, followed by another for Cranbourn Street a year later. The Commissioners found it very difficult to borrow the money, and it was not until further legislation in 1841 that work could start on acquiring the property, a process which involved two years of minutely detailed haggling. Several awards were disputed, and when the cases went to arbitration the juries often gave higher awards to freeholders and lessees than the government had expected. Especially high sums were extracted for 'goodwills' of shopkeepers who feared losing their trade. These high awards made it impossible to keep within the original estimates. By the spring of 1843 all the money borrowed in 1841 had been used up before work had even begun on the construction of the streets themselves, and the final cost was more than twice that envisaged in 1840.[24]

Demolitions began early in 1843 to a chorus of complaints from the local people. A resident of St Martins Court, in the line of Cranbourn Street, complained to *The Times* in September that it had been impossible to let houses in the area for the past four years and that the 'fancy trades' had been ruined from the clouds of dust from falling buildings. Thirteen building lots in Cranbourn Street and thirty-five in New Oxford Street were advertised on eighty-year building leases in 1845, with the aim of selling the ground rents after they had improved in value. The negotiations with the builders were handled by Pennethorne, Chawner having just retired. His main tasks were to fix the ground rents, to set out the terms of the leases, to impose restrictive clauses to deter the wrong sort of tenant, to vet the elevations and to ensure that the buildings were properly constructed. He did not insist on 'symmetrical Architectural Elevations for any particular number of Houses', and told prospective builders in New Oxford Street that he would welcome facades in the Elizabethan style[25] – an indication of what was to become a new stylistic pluralism in the streets of London. In one or two cases he was asked to alter elevations sent in

23 'Metropolitan Improvements', *The Westminster Review*, 36 (1841), pp. 424–6.
24 PRO, Work 6/99, pp. 350–1; Return of Cost of Met. Improvements, *PP* 1847–8, 39 [440].
25 PRO, Cres 2/670.

23. Cranbourn Street, looking west from St Martin's Lane. Most of the buildings in the block on the left still survive, including the central turreted structure which was designed and built by William Dent in 1845.

by the builders and their architects, and to this extent the streets can be said to have embodied his taste to a small degree.

Cranbourn Street was the first of the streets to be completed (Plate 23). The new blocks had shops on the ground floor and either 'chambers' or storage spaces for goods on the floors above. Shopkeepers were now demanding large plate-glass windows in which to display their wares, and developers were beginning to vie with each other in attracting tenants by building ever more ornate facades. Londoners were turning against the relative blandness of the ordinary street architecture of the Nash era, and Pennethorne encouraged this trend towards a richer and more plastic treatment of facades, telling some of the builders to add heavier cornices and other enrichments to otherwise plain brick or stucco facades. But the Cranbourn

24. New Oxford Street, looking east from Tottenham Court Road. The building on the left was part of Messrs Meux's brewery and was remodelled by Samuel Beazley in 1850. That on the right (on the site of Centrepoint) dates from the late nineteenth century. The former Royal Bazaar is in the middle distance. It has been demolished, along with most of the buildings seen here.

Street shops never attracted a fashionable clientele, and in March 1850 Pennethorne confessed that 'to a certain extent the Speculation has failed; perhaps from the depression of the times – or that the Shops are too good for the neighbourhood – or that they are out of the line of Retail traffic, or from these and other causes unitedly'.[26]

New Oxford Street (Plate 24) was always a more important street than Cranbourn Street. It became a major through route as soon as it was opened in 1847,

---

26 *Ibid.*, 2/671.

and its value was later increased when the Metropolitan Board of Works took up Pennethorne's suggestion of extending Hart Street (now Bloomsbury Way) through Theobalds Road to Clerkenwell Road, Old Street and the East End. Already in 1847, according to one commentator, the area had become 'civilised – which it hardly was before – and has put on not only a cheerful but an unusually attractive aspect'. The architecture, moreover, was 'incomparably superior to that of Regent Street, which is excessively flimsy and jejune'.[27] The writer of an article in *The Lady's Newspaper* was moved to hyperbole by the comparison with the squalor of the Rookery which had stood on the site:

On the very spot . . . have arisen mansions and stores vying in architectural splendour with palaces . . . Peter the Great on a low marsh founded the splendid imperial city of St Petersburg; our merchant princes on the most malignant spot in the metropolis have created a broad, elegant and noble street, designated New Oxford-Street . . . The foot of beauty will trip, the elegances of life be displayed, the language of gentleness be musically uttered, where the antipodes of the fascinations of life but a few short months ago were rude and rampant.[28]

Though less impressive than the slightly earlier Grey Street in Newcastle – perhaps the most impressive English urban improvement of the post-Nash era – the new street certainly boasted some striking buildings. At the western end there was a shopping arcade or 'bazaar' designed in 1848 by Thomas Marsh Nelson for John Merrick, owner of a paper-staining factory in Soho.[29] This long-forgotten structure was influenced by the Lowther Arcade, part of the West Strand improvement scheme. It consisted of two rows of shops behind an enriched street front of the kind Pennethorne had advocated, with a glass-roofed passageway between them (Plate 25). Further east, on the site of an old stone yard stretching south to Broad Street, the religious needs of the neighbourhood were catered for by no fewer than three adjacent churches in contrasting styles: the Gothic French Protestant chapel (by Ambrose Poynter, 1845), the neo-Romanesque Bloomsbury Central Baptist Chapel – the only one to survive – designed by John Gibson in 1845–8, and the classical Bedford Chapel, remodelled in 1846 by H. E. Kendall, the district surveyor of St Martin-in-the-Fields. Pennethorne added to the stylistic diversity in 1845 by designing a block of neo-Jacobean shops and offices on a patch of ground to the south of this tongue of land with a frontage to Broad Street (Plates 26–7). This carefully proportioned building, coming only a few years after Pennethorne's last country houses, represented one of the first uses of the 'Jacobethan' style for commercial purposes, its red brick walls, stone dressings and strapwork flourishes on the roofline anticipating the 'Queen Anne' revolution of the 1870s.[30] The building was

---

27 *Companion to the Almanac* (1847), p. 231; (1850), p. 227.
28 *The Lady's Newspaper*, 21 Dec. 1850.   29 PRO, Cres 2/672.
30 It was demolished in 1885; H. B. Wheatley and P. Cunningham, *London Past and Present*, 3 vols (1891), I, p. 209.

25. The interior of the Royal Bazaar, New Oxford Street, designed by Thomas Marsh Nelson and built in 1848.

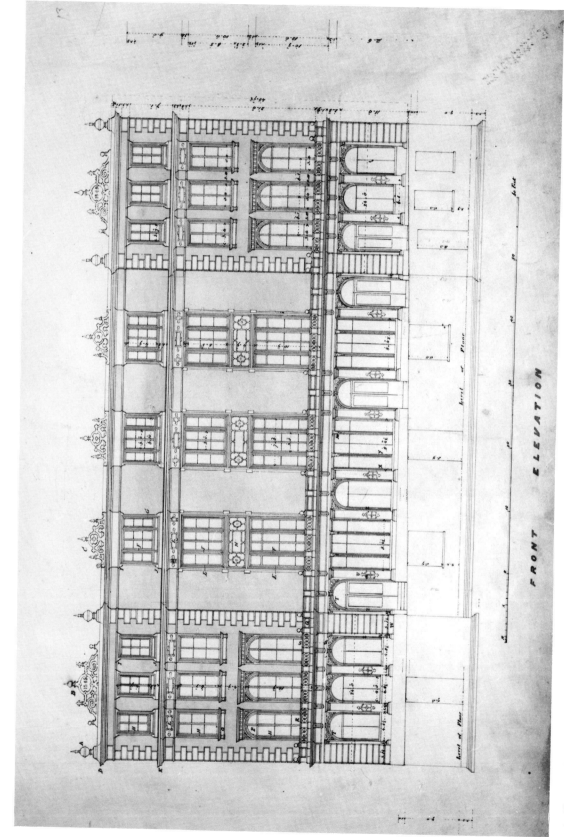

FRONT ELEVATION

26. Shops and offices at the corner of Bloomsbury Street and Broad Street, built to Pennethorne's designs in 1845. The building was demolished to make way for Shaftesbury Avenue in 1885.

27. Broad Street in the late 1840s, looking west towards St Giles parish church, with Pennethorne's neo-Jacobean block on the right. The 'Middle Row' which formerly blocked the street has been removed, much of the traffic siphoned off into New Oxford Street, and inhabitants of the Rookery mingle with more 'respectable' pedestrians.

intended to be a design 'after which others are to be erected in the neighbourhood', and a second neo-Jacobean block was indeed built to the designs of James Stansby in the eastern part of New Oxford Street (since demolished).[31] But the other developers and their architects remained faithful to the conventional stuccoed classicism of the time (Plate 28).

Hopes that New Oxford Street would become another Regent Street were never realised. As Pennethorne had feared, the continued presence of the remains of the Rookery to the south deterred prospective shoppers, and despite a reduction in rents the street remained 'seriously depressed' for some years. John Merrick, the owner of the 'Royal Bazaar', went bankrupt in 1854, and the street soon developed a solidly respectable but hardly glamorous character best exemplified by Mudie's famous circulating library at the junction with Museum Street.[32] A few of the original buildings remain, but most have now been replaced by offices of numbingly mediocre quality, and today it is hard to recapture the enthusiasm with which most contemporaries viewed the street.

New Oxford Street played an important part in alerting public opinion to the limitations of street improvements as a means of solving the problems of the slums. A writer in *Punch* drew attention to the problem in 1845:

While the battle of the gauges is dividing the railway world, the battle of the streets . . . is revolutionising the metropolis. Unfortunately for the narrow, the broad carries, or rather knocks down, everything before it. We shall soon be utterly without a lane or alley throughout the whole of London; while as to architecture, the old brick and tile order will be utterly superseded by the modern stuccoite. It is all very well to enlarge the streets if we can sufficiently enlarge the means of the people to enable them to live in them; but . . . [the] old police principle of 'move on', 'you can't stop here', seems to be now generally applied to those of humble means, and the question is, 'where are they all to go to?' So as they are got rid of somehow, this is a question which gives little trouble to those who are bent on 'improving' a neighbourhood.[33]

Most of the 5,000 or so displaced inhabitants of the Rookery moved to other poor areas, especially in the parishes of St Marylebone and St Pancras, where overcrowding increased. As a writer in the *Illustrated London News* put it:

Like a nest of ants, they are turned loose to overrun other neighbourhoods: the new houses and splendid streets which have risen above the old sites of sorrow, misery and wretchedness, have but driven them from their ancient haunts . . . and compelled them to seek shelter in other quarters where the poverty-stricken population 'most do congregate'.[34]

---

31 *The Builder*, 7 Dec. 1844, 611. Stansby was also responsible for an impressive block in the enriched Renaissance manner which still survives at the corner of Coptic Street.

32 PRO, Cres 2/672, 2/706; *The Builder*, 1 Dec. 1866, 878; W. Thornbury and E. Walford, *Old and New London*, 6 vols (1873), IV, pp. 487–9.

33 *Punch*, 9 (1845), 64.

34 *ILN*, 22 Sept. 1849, 197–8. See also H. Jephson, *The Sanitary Evolution of London* (1907), p. 29.

28. The corner of New Oxford Street and Hart Street (Bloomsbury Way), with the tower of Nicholas Hawksmoor's St George, Bloomsbury, in the background. The new buildings (by the builders John Hill and Samuel Brooking) are taller and more richly embellished than the eighteenth-century houses in Hart Street; all were demolished between the Wars.

Some of the displaced poor of the Rookery moved no further than the adjoining streets, which became even more crowded than they had been before, with some houses containing sixteen or more people to a room. One solution to this problem was to provide improved artisan housing in the immediate area – albeit at higher rents than the most desperately poor could afford – and in 1850 the Society for Improving the Conditions of the Labouring Classes built one of the first blocks of model dwellings in London on ground belonging to the Duke of Bedford in Streatham Street, just to the north of New Oxford Street. At the same time the landlords of the remaining parts of the Rookery began to improve their property in the hope of attracting a 'better class' of inhabitant, and in 1861 it was reported that 'the district is considerably changed, the inhabitants are rapidly rising in decency, cleanliness and order, and the Rookery of St Giles will soon be ranked among the memories of the past'.[35] But the problem of rehousing those displaced by street improvements remained to haunt future generations.

Even more than Cranbourn Street and New Oxford Street, Endell Street suffered from the spending cuts forced upon Pennethorne in 1840. The tortuous line insisted upon by Higgins and Jones deterred through traffic, making it difficult to let the building sites, and the street, which should have become part of a through route leading north from Waterloo Bridge past Covent Garden to Bloomsbury, was in 1851 a 'sinuous avenue of ruins'. The western side still retained its shabby eighteenth-century houses, and in the end the ground on the east was filled by institutions catering for the working-class inhabitants of the neighbourhood: a Gothic church designed by Benjamin Ferrey in 1845, a neo-Elizabethan maternity hospital (1849), Italianate public baths (1852) and a workhouse. The ensemble was completed with the construction of the impressively polychromatic Gothic stained-glass factory of Messrs Lavers, Barrauld and Westlake in 1859. Today most of these buildings (though not the glass factory) have gone and the street is largely closed off to through traffic – a monument to thwarted endeavour.

Commercial Street (Plate 29) eventually became a major through route, as anyone contemplating the endless procession of heavy lorries today can testify, but for a long time it also presented a distinctly forlorn appearance. By 1849 only one site had been leased, and a large number of the plots were eventually disposed of at very low rents. Most of the street was not built up until the 1850s and the unsold sites were finally sold off in the 1860s. By this time the street had been continued north to the railway terminus in Shoreditch. Pennethorne first drew up plans for this extension in 1839, but it was not until the passing of a new Act of Parliament in 1846 and the raising of a loan by the Bank of England two years later that work could begin.[36] The usual delays and difficulties intervened, and the street was not opened until 1858, the costs having doubled in the meantime. Pennethorne hoped to create an impressive *rond-point* outside Shoreditch railway station in connection with his plan to make Commercial Street 'part of a great thoroughfare all round London, one of the main arteries'.[37] This eastern Piccadilly Circus was never built, but with the construction of Great Eastern Street by the Metropolitan Board of

---

35 H. Mayhew, *London Labour and the London Poor*, IV (1861), p. 301.

36 4th Rep. Commrs. for Improving the Metropolis, *PP* 1845, 17 [627], p. 9; 26th Rep. Commrs. of Woods, Forests, *PP* 1849, 27 [611], p. 11.

37 Rep. Commrs. for Establishing Railway Termini in the Metropolis, *PP* 1846, 17 [719], p. 60.

29. The central part of Commercial Street, with Spitalfields Market to the left and Christ Church, Spitalfields just out of the picture to the right. Two pubs of the 1840s are visible, and in the background is the northern extension of the street completed in 1857. The view remains substantially unchanged today, apart from the replacement of carts and trams by cars and heavy lorries.

Works in 1872–6 traffic could at last pass directly to Old Street, City Road and the West End as Pennethorne had envisaged.

The difficulty of attracting tenants to Commercial Street made it impossible and perhaps unnecessary for Pennethorne to exert much influence over the architectural elevations. His concern was chiefly to encourage the building of churches and schools and to keep out 'bad influences' like theatres. Architecturally, the main interest lies in the presence of some impressive brick-built warehouses (Plate 30). As in New Oxford Street, the making of the street led to changes in the character of the surrounding areas. In the short term overcrowding increased, but in time gaunt blocks of improved housing began to replace the worst slums, starting with London's first Peabody Buildings in the northern part of the street in 1864. The process culminated in 1889 with the construction of a series of larger and even more austere blocks (since demolished) by the Four Per Cent Industrial Dwellings Company in and around Flower and Dean Street further south.[38] Writing in 1902, Charles Booth observed:

[It] is difficult to over-estimate the importance of this improvement in the later structural changes in Whitechapel . . . The clearances and rebuilding have . . . not cured and may even have aggravated, crowding, but still the effect on the character of the inhabitants has been good. 'As poor as ever, but old rookeries destroyed, black patches cleared away, thieves and prostitutes gone, a marvellous change for the better', is the opinion of one as to the results in his neighbourhood.[39]

There spoke the authentic voice of Victorian improvement.

LATER PROJECTS

Pennethorne's new streets did little more than scratch the surface of London's traffic problems, let alone the more fundamental problems of poverty and disease. Even before work began there was pressure to extend the improvements to other parts of London. A Metropolitan Improvement Society was formed in January 1842, the year of Edwin Chadwick's influential *Report on the Sanitary Condition of the Labouring Population*, and later in the same year a Royal Commission was appointed, made up of some of the MPs who had served on earlier Select Committees, together with the three Commissioners of Woods and Forests and two architects, Sydney Smirke and Charles Barry. Pennethorne was not a member, but he acted as 'professional adviser'[40] and was called in to judge upon the practicality of the schemes discussed.

The Royal Commission's recommendations had, in the long term, as important

---

38 J. N. Tarn, *Five Per Cent Philanthropy* (1973), pp. 45, 87–9.
39 C. Booth, *Life and Labour of the People in London*, 3rd series, II (1902), p. 61.
40 5th Rep. Commrs. for Improving the Metropolis, *PP* 1846, 24 [682], p. 3.

30. The southern part of Commercial Street in the 1920s. The church of St Jude was part of the attempt to use the new streets to bring civilising influences to bear upon the poor. Canon Samuel Barnett, the incumbent at the end of the nineteenth century, was a noted philanthropist and founder of the University settlement, Toynbee Hall. It still survives, but the church has gone. The warehouse on the left is typical of those built along the street.

an effect on Victorian London as Nash's plans had had on the London of the Regency. The north bank of the Thames was to be embanked from Blackfriars to Chelsea, a new park to be formed on the South Bank at Battersea, with a bridge linking it to Chelsea, and new streets constructed in Westminster and the East End. A new Public Record Office would also be built in Chancery Lane with Pennethorne's 'Great Central Thoroughfare' re-routed to run along its north flank, from which point it would strike eastwards to join up with a route already projected by the City's surveyor, J. B. Bunning.

Pennethorne played a major part in carrying out these proposals. He was responsible for the northern extension of Commercial Street from Spitalfields to Shoreditch. He laid out Battersea Park and Chelsea Bridge Road, which led north from the bridge to Sloane Street (see p. 105). He also designed the Public Record Office (see pp. 145–62), but although compulsory purchase orders were given for the part of his new street which was to run alongside the new building, successive governments balked at the cost and it was never built.[41]

One of the most ambitious of the proposals recommended by the Royal Commission was for a new route (Victoria Street) from Westminster to the rapidly expanding districts of Pimlico and Belgravia. First formulated by Rigby Wason, MP for Ipswich, in 1832, this project foundered for lack of money, but it was revived in 1845 and Pennethorne's advice was sought on the route. His aim was 'to ascertain how best to improve the condition of the inhabitants of Westminster by improving the buildings, the levels and the sewers, and by opening communications through the most crowded parts' – a concise summary of the aims of most Victorian street improvement schemes. With these objectives in mind the street was realigned through Palmers Village, a particularly noxious slum near Westminster Abbey. The street – never one of London's more cheerful thoroughfares – was finally completed by the Westminster Improvement Commissioners with financial help from the Government in 1851 under the supervision of their architect, Henry Ashton, and he was responsible for lining the street with the first blocks of middle-class flats seen in London.[42]

Pennethorne also modified the line of Garrick Street. This was first planned by the parish surveyor of St Paul's, Covent Garden, to lead from the eastern end of Cranbourn Street towards Covent Garden Market, levelling on its way a congeries of courts which sheltered 'strange chaotic trades' and 'low gambling houses', and easing access both to the market and to the Covent Garden and Drury Lane theatres. The street was not built until 1859–61, by which time the Metropolitan Board of Works had taken over from the Commissioners of Woods and Forests as the main agency for building new streets in London. But their architect, Frederick

41 PRO, Work 6/157/1.
42 F. Barker and R. Hyde, *London as it Might Have Been* (1982), pp. 165–8; 3rd Rep. Commrs. for Improving the Metropolis, *PP* 1845, 17 [619], pp. 1–3, 22–5; *ILN*, 6 Sept. 1851, 275.

Marrable, retained Pennethorne's route and the street remains one of the least altered of its date in central London.[43]

In 1846 Pennethorne was drawn into preparing new plans for streets south of the Thames (Plate 31). The 1840 Select Committee on Metropolitan Improvements had recommended government help for the building of a new street through 'the Mint' in Southwark, one of London's worst slums, but no funds were forthcoming, and a local improvement act passed in 1842 remained ineffective through lack of money.[44] Southwark suffered from the same problems as many areas north of the river. Factories, slum houses and prisons, such as the notorious Marshalsea, stood side by side. The adjacent parishes of Bermondsey and Lambeth were equally poverty-stricken. The building of bridges over the Thames increased the amount of traffic through the area, but there was no main thoroughfare running parallel to the Thames – the shortest route from Westminster to the City. Pennethorne's involvement stemmed from the need to replace the eighteenth-century Westminster Bridge, which by the 1840s was showing severe signs of strain. He proposed building two new bridges, one on the site of the present Lambeth Bridge and the other slightly to the south of Isambard Kingdom Brunel's elegant Hungerford foot-bridge of 1841–5. New streets would lead from Trafalgar Square and Whitehall to the new 'Charing Cross Bridge', anticipating the present Northumberland Avenue and Horse Guards Avenue, and embankments would be constructed on both sides of the river, flanked by blocks of new terraced houses set among gardens and overlooking public walks. There would be two new streets on the south bank, one heading south towards Kennington and Camberwell, and the other leading in a direct line to Southwark and Bermondsey.[45]

This bold and imaginative plan came to nothing. Pennethorne's proposals were discussed by a Commons Select Committee in 1847 after one of the piers of Westminster Bridge collapsed, but they were rejected in favour of building a new bridge on the site of the old one to the designs of the engineer Thomas Page. In 1853 the Southwark Improvement Commissioners proposed building a new street themselves and funding it out of the local rates, with the help of a government grant. Their plan was submitted to Pennethorne, who responded by producing a revised plan of his own, under which Hungerford Bridge would be widened to take road traffic and the street built in a straight line through the heart of the slum courts.[46] But once again there was no money, and Brunel's suspension bridge was eventually replaced by the present Charing Cross railway bridge, completed in 1864 – one of the most insensitive Victorian additions to the capital. The new street (Southwark

---

43 7th Rep. Commrs. for Improving the Metropolis, *PP* 1851, 29 [1356], pp. 6–19; *RIBA Transactions* (1856–7), p. 89.
44 *The Times*, 9 Aug. 1842; PRO, Work 6/147/4.
45 3rd Rep. Sel. Cttee. on Westminster Bridge and New Palace, *PP* 1846, 15 [574], pp. 159–60.
46 PRO, Work 38/92; Rep. Sel. Cttee. on Metropolitan Communications (1854–5), pp. 168–9.

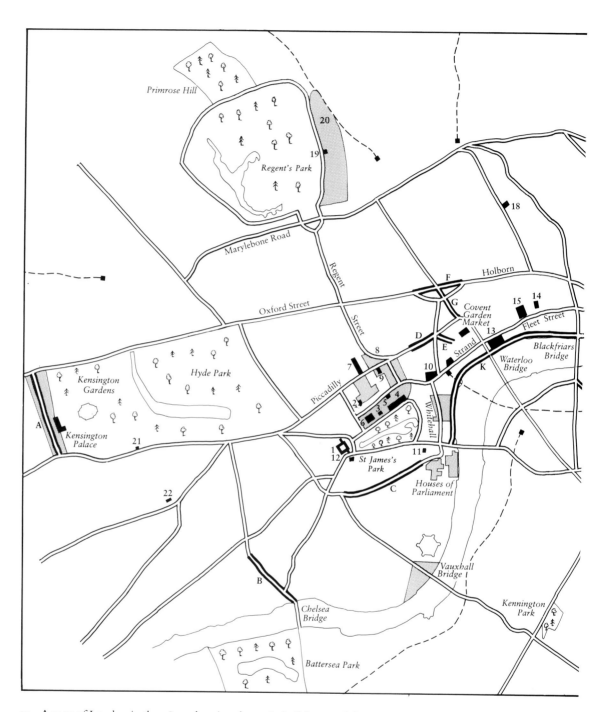

31. A map of London in the 1870s showing the main buildings and the Metropolitan Improvement schemes projected or carried out by James Pennethorne, or with which he was associated.

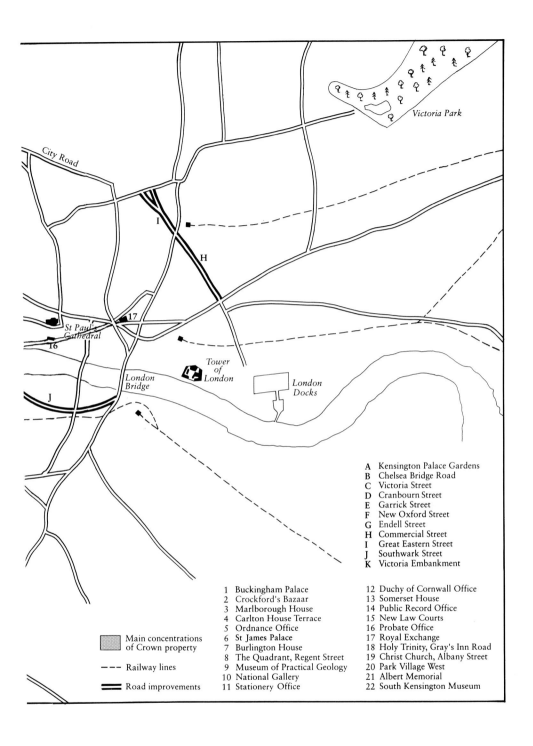

A Kensington Palace Gardens
B Chelsea Bridge Road
C Victoria Street
D Cranbourn Street
E Garrick Street
F New Oxford Street
G Endell Street
H Commercial Street
I Great Eastern Street
J Southwark Street
K Victoria Embankment

Main concentrations
of Crown property

- - - Railway lines

Road improvements

1 Buckingham Palace
2 Crockford's Bazaar
3 Marlborough House
4 Carlton House Terrace
5 Ordnance Office
6 St James Palace
7 Burlington House
8 The Quadrant, Regent Street
9 Museum of Practical Geology
10 National Gallery
11 Stationery Office

12 Duchy of Cornwall Office
13 Somerset House
14 Public Record Office
15 New Law Courts
16 Probate Office
17 Royal Exchange
18 Holy Trinity, Gray's Inn Road
19 Christ Church, Albany Street
20 Park Village West
21 Albert Memorial
22 South Kensington Museum

Street) was finally built by the Metropolitan Board of Works in 1862, but in order to keep the demolition of houses to a minimum, Pennethorne's route was abandoned in favour of a curving route which left much of the slum property intact.[47]

London's traffic problems were magnified by the coming of the first railways. By the mid 1840s seven termini had opened, each of them generating increasing quantities of both passengers and freight through the already crowded streets of the City and West End. With the 'Railway Mania' spreading, a Royal Commission was appointed in 1846 to investigate projects for establishing new termini in central London, and for concentrating the existing ones.[48] Pennethorne believed that the coming of the railways presented an opportunity for finally rationalising the streets of central London. He suggested building a new central terminus shared by several railway companies at King's Cross or Clerkenwell Green – a project which echoes the abortive proposal put forward by the City solicitor, Charles Pearson, for a 'Grand Central Terminus' – and another alongside his proposed new street on the South Bank. These stations would be served by an improved network of streets financed by the railway companies which would channel the traffic they generated away from the congested central area.[49] Nothing came of these proposals, and before long the railways, eager to exploit the growing suburban market, were pressing into the heart of the City and Westminster.

THE CROWN ESTATE AND THE WEST END

As well as being the government surveyor for Metropolitan Improvements, Pennethorne was also responsible, as surveyor to the Crown estate, for the maintenance of a large area in the heart of the West End. The Crown estate was made up of several patches of land, each of which had its own distinct character.[50] There was a large tract of land on the site of the old Palace of Whitehall, between Whitehall and the River Thames. To the north of St James's Park there was another block of land including much of Pall Mall, St James's Street, Jermyn Street and the southern side of Piccadilly. Most of this area consisted of relatively modest eighteenth- or early nineteenth-century houses and shops, with some noblemen's houses and club houses along the main street. Then there were the areas which bore the mark of John Nash: Regent Street, the Haymarket, the block of land

---

47 *RIBA Trans.* (1856–7), p. 90; GLRO, *1st Rep. Metropolitan Board of Works* (1857), pp. 7–8.
48 S. R. Hoyle, 'The First Battle for London: A Case study of the Royal Commission on London Termini 1846', *London Journal*, 8 (1982), 140–52.
49 Rep. Commrs. for Railway Termini (1846), pp. 56–62, 204–7.
50 2nd Rep. Sel. Cttee. on Woods, Forests (1849), Appendix A; PRO, LRRO 1/2440. For the Crown estate in general, see R. B. Pugh, *The Crown Estate* (1960).

comprising the 'West Strand' improvement, the Regent's Park terraces, the Park Village, and the largely working-class district around the Cumberland Basin and Market. There were also pockets of land around the royal parks and elsewhere, notably at Millbank, close to the recently opened Vauxhall Bridge.

Pennethorne had none of the opportunities seized so spectacularly by Nash for redeveloping the Crown lands in London. The central core of the estate was already built up and its traffic problems largely solved by the building of Regent Street. It was only on the fringes that the Commissioners of Woods and Forests were prepared to contemplate new housing developments. The most ambitious of these developments was in Kensington Palace Gardens. Speculative building was spreading westwards along the Bayswater Road towards Notting Hill Gate in the 1830s and 40s, and in 1838 the Commissioners mooted the idea of building on the 28-acre (11-hectare) kitchen gardens to the north of Kensington Palace; the garden activities would meanwhile be concentrated in Windsor Great Park. At first envisaged by Chawner, there would be a wide, straight tree-lined street leading from Kensington High Street north to Bayswater Road with substantial houses on either side. The project was opposed by the gardener John Claudius Loudon, who lived in Portchester Terrace, a short distance away to the north, and wanted the land to be incorporated into Kensington Gardens.[51] But pecuniary considerations prevailed, and in 1841 Pennethorne helped Chawner draw up the stipulation for leases, together with a detailed plan showing thirty-three building plots.

Development only got off the ground when John Marriott Blashfield, a pioneer of terra-cotta and a manufacturer of mosaic pavements, agreed to take twenty plots in September 1843.[52] He went bankrupt in 1847, and the remaining plots were filled in the more favourable economic climate of the 1850s. Several of the designs of the houses emanated from the office of Charles Barry, and there are good examples of his Italian *palazzo* manner. But Pennethorne, in his supervisory role, also allowed some lapses from strict stylistic purity, both in the 'Moresque' (Moorish) external decoration proposed by Owen Jones – one of the architects introduced by Blashfield – for two of the houses (nos. 8 and 24) on the western side of the street, and in the Tudor style employed by Lord Harrington in his house (no. 13), designed by C. J. Richardson on the east. By the 1850s the development had succeeded in attracting a phenomenally wealthy *nouveau riche* clientele, and was well on its way to becoming 'Millionaires' Row'. And, despite the conversion of many of the houses into embassies, it still – almost alone among the housing developments of West London – retains its original character of jealously guarded privacy and restrained opulence, down even to its entrance gates with porters to keep out undesirable visitors (Plate 32).

---

51 Kensington Public Library, local history section, 39321–3.
52 PRO, Cres 35/2116.

32. Kensington Palace Gardens in 1845, looking south from Bayswater Road. The gates, by T. H. Wyatt and David Brandon, still survive and in general the scene has changed little.

The other main housing development of the 1840s was on a marshy tract of land on either side of the approach to Vauxhall Bridge, stretching north to the grim Millbank Penitentiary of 1813–21 which stood on the site of the present Tate Gallery. This project only became feasible after property values rose following the building of the adjacent Grosvenor estate in Belgravia and Pimlico, and it was the developer of that estate, Thomas Cubitt, who built the relatively modest terraced houses, starting in 1842.[53] They consist of three-storied stuccoed blocks with round-arched windows in the Nash manner facing the river, with plainer houses in the streets behind. In 1842 Pennethorne produced a plan for laying out the ground to the north and west of the prison, but it was not carried out, and today much of that area is occupied by one of the first of the London County Council's housing estates, a landmark in the history of publicly financed housing in England.

Elsewhere on the Crown estate, Pennethorne's task was to supervise alterations to, and, in some cases, the replacement of, existing buildings. He was enthusiastic in recommending the removal of the slum courts which still survived close to some of the main streets, like Darby's Court, off Piccadilly, which disappeared in 1846 to make way for his own Museum of Practical Geology. And he thought it important to take particular care over the facades of new buildings. Architects of his generation rejected the blandness and sheer dullness of much of the architecture of the previous generation – epitomised for many of them by Gower Street in Bloomsbury – and believed that they could introduce a new liveliness and majesty into the streets of the capital, befitting its role as one of the great cities of the world. The buildings on the Crown estate, in Pennethorne's view, 'ought to be designed with peculiar regard to Architecture for the improvement of the appearance of the Town generally . . . such views were I know entertained by Mr Nash and by former Boards of Works who concurred with him in endeavouring to improve the Architecture of London – and whose exertions certainly infused a new spirit into our Street Architecture'. In private houses or commercial buildings he thought that architectural considerations 'ought not to be allowed to interfere to any great prejudice of Speculators or with the requirements or profits of Trade'. But he was convinced that 'the guardianship of the Commissioners of Woods does extend to the Architecture of Public Buildings on the Crown Estate and is not confined merely to pecuniary considerations, regarding the Land Revenues'.[54]

He took a particular interest in the architectural development of Pall Mall, where the Crown owned all the land on the southern side of the street. Nash had been involved in the original decision to house clubs here, and had designed the first of them, the [Senior] United Services Club (now the Institute of Directors), in 1826–8. The Travellers', Athenaeum, Reform, and Oxford and Cambridge clubs followed

---

53 *Ibid.*, MPE 813, MPEE 42/17; H. Hobhouse, *Thomas Cubitt, Master Builder* (1971), p. 220.
54 PRO, Cres 35/2227; *Survey of London*, 29 (1960), p. 12.

in rapid succession, giving London a display of revived Italian Renaissance architecture second to none in Europe. Pennethorne favoured housing yet more clubs in Pall Mall and St James's Street, believing that '[the] Club Houses . . . are usually built so solidly, and so regardless of expense, that the rents they will command at the end of the several leases will be very large – probably much higher and much better secured than any Rents, which would be derived from Trade or Dwelling Houses built on the same site'.[55] He oversaw the building of Sydney Smirke's splendidly Venetian Carlton Club next to the Reform Club in 1847, and enhanced the Italianate character of the street with his own *palazzo*-like addition to the Ordnance Office further west in 1850–1 (Plate 33), preparing magnificent designs for a new War Office on the adjoining site in 1856. He also kept a close watch on anything which might spoil the appearance of the existing club houses. In 1854 he successfully opposed plans to build a bow window onto the Pall Mall front of Decimus Burton's Athenaeum, and in 1858 he suggested alterations to Burton's own proposals for removing the portico of the United Services Club. In 1868 he even forced the Travellers' Club to reinstate the stone balustrades on the balconies of the garden front which had been replaced by iron bars, on the grounds that

connoisseurs in Architecture must be offended, and that great injury would be done to the reputation of Sir Charles Barry if the iron railing were allowed to remain; also, considering how little good Architecture there is in London, and how much care is bestowed in the first instance upon the selection of a design for these Club Houses . . . I think it is incumbent upon the Crown . . . to protect such Buildings from mutilation.[56]

The greatest architectural showpiece on the Crown estate in central London was Regent Street. Here Pennethorne faced pressures of another sort. The street was commercially highly successful, but by the 1840s the tenants were clamouring for more enticing shop fronts. Swan and Edgar's received a spectacular new front with plate-glass windows to Piccadilly Circus in 1841, and in 1846 the shopkeepers in the nearby Quadrant were complaining that the Doric colonnade – one of Nash's master-strokes – was preventing them from sharing in the general prosperity. According to one tenant, the covered walk afforded 'haunts of vice and immorality . . . which no police or watchfulness can prevent', while another complained that it was 'almost impossible to procure lodgers for the upstairs apartments'. On one estimate the Crown was losing £10,000 a year in rents, and the tenants a comparable sum in trade. Impressed by these calculations, the Commissioners of Woods and Forests obtained an Act of Parliament enabling them to remove the colonnade. Pennethorne supplied drawings for the remodelled facades in September 1848, and by November the demolition was completed, to the satisfaction of the shopkeepers

---

55 PRO, Cres 35/2453.
56 *Ibid.*, 35/2226–7; *Survey of London*, 29 (1960), pp. 392, 396, 404.

33. Pall Mall in the second half of the nineteenth century, showing buildings erected on the Crown land on the southern side of the street. The Carlton Club (Sydney Smirke 1847) is in the foreground, and beyond that is Buckingham House (Sir John Soane 1792–5), which became part of the War Office in 1855. Behind the lamp-post is Pennethorne's Ordnance Office extension. All these buildings have now gone.

and the fury of those few who still cherished Nash's vision.[57] Pennethorne's own feelings on the removal of one of his mentor's most imaginative pieces of urban design are not recorded, but he certainly acquiesced in it, and did his best to mitigate its effects by designing the new frontage to the street. A cantilevered balcony was added to the first floor, the windows given prominent architraves, and enriched ornamental panels separated by pilasters decorated with arabesques were placed at mezzanine level (Plate 34). These alterations gave the Quadrant a more Italianate character in keeping with most of the newer London street architecture of the time,

---

57 *PP* 1847–8, 60 [519], pp. 399–407; *The Builder*, 4 Nov. 1848, 530; H. Hobhouse, *A History of Regent Street* (1975), pp. 72–3.

but they can hardly be called an aesthetic improvement and the removal of the colonnade seems to have had little effect on the morals of London. It was perhaps no great loss therefore when the original ninety-nine leases fell in and the Pennethorne facades disappeared to make way for the massive blocks by Norman Shaw and Reginald Blomfield which line this part of the street today.

In 1851 Pennethorne became involved in a scheme for improving the Crown property to the south of Buckingham Palace. The origins of what was known as the 'Pimlico Improvement' lie in a proposal of 1832 by Rigby Wason and William Bardwell, the first promoters of Victoria Street, for driving a new thoroughfare through the warren of narrow streets and courts which disfigured the southern approaches to the Palace. An inn, the Gun Tavern, faced the grounds, and the area was crossed by the open Kings Scholars Pond Sewer, notorious for its 'disgusting and dangerous effluvia'; as so often, it was hoped that the building of a new street would improve communications, in this case between the rapidly expanding Grosvenor estate in Belgravia and Westminster, and at the same time ameliorate the general sanitation of the area, including that of the Palace itself.[58] The Commissioners of Woods and Forests therefore bought a block of land to the south of James Street in 1838–40, but nothing was done until 1851, when the government agreed to build a new south-west wing onto the Palace, for which Pennethorne was chosen as architect in the following year. With Victoria Street completed and Belgravia largely built up, the area was clearly poised for profitable development, and he prepared a new plan showing a broad street with a square in front of the new service courtyard and substantial houses facing the Palace gardens.[59] An Act of Parliament was passed in 1852 but the plans were changed a year later to allow more space around the Palace, with a new office for the Duchy of Cornwall (also designed by Pennethorne) occupying the angle formed by James Street and the new street, which became known as Buckingham Gate. As so often, the costs escalated as a result of excessive awards by juries to shopkeepers for the loss of 'goodwill', and the whole street was not finally completed until the end of 1858.[60]

Pennethorne prepared a plan in 1859 for letting the ground facing the Palace on building leases, with substantial 'first-rate' houses next to the Duchy of Cornwall office and a new district post office and a large hotel further south. His architectural contribution was limited to the design of the Post Office (since demolished), a plain well-proportioned Italianate building completed in 1861. He also supplied an elevation showing a proposed treatment of the house facades, in which they would form part of a single composition as in the Regent's Park terraces. But he

58 2nd Rep. Sel. Cttee. on Westminster Improvements, *PP* 1831–2, 5 [614], p. 3 and Plan A; PRO, Cres 19/35, p. 54.

59 PRO, Cres 2/1735; Work 19/9, f. 3024.

60 *Ibid.*, Work 2/10, pp. 291–5; Work 6/156/8; Copy of Rep. on Pimlico Improvements, *PP* 1856, 52 [193 (i)] pp. 1–3.

34. The Quadrant, Regent Street, from Piccadilly Circus in 1852, soon after the removal of the colonnade. Pennethorne was responsible for the balconies and other embellishments added to Nash's plain stuccoed blocks, but the ornate facade of Swan and Edgar's shop in the foreground was built earlier, in 1841.

was not powerful enough to force his impressive French-inspired design (Plate 35) on the builders, Messrs Trollope and Kelk, and in the end the houses were built individually in the conventional stuccoed Italianate manner adopted by builders all over the smarter parts of west London in the 1850s and 60s. The promoters of the hotel chose a restrained *palazzo*-like design by James Murray, a pupil of Sir Charles Barry, finished in 1861 after Pennethorne had been reprimanded for allowing the upper storey to overlook the Palace gardens.[61] Today

---

61 PRO, Work 6/155/18; 6/147/3, f. 56; *BN* 28 Sept. 1860, 748.

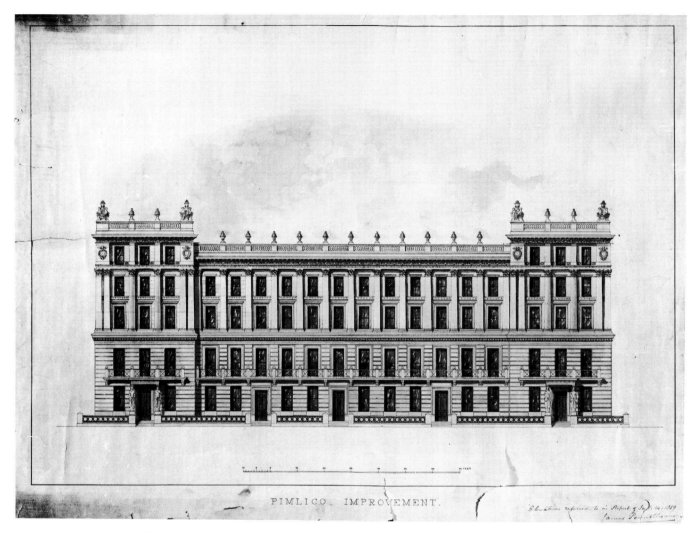

PIMLICO IMPROVEMENT.

35. Design for a terrace of houses in Buckingham Gate, 1859. The houses would have stood on the site adjoining the Duchy of Cornwall Office, facing Buckingham Palace. They were never built and the present houses on the site were designed by the builders.

the street is a largely unchanged example of a Pennethorne-inspired townscape (Plate 36).

The Pimlico improvement eased communications between Westminster and the western and south-western suburbs, but St James's Park and Green Park still presented an impenetrable barrier to traffic wanting to reach the West End. Birdcage Walk was closed to through traffic and the Mall was still an avenue of trees open only to pedestrians. Vehicles therefore had to clog an already crowded Whitehall. In 1844 Pennethorne made plans to drive a new road from St James's Street to Westminster, cutting through the fire-damaged eastern quadrangle of St James's Palace, levelling Inigo Jones's Queen's Chapel on its way and crossing the

36. Buckingham Gate, showing Pennethorne's Pimlico District Post Office and James Murray's Palace Hotel in the foreground and the Riding House of Buckingham Palace in the distance.

park with a new bridge over the lake; at the same time Pall Mall would be extended west to Green Park.[62] Fortunately nothing came of these ambitious proposals, but in 1855, in response to a request from Sir Benjamin Hall, the First Commissioner of Works, Pennethorne revived his plan for the road across St James's Park. The most striking feature of the revised scheme was a monumental bridge across the lake

---

62 PRO, Work 34/888; Rep. Sel. Cttee. on St James's Park, *PP* 1856, 7 [85], p. 8.

37. Design for a bridge over the lake in St James's Park, made in connection with plans for a new road from Pall Mall to Westminster in 1855. Sir Benjamin Hall rejected this scheme in favour of one by James Rendel for an all-iron footbridge, which lasted until it was replaced by the present footbridge in 1956–7.

(Plate 37), with three low arches of iron and massive piers surmounted by pedestals supporting hefty gesticulating figures – an echo of Schinkel's Schlossbrücke in Berlin. At the same time Lower Regent Street was to be extended down to the Mall between the two blocks of Carlton House Terrace, enabling traffic from Piccadilly Circus to reach Westminster via Horse Guards Parade.[63]

These proposals were supported by the Queen and Prince Albert, but were vociferously opposed by *The Times* and some MPs, and their criticisms led to the appointment of a Commons Select Committee early in 1856.[64] They would have involved expensive compensation of Crown tenants, and the committee recommended building only the road through St James's Palace to the Mall and the southern extension of Lower Regent Street – a proposal that was later abandoned. The road through the park was also scrapped, and an iron footbridge built over the lake on the initiative of Hall, who 'over-rode the Palladian form altogether'.[65] Thus the seclusion of the park was preserved. The part of Pennethorne's scheme to survive was the road through St James's Palace (Marlborough Road), which he now redesigned to pass beside the west wall of the Queen's Chapel, between the truncated eastern courtyard and Marlborough House. Here he designed a plain single-storied lodge and gates to Marlborough House, where he later carried out important alterations for the Prince of Wales.

Despite the introduction of new and more ornate buildings like the later Pall Mall clubs, the main streets in the West End generally retained their late-Georgian proportions until the 1860s. It was only in the last decade of Pennethorne's life that there was a dramatic change in scale. The demand was now growing for hotels and places of entertainment catering for a wider clientele than the socially exclusive clubs of Pall Mall, and these buildings were bound to be larger and brasher in appearance than their predecessors. A comparable change was taking place in the City, where massive offices and warehouses were taking the place of Georgian houses. Pennethorne could do little to turn back the tide of social change, and he was happy in 1865 to recommend the demolition of the shady White Bear inn in Piccadilly Circus, a former coaching inn but now 'extremely old and worn out and unworthy of its locality'. Its replacement was the Criterion Restaurant and Theatre, built to the designs of Thomas Verity in 1870–4.[66] This heralded the creation of Piccadilly Circus in its present form, a development which, perhaps mercifully, Pennethorne was never to see. The character of the northern end of Regent Street also began to change with the building of St George's concert hall near the present

---

63 PRO, Work 16/298; Work 32/225.

64 Broadlands Papers GC/HA/10, 21 Sept. 1855; *Hansard*, 140 (25–7 Feb. 1856), 1389–90, 1429.

65 Rep. Sel. Cttee. on St James's Park, pp. iii–iv, 1–10; *Hansard*, 141 (10 Apr. 1856), 768–9; 142 (13 and 17 June 1856), 1138, 1141–6, 1569; *BN*, 13 March 1857, p. 258. The bridge was designed by the engineer James Rendel with the assistance of Matthew Digby Wyatt.

66 *Survey of London*, 29 (1960), p. 254; Hobhouse, *Regent Street*, pp. 76–8.

BBC building in 1865, and the gargantuan Langham Hotel at the southern end of Portland Place in 1864–6 – a grim foretaste of future developments. These huge buildings pointed the way towards the total rebuilding of Regent Street in the early twentieth century.

Away from the main streets, Pennethorne was generally content to allow repairs or rebuilding to take place without imposing strict controls. The plain brick houses which covered much of the Crown estate would be valued today, but they were not considered worth preserving in the mid nineteenth century, and there was some piecemeal rebuilding in the area between Piccadilly and Pall Mall in the 1860s. Some of the new buildings in this area were designed by Pennethorne's assistant, Arthur Cates, but none of his buildings rose above the normal level of the commercial architecture of the time.[67] Rebuilding gathered momentum after Pennethorne's death as the leases of the eighteenth-century houses fell in, and today the area contains a mixture of buildings of different dates with little architectural coherence.

THE METROPOLITAN BOARD OF WORKS

Throughout the 1850s Pennethorne continued to argue vainly in favour of a comprehensive scheme of street improvements financed out of an extended coal tax, together with government contributions from the Consolidated Fund. The improvement of London, he told the Select Committee on Metropolitan Communications in 1854, was more than a matter of merely local concern:

I look upon the Metropolis as belonging to the Empire altogether; I think the empire ought to a certain extent to pay for beautifying the metropolis . . . It is visited perhaps by a million of people out of the country and foreigners every year; and every man in the empire is interested in the appearance generally, and the open space and public buildings of the Metropolis.[68]

His pleas fell on deaf ears. In 1848 the First Commissioner of Woods and Forests, Lord Morpeth, had announced that further street improvements could not be contemplated until new funds were found.[69] The new streets of the 1840s and 50s, it was later calculated, had cost a staggering £359 per yard for a mere three and a quarter miles of new thoroughfare.[70] The transference of street improvements to a revived Office of Works in 1851 did nothing to break the impasse, and a writer in *The Builder* subsequently bemoaned the fact that the lack of a fund for Metropolitan

---

67 There are drawings by Cates in PRO, LRRO 1/2158, 1/2283, and RIBA drawings collection W3/17–20.
68 Rep. Sel. Cttee. on Metropolitan Communications (1854–5), pp. 164–70.
69 *Hansard*, 98 (12 May 1848), 932; *The Builder*, 20 May 1848, 250.
70 *BN*, 1 Nov. 1861, 870. This included the new streets in the City.

Improvements had 'prevailed against all the ideas of a comprehensive scheme of London street improvement . . . and has delayed and ultimately crippled nearly every isolated work since the time of Nash'.[71]

The easiest solutions to the problem of funding were to extend the coal duty or to levy local rates. The latter course of action had the greatest appeal to the governments of the 1850s, since it satisfied the principle of 'local self-government'. But before this could happen there needed to be a single representative local authority for the whole of London with the energy and resources to carry the improvements through. The formation of the Metropolitan Board of Works was intended to solve this difficulty. It was the brainchild of Sir Benjamin Hall, MP for Marylebone and 'an unsparing searcher after and exposer of abuses'.[72] One of the most shocking of these abuses was the worsening state of London's public health, due to the continuing lack of good sanitation. As President of the General Board of Health, Hall had succeeded in persuading Lord Aberdeen's government to abolish the ineffective London Commission of Sewers and to replace it with an elected body which would manage the sewers, oversee the London Building Acts – revised in 1844 but still in need of improvement[73] – and relieve the Office of Works, and thereby the British taxpayer, of the responsibility for planning and financing street improvements. The only improvements remaining in government hands were to be those in and around the Royal Parks. Pennethorne was therefore finally relieved of his responsibility for Metropolitan Improvements. The new Board was to cover almost all the built-up area outside the City and to have the power of levying local rates and borrowing money.[74] With its creation in 1855 London had, for the first time, a unified agency capable of carrying out the street improvements which Pennethorne and others had long urged.

The greatest achievements of the Metropolitan Board of Works were the provision of a modern system of sewers and the building of the Victoria Embankment – the most ambitious of the proposals recommended by the recently disbanded Royal Commission on Metropolitan Improvements. Work on the Embankment began in 1862, laying the way open for the architectural transformation of the river front. The Embankment also eased traffic congestion in the Strand and Fleet Street and finally killed off Pennethorne's project for an inevitably expensive new street from Piccadilly to St Paul's Cathedral, while the building of Holborn Viaduct by the City Corporation in 1863–9 removed the worst of the remaining obstructions along the route from Oxford Street through New Oxford Street to the City. The

71 *The Builder*, 1 Dec. 1866, 877.

72 *ILN*, 30 April 1859, 429. See p. 68.

73 I. Darlington, 'The Metropolitan Buildings Office', *The Builder*, 12 Oct. 1956, 628–32. Pennethorne was an Examiner under the Act.

74 F. Sheppard, *London 1808–1870: the Infernal Wen* (1971), pp. 277–8; D. Owen, *The Government of Victorian London* (Cambridge, Mass., 1982), pp. 23–32.

Metropolitan Board of Works continued Pennethorne's policy of building more new streets through poor neighbourhoods, notably Shaftesbury Avenue, Charing Cross Road and Rosebery Avenue, and this succeeded in clearing the worst remaining slums from central London.[75] The end result was the social and architectural transformation of a large area in the very heart of the capital.

But, for all their social significance, the streets built by the Metropolitan Board of Works added little to the beauty of London. The Board had only limited borrowing powers and costs had to be kept to a minimum. There was none of the cheerful tree-lined expansiveness of the boulevards of Paris or Vienna. In the free-for-all aesthetic climate of the later nineteenth century, even the rudimentary architectural control exercised by Pennethorne in the 1840s was jettisoned. Grim 'mansion' blocks of flats share the street frontages with the even grimmer tenement blocks of working-class housing erected by the philanthropic societies. The more expansive Edwardian era brought a temporary return to the grander visions of Nash and Pennethorne in the building of Kingsway and Aldwych in 1905. These finally succeeded in opening up a major route leading north from Waterloo Bridge. But generally speaking the vexations which Pennethorne encountered in his efforts as a street planner have continued to dog his successors, and today the lover of London is well advised to seek his aesthetic pleasures away from the grimy, fume-filled and traffic-laden main thoroughfares.

---

75 See P. J. Edwards, *The History of London Street Improvements* (1898).

3

PARKS FOR THE PEOPLE

THE URBAN PARK in its present form is a creation of the nineteenth century. The vast growth of cities had barred many people from easy access to the countryside. It was generally believed that the lack of fresh, pure air and open space contributed to a deterioration in public health and to that restless *anomie* which has always affected some of the poorer inhabitants of the central areas. This frame of mind could discourage self-improvement and, at worst, feed those disorderly impulses which threatened social stability and harmony. By encouraging 'rational amusements' in discreetly supervised surroundings, parks could contribute to the creation of a balanced and orderly society. And, together with well-planned streets, they could point the way towards the development of cities along aesthetically more pleasing lines.

Early nineteenth-century London did not lack public open spaces, but they were not situated in those parts of the city where they were needed most. The royal parks formed a wedge of greenery stretching from Bayswater and Kensington to the very heart of government in Whitehall, but the City, the East End, and the northern and southern suburbs were much less well supplied. The squares in the smarter districts were not open to the general public. Private pleasure gardens, like the once-fashionable Vauxhall Gardens and the more plebeian Eagle of nursery-rhyme fame ('Pop goes the weasel') in the City Road were disappearing under the rapid advance of housing. A witness to the Commons Select Committee on Public Walks in 1833 bemoaned the fact that 'the little tea-gardens round about London, in my time, have all gone to decay for want of encouragement'. Working-class youths and their girlfriends who had patronised them at weekends now had nowhere to go but the public houses. Commons and open grasslands and meadows were equally threatened. Moorfields, for long a favourite resort of City-dwellers, had been leased for building by the City Corporation. As more and more people found it difficult to walk out of London into the country for recreation, influential citizens began to call on the government to set aside suburban areas for new parks.

The government's initial involvement in the provision of metropolitan parks sprang not out of altruism but from a wish to develop the Crown estates on profitable and visually satisfying lines. The result was Regent's Park. Visually the park represented a new departure, with its irregularly shaped lake, winding walks and artfully positioned clumps of trees. Such features were familiar in the landscaped grounds of country houses, but had hitherto been unknown in an urban setting. The surrounding terraced housing served not only to provide an appropriately stately backdrop to the picturesque landscape, but also to bring in an income which would, it was hoped, increase over the years and help defray the cost of making the park. Pennethorne had nothing to do with the formation of Regent's Park, but he was closely involved in a subordinate capacity in the remodelling of St James's Park, where the formal straight 'canal' was converted into the present irregular lake and curving paths formed in place of the earlier straight lines. It was through this project that he acquired his first experience of landscape design.

However, Regent's Park and St James's Park did relatively little to remedy the chronic and increasing lack of open space for the inhabitants of London's poorer areas. Interest in questions of public health and environmental issues increased in the aftermath of the 1832 Reform Act and the first visitation of cholera in the same year. In 1833, therefore, a Commons Select Committee was set up to investigate the provision of 'public walks' in London and other larger towns. Its members, who included Lord Duncannon, the First Commissioners of Woods and Forests and Lord Morpeth, a future First Commissioner, investigated the provision of open spaces in the capital and recommended the opening of the whole of Regent's Park to the public and the acquisition of Primrose Hill to the north. New parks should be created to serve the inhabitants of the East End, and 'open quays' provided on the banks of the Thames. These new open spaces would, it was hoped, help wean the poor from 'low and debasing pleasures' like dog-fights and boxing matches. The committee concluded that public money should be used in furtherance of these aims, since 'it seems the duty of the Government to assist in providing for the Health of the People by whose efforts they are supported'.[1]

PRIMROSE HILL

The first tangible result of the Select Committee's deliberations was the acquisition of Primrose Hill. An 'open healthy spot which the humbler classes have been in the habit of visiting with their families in fine weather time out of mind', the hill commanded a view over Regent's Park and the rest of London to the south. It belonged to Eton College, which was just about to develop its extensive north London estates for building, but early in 1841 the Treasury approved an

---

1 Rep. Sel. Cttee. on Public Works, *PP* 1833, 15 [448], pp. 5–10, 20–8.

arrangement under which the Crown would exchange some of its property at Eton with the College in return for the acquisition of the hill.[2] Pennethorne had already prepared a plan of the ground showing a rudimentary layout of walks and plantations and, at the highest point of the hill, a level terrace, crowned by a monstrous figure of a seated Britannia. This plan was not implemented in full, and the ground was allowed to remain in the relatively 'unimproved' state which it still preserves today.[3] The opening of the whole of Regent's Park to the public in 1841 completed the process of creating a large public open space to serve the inhabitants of north-west London.

VICTORIA PARK

The need for new parks was most marked in the crowded streets and squalid courts of the East End. The question of creating a park here was raised in 1838 by Joseph Hume, the radical MP for Middlesex and a member of the 1836 Select Committee on Metropolitan Improvements. A disciple of Francis Place and an energetic reformer, Hume had been interested in the provision of parks for the poor since 1832.[4] His appeal for a park in the East End was reinforced by the publication of the first report of the Registrar General of Births, Deaths and Marriages in 1839, which contained a statement by the statistician William Farr, that

[a] good general system of Sewers, the intersection of the dense crowded districts of the Metropolis by a few spacious streets, and a park in the East End of London would probably diminish the annual deaths by several thousands, prevent many years of sickness, and add several years to the lives of the entire population. The poorer classes would be benefited by these measures and the poor rates reduced, but all classes of the community are directly interested in their adoption, for the epidemics whether influenza or typhus, cholera, small pox, scarlatina or measles, which arise in the East End of the town, do not stay there, they travel to the West End and prove fatal in the wide streets and squares.[5]

Hume now began a campaign to attract public support for his proposal, and in June 1840, with Chartism in the air, a public meeting was held in Limehouse and a petition circulated.[6] The idea was supported in Parliament by Lord Duncannon and by Charles Blomfield, Bishop of London, and their advocacy no doubt helped persuade the Melbourne administration to take it seriously. The Whigs had already taken the first steps towards implementing a coherent system of street improvements

---

2 PRO, T 25/18, pp. 125, 318; Work 6/180.

3 *Ibid.*, MPE 1608; *The Builder*, 24 March 1849, 140. Pennethorne is credited with the layout of the ground in *Mechanics' Magazine*, 26 (1871), 285.

4 A. Fein, 'Victoria Park: its Origins and History', *East London Papers*, 5 (1962), 74.

5 PRO, Work 6/99, pp. 54–5.

6 G. F. Poulsen, *Victoria Park* (1976), pp. 17–20; *BN* 16 Oct. 1857, 1083.

in central and east London. The creation of a new park in the East End could be presented as a token of their concern to help eradicate some of the worst evils of modern urban life. Pennethorne, who had already prepared schemes for the new streets, was an obvious choice to investigate possible sites. His report, presented in April 1841, marked the first stage in the formation of what became Victoria Park, the first park specifically intended for the Poor in any capital city.

Pennethorne suggested two possible sites: one near Bow Common not far from the River Thames, and the other further north at Bonners Fields, near the rapidly expanding artisan suburb of Bethnal Green. East London was expanding very rapidly, and the two sites offered the closest open space available for purchase at a reasonable price. Pennethorne's own preference was for the first site, because it could be easily reached by larger numbers of people. The acquisition of the land would involve the compulsory purchase of some factories and about a hundred small cottages, but the social advantages would outweigh the high cost and the 'trifling (if any) advantages derivable from the picturesque beauty of the other site'.[7]

It was the cost which made the Commissioners of Woods and Forests ignore Pennethorne's advice and plump for the northern site. Although it was further from the main centres of population, there were no buildings to purchase. The land was completely flat and had the rather down-at-heel appearance characteristic of many areas on the edges of large towns, with grave-diggings, brick pits, and impoverished hamlets clustering close by. Pennethorne proposed to form the park to the south of one such hamlet, known popularly as Botany Bay, on a boot-shaped site of 237 acres (96 hectares), in an angle formed by the Regent's Canal and a cut (now called the Hertford Union Canal) which linked it to the River Lea. It was crossed by a lane (Grove Road) linking Hackney, soon to become a haven for lower-middle-class commuters, with the Mile End Road.[8] On the western or London side of the Regent's Canal stood Bonner's Hall (Plate 38), the former manor-house of Stepney, a 'curious old-fashioned structure of plaster and brickwork', named after the notorious sixteenth-century bishop who was said to have imprisoned and tortured Protestants in a building on the site.[9] Around it stretched a tract of meadow-land called Bonners Fields, over which the public claimed a right of access. Pennethorne proposed to create the park for £75,075, little more than half the cost of a park on the Bow Common site; he pointed out, though, that another £5,000 at least would need to be spent on providing better access roads, especially from the poor districts to the south, and that before the surrounding ground could be let for housing the government would also need to spend extra money on providing roads and sewers.

In its dying days Lord Melbourne's government decided to pay for the park out of the proceeds of the sale of York House – now Lancaster House – on the edge of

---

7 PRO, Work 6/99, pp. 58–68.
8 *Ibid.*, MPE 837.
9 W. Thornbury and E. Walford, *Old and New London*, 6 vols. (1873), v, p. 508.

38. Bonner's Hall, shortly before its demolition to make way for the Victoria Park approaches. The house clearly dates from the second half of the seventeenth century and the sign advertises 'ginune ales'.

Green Park. This magnificent residence had been beautified by George IV's younger brother the Duke of York, but with his death it was no longer needed by the royal family, and it was purchased by the prodigiously wealthy Duke of Sutherland who proceeded to embellish it further. Because of this fortunate windfall the government did not need to resort to taxation to finance the park, and the difficulties encountered with the concurrent programme of street improvements were avoided. The first plan for laying out the ground was submitted with the signatures of Pennethorne and Chawner in June 1841, but, as with the street improvements, it is obvious from the correspondence that Pennethorne was the guiding spirit. The design, intended 'more as a means to bring certain points under the Consideration of the Board, than as a plan suggested to be acted upon', showed a rudimentary layout of trees in clumps, bounded by a drive around the perimeter, beyond which houses were arranged in terraces 'as in the Regent's Park'. As one later writer put it: 'The formers of the park can thus shut out what is disagreeable and obtain, by judiciously placing these structures and adapting the plantations to them, and keeping a control over the elevations, a series of delightful and ornamental accompaniments'.[10] In the same spirit Pennethorne persuaded the commissioners to turn down proposals for a private zoo on the grounds that it would encourage 'fireworks and evening assemblages'.[11]

A draft Bill for acquiring the land was prepared at the beginning of 1842 and became law in the summer, but plans to start work were delayed by some of the twelve freeholders who submitted wildly excessive claims in order to cash in on the improved value of their property. A brick-maker who owned 22 acres (9 hectares) in the middle of the park demanded £19,000 and was not persuaded to accept a lower adjudication of £800 until late in 1844. By then work could begin on preparing the ground, and early in 1845 Pennethorne prepared designs for the approach roads and for the main entrance lodge. The lodge was to form a focal point at the end of a wide approach road on the line of a former footpath leading north-east across Bonners Fields from Old Ford Road, the country lane which ran east from Bethnal Green. The streets on either side were to be lined with terraced housing, and part of the ground laid out as an ornamental garden – an echo of fashionable Belgravia. At a later stage the approach road would be extended south-west across Bethnal Green in the direction of the City, making the park more accessible to potential users and more closely integrated into the fabric of London as a whole.[12]

The lodge and gate-piers were designed in the florid Jacobean manner which Pennethorne was currently recommending as a model for the development of New Oxford Street. The lodge, destroyed in the Second World War, was a substantial two-storied red brick building with a low tower capped by a parapet with strapwork ornament and obelisks (Plate 39). Its style of architecture alluded to the early history of the site and provided a suitably picturesque introduction to the scenes which would unfold within the park. More importantly, its presence gave an elevated aristocratic character to the park which distinguished it from a mere piece of common ground and enabled some control to be kept over who came in and out. According to one account:

The regulations of St. James's Park, with regard to the admission of visitors, are observed as far as possible, the park-keepers having orders to exclude all disorderly and drunken persons,

---

10 E. Kemp, *The Parks, Gardens . . . of London and its Suburbs* (1851), p. 18.
11 GLRO, Victoria Park Papers (VPP), vol. 1; 18th Rep. Commrs. of Woods, Forests, *PP* 1841, 12 [426], Appendix 20; PRO, Work 6/99, pp. 112–16.
12 VPP plans, nos. 15, 19 and 31; PRO, LRRO 1/2037/3.

39. The lodge and gates at the main entrance to Victoria Park, on the site of Bonner's Hall, in 1936. The gates have recently been restored, but the lodge, which was the home of the park-keeper, was destroyed in the Second World War.

itinerant vendors, and dogs. During the recent holidays, notwithstanding the crowds of visitors, excellent order was kept by an efficient staff of park-keepers, under the direction of Mr. Mobbs, the chief gate-keeper, and very trifling injury or damage was done.[13]

Victoria Park was intended to improve the moral as well as the physical conditions of the poor, and the lodge played an important part in that ambitious aim. With the completion of the lodge and main approach road at the end of 1845, it became possible to plan the layout of the park itself (Plate 40). Pennethorne's general plan showing the proposed disposition of drives, paths and plantations was accepted by the Commissioners of Woods and Forests with the sensible observation that 'the proper direction for [the] paths will be found to be best ascertained by the Lines, which the Public work out for themselves', and the detailed management of the planting was placed, on the recommendation of Sir William Hooker, director of

---

13 Newspaper cuttings, Bancroft Library, London Borough of Tower Hamlets.

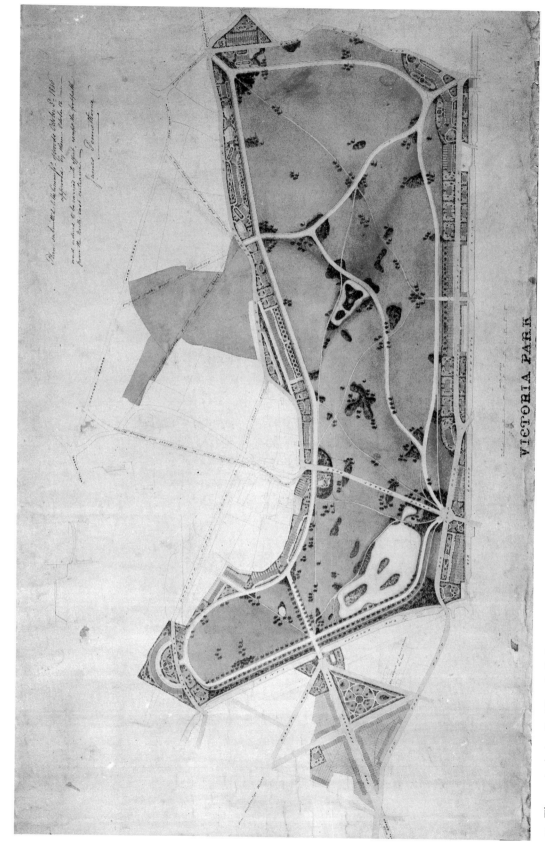

VICTORIA PARK

40. The revised plan for Victoria Park, 1846. Two lakes are shown (a third was dug slightly later) and so too is the carriage drive around the perimeter. This layout remains virtually unchanged today. Pennethorne wanted the park to be overlooked by smart terraces and semi-detached villas with gardens, but these were never built, at least in the form intended. The Approach Road from Bethnal Green is on the left; a hospital replaced the ornamental garden shown here.

Kew Gardens, in the hands of Samuel Curtis.[14] The ground was thrown open to the public as work proceeded, and, according to *The Times*, 25,000 people went there on Good Friday 1846.

The main change to Pennethorne's original plans for the layout came with the decision to form a lake, to 'suit the present forms and levels of ground, and to produce as much variety of scenery as may be obtained in the limited space without any great increase of cost'[15] There was some popular pressure for a boating lake, and Pennethorne reminded the commissioners of

the good effect which rational amusements produce on the lower orders – and the ornamental water in St James' Park, Hyde Park and the Regent's Park have been the source of such enjoyment to the Public as to induce a general feeling that ornamental water is almost an integral and indispensible part of a Royal Park.

In 1842 he had produced a plan jointly with Joseph Paxton, the greatest park designer of the mid nineteenth century, for Prince's Park, Liverpool – a park very similar in its general principles to Victoria Park – with an irregular lake in one angle.[16] He proposed putting the Victoria Park lake on some brick pits in the southern angle, with a museum on the north bank. But although the lake was approved by the Commissioners in October 1846 the museum was never built.[17]

In his final design for the park Pennethorne achieved a satisfying balance between formality and irregularity. The broad 'carriage drive' around the perimeter and the straight avenue leading north across the park from the entrance gates towards Hackney imparted a note of elevated grandeur noticeably absent from most of the East End (Plates 41–2). The drives and pathways were liberally planted with trees and shrubs which now, in their maturity, convey a sense of expansiveness, and further variety came from the lake, dotted with islands to give that effect of 'intricacy' so admired by Humphry Repton and his successors. The purchase, on Pennethorne's recommendation, of a Chinese pagoda of iron (since destroyed) for one of the islands added to the picturesque charm (Plate 43), which would have been further enhanced if the commissioners had allowed him to build a Chinese footbridge to the island.[18] The rest of the landscape was crossed by winding paths and broken up with clumps of trees. A second lake in the northern portion of the park, approved by the commissioners in mid 1847, was eventually used for bathing, despite objections from Pennethorne that it would 'quite destroy the value of the

---

14 VPP, vol. 2, 27 June 1845; PRO, Cres 19/32, pp. 100–2.

15 *Ibid.*, 18 May 1846.

16 G. F. Chadwick, *The Works of Sir Joseph Paxton* (1961), p. 47. Pennethorne played no part in the subsequent layout or execution of the park, a plan of which survives in the Liverpool Record Office.

17 PRO, LRRO 1/2036/1.

18 VPP, vol. 3, 2 Feb. 1849; PRO, LRRO 1/2046; Cres 19/35, p. 435.

41. An early view of Victoria Park. The trees are placed at regular intervals along the wide pathways and there is an ample display of bedding plants.

Park as a place of residence', and a gymnasium and a second boating lake followed later.[19]

Like Nash, Pennethorne was not a plantsman. So he left the important decisions about planting to Curtis, who turned out to be negligent and was dismissed in May 1849. A few years later Joseph Paxton was quoted in Parliament as saying that the planting had been done by 'men who did not know the names of half-a-dozen kinds of trees they were planting'.[20] Most of the imperfections were remedied by Curtis's successor, John Gibson, a Paxton pupil and protégé who had been trained at Chatsworth and had gone to South Africa and India to collect orchids for the Duke of Devonshire in 1835–7. He was given a relatively free hand, and, while making

19 PRO, Cres 19/34, pp. 144–5; *ILN*, 20 Sept. 1851.
20 *Hansard*, 142 (18 July 1856), 1433–5, 1563.

42. Avenue and boating lake, Victoria Park. The spacious layout and generous planting provide a dignified backdrop to the recreations of a group of East Enders.

few alterations to Pennethorne's layout, he introduced beds of flowers, flowering shrubs and exotic trees which undoubtedly improved the appearance of the park. Pennethorne's own final contribution was an attractive round-arched arcade built as a place of shelter in 1861, but destroyed after the Second World War.[21] Like the splendid Gothic drinking fountain, given by the well-known philanthropist Baroness Burdett-Coutts in 1862 and designed by her architect H. A. Darbishire, this exotic structure added an appropriate note of gaiety to a park which succeeded in bringing to the poor of east London some of the enjoyments formerly available only to the few.

Socially as well as aesthetically, Victoria Park was a great success. By the late 1850s

---

21 PRO, Work 1/68, p. 273; VPP plans, no. 14.

an estimated sixty to seventy thousand people were visiting it each Sunday.[22] As a symbol of enlightened government action it demonstrated to one contemporary commentator

that the rich and powerful no longer deem the poor beneath their contempt . . . No nobler monument exists of the kindly disposition which now generally prevails, for ameliorating the condition of the operative classes; no surer antidote is found to the incendiary harangue, which would make the humble discontented with their governors, than Victoria Park.[23]

The park did in fact later become the scene of 'incendiary harangues' in the form of mass Trades Union meetings, but in general it contributed in a small way to the softening of manners among the mass of the people which marked the century or so after 1850. Conceived in the troubled early 1840s, it is a monument to the increasing social cohesion which began to be evident in England in the post-Chartist period. Even today, despite later and not always sympathetic alterations, it remains a benign influence among the high-rise blocks and shabby streets of the East End.

Once the park had been completed, Pennethorne's attention was directed to the development of the building estate around the edge. He told the Commissioners of Woods and Forests in October 1846 that the area to the north, towards Hackney, was assuming 'a new and improved aspect', and that he hoped that the sites might be let in the following spring.[24] His first proposals now seem absurdly optimistic. Detached and semi-detached houses were to line both sides of a new road running parallel to the Hertford Union canal, and terraces built along the whole of the northern side of the park, with a crescent around the 'toe' at the western end. These plans were obviously influenced by those for Regent's Park, but there was never any likelihood that the rich would be persuaded to live so far from their accustomed haunts. The best hope lay in attracting the growing army of Samuel Pooters emerging from the offices of the City.

The letting of the sites, even to builders catering for this much maligned class, depended on the construction of suitable access roads. According to *The Builder*: 'Where is Victoria Park? is not at all an infrequent question, even within a hundred yards of the gate, so obscured and hidden is it . . . The land in Victoria Park will *not let* for building purposes until the public know and can see the way to it'.[25] Early in 1847 therefore Pennethorne submitted estimates to the Royal Commission for Metropolitan Improvements for building three such thoroughfares: one crossing Bethnal Green, another leading to the northern side of the park from Cambridge Heath Road, and a third running south to Mile End Road and Limehouse. The road on the north side of the park (now Victoria Park Road) was built in 1850–1 with the help of the trustees of the Sir John Cass charity, which owned much of the

---

22 *The Builder*, 5 June 1858, 389.
23 W. Gaspey, *Tallis's Illustrated London* (1851) II, p. 254.
24 VPP, vol. 2, 3 Oct. 1846.   25 *The Builder*, 9 Jan. 1847, 11.

43. Ornamental features of Victoria Park. The swings, boating lake and wooden refreshment pavilion enhance the park's popular appeal, while the pagoda and cascade add a note of the exotic.

land, and its construction succeeded in sweeping away the 'wretched village of houses (or hovels more properly) formerly known as Botany Bay'.[26] Pennethorne wanted the southern road to Limehouse to be a broad tree-lined boulevard 'assuming so much the character of part of the park, that those who were unable to walk far enough actually to reach it, might still fancy themselves almost within its precincts as soon as they entered the road itself'[27] – an imaginative idea which calls to mind the spacious layout of the streets in nineteenth-century Berlin. But the project languished for lack of funds, and the Bill for purchasing the ground was never introduced. A less ambitiously conceived thoroughfare called Burdett Road from Mile End to Limehouse was built by the Metropolitan Board of Works in 1862, but it bore no relationship to Pennethorne's proposals, and the road across Bethnal Green was never built at all.

The development of the building land dragged on throughout Pennethorne's life. After complaints in 1848 about the use of Bonners Fields for Sunday Chartist meetings, held by people with 'irreligious or democratic principles', he recommended enclosing the ground and letting some of the sites for building.[28] But the building trade was depressed and nothing was done until 1850, when a large site to the east of the approach road, originally intended for an ornamental garden, was leased as the site of the City of London Hospital for Diseases of the Chest. Here in 1851 F. W. Ordish designed a neo-'Queen Anne' building, stylistically unusual for its time. The opening of Victoria Park Road in the same year at last made the northern side of the park available for 'good Houses and Villas', and an Act was finally passed in mid 1852 setting aside 45 acres (18 hectares) on which building would take place. Pennethorne thought that it would be unwise to let the ground until land values had risen to the point where substantial middle-class houses could be contemplated, and he believed that this point had been reached in 1853. The area around Bonners Fields was beginning to be developed by the neighbouring landowners, and Hackney, to the north-west, was already accessible to City clerks by the new North London Railway, albeit by a circuitous route. Only the northern and eastern extremities still abutted on open country. Streets were therefore laid out in Bonners Fields and to the south of Victoria Park Road, and in February 1854 Pennethorne prepared a series of detailed plans showing a division of all the building sites into 173 lots.[29]

The response was very disappointing. Builders were deterred by the state of the money market and the availability of similar ground nearer London. Smaller houses for artisans could, no doubt, have been built more rapidly, but neither Pennethorne nor the Commissioners of Woods and Forests thought that this was an appropriate

---

26 *Ibid.*
27 VPP plans, nos. 20–1; *BN*, 16 Oct. 1857, 1084.
28 VPP, vol. 3, 30 June 1848.
29 PRO, LRRO 1/2043, 1/2115; MR 55/8; T 1/5806A, 1/14661.

way to develop what was now part of the Crown estate. The curving roads south of Victoria Park Road (Gore Road, Morpeth Road, etc.) were finally completed in 1858, but despite the granting of a few building leases in the former Bonners Fields the building sites were still only bringing in £200 a year by the middle of 1859 instead of the £6,000 Pennethorne had anticipated.[30] Even by 1863 development was still distinctly patchy, but by then the park was finally achieving its effect of raising property prices in the area around, and one writer could draw attention to the 'new town of villa residences [which] has sprung up where before there were open fields, waste land and miserable rookeries, tenanted by a squalid, criminal population'.[31] Most of the remaining building plots were leased in the next few years. But the ground on the north-eastern side was not built up until well after Pennethorne's death, and his proposal to build a road parallel to the canal was fortunately abandoned in 1872, when an Act was passed incorporating the remaining building ground into the park itself.

The houses which overlook the park and line the broad approach road are of the two- or three- storied terraced type, some of them with basements, popular with the better-off City clerks of the time (Plate 44). The builders were local men, but the designs were all submitted to Pennethorne for approval, and when necessary, modification. Because of the reluctance of small-scale builders everywhere to engage on large-scale projects, the houses were built in small groups, and there was little architectural uniformity. The streets around the park nevertheless provide an attractive, if unremarkable, example of the suburban architecture of the time.

KENNINGTON PARK

The creation of Victoria Park raised the expectations of the poorer inhabitants of the rest of London. As in the East End, the rapid spread of building was daily reducing the amount of accessible open space and placing what remained under constant threat. Pennethorne and Chawner were asked to investigate possible sites for parks in other parts of London as early as the autumn of 1841. They suggested four sites north of the Thames and six to the south.[32] The need for a park to serve the expanding areas south of the river seemed most urgent, and here the architects suggested making a park on 55 acres (22 hectares) of ground which included Kennington Common, at the then edge of the built-up area, 'a dreary place of waste land, covered partly with short grass, and frequented only by boys flying their kites or playing at marbles'. Plans to acquire the whole area foundered in 1842 because

30 *Ibid.*, Cres 19/48, p. 51
31 G. R. Emerson, *London: How the Great City Grew* (1862), p. 272. See also M. Hunter, *The Victorian Villas of Hackney* (1981).
32 PRO, Work 6/99, pp. 160–5.

of the extravagant claims for compensation made by the main landowners, the Dean and Chapter of Canterbury. The ground surrounding the Common was built on during the 1840s, and the Common itself played host to the final Chartist rally in 1848, attracting adverse comments on account of its 'dirty unwholesome state', due in part to the presence of a vitriol works nearby. It was finally acquired by the government and laid out as a park in 1852–3, after Pennethorne had made 'detailed plans and schedules' for the site. None of his plans survive, and he was not responsible for the rather conventional scheme of planting which turned the common into a 'pretty promenade . . . intersected by broad and well-kept gravelled walks bordered with flower-beds', noteworthy mainly for the entrance lodge designed by Henry Roberts for Prince Albert as one of a pair of model cottages at the Great Exhibition of 1851.[33]

BATTERSEA PARK

Pennethorne played a much more significant role in the formation of the other government-sponsored park in south London, at Battersea Fields. The idea of making a park out of this low-lying tract of land on the banks of the Thames originated with the philanthropic impulses of the great builder Thomas Cubitt. In the early 1840s Cubitt was deeply engaged in the development of the Marquess of Westminster's estate on the opposite side of the river in Belgravia and Pimlico. Through this project he became interested in the idea of making an embankment and a new bridge (Chelsea Bridge) which would open up the area south of the river to building, and in 1843 he put a proposal for a park to the Royal Commission on Metropolitan Improvements. The proposal was warmly backed by the Rev. the Hon. Robert Eden, vicar of Battersea, and in November 1843 he wrote to the Prime Minister, Sir Robert Peel, urging the immediate purchase of what he called 'a lung that is almost necessary to the health of the Neighbourhood'.[34]

The ground formed part of the former common fields of Battersea, still in the 1840s an isolated village grouped around its eighteenth-century church within a bend of the Thames. The fields had largely escaped enclosure, and parts were still subject to common grazing rights. Herds of cows were pastured there from September to November each year, but otherwise the land was used for growing hay and for market gardening. To the west was the wooden Battersea Bridge, immortalised in Whistler's poetic 'Nocturnes'; to the east a waterworks; and to the south the main line of the London and South Western Railway, opened in 1838. Small factories and workshops lined the river banks. There were no fewer than 364

33 GLRO, Kennington Park papers; PRO, Work 2/10, pp. 139–41, 531; *RIBA Transactions* (1856–7), 10; Thornbury and Walford, *Old and New London*, VI, pp. 334–8.
34 5th Rep. Commrs. for Metropolitan Improvements, *PP* 1846, 24, p. 3; PRO, Work 6/102, p. 142.

44. Approach Road, Victoria Park in the early twentieth century. The grounds of the hospital are on the right, terraced houses of the late 1850s and 1860s on the left and the entrance gates in the middle distance. The street is unusually wide for this part of London.

separate parcels of land, most of them small strips known as 'marshes' or 'shots'.[35] The persistence of common rights and the difficulty of access from central London prevented large-scale building, and in the 1840s there were only a few dwellings. But with the sale of the manor by Lord Spencer in 1835 pressure on the small free-holders to sell their land for housing began to increase.

Battersea Fields were already a place of popular resort by the 1840s, but they had acquired an unsavoury reputation which the promoters of the park wished to eradicate. Duels had long been fought there, one of them involving the Duke of

---

35 PRO, Work 32/660.

Wellington, and on Sundays much of the area was given over to fairs which attracted large numbers of dubious characters, including

costermongers and roughs, and those prowling vagabonds who call themselves gipsies. The weekday scenes here were bad enough, but on Sundays they were positively disgraceful, and to a great extent the police were powerless, for the place was a sort of no man's land, on which ruffianism claimed to riot uncontrolled by any other authority than its own will. Pugilistic encounters, dog-fights, and the rabble coarseness of a country fair at its worst were as common as blackberries in autumn.[36]

By the bank of the river, close to the present Chelsea Bridge, there was an inn called the Red House 'the 'Red'us', mentioned by Dickens in *Sketches by Boz*. It served as a resort for pigeon shooters and acted as 'a second Vauxhall Gardens' for visitors who came by river in increasing numbers with the expansion of steamboat traffic in the 1840s. Rival beerhouses and tea gardens now sprang up to attract customers, some of whom bathed naked in the river. A writer in the *London City Mission Magazine* thought that 'if there was a place out of hell that surpassed Sodom and Gomorrah in ungodliness and abomination, this was it'. But according to the vicar of Battersea:

many of these persons would become orderly if pains were taken to provide for them healthful recreation . . . By encouraging healthful recreations [like skating, cricket, archery and boating] the Commissioners [for Metropolitan Improvements] will promote social and domestic happiness; they will implant feelings which are now deadened by dirt, by drink, and by discomfort.[37]

The question of designing and funding the park was taken up seriously by the commissioners in 1845. Thomas Cubitt was not prepared to pay for the park himself, and even Charles Trevelyan, the usually parsimonious Assistant Secretary to the Treasury, urged the government to buy the land. He walked across Battersea Fields daily from his home at Clapham, and concluded that

it would not only be the most complete, but also, in the end, the most economical plan to buy the whole of the unoccupied portion of the Fields between the River and the Railroad and to lay out the portion bordering on the new Park in Villas with ornamental shrubberies and gardens so that the Park should be bounded only by the River and by detached buildings of a kind calculated to add to the general effect.[38]

The vicar of Battersea had already prepared a plan for a 315-acre (127-hectare) park, but the commissioners did not trust his estimate of the cost and turned to Pennethorne, who was asked to prepare a detailed plan of his own under which a

---

36 Thornbury and Walford, *Old and New London*, VI, p. 476.
37 PRO, Work 6/102, p. 295; J. J. Sexby, *The Municipal Parks, Gardens and Open Spaces of London* (1898), p. 10; *PP* 1846, 24, pp. 10–11.
38 PRO, Work 6/103, pp. 85–6.

third of the ground would be used for houses. As at Victoria Park, the intention was to attract middle-class people to the building land, so defraying some of the cost through rents. The building of Chelsea Bridge would help make the ground attractive to potential suburbanites who, until then, had shunned the south bank of the river.

Pennethorne's plan shows an ambitious layout of terraces and villas around a rectangular open space with a terrace along the river bank, a large lake in the centre and a grand public building on its northern shore, close to the river (Plate 45). The surrounding roads converge on *rond-points* by the new Chelsea Bridge and by the site of Albert Bridge (not yet proposed) further west. The layout of streets and houses, had it been carried out, would have provided a visually attractive mixture of large and smaller houses (21 terraces and 146 villas), rather along the lines of the Ladbroke estate in north Kensington. Pennethorne told the commissioners that, if the site were developed as he proposed, it would make a profit of about ten per cent of the estimated outlay of £145,250. But before that could happen Chelsea Bridge had to be built, and the promoters did not want to proceed until the embankment had been constructed. The commissioners assumed – wrongly – that these obstacles would be easily overcome, and recommended the government to go ahead on the basis of Pennethorne's scheme. Peel communicated the report to the Queen, and in October 1845 the government decided to introduce a Bill in the next session.[39]

From the very beginning the plans were thwarted by a lack of money. The Act passed in August 1846 for Battersea Park and Chelsea Bridge authorised the Commissioners of Woods and Forests to borrow £200,000 for making the park and £120,000 for the bridge. The original intention was to raise the money by selling Crown property on the foreshore at Birkenhead (Merseyside), but that plan came to nothing because the government refused to place further charges on the Crown's land revenues, which were not subject to direct Parliamentary control.[40] The commissioners were therefore obliged to resort to loans, using the expected rents and bridge tolls as security.[41] Rather than raising the loan on the open market – a tactic which had already proved all but impossible in the new streets – the Treasury told the commissioners to apply to the Exchequer (or Public Works) Loan Commissioners. They controlled a fund of some £360,000 designed to provide capital for public works undertaken by local authorities, but because of other demands on the fund the Loan Commissioners felt obliged to lend the money only in small instalments; the purchase of the ground therefore took a very long time, during which the owners and occupiers of the land took the opportunity to increase their claims for compensation. The result of this delay was all but disastrous.

---

39 GLRO, Battersea Park Papers (BPP), vol. 1, 3 Oct. 1845.
40 There is a detailed account of the formation of the park in Copy Rep. on Battersea Park, *PP* 1856, 52 [193], pp. 14–15 and Rep. Sel. Cttee. on Chelsea Bridge Bill, *PP* 1857 (2), 41 [251], pp. 2–20.
41 *Hansard*, 118 (16 July 1851), 851; 129 (5 Aug. 1853), 1409.

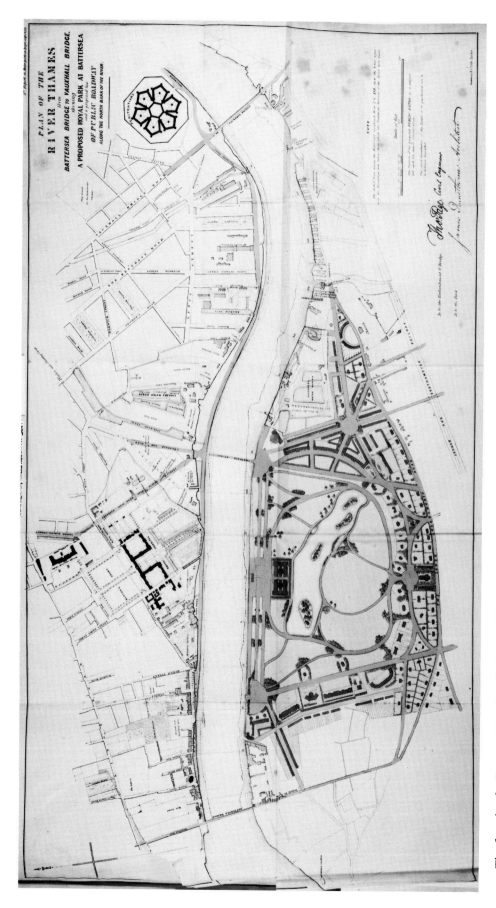

45. The first plan for Battersea Park (1845). Much of the area inside the park is taken up by a lake. New roads flank the open space with terraces of housing beyond them, and to the south there are spacious villas set amidst gardens; these features were nearly all omitted when the park was eventually laid out. The Chelsea Embankment runs along the opposite side of the river and Chelsea Bridge Road links Chelsea Bridge to Sloane Street.

When Pennethorne started preparing detailed estimates of the value of the ground in September 1846 he discovered that both freeholders and leaseholders were demanding twice what he had estimated a year earlier; these claims, he later said, had been orchestrated by some of the larger property owners, including the parish surveyor. Since the decision to make the park was made public, some of the freeholders had built houses on their land. Some of the leaseholders had sub-let their property to builders, and the new houses were so badly built that they were on the point of falling down. A Mr Hart Davies had leased 3 acres (about a hectare) for £90 a year and was sub-letting the land for £1,000. Others, like the owners of the Red House, were making extravagant claims for the loss of 'goodwill' during the summer months when crowds flocked to the area. Claims for compensation in cases of compulsory purchase were always high, but those of the Battersea freeholders were 'unprecedented', averaging £1,000 per acre, compared to less than £100 when the ground was sold by the lord of the manor in 1835, or the £450 which Pennethorne thought was reasonable.[42] Decisions to add an extra 10 acres (4 hectares) to the site for public baths, and to purchase the neighbouring wharves and vitriol works added to the estimated cost, which Pennethorne revised upwards to £265,933 in 1847. He still believed, though, that the proposed housing would more than pay for the expense of forming the park, and would in the end yield a handsome profit of £322,189 over a 25-year period.

It took seven years to obtain all the ground. The first disputed case was brought before a jury in December 1847, but soon after granting this first loan the Public Works Loan Commissioners announced that no more money was available, and in May 1848 Pennethorne had to cease buying the land. Some of the occupiers now started building houses again. In September 1848 Pennethorne finally obtained permission to raise outside loans on the security of the Crown's land revenues, and soon afterwards the Loan Commissioners resumed their payments. Two years later, with a third of the ground still unpurchased, the government tried to abandon the project completely before discovering that it had entered into so many agreements that it would be cheaper to go on. By 1851 the compulsory powers of the original Act were on the point of expiring, and a new Act was passed, extending the powers to 1853, at the same time placing the park under the management of the newly reconstituted Office of Works.[43] A scheme by Joseph Paxton to move the Great Exhibition building to the site came to nothing despite the support of Prince Albert and the great glass shed went to Norwood instead.[44] The landowners who

---

42 BPP, vol. 1, 22 Feb., 13 March 1847; PRO, Work 32/667.

43 *Hansard*, 134 (7 July 1854), 1402. Victoria Park, still technically a royal park, remained under the control of the Office of Woods and Forests.

44 BPP, vol. 1, 9 Aug. 1851; PRO, Work 32/3; *Getting London in Perspective* (Barbican Art Gallery exhibition catalogue, 1984), pp. 67–8.

had held out now increased their claims for compensation in the knowledge that the compulsory powers would soon run out.

By the beginning of 1853 it had become clear that nearly all the money permitted to be borrowed in 1846 had been used up, and that there would be no funds available to form the park itself or even to complete the remaining purchases. Work was therefore held up yet again. The project was seized upon by Benjamin Disraeli, Chancellor of the Exchequer in Lord Derby's new government, as an example of Whig profligacy, but the Tories fell before they could sabotage it completely and in February 1853 Thomas Cubitt offered to take the site over himself at cost price. His offer was turned down after Pennethorne made it clear that the government would still be responsible for forming the roads and river embankment, from which it would get no financial return. Sir William Molesworth, the new First Commissioner of Works, now pressed ahead to ensure that the park was completed as quickly as possible. With almost no money in hand and the extended compulsory powers about to elapse, he was forced to ask Parliament for extra funds out of general taxation to complete the remaining purchases and to carry out the very large works needed to convert what was still a collection of desolate, marshy fields into an attractive landscape. Despite complaints from provincial MPs the money was voted, and by the middle of 1854 all but one of the purchases had been completed. Work could now begin on forming the park itself.[45]

Extensive earthworks were needed before any planting could take place. Much of the ground was below river – a 'perfect swamp' in the words of one MP – and two or three years' work was needed to raise the level so as to create the undulating surface necessary for a picturesque landscape. Even greater efforts were required to build an embankment and terrace along the river front and to construct the roads. By June 1855 twenty barges were coming daily bringing spoil from dock excavations to construct the new road (now Queenstown Road) which was to lead south from Chelsea Bridge. Much of the earth was supplied free of charge by William Cubitt and Company, and transported by wagons on rails supplied by the contractors, Messrs Kelk.

Pennethorne's original proposals for the roads had to be drastically modified as the result of a successful application by the West End of London and Crystal Palace Railway Company in 1853 for powers to build a terminus close to the southern end of Chelsea Bridge, with a wharf and pier adjoining. The line, which was extended in 1860 to Victoria Station, went through property which the government had purchased, and on which Pennethorne had proposed to build smart houses. Queenstown Road now had to be realigned parallel to the proposed railway line, and the idea of building the houses was abandoned. The remaining ground was incorporated within the park, and trees were planted to shield it from the railway.

---

45 *Hansard*, 134 (7 July 1854), 1396; PRO, Work 1/43, pp. 163–5; BPP, vol. 2, 29 March 1854.

Pennethorne also decided to leave out the villas which would have lined the southern edge of the park. So Battersea Park became much more self-contained than Regent's Park or Victoria Park, where views to the surrounding houses were an integrated feature of the landscape.

With the main roads completed, Pennethorne could turn his attention to the design of the park itself (Plate 46). In April 1856 he told the new First Commissioner of Works, Sir Benjamin Hall, that work could start on making the lake, together with an esplanade along the river, a drive around the circumference of the park, an avenue in the centre and plantations around the edge. The shape and position of the lake were modified after the discovery of a sand bank; it was finally made by the junction of two ditches in the south-eastern corner of the park, and the paths were correspondingly realigned. The lake was filled at the end of 1856 and by the spring of 1857, after a lengthy and expensive programme of earth-moving, Pennethorne claimed that 'variety and undulation have been given to the surface; and the whole has been so divided and the vistas have been so arranged that when the plantations shall have grown the comparative lowness of the site will pass unnoticed from the higher ground by the river side'. When completed, the park would be a major asset for London:

In a few years, after the plantations shall have been formed, there will probably not be a park near London presenting more attractions of Scenery or more sources for the enjoyment and recreation of the Public than Battersea Park – and the locality altogether, instead of being (as would have been the case) a hot bed of malaria, fever and crime, will be, as I firmly believe, a Suburb worthy in every respect of the West End of London.[46]

Pennethorne called in John Gibson from Victoria Park to supervise the detailed planting. Gibson, he said, had 'always shown himself anxious to carry out my original intentions', and possessed 'such taste and knowledge as will enable him to carry out the Plan according to the instructions I shall give him respecting the levels, the choice of Trees, &c. &c.'. Gibson visited nurseries at Liverpool and Chester to choose the trees in October 1856, but two months later, with costs rising rapidly, the work was brought to a halt because of a decision by Sir Benjamin Hall to cut off the funds. Soon after taking over office in 1855 he had begun a wide-ranging investigation into the management of the various Metropolitan Improvement schemes still being carried out by the Office of Works, telling Pennethorne to finish the park by August 1857 and not on any account to exceed the money voted by Parliament. He now demanded a new and detailed account of how much money had been spent over and above the original estimate, and how much more would be needed. Pennethorne refused to accept responsibility for the overspending, but Hall nevertheless relieved him of further control over the park in

---

46 Copy Reps. on Metropolitan Improvements, *PP* 1857 (2), 41 [130], pp. 12, 20.

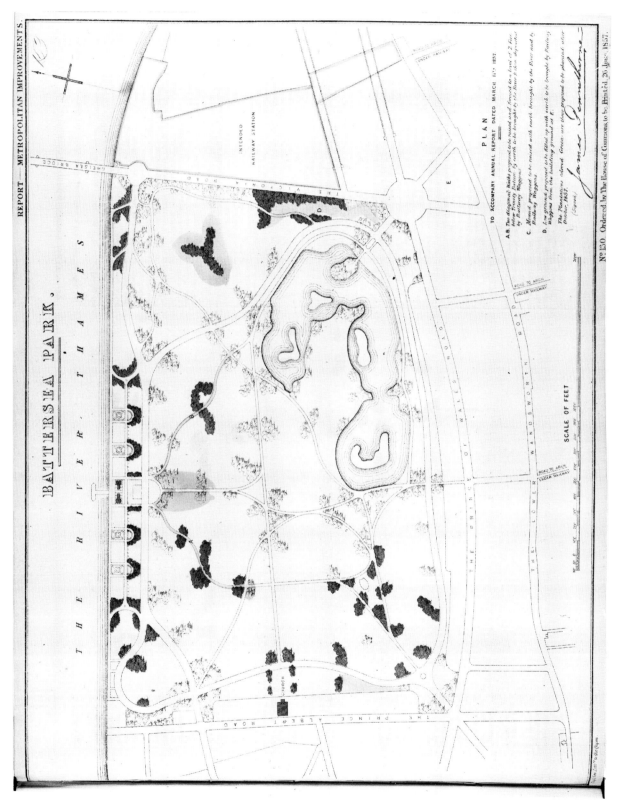

REPORT—METROPOLITAN IMPROVEMENTS.

BATTERSEA PARK.

THE RIVER THAMES

PLAN
TO ACCOMPANY ANNUAL REPORT DATED MARCH 11ᵀᴴ 1857

Nº 130. Ordered, by The House of Commons to be Printed, 26 June, 1857.

SCALE OF FEET

46. Revised plan for Battersea Park. Pennethorne produced this plan shortly before his replacement by John Gibson. It shows that he was responsible for the main features of the present layout, including the lake and carriage drive, although Gibson carried out the planting; the shading indicates work still to be undertaken. The ground to the east, originally intended for housing, is set aside for a railway station which was abandoned when the line was taken across the river to Victoria.

47. Battersea Park in 1858, looking towards the newly-completed Chelsea Bridge. It is difficult when surveying this desolate scene not to feel some sympathy with Sir Benjamin Hall in his determination to ensure the speedy completion of the park.

July 1857.[47] He was replaced by John Gibson, who now gave up his responsibilities at Victoria Park.

Twelve years had passed since the park had first been planned and it still presented a very bleak impression to the visitor (Plate 47). Gibson reminded Hall that the disparity between the effort expended and the disappointing results was the result of having to move an 'almost incredible quantity' of earth to the site, amounting to some three-quarters of a million cubic yards (about half a million cubic metres). An open sewer still had to be removed, the level of water in the lake raised, and

47 PRO, Work 1/50, p. 381; 1/55, pp. 43, 62.

extensive plantations made before the desolate effect could be removed. The park also suffered at first from poor communications, as Lord Palmerston reminded MPs in 1858:

On one side of the river there was a park which had been formed for the recreation and benefit of the health of the people; on the other side were the people wandering about like shades on the banks of the Styx . . . They and their wives and children were tantalised with the sight of a park which they could not reach.[48]

Many of these problems were solved by the opening of the new Chelsea suspension bridge and Chelsea Bridge Road, which was laid out alongside the grounds of Chelsea Hospital to Pennethorne's design in 1857–8 and opened up a direct communication to the rapidly developing suburbs of Chelsea and Kensington.[49]

The remaining work on the park itself, together with the building of the river wall, was eventually carried out with the aid of yet more money voted by Parliament, some of it repaid by the sale of land, including the 21 acres (8 hectares) to the east where the railway company was planning to build its station. This work continued well into the 1860s, and as a result of Gibson's careful management the park was finally transformed into a varied and picturesque landscape with an exotic 'tropical garden', a grotto and profuse flower beds. Despite some unsympathetic later alterations there is still a sense of scale and of care in the management of vistas which make it an attractive successor to Victoria Park, Regent's Park and the famous landscapes of the eighteenth century (Plate 48). And in its long frontage to the river it possesses an asset shared by none of the other parks of London. It has played a similar role in the lives of the working-class inhabitants of south-west London to that of Victoria Park for the East Enders, and from time to time it has attracted people from farther afield. Cyclists flocked there in the 1890s after being forbidden from riding in Hyde Park, and the Festival of Britain Gardens were laid out there in the 1950s, their remnants still surviving as a forlorn reminder of the taste of that vanished era.

As in Victoria Park, Pennethorne remained involved in the management of the building estate until his retirement. There were still 83 acres (34 hectares) left after the sale of the ground to the east to the railway company, and Pennethorne proposed to let this ground to builders for villas and terraces, with some smaller houses for the artisan population which was beginning to cluster near the railway line.[50] These plans were thwarted by the retention of tolls on Chelsea Bridge (they were not removed until 1879) and by the activities of the railway companies, which in a few years turned the whole of the land at the eastern and south-eastern ends of the park into a skein of lines criss-crossing each other on viaducts. The remainder

---

48 *Hansard*, 40 (11 June 1858), 1995.
49 PRO, Work 6/139/1; 6/139/15. The bridge was designed by Thomas Page.
50 Rep. Sel. Cttee. on Chelsea Bridge Bill, pp. 1–6.

48. The lake of Battersea Park. John Gibson must be given the credit for the planting which makes the park, even in its present rather run-down state, such an asset to south London. Trees, rocks and water combine to produce those effects of 'roughness', 'intricacy' and irregularity extolled by the theorists of the Picturesque at the end of the eighteenth century.

of the ground to the east of the park was therefore sold off, some in 1863 to the Southwark and Vauxhall Water Company, and the rest in 1865 for the construction of a proposed 'metropolitan Western Docks'. Originally intended by Pennethorne to become part of a fashionable residential neighbourhood, this land was in time almost completely taken over by the now derelict Battersea Power Station, which since 1937 has loomed magnificently over the eastern part of the park.

The land to the south and west of the park remained undeveloped until long after Pennethorne's death. With speculative building spreading rapidly into the area, 57 acres (23 hectares) were vainly advertised in 1864, despite a warning from Pennethorne that 'the system of letting lands by Public Tender has frequently been tried and has always proved a failure: and the effect of the Competition in all the

New Streets and in Victoria Park was to depreciate the value of the lands'.[51] These fears proved justified and it was not until the 1890s that the remaining sites around the edge of the park were covered with the 'mansion' blocks of red brick middle-class flats which still overlook the landscape Pennethorne designed.[52]

ALBERT PARK

While Battersea Park was being created, the countryside around London's northern periphery was disappearing inexorably. Nowhere was this more noticeable than in the drab expanses of the ancient parish of Islington. The loss of open spaces in this area prompted some inhabitants of the City and the densely packed borough of Finsbury to circulate a petition in 1841 calling for the formation of a park to promote 'the health and improvement of the moral condition of the middling and poorer classes . . . and as the only means of affording that healthful exercise and recreation to the classes and industrious population located in these confined districts, from which they have been within the present Century almost entirely deprived'. The petition was sent to the Commissioners of Woods and Forests and forwarded to Chawner and Pennethorne, who suggested four possible sites, all of which were built over in the next few years.[53] The failure to secure one of these sites, Copenhagen Fields – later the site of the Metropolitan Cattle Market – led one correspondent to *The Builder* to exclaim:

I have visited [the site] and am sorry to find that all hope of saving it from the sulphurous vapours of the brickmaker and the fencing-in of the bricklayer must be given up, and in a short time the whole space between Holloway and Camden Town . . . will be covered with houses . . . To think that the expenditure of a few thousands might have saved those green fields and hedgerows from encroachments, seems to throw some doubt on the consistency of those who talk much of Schools of Design and a 'Health of Towns' Bill, whilst they neglect obvious opportunities of securing healthy recreation and the sight of beautiful Nature to our working classes, who can ill afford the expense of railway excursions'.[54]

The building of the North London Railway through the northern parts of Islington to Camden Town in 1850 opened up more land to the attention of the developers, and supporters of a North London park now concentrated their efforts on securing a site to the north of the line. A proposal for a park at Highbury had already been mooted by a local inhabitant, James Lloyd, in 1844, and in 1845 T. E. Maslem of Tottenham prepared a plan for an 'Albert Park' in the area. Lloyd revived

---

51 PRO, Work 16/22/6, ff. 1–4; Work 2.28, p. 261.
52 The development of the estate was carried out under the supervision of one of his former pupils, Charles Frederick Reeks.
53 PRO, Work 6/99, pp. 154–6; Work 16/34/4, f. 1.
54 *The Builder*, 27 Nov. 1847, 565.

his idea early in 1850 and publicised it by holding public meetings, organising a petition which attracted the support of Lord Robert Grosvenor – an enthusiastic supporter of Metropolitan Improvements – and commissioning a surveyor, John Barnett, to prepare plans for the layout.[55]

The proposed site consisted of over 500 acres (200 hectares) of meadow land, stretching north from the railway line at Highbury and Canonbury to the present Finsbury Park and the New River Company's reservoirs at Woodberry Down; to the east lay the expanding suburban villages of Stoke Newington and Newington Green, and to the west Holloway and the Seven Sisters Road. The land was bound to be expensive because of its potential for building, and from an early stage the promoters tried to enlist government help. Pennethorne inspected the site in August 1851 with a view to negotiating with the owners and occupiers of the land. Some owners had already prepared plans for building, especially in Highbury New Park to the south-west, where a speculative builder, Henry Rydon, was proposing to construct five hundred middle-class villas.[56] Pennethorne recommended purchasing 467 acres (189 hectares), a third of which, as at Battersea, would be laid out in building sites, and in November, after the Treasury had given permission to the Office of Works to apply for an Act of Parliament, he began to 'elaborate' the existing schemes for the park. The result of his efforts was a large but unsigned plan (Plate 49) which, had it been carried out, would have given London its most impressive open space to date.

'Albert Park' is one of the most tantalising of London's many abandoned planning schemes. It is shaped rather like Regent's Park, but the narrow southern part, north of the railway, is made up of a long rectangular stretch of water flanked by intricately designed gardens overlooked by terraces of houses and reached by a broad approach road. To the north the park broadens out into a large oval-shaped tract of ground landscaped with clumps of trees and sinuous lakes formed out of the meanderings of the New River, constructed in the seventeenth century as an aqueduct to bring water to the City. This part of the park is shown surrounded by substantial detached villas in their own gardens, like those in the original scheme for Battersea Park or around Paxton's influential Birkenhead Park, and a broad road sweeps around the perimeter. Compared to Victoria and Battersea Parks, which did not depart significantly from the Nash/Repton tradition, the plan shows the influence of formal garden design, already seen in the country-house gardens of Charles Barry and W. A. Nesfield. With his training in Rome and Paris, Pennethorne was naturally sympathetic to this new influence, and he was soon to design elaborate (and equally abortive) formal gardens as part of his plan for developing the South Kensington estate. The combination of formality with the

---

55 *Ibid.*, 30 March 1850, 148; PRO, Work 16/34/4, ff. 24, 121; Work 6/103, p. 87; Work 32/1.
56 *The London Journal*, 7 (1981), 29–32.

picturesque tradition is what gives the project its interest in the history of English park design.

Pennethorne estimated the cost of forming the park and realigning the roads at £430,000, much more than Victoria or Battersea parks, with a net loss to the government of £117,000 after the disposal of the building sites. In the climate of strict economy which prevailed at the time this alone was sufficient to doom the project. As so often, though, a change in government administered the final *coup de grâce*. The Derby administration, which took over from the Whigs early in 1852, decided to cut back the park by excluding the more expensive southern part of the site. Pennethorne now submitted a plan for a park on the reduced site, but the minority government, already embroiled against its will in Battersea Park and fearful of trying to persuade Parliament to vote money for a loss-making enterprise, decided to delay the introduction of the Bill. The government finally fell in December, a month after the Treasury decided to discharge claims and to pay Pennethorne's bills.[57]

An attempt was made by James Lloyd and others to persuade the next government to revive the park, but Lord Aberdeen, the new Prime Minister, and his economy-minded Chancellor, William Ewart Gladstone, decided that they would do no more than make a grant in aid of locally raised funds. The responsibility for designing the park was therefore returned to the park's original promoters, and Pennethorne was asked in July 1853 to report on a new scheme sent in by Lloyd and Barnett. He was sceptical about the likelihood of the funds being raised locally, and suggested the introduction of a 'Metropolitan Improvement Rate' for works of this kind – a foretaste of the solution adopted when the Metropolitan Board of Works was formed in 1855. After further pressure from Lord Robert Grosvenor, the government agreed in December to grant £50,000 to supplement the £100,000 which the ratepayers of the Borough of Finsbury were expected to find. But, as Pennethorne had anticipated, their enthusiasm for the park waned when they were asked to pay for it, and since the money was not raised the scheme was dropped.[58] It was revived again by the new Metropolitan Board of Works in 1857, only to founder once more after Palmerston's government went back on its earlier undertaking to contribute £50,000.[59] When the Metropolitan Board of Works finally made up its mind to make a north London park in 1869, a much smaller site to the north-west of Seven Sisters Road was chosen, and named Finsbury Park out of deference to the origins of the project. It is a poor and paltry reflection of the original scheme. Meanwhile the rest of the original site was gradually built over.

---

57 PRO, Work 16/34/4, ff. 33–141; Papers concerning a projected park in North London, *PP* 1854, 67 [409].

58 PRO, Work 16/34/4, ff. 150–62; *The Builder*, 17 Dec. 1853, 762; *Hansard*, 134 (7 July 1854), 1394–6.

59 *BN*, 12 June, 3 July 1857, 618, 699; 2nd Rep. on Hungerford Bridge, *PP* 1868–9, 10 [387], p. 27.

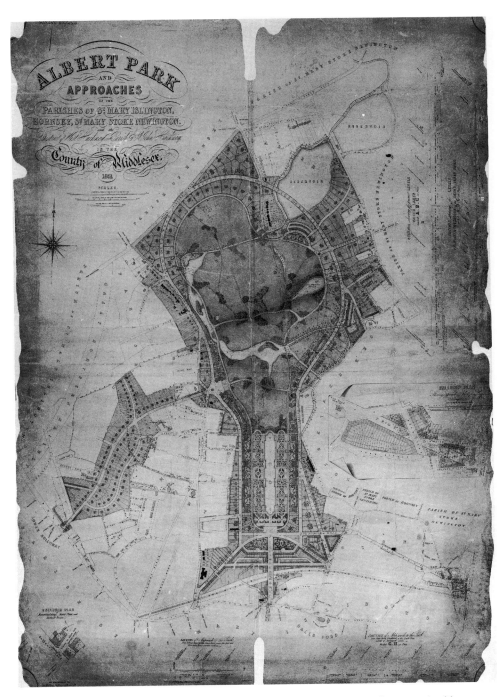

49. The plan for Albert Park, 1851. Here Pennethorne refined a scheme first conceived by an earlier surveyor, and in so doing produced a design for what would surely have been the most magnificent of all London's suburban parks. The open space stretches from the North London Railway at Canonbury in the south to the Woodberry Down reservoirs, north of Stoke Newington, in the north. Most of the ground is laid out in the picturesque tradition of Victoria and Battersea Parks, but the narrower portion to the south is a French- or Italian-inspired formal garden.

The only part of the site to survive as an open space is a tract now called Clissold Park, close to the former village of Stoke Newington, which was opened by the Metropolitan Board of Works in 1889.

Pennethorne was one of the most important park designers of the nineteenth century. His parks, like those of the better-known Joseph Paxton, are an urbanised version of the great country-house landscapes of the eighteenth century, with lakes, carriage drives, and carefully managed surprises. They were intended to elevate the poor by giving them some of the benefits formerly confined to the rich – an admirable idea. Historically they bridge the gap between the bold projects of Nash and the more mundane, but socially equally valuable, creations of the Metropolitan Board of Works. They still enhance the lives of south Londoners and East Enders, and their successful completion set a valuable example for town planners throughout England and abroad, especially in the USA. Of all his achievements, they surely had the greatest beneficial influence.

4

ARCHITECTURE AND POLITICS

IF ANYONE COULD be called the government architect of the mid nineteenth century it was James Pennethorne (Plate 50). His first public buildings date from the late 1840s and from then until his retirement in 1870 he was more closely involved than any other architect with the planning and design of official buildings in London. In many respects he was the successor of Inigo Jones and Sir Christopher Wren and the counterpart of Karl Friedrich Schinkel in Prussia and Leo von Klenze in Munich. In practice, though, his position was more precarious than theirs, and his architectural opportunities correspondingly more limited. In this respect he was the victim of social and political forces which neither he nor his employers could control.

Ever since the Middle Ages the design and maintenance of official buildings and the royal palaces had been the responsibility of the Office of Works. The department came into being because of the needs of the Crown, but as the powers and resources of the monarchy waned it was brought under ever more stringent Parliamentary control. In 1832, as an economy measure, it was united with the Office of Woods and Forests under a single board headed by three commissioners: the First (or Chief) Commissioner, a politician who took responsibility for general policy and its presentation to Parliament, and the Second and Third Commissioners, who were civil servants, the former looking after public buildings and metropolitan improvements and the latter managing the Crown estates. When Pennethorne started working for the government, the Whigs were still in power under Lord Melbourne, and the First Commissioner was Lord Duncannon, former Home Secretary and subsequently, as the Earl of Bessborough, Lord Lieutenant of Ireland. The Second Commissioner was Alexander Milne, who had worked closely with Nash, and the Third was Charles Gore, former secretary to Lord John Russell. The most important subsidiary officer was Trenham Philipps, the First Commissioner's secretary, and he was responsible, at least in part, for Pennethorne's advancement in the Office, even becoming godfather to one of his children.

The combined Office of Woods and Works occupied a pair of plain late-eighteenth-century houses, 1–2 Whitehall Place, opposite the Admiralty on the eastern side of Whitehall.[1] From these modest premises the commissioners exercised a bewildering range of responsibilities, from the upkeep of the royal palaces to the management of the London to Holyhead road and the lordship of manors which had escheated to the Crown. According to Sir Robert Peel in 1844: 'Where there is anything to be done which is not immediately within the functions of some other established public department, the general rule seems to be to devolve it on the Woods and Forests, and consider that office the Common Sewer of the flotsam and jetsam of other offices.'[2] There were three sub-departments: Works and Buildings; Forests, Land Revenues and Accounts (including Metropolitan Improvements and the Crown estate in London); and Irish and Scottish. The Office was a sub-department of the Treasury, not a ministry with its own budget. The commissioners were not fully autonomous, and their decisions could be overruled by the Chancellor of the Exchequer and by Treasury officials, so that in 1848 the then First Commissioner, Lord Morpeth, could say that 'the Chancellor of the Exchequer was responsible for expenditure on works, and the Commissioners merely ensured that they were carried out'.[3] Ordinary requests for spending were channelled through the Treasury in estimates submitted at the beginning of each Parliamentary session and then submitted to Parliament in the annual request for Miscellaneous Expenditure. Large-scale projects, like those for new streets, parks and public buildings, were submitted and voted upon separately, and if other calls on the public purse intervened they were postponed, often indefinitely. The Treasury also regulated the Office's establishment.

Treasury control reflected the political and economic preoccupations of the time. Conventional wisdom had it that public spending should be kept as low as possible so that, in Gladstone's words 'money should be left to fructify in the pockets of the taxpayer'.[4] Backed by a stable currency, with balanced budgets at home and free trade abroad, the nation could then fulfil its destiny of capturing the world markets and thus increasing its prosperity. Half of all government expenditure in the mid nineteenth century went on servicing the National Debt, and much of the rest was earmarked for the armed forces. So, encouraged by an ever more powerful Treasury, successive governments developed official economy to exquisite levels of refinement.

The Treasury was answerable to Parliament, which was susceptible to an ever more vociferous and highly articulated public opinion. George IV was the last King who could initiate and carry through major building projects in the heart of

---

1 J. M. Crook and M. H. Port, *The History of the King's Works*, VI (1973), p. 542; *Survey of London*, 16 (1935), pp. 194–6.
2 BL, Add. MS 40481, f. 289.
3 *Hansard*, 97 (2 March 1848), 142–3.
4 M. Wright, *Treasury Control of the Civil Service* (1969), pp. 329–30.

50. A portrait of James Pennethorne in early middle age.

London on the strength of his own personal power and prestige. Recent historical writing has tended to play down the effects of the Reform Act of 1832, but in government architecture at least there was a noticeable change of mood. Governments now had to listen more carefully to the opinions of backbench MPs, some of whom were advocates of the 'strict economy' doctrines of the classical economists and resented any spending on projects whose usefulness could not be immediately demonstrated and quantified. Others were equally zealous in championing provincial over metropolitan interests. Prince Albert, a great believer in the benefits of enlightened state patronage, wrote in 1853 about the 'increasing dislike of the large provincial Towns to the monopoly in London of great Institutions to be paid for by money collected by the general taxation of the Country – The feeling is growing rapidly that such great works should be executed when they are called for, and be enjoyed by those who are willing to pay for their use'.[5] Given the growing economic and political strength of the 'manufacturing districts', official architecture was bound to be affected by such attitudes.

In choosing designs for buildings, Victorian governments could not help being influenced by changing public taste. Prince Albert and others might call on governments to do more to beautify London, as foreign rulers were beautifying their own capital cities. But there was now no longer, as there had been in the eighteenth century, a visual culture shared by all the ruling class. The pluralism and individualism which impressed foreign observers as so marked a feature of English life extended to the arts. Arguments over style were carried on in the newly established architectural press – *The Builder* was founded in 1843 – and spilled over into journals, newspapers and into the chamber of the House of Commons, where Lord Lincoln, Sir Robert Peel's First Commissioner of Works, deplored in 1848 'the practice of that House resolving itself into a dilettanti society, with a view of discussing matters of taste'.[6] Select Committees and Royal Commissions proliferated, their lengthy deliberations enshrined in Parliamentary 'Blue Books'. Government architecture thus became a battleground in which the practical and artistic merits of buildings were sometimes forgotten amid the fierce partisanship of rival factions.

The abolition of the system of 'attached architects' in the Office of Works in 1832 led to a change in the method of appointing architects and choosing designs. The routine maintenance and repair of government buildings and the royal palaces remained in the hands of a salaried surveyor of works and buildings, Henry Seward, a former pupil of Sir John Soane; he retired in 1844 and was replaced by the equally obscure William Inman. There was also an assistant surveyor, John Phipps, who had special responsibility for the maintenance of buildings in London. But architects for new government buildings were now chosen by the First Commissioner from outside the Office, the original intention being that the most important commissions would be opened up to competition. The worst excesses of patronage would thus be avoided and a wider range of talents enlisted than ever before. Charles Barry became the designer of the Houses of Parliament through victory in a competition in 1835, but subsequently the rule was 'tacitly set aside'.[7] Competitions were time-consuming and often rancorous, and for the rest of the 1830s and 40s First

---

5 Royal Archives, Add F25/171, 26 Sept. 1853.
6 *Hansard*, 97 (2 March 1848), 142.   7 PRO, T 1/6693A/3774.

Commissioners found it easier to select architects by informal patronage, a system which was still very much alive in the civil service. Patronage accounted for Barry's later official commissions, for the layout of Trafalgar Square (1840) and the remodelling of Soane's Board of Trade and Privy Council offices in Whitehall (1844–5). Other architects who benefited from government patronage were Decimus Burton, an almost exact contemporary of Pennethorne who designed buildings in Regent's Park and Kew Gardens for the government-sponsored Royal Botanic Society; Edward Blore, who remained in control at Buckingham Palace after Nash's departure and built a new east range to the Mall in 1847–50; and Nash's former pupil Anthony Salvin, who became involved in castle restoration for the government in 1844 and later did extensive work at the Tower of London and Windsor.

These architects all drew the normal fee of five per cent on the total cost of the building, a system which began to come under attack in the 1840s. The high cost of public buildings such as Buckingham Palace, the new Board of Trade and, above all, the Houses of Parliament led Charles Trevelyan, the formidable Assistant Secretary to the Treasury, to remark in 1846 that:

. . . no system can be more absurd or contrary to economy than that of a percentage upon the ultimate charge, which makes it in the interest of those who conduct extensive works to render them as expensive as they can, and offers them a premium on their own unrestricted inaccuracy and extravagance.[8]

Here was a potential conflict between the professional status of architects, newly enshrined in the Institute (later the Royal Institute) of British Architects, founded in 1834, and the exigencies of government. James Pennethorne's career cannot be understood without bearing this conflict in mind.

Pennethorne's employment as architect for government buildings came about more by accident than design. For the first four years of his official career his responsibilities in the Office of Woods and Forests were limited to Metropolitan Improvements and work on the Crown estate. But in 1843 and 1844, with work on the new streets well in hand, he began to be employed on other tasks. In October 1843 he was sent to Ireland by Lord Lincoln to investigate the construction of the new workhouses built there in the wake of the passing of the new Poor Law. He visited sixty-two of these spartan buildings in the last two months of 1843, and told Trenham Philipps that:

a more monstrous proceeding you cannot imagine. They are all built from the same plans and the same specification . . . and now I would undertake to walk blindfolded over every

---

8 PRO, T 25/19, pp. 468–9.

Poor House in Ireland and make out for the Constructor his Bill of extra works without looking to plan, specification or contract.[9]

Shortly before he left Ireland, his partner Thomas Chawner fell ill, and in 1844 gave notice of his impending retirement. The Commissioners of Woods and Forests decided not to appoint anyone in his place and told Pennethorne that he could continue as sole architect for Metropolitan Improvements and the Crown estate. When Chawner formally retired at the end of 1845, Pennethorne therefore gave up his remaining private practice in order to work full-time for the government. He had already turned down several private commissions in order to concentrate on official work, and now had only one still in hand, the enlargement of a house in Seymour Place, Marylebone, for the son of his first patron, William Crockford, which he was undertaking 'more as a friend than an architect'. With this completed, the Treasury agreed to give him the same semi-official position as Chawner, including rights to a pension.[10] He now drew not only fees for individual transactions but also a salary of £100 for, as he later put it, 'a great many services for which I would not make a charge; for being always within call, and also to give the Commissioners some sort of power over me, which they would not have unless I were on the establishment'.[11]

Pennethorne's first designs for a government building were made in 1843, when he was asked to prepare the first of several unexecuted plans for additions to the National Gallery in Trafalgar Square. A year later he was given his first commission for a complete new building, the Museum of Practical Geology in Piccadilly, work on which was delayed until 1847–51. These commissions came about in a haphazard, *ad hoc* manner which reflected a wish on the part of Philipps to 'keep the work as much as possible in the Office'. Pennethorne later told a Treasury committee that he had given up his private practice

upon the distinct understanding that I should have quite sufficient business to give me a very good income . . . I remember perfectly that they kept me in suspense a long time as to what they meant to do. I was six months in Ireland – and after I came back I was kept in suspense, and the observation at the time was that they intended to give me a good thing.[12]

There were obvious advantages in employing the man on the spot. Time could be saved and costs kept under stricter surveillance. But Pennethorne's new position was less secure than he thought. Neither Lord Lincoln nor his masters in the Treasury were officially involved in changing the terms of his employment. Nothing was written down, and when his position came under official investigation

---

9 House of Lords Record Office, Willis MSS 2/168; Rep. Commission for inquiring into the execution of certain Union Workhouses in Ireland, *PP* 1844, 30 [562], pp. 1, 23–4, 83–4.
10 PRO, Cres 19/32, p. 152; T 25/19, p. 304.
11 2nd Rep. Sel. Cttee. on Woods, Forests, *PP* 1849, 20 [574], p. 128.
12 PRO, T 1/6693A/3774.

fifteen years later it was soon made clear that he had never been given an open-ended promise to design government buildings *in perpetuum* – a promise which would have run directly counter to the spirit of the Office reorganisation of 1832. Ultimately his status as government architect depended on his satisfying the First Commissioner of the day. Commissioners came and went, and for the rest of his career Pennethorne was dependent not only on their views but also on the political pressures to which they were subject.

Despite the weaknesses in his position, Pennethorne was looked upon for more than ten years as 'the general advisor of the Department on matters relating to public works'. In this respect he filled a real gap. The First Commissioners of the 1840s were chosen more for their political usefulness than for any aesthetic insights they might be able to bring to the subject of government architecture. They could take advice from anyone, but there was much to be said for employing an experienced man to give a synoptic view of the whole question of Metropolitan Improvements and public buildings, to report on how plans and schemes related to each other, on where accommodation could be found, and on how much new buildings might be expected to cost. It was through making reports of this kind, many of them verbal and informal, that Pennethorne got drawn into designing many of his buildings.

Pennethorne's decision to work full-time for the government assured him of a steady income. In the fifteen years from 1844 to 1858 he received an average of £3,802 a year in professional fees, of which an increasing amount (though only about a third *in toto*) came from commissions for buildings, and the rest from surveying, street improvements and park design (see Table 1). Despite the need to deduct the rent of his office and the salaries of his assistants, this was a very respectable upper-middle-class income, and it enabled Pennethorne to move, in the late 1840s, with his growing family to Elms Court (Plate 51), a rambling old-fashioned house at the top of Highgate Hill, between the seventeenth-century Lauderdale House and a cottage which had reputedly been the home of the poet Andrew Marvell.[13]

Pennethorne had to pay an artistic price for his reliable income. The office routine connected with the Metropolitan Improvements and the Crown estate was time-consuming and, from a creative point of view, often stiflingly tedious. During the 1840s, when his contemporaries were designing major buildings, he was still preoccupied for much of his time with the demands of evicted tradesmen in the lines of new streets, the questions of Parliamentary Select Committees, and the valuing of Crown property. Official reports had to be written for all the tasks on which he was employed. By the time his first large public buildings were designed,

---

13 *Survey of London*, 17 (1936), p. 16. Elms Court was later demolished and its site incorporated into Waterlow Park.

Table 1. *Sources of Pennethorne's income (in £), 1844–1858*[14]

	Buildings	Surveys	Metropolitan Improvements	Parks	Crown Estate	Total
1844	366		523		1168	2057
1845	124	263	1656		170	2213
1846	115	9	2017	741	1145	4027
1847	106	169	500	830	1088	2693
1848	801	145	1200	250	483	2879
1849	413	92	801	807	662	2775
1850	1475	154	170	710	1789	4298
1851	200	27	1873	311	785	3196
1852	1200	700	800	1000	1491	5191
1853	2229	500		819	600	4148
1854	1935	4	900	600	1341	4780
1855	2500	1320		860	846	5526
1856	3292	63	300		852	4507
1857	4241				1101	5342
1858	798	249	57	1500	794	3398
Fees still unpaid in 1858	5546	1444	1354	6359	789	15492

a new generation of architects with very different artistic ideals was ready to challenge him.

Pennethorne ran his practice from 7 Whitehall Yard (Plate 52), an insignificant-looking house rented from the Crown in a picturesque backwater between Whitehall and the river. Just to the south was Inigo Jones's Banqueting House, then used as a chapel, in which Pennethorne rented a pew. At the end of the 1840s he was employing five or six clerks, who helped in the preparation of the detailed working drawings which were increasingly required by builders and surveyors. Some of the clerks stayed with him for only a short time: Charles Frederick Reeks went into partnership in 1848 with Alfred Humbert, the architect of the Royal Mausoleum at Frogmore and Sandringham House; and Henry Saxon Snell later became well known as an architect of hospitals and workhouses.[15] Others stayed with him throughout his career, notably Arthur Cates, a pupil of Sydney Smirke, who eventually succeeded Pennethorne as architect to the Crown estate in London and subsequently played an important part in establishing a system of examinations in the Royal Institute of British Architects.[16] There was only one articled pupil,

---

14 PRO, T 1/6693A/3774. Figures after 1858 are not available.
15 *RIBA Journal*, 25 April 1908; *The Builder*, 16 Jan. 1904, 64.
16 *The Builder*, 18 May 1901, 494. In 1859 Cates was one of four clerks, the others being William Perkins, a Mr Robertson and a Mr Slack: PRO, T 26/1, pp. 403–4.

51. Elms Court, Highgate, with members of the Pennethorne family.

John Robinson, who was awarded the Royal Academy gold medal for architecture in 1851 and later won the Academy's travelling studentship to Italy.[17] He became Pennethorne's chief architectural assistant after returning from the Continent in the mid 1850s, but designed no major buildings and was heard of no more after Pennethorne's death.

The scope of Pennethorne's architectural activities widened at the end of the 1840s. Lord John Russell's First Commissioner, Lord Morpeth (later Earl of Carlisle), a serious-minded advocate of public health reforms, faced pressing demands for new public buildings, above all for a new Record Office to house the nation's archives, a project recommended by the Royal Commission on

17 *The Builder*, 16 Sept. 1871, 718.

Metropolitan Improvements. Like his predecessor, Lord Lincoln, he fought shy of holding competitions or bringing in outside architects, and turned to Pennethorne, who early in 1847 submitted a scheme for a massive Gothic building on the Rolls Estate in Chancery Lane. After severe cuts, work began in 1851 and continued on and off for the rest of Pennethorne's life. Morpeth also gave Pennethorne his first commissions for government offices: an extension to the Ordnance Office in Pall Mall, built in 1850–1, and a western extension to Somerset House for the new Inland Revenue department, designed in 1849 but not begun until 1852.

These projects were all plagued by delays and financial difficulties. At the end of the 1840s the economy entered into depression and Russell's government found it increasingly difficult to balance the budget. Public works suffered immediately. The London street improvement programme ground to a halt, and in 1848, with the Chancellor of the Exchequer threatening to increase the newly imposed income tax, Parliament limited the annual vote for ordinary repair and maintenance works on public buildings to £100,000, two-thirds of its level for the previous year. Encouraged by radicals like Joseph Hume, a notorious scourge of public spending, Select Committees were established to examine the management of the Crown estates and the ordinary expenses of the works department. The main result of these inquiries was to convince Russell and his Cabinet of the need to separate the works department from the Woods and Forests.[18] There was certainly an inbuilt paradox in the union of a spending department with one which was primarily concerned with managing the revenues of the Crown estates. In periods of financial stringency it was only too easy to transfer money from one section to the other, making Parliamentary supervision very difficult. The Geological Museum, for instance, was financed out of the Crown's Land Revenues, and parliament was only consulted when the building was well under way. Charles Gore, the Third Commissioner, admitted in 1849 that such 'extraordinary payments' had increased threefold in the previous four years.[19] So in February 1850 Russell introduced a Bill to separate the Woods from the Works and after some revision it was passed in the summer of 1851.

The main aim of the new legislation was 'to bring the expenses incurred in public works more specifically under the notice of Parliament, and to secure a better management of accounts'. The Office of Woods and Forests now became a purely revenue department like the Post Office, spending no more money than was necessary to improve the Crown estates. Its revenues were placed straight into the Exchequer and its expenditure was made the subject of an annual Parliamentary grant. Its head was the former Third Commissioner, Charles Gore, and it was represented in Parliament by Treasury spokesmen. All other spending activities,

18 Rep. Sel. Cttee. on Miscellaneous Expenditure, *PP* 1847–8, 18 [543], pp. ix–xi; Rep. Sel. Cttee. on Woods, Forests, *PP* 1847–8, 24 [538], pp. iv–v; 2nd Rep. on Woods, Forests (1849), pp. 127–30.
19 2nd Rep. on Woods, Forests (1849), p. 50; Crook and Port, *King's Works*, VI, pp. 209–10.

52. Whitehall Yard looking west. Pennethorne's office is the low stuccoed building in the centre of the picture, with the Royal United Service Institution (built by Sir John Vanbrugh as his own residence) to the right and Carrington House (Sir William Chambers 1765–74) to the left; these buildings were all demolished to make way for the new War Office soon after this photograph was taken by Bedford Lemere. The Horse Guards can be glimpsed on the extreme left.

including the remaining Metropolitan Improvements and the maintenance of the royal parks, came under the new Office of Works, headed by a politician whose task was to 'exercise a control over public works which have of late years occasioned very considerable expense'. Since it would no longer be possible for works to be financed out of the Land Revenues, all large proposals for spending would now have to come under the scrutiny of Parliament, as had been intended in 1832. The Office would still be supervised by the Treasury, but the concentration of responsibility under a single head would give it something of the character of a modern ministry. The corresponding growth in the influence of the First Commissioner on government architecture soon became apparent.[20]

After this reorganisation, the Office of Woods and Forests remained in its old premises in Whitehall Place, which were remodelled and extended by Pennethorne in 1856 and 1861.[21] The Office of Works moved to another house on the opposite side of the street, 12 Whitehall Place, and expanded in 1854 into no. 13.[22] The staff of the old combined office was divided between the two new departments. The new Office of Works retained Trenham Philipps as secretary in charge of the 'general branch', and the 'professional branch' was headed, as before, by Inman, with Phipps and his assistant James Williams taking responsibility for the maintenance and repair of buildings in London.[23]

Pennethorne's official standing after 1851 was ambiguous. He retained his surveyorship to the Crown estate in London under the Woods and Forests, but his only official foothold in the Office of Works derived from his responsibility for the now largely completed Metropolitan Improvements. The appointment of architects remained the prerogative of the First Commissioner, subject to the approval of the Treasury, and successive commissioners continued to make use of Pennethorne's advice, while admitting that his employment to design buildings was 'as much a matter of selection by this Board as would have been that of any other member of his profession'.[24] The difficulty lay in making clear dividing-lines between giving advice on the design and layout of new buildings and preparing detailed designs which, once made, had to be paid for. Once Pennethorne had made preliminary designs it was both easier and cheaper to employ him than to go through the whole process again by holding a competition. So for a time he remained government architect in fact, if not in name.

The first head of the new Office of Works was a Whig nobleman, Lord Seymour (later Duke of Somerset), who replaced Lord Morpeth as First Commissioner of the old combined department in 1850. He remained in office until the fall of Russell's government in February 1852, when he was succeeded by the 33-year-old Lord John Manners, a former member of the 'young England' group. His social and political philosophy is perhaps best summed up in the lines he himself wrote:

> Let wealth and commerce, laws and learning die,
> But leave us still our old nobility.

---

20 Crook and Port, *King's Works*, VI, pp. 244–6; *Hansard*, 118 (3 July 1851), 175–80, 620, 1318–20; Rep. Sel. Cttee. on Misc. Expenditure, *PP* 1860, 9 [483], pp. 76–9.
21 PRO, Cres 19/44, p. 245; 19/48, p. 120; 19/49, pp. 136, 352; LRRO 1/2177.
22 *Ibid.*, Work 2/11, pp. 51, 585–7; T 26/1, pp. 82, 86, 151.
23 *Ibid.*, Work 2/10, pp. 778–80; Work 22/2/10, f. 5.
24 *Ibid.*, T 1/6041A/20465; T 1/6693A/3774.

Described by some as 'the Philip Sydney of our generation', Manners confessed soon after accepting office that he was 'entirely ignorant of the very first principles of Art'. He therefore relied heavily on the advice of his political mentor Benjamin Disraeli, the new Chancellor of the Exchequer, and of Prince Albert, who had already argued unsuccessfully for the appointment of an unofficial council of experts and art-lovers like himself to advise the First Commissioner of the day.[25]

Lord Derby's minority Tory government fell at the end of 1852, and the new Prime Minister Lord Aberdeen, a connoisseur of Grecian art – appointed a scholarly free-thinking radical, Sir William Molesworth, in Manners's place. He brought more intellectual energy and aesthetic understanding to the post than his aristocratic predecessors. As a young man he had come under the influence of James Mill, had owned *The Westminster Review*, and had edited the works of Hobbes. He was a man of some artistic sensibility, and had effected alterations to his country house, Pencarrow (Cornwall) in the 1840s, but he saw his appointment as a means to political advancement rather than an end in itself. The appointment, Molesworth said, was 'not a very important or highly paid one . . . but accompanied by a seat in the Cabinet it is one of much dignity bringing me into frequent contact with the Queen . . . and in all probability will eventually lead to one of the higher offices in the Government of our country'[26] – a prediction which was realised when he became Colonial Secretary in 1855, only to die a few months later.

Pennethorne's first new commission under the reorganised Office of Works was for the construction of a new Stationery Office near Westminster Abbey. Other work followed rapidly in the relatively buoyant financial climate of the early 1850s: a new wing at Buckingham Palace, containing a magnificent new ballroom and supper room, which was finally completed in 1856, and a new office for the Duchy of Cornwall on ground opposite. He also became involved in 1853 in two larger but abortive schemes: the layout and development of the South Kensington estate, bought by the Commissioners of the Great Exhibition of 1851, and the provision of new blocks of government offices, including a new Foreign Office, on the western side of Whitehall. Had either project been carried out his place in the architectural history of London would have been secured at a stroke, but in the end there was only one building to show for his efforts: a modest and short-lived extension to the recently established South Kensington Museum in Brompton Road.

Pennethorne's more ambitious proposals were put in jeopardy because of changes in the way in which the Office of Works chose its architects.[27] With Sir William Molesworth in command, he enjoyed a considerable degree of security and respect. Business was increasing, and he even acquired an assistant, William Smith, who had

---

25 C. Whibley, *Lord John Manners and his Friends*, II (1925), p. 49.
26 Mrs Fawcett, *Life of the Rt. Hon. Sir William Molesworth, Bart.* (1901), p. 307.
27 M. H. Port, 'A Contrast in Styles at the Office of Works', *Historical Journal*, 27 (1984), p. 151.

worked with him in 1840–1 and returned in 1853 after spending twelve years in Constantinople.[28] But Molesworth's departure in July 1855 left the way open for a very different regime. The Prime Minister was now Lord Palmerston, and his choice as First Commissioner was Sir Benjamin Hall (Plate 53). Hall was a domineering, energetic and abrasive man who owned large estates at Llanover (Monmouthshire, now Gwent), where his wife made widely-publicised efforts to preserve the Welsh language and to revive Welsh dress.[29] As MP for Marylebone in the 1830s and 40s, he had joined Hume and other radicals in attacking government extravagance, not least in architecture, where he publicly deplored the high costs of the Houses of Parliament. He had built up a reputation as a champion of 'local self-government' against centralisers like Edwin Chadwick, and had succeeded in putting that ideal into effect in London by the formation of the Metropolitan Board of Works. This relieved the taxpayer of a burden which had hitherto distorted the expenditure of the Office of Works, leaving it free to concentrate on its main responsibility of providing dignified and serviceable buildings for the many government departments and public institutions which were clamouring for space.

Hall saw the Office of Works as an Augean stables awaiting its Hercules. Certain aspects of the Office were bound to irritate any champion of administrative efficiency. Philipps, the secretary for forty-two years, had been unable to work for nearly a year because of ill health; he died in November 'worn out in the public service'. His assistant, John Thornborrow, appointed by Molesworth, had proved unfit for the task and had had a nervous breakdown. The accounts were therefore in disarray. The 'professional branch' was equally run-down. Soon after taking over, Hall asked Phipps, the assistant surveyor of works, about his work, and was told that 'he had nothing to do at that time particularly'. Hall believed that 'the state of things [was] so bad, that it was my duty to give up everything for the purpose of remodelling the department'. His recommendations were embodied in a report submitted to the Treasury in November 1855. They included the appointment of a new secretary, Alfred Austin, a former Poor Law inspector recommended by Charles Trevelyan; he was later given an assistant, George Russell. Routine business was left in the hands of Phipps, who was given a second assistant surveyor, but Pennethorne's assistant William Smith was dismissed, and a new part-time surveyor of works appointed in place of the ineffective Inman.[30] These reforms helped Hall to impose a stricter financial control. The annual cost of official furniture halved as a result of Hall's reforms and for the rest of the 1850s and 60s ordinary expenditure

---

28 PRO, T 1/6041A/20465.
29 The best account of Hall's life and career is in a series of articles by Maxwell Fraser in *National Library of Wales Journal*, 13 (1963–4); 14 (1965–6), and 15 (1967–8); and *Transactions of the Honourable Society of Cymmrodorion*, 1963 (1), 70–81.
30 *PP* 1860, 9, pp. 89–91, 112–14, 143; PRO, T 26/1, pp. 299–300; T 1/6041A/20465.

53. Sir Benjamin Hall.

on maintenance of public buildings increased at a much slower rate than government spending as a whole.[31]

The new surveyor of works, appointed early in 1856, was William Henry Hunt, son of a builder and principal partner in the firm of Hunt and Stephenson of 45 Parliament Street. A leading member of the relatively new profession of quantity surveyors, Hunt had enhanced his reputation by his accuracy in surveying the new Houses of Parliament, through which he must have first come into contact with Hall.[32] He soon built up a position of considerable influence in the Office, and was consulted by Hall on 'every question of the slightest importance'. He became responsible for estimating the cost of proposed public buildings, and for supplying the names of builders invited to tender for public works[33] – tasks formerly undertaken by Pennethorne who, after the death of Phillips, had lost his most influential supporter in the Office.

Hall was no lover of architects, and carried out a long vendetta against Charles Barry over his fees for the Houses of Parliament. In March 1856 he accused Pennethorne of spending money on Buckingham Palace without consent, and told him in future to

draw up your Specifications so fully that they will include, so far as possible, all contingencies . . . and that on no account, or under any circumstances [to] deviate from the Plans once approved without requesting the expediency or necessity of such deviations, and having the authority in writing of the Chief Commissioner for the alterations you may suggest.[34]

In the same month Hunt was asked to investigate the remaining Metropolitan Improvement schemes which had been begun before the Metropolitan Board of Works was set up. The most important of these was Battersea Park. Hall took a great interest in London's parks, introducing flower beds into the royal parks for the first time and inaugurating Sunday afternoon band concerts, to the horror of Sabbatarians. But he believed that, by consistently underestimating the sums of money needed for Battersea Park and other metropolitan improvement projects, Pennethorne had delayed their completion and embarrassed the government. Pennethorne regarded the enquiry as an infringement of his professional status and refused even to meet Hunt, although he had originally backed his appointment. When he was finally persuaded to submit detailed reports on the works in progress, Hall took them as confirmation of his suspicions. Further complaints in 1857, inspired by backbench questioning of the continuing high costs of Battersea Park,

31 Wright, *Treasury Control of the Civil Service* (1969), pp. 373–4.
32 F. M. L. Thompson, *Chartered Surveyors* (1968), pp. 86–90, 365; M. H. Port (ed.), *The Houses of Parliament* (New Haven and London, 1976), p. 77.
33 Rep. Sel. Cttee. on Miscellaneous Expenditure, *PP* 1860, pp. 83–91, 118–25, 135–44.
34 PRO, Work 1/49, pp. 8–9.

provoked a long and detailed rejoinder from Pennethorne, but this did not prevent the completion of the park from being taken out of his hands.[35]

An even greater blow came when Hall decided early in 1856 to reverse recent Office of Works practice by holding competitions for 'Architectural works of magnitude'. In a return to the policy of the Office of Works reformers of 1832 he disclaimed any responsibility for jeopardising Pennethorne's official position, insisting that 'he ought to get as much talent as he can in the execution of Public Buildings, so that they may be an ornament to the Metropolis'.[36] Hall was no penny-pinching philistine. He had designed a church at Abercarn on his Welsh estate, and was prepared to use government patronage to rebuild Whitehall as a counterpart to Napoleon III's rebuilding of Paris; one peer even accused him of 'wishing to become another Lorenzo, to go down to posterity as Benjamin the Magnificent'.[37] But he saw Pennethorne as an incorrigible product of the discredited patronage system which had come under widespread attack by radicals and their friends in the press as a result of the inefficiencies exposed by the Crimean War. His point of view was supported by *The Saturday Review*, a journal newly founded by Alexander Beresford Hope, the former Tory MP for Maidstone and 'the Nestor of Ecclesiology'. Hope was the guiding spirit behind William Butterfield's 'model church', All Saints, Margaret Street, and he was now prepared to use his formidable argumentative powers and knowledge of architecture to attack the last relics of the old regime in the Office of Works, while at the same time pleading the case for the adoption of Gothic for large public buildings – a cause much nearer to his heart.[38] Pennethorne was an easy target. A writer in *The Saturday Review* in November 1855 dismissed him as 'an inheritance of the Georgian era, when the divorce between political administration and artistic refinement was complete'.[39] Hall did not share Hope's politics, but he was happy to enlist his help in a campaign against what he saw as favouritism and jobbery. The result was that Pennethorne lost the commissions for the two major government office buildings currently under consideration, a new Foreign Office in Whitehall and a War Office in Pall Mall. Competitions were announced for these buildings and Pennethorne, who refused to enter them, found himself for the first time for some years without any major public buildings to design.

With his architectural practice diminished, Pennethorne was forced back to rely on surveying work. Even here he faced a threat from Hall, who announced in May 1856 that he was transferring to Hunt the remaining surveying business of the

---

35 Copy Rep. on Metropolitan Improvements, *PP* 1857 (2), 41 [130]. See p. 109.
36 PRO, Work 1/49, pp. 116–17.
37 *Hansard*, 145 (15 May 1857), 286–91, 1674–88.
38 H. W. and I. Law, *The Book of the Beresford Hopes* (1925), pp. 214–22; A. B. Hope, *Public Offices and Metropolitan Improvements* (1857).
39 *The Saturday Review*, 17 Nov. 1855, 48–9, 64–5.

Office, most of it connected with the acquisition of sites for new public buildings. Pennethorne would be allowed to remain architect in the Office, but his work was not to include 'buildings . . . the design of which ought to be thrown open to limited or unlimited competition'.[40] This proposal would, in Pennethorne's view, have been 'a direct violation of the terms of my employment under which I agreed to abandon all private professional practice'. He therefore appealed over Hall's head to the Treasury, where he found support from the Chancellor of the Exchequer, Sir George Cornewall Lewis. Lewis thought that Pennethorne 'could not be set on one side without a breach of faith. He is not a person whom I would go out of my way to serve, but I think that every public servant has a claim to be protected from injustice'. Hall was told that while Pennethorne had no right to be employed to design public buildings, he should not be deprived of surveying work unless found guilty of inefficiency or misconduct.[41] His status as a civil servant – though not as government architect – was therefore confirmed.

Hall was delivered a further snub by the architectural profession in July 1856 with the award of an RIBA Gold Medal to Pennethorne after the recent successful completion of his extension to Somerset House. The citation was signed by seventy-five architects whose names read like a roll-call of the Victorian architectural establishment: Charles Barry, C. R. Cockerell, William Tite, Sydney Smirke, P. C. Hardwick, Owen Jones, Matthew Digby Wyatt, Anthony Salvin, T. L. Donaldson, and others now known only to the *cognoscenti*. Only the Young Turks of the Gothic revival were missing, though their day was soon to come. The architects referred pointedly to 'the skill and intelligence which you have habitually brought to bear upon complicated and difficult questions of a technical nature, and the most anxious attention to protect the public interests in the very extensive purchases of property entrusted to your care', and in the accompanying discussion Tite praised the metropolitan improvement schemes carried out by Nash and Pennethorne and called for the adoption by the government of 'a distinct and well-chosen plan, as in Paris'. The award is a reminder of Pennethorne's high status in the British architectural establishment and of the continuing importance of the classical ideal to which he bore witness.

Palmerston's government fell in February 1858 and Hall was replaced by Lord John Manners, prompting the comment from *Building News*:

We know of no qualifications he had for the office; nor do we suppose that any other member of the Derby administration will be found at all more fitted for an office which is not one of mere clockwork or administration, but which requires some professional knowledge . . . The notion that public buildings are to depend on Whiggism or Toryism is absurd,

---

40 PRO, Work 1/49, pp. 151, 399.
41 *Ibid.*, T 1/6693A/3774; T 26/1, p. 369; Rep. Sel. Cttee. on Foreign Office Reconstruction, *PP* 1857–8, 11 [417], pp. 182–4, 196.

unless Young England really does represent a belief in art, and threatens us with the universal application of Gothic or the Christian Style.[42]

Manners reverted to the practice of Hall's predecessors by asking Pennethorne to design an important new public building, the Staff College at Camberley, and commissioning him to prepare a plan for the layout of the Burlington House site in Piccadilly, purchased by the Government in 1854. But hopes of gaining grander commissions were short-lived. In the last months of the Palmerston administration the Treasury had attempted to reinstate Pennethorne as architect of the Foreign Office against the wishes of Hall. When this became known Gilbert Scott, one of the prizewinners, protested, and the subject was referred to a Commons Select Committee chaired by Beresford Hope, now back in Parliament as a Tory MP. Its report, published in July 1858, backed Scott and, doubtless in order to persuade Manners to abide by the recommendations, *The Saturday Review* published a vicious attack on Pennethorne, claiming that 'the national surveyor and architect is the only national institution that defies the law of progress', that he had designed 'the very worst buildings, and in every variety of style, in London', and that he had 'proved himself to be incapable of a great or even a decent architectural work'.[43] Pennethorne's 'sensitive nature' was 'deeply grieved' by the attack,[44] but Manners dismissed his claim and awarded the Foreign Office to Scott.

Still smarting under his treatment by Hall, and worried about being 'put upon the shelf', as he put it, Pennethorne now appealed to Manners for 'full employment' with a guaranteed income and security from the whims of awkward politicians. The question was referred to the Treasury, which held an internal inquiry into Pennethorne's position in June 1859. The mandarins concluded that while Pennethorne did not have a claim to a salary comparable to the fees he had received in the past, or to compensation for loss of work, he should be given a £1,500 salary for his 'general services' for the Office of Works, including the giving of architectural advice, the valuation and purchase of property for new government buildings (including the Foreign Office), and negotiations with railway companies when their new lines passed through government-owned land. He would still receive a salary of £850 from the Woods and Forests for his work on the Crown estate, and would be paid the usual percentage fees for any major new buildings he might be asked to design, but would continue to pay his own office expenses, which amounted in the 1860s to some £600 a year.[45] In another development James Williams, the assistant surveyor in the 'professional department' was made surveyor for Post Offices, a

---

42 *BN*, 26 Feb. 1850, 202.
43 *The Saturday Review*, 24 July 1858, 82–3.
44 *RIBA Transactions*, 1st series, 22 (1871–2), 60.
45 PRO, T 1/6693A/3774; T 26/2, p. 400; Cres 19/47, pp. 289–90; *The Builder*, 3 June 1865, 400; Copy of Papers relating to recent changes in the Establishment of the Office of Works, *PP* 1868–9, 24 [336], p. 4.

position which he filled with 'conspicuous zeal and ability' for twenty-five years, and a new assistant surveyor, John Taylor, was appointed in his place.[46]

The new arrangement finally removed the ambiguities in Pennethorne's position. He later claimed that he did 'not covet employment as a Surveyor. I was educated as an Architect; I greatly prefer that Profession; I gave up my private practice as an architect on the assurance of full employment from Public Buildings.' But it was clear that Hunt, with his large private practice, could not handle all of the rapidly increasing surveying work emanating from the Office of Works, and Pennethorne had no option but to accept what the government offered him. With the failure of Hall's attempt to concentrate all the surveying work in Hunt's hands, a *modus vivendi* was worked out under which Hunt framed competition specifications, worked out quantities for new buildings, and checked the architects' accounts. Pennethorne carried out many of the surveys for new buildings, and was once more consulted as an adviser 'on general questions relating to Works and Public Buildings'.[47] He later claimed that his salary was paid in part 'for being constantly at the command of the First Commissioner, and for advising the Board generally on such architectural and surveying questions as may be referred to me relating to Works and Public Buildings'; and during the 1860s he was repeatedly described as surveyor and architectural adviser to the Office of Works. In effect he became one of a semi-official council advising the First Commissioner on matters relating to public works, along with Hunt, Austin and the assistant secretary, Russell. This role lasted until 1869.

Manners stepped down as First Commissioner when Lord Derby's second government fell in May 1859. His successor in the second Palmerston administration, Lord Henry Fitzroy, died in December after only six months in office, and was succeeded in February 1860 by Palmerston's stepson, William Cowper. Cowper was an experienced though not very ambitious politician, whose languid and relaxed manner charmed some and infuriated others. He had been private secretary to his uncle Lord Melbourne, and later held junior positions in various government departments before succeeding Sir Benjamin Hall as President of the Board of Health in 1855. He continued to show an interest in social and philanthropic legislation, became the first president of the Commons Preservation Society and shared Hall's interest in improving the royal parks. A friend of Dante Gabriel Rossetti and John Ruskin, with whom his wife corresponded, he showed more enthusiasm for contemporary art than most of the holders of his office, and later became one of the first trustees of Ruskin's St George's Guild,[48] even choosing the

---

46 *RIBA Journal*, 24 Nov. 1892, p. 68; *Dictionary of National Biography 1911–1921*, p. 524. Taylor was described as 'sometime a carpenter in the employment of Mr George Smith the Contractor', *The Builder*, 14 May 1870, 379.

47 *The Builder*, 8 Sept. 1877, 897.

48 [Lady Mount Temple] *Memorials* (privately printed 1890), pp. 51–6.

William Morris firm to carry out a redecoration of two of the state rooms in St James's Palace in 1866–7.

Cowper remained First Commissioner until the Liberal government fell in 1866. During this time he faced contradictory demands to reduce expenditure on buildings on the one hand and to take an active lead in beautifying London on the other. Palmerston's determination to re-equip the armed forces put a strain on the national finances at the same time as Gladstone, once more Chancellor of the Exchequer, was trying to reduce government spending in order to introduce tax cuts. Against this background, a Commons Select Committee was appointed in 1860 to examine expenditure in the Office of Works. Cowper and other witnesses pointed out the wastefulness of renting offices for government departments, and Sir Benjamin Hall (who had gone to the Lords as Lord Llanover) argued in favour of placing the Office under a permanent head who would not be a politician – a proposal which was approved but never implemented.[49] Meanwhile, with work beginning on Scott's Foreign Office, expenditure on new buildings began to rise, and there were ever more clamorous calls for a solution to the chronic problems of overcrowding in the older Whitehall offices and the headquarters of the major national institutions. With Napoleon III's Paris in mind, Alexander Baillie-Cochrane, a 'Young England' crony of Manners and Disraeli, put forward a motion in 1862 for a Royal Commission which would review the operation of the Office of Works and work out a 'comprehensive plan' for London, and in the following year he revived, unsuccessfully, the proposal for appointing a permanent First Commissioner.

These arguments cut little ice with Palmerston, who told MPs in 1863: 'If anyone will go to Liverpool, to Leeds, to Manchester, and to other great towns, he will see buildings of the most beautiful description erected, not under the control of Government, but by persons employed by the municipalities themselves.'[50] The government nevertheless decided to go ahead with competitions for three important new buildings: a Natural History Museum at South Kensington, a new Law Courts in the Strand, and an extension of the National Gallery at Trafalgar Square. Pennethorne played no active part in these frustrating contests, but Cowper asked him to design a number of buildings where a competition was not thought to be necessary. They included a new picture gallery at the National Gallery constructed in 1860–1 when the long-term future of the Trafalgar Square building was still uncertain, the remodelling of Marlborough House and the building of a new stable block for the Prince of Wales, extensions to the Principal Probate Registry at Doctors Commons in the City, a new Library at the Patent Office, the east range and tower of the Public Record Office and, most important of all, the new Senate

49 Rep. Sel. Cttee. on Miscellaneous Expenditure, *PP* 1860, 9, pp. iv, 77, 118–19.
50 *Hansard*, 171 (1 June 1863), 207.

House for the University of London at the back of Burlington House which the government had acquired in the 1850s. This was his last building. In 1865 his status as an elder statesman of the profession was marked by the award of the RIBA Royal Gold Medal, and in an extraordinary *volte-face* the medal was presented by none other than Beresford Hope, the first non-architect President, who in his address praised him for encouraging 'the revival of art-conscience on the part of our rulers'.[51]

Palmerston died in 1865 and the Liberal government fell in the following year. Lord John Manners now returned to the Office of Works for the third and last time. His tenure was not marked by any important policy changes, but the fall of the Conservatives in the first general election after the 1867 Reform Act signalled another upheaval in the Office of Works. Gladstone, who became Prime Minister in the new Liberal administration at the end of 1868, regarded the popular vote in his favour as a mandate for enforcing more of the 'strict economy' policies with which he had been associated in the past. For the Office of Works this meant the application of an even harsher regime of Treasury control over spending. Writing to the new Chancellor of the Exchequer, Robert Lowe, Gladstone expressed the fear that '[the] great danger is excess in the buildings we raise and the affectation of a Palatial style in what are after all workshops'. The instrument for enforcing this bleak doctrine was the new Financial Secretary to the Treasury, Acton Ayrton, barrister MP for Tower Hamlets. Under a ruling from Lowe, Ayrton, aptly described as 'the man who had assumed the mantle of Joseph Hume', now had to approve all proposals for new spending on public buildings.[52]

Gladstone's choice as First Commissioner of Works was Alfred Henry Layard, a man of scholarly tastes and refined aesthetic sensibilities, who possessed many of the qualities of artistic judgement which the critics of the Office of Works had long demanded in a First Commissioner. Best known as the excavator of Nineveh, he had made a career in politics and had been an under-secretary in the Foreign Office under Palmerston and Russell. In an article published in *The Quarterly Review* in 1859, he had argued in favour of an appropriate functional style for public buildings, and on assuming office he tried to institute a series of reforms intended not only to increase the efficiency of the office, but also to enable it to exercise its role as public patron of architecture more effectively. Like Beresford Hope, he believed that the government should do more to set standards for beautifying London, though unlike him he was temperamentally inclined to look to classical models for inspiration. The imminent need to settle the design of important public buildings – the long-awaited National Gallery extension, the new Law Courts, the Natural History Museum, where work had still not begun – together with the

---

51 *RIBA Transactions* (1864–5), 1–2.   52 Port, *Historical Journal*, 27 (1984), 151–4.

recent completion of the Victoria Embankment, gave him an opportunity, as he saw it, to 'do something for the improvement of our public buildings and monuments, and for the embellishment of the metropolis'. His ideas were upheld by a Commons Select Committee, heavily influenced by Hope, which advocated that railway companies and other bodies preparing large-scale works in London should submit their plans for approval to the First Commissioner.[53]

Like others before him, Layard was frustrated in his aim of imposing a coherent plan on London. But he managed to bring about another reform of the Office of Works, one of the results of which was the final departure of Pennethorne. The occasion was the resignation of Alfred Austin as secretary in 1868. In view of the great increase in the responsibilities of the Office, Layard now proposed appointing two secretaries: a general secretary to control finance and normal correspondence, and a 'Secretary of Works and Buildings' who would superintend the preparation of architects' plans and give general advice to the First Commissioner. This advice was normally given by Hunt and Pennethorne, but they were professional men, paid by percentage fees, and in Layard's view they could not be expected to be totally impartial. Pennethorne had felt professionally debarred from giving opinions on other architects' plans and estimates, and as a result there was no built-in check on expenditure. Layard thought that 'the wasteful and unnecessary expenditure on the New Foreign Office [and] the manner in which space has been thrown away in providing for the different scientific societies on the Burlington House site . . . might be mentioned in proof of the necessity for this control'.[54]

Layard's candidate for the post of Secretary of Works and Buildings was James Fergusson, an authority on oriental architecture, author of the *History of the Modern Styles of Architecture* (1862), and a man 'carrying with him a certain weight with the public and with the architectural profession, and of business-like habits'. He was appointed in January 1869. Layard believed that 'the system was a bad one which led to the employment of Mr. Pennethorne to check the expenditure on buildings which he himself was erecting for the government'.[55] He therefore recommended the Treasury to discontinue Pennethorne's salary, and with it the post of 'Salaried Architect and Surveyor'. The Treasury had saved his post from extinction under Hall. Anxious about some of Layard's other proposed reforms, it now appointed a Committee of Inquiry, which agreed in March 1869 to the abolition of Pennethorne's appointment, but insisted on modifying Layard's reforms by appointing an assistant secretary to scrutinise the official coal, candles and furniture which the First Commissioner had hoped to remove from the purview of the Office. To finance this new post, Fergusson's salary would be reduced. Hunt was to continue

---

53 PRO, Work 22/2/6, pp. 1–2; 2nd Rep. Sel. Cttee. on Hungerford Bridge, *PP* 1868–9, 10 [387], p. iii.
54 PRO, Work 22/2/6, p. 1.
55 *Hansard*, 118 (22 July 1869), 516.

as surveyor, but was now to perform some of the surveys for large sites which had in the past been delegated to surveyors outside the office.[56]

Pennethorne had no choice but to accept the new arrangement, but he did not do so without some bitterness. For thirty years his life had centred around his official duties, and he seems to have had few other interests. He was now obliged to abandon his architectural practice and dismiss his staff, since it was clearly impossible to start a new private practice. As he told Charles Gore: 'Being now under 68 years of age with (as I hope) my intellect and powers of exertion equal to the performance of [my] duties, I had expected to continue to serve both offices some years longer, and it is painful to me to have that connection severed so suddenly and without cause assigned'.[57] Gore failed to persuade the Treasury to continue Pennethorne's salary from the Office of Woods and Forests, but his retirement was postponed until June 1870 to allow him to complete the London University building, the current extension of the Public Record Office and some surveying work. Concerned that earlier accusations of incompetence would affect his reputation after retirement, Pennethorne asked the Treasury 'to place on record that I have not been dismissed but retire with honour, and only in consequence of the reorganisation of this department having rendered necessary the abolition of my office'. This request was granted, the Treasury noting that he would 'leave the Public Service . . . with honour and credit to himself'.[58]

Pennethorne's retirement marked the end of an era in the Office of Works. Layard had hoped to use Fergusson's advice to increase the public standing of the Office. In fact the reverse happened. Angered by the Treasury's refusal to countenance his schemes for improving London, Layard resigned in October 1869, claiming that the Office of First Commissioner had become 'little better than that of a clerk in the Treasury'.[59] His successor was none other than Acton Ayrton, chief wielder of the Treasury axe. Ayrton's appointment was followed by the resignation of Fergusson, who resented being asked to perform petty secretarial duties. His post was now abolished, leaving Ayrton with the prospect of having no architectural adviser within the Office, though Hunt continued to advise on surveying matters and eventually received a knighthood for his services. As an enthusiastic retrencher, Ayrton was appalled at the high spending on architects' fees in recent years and agreed to a suggestion from the Chancellor of the Exchequer, Robert Lowe, for the appointment of Captain Douglas Galton, a Royal Engineer officer who had designed the Herbert Military Hospital at Greenwich in 1860, as 'Director of Public Works and Buildings'. He was charged with the responsibility for

---

56 2nd Rep. on Hungerford Bridge (1868–9), pp. 28–9; *PP* 1868–9, 24, pp. 2–10; BL, Add MS 39053, 22 July 1869.
57 *PP* 1868–9, 24, p. 11.
58 2nd Rep. on Hungerford Bridge (1868–9), p. 14; PRO, T 26/4, p. 297.
59 BL, Add MSS 38997, f. 17; Port, *Historical Journal*, 27 (1984), 160–1.

supervising the construction of new government buildings, the preparation of contracts, and the payment of architects. He too resigned in 1875 and was not replaced. Two years later a writer in *The Builder* thought that the Office of Works was 'not artistically so well off as it was twenty-five years ago, when its . . . chiefs had the advantage of an accomplished architect's advice'.[60] The mediocre quality of some of London's public buildings of the 1870s and 80s bears out this complaint.

Under Ayrton and his successors, major government buildings continued for some time to be put out to competition. But, as an economy measure, Ayrton tried to concentrate the less prominent architectural work of the Office in the hands of the assistant surveyors, who received salaries and not professional fees. After Pennethorne's retirement several important jobs, including the completion of the Public Record Office and the remodelling of the central part of the National Gallery, were given to John (later Sir John) Taylor, who succeeded John Phipps as surveyor of works in London in 1866 and later gave 'sound and cautious' advice to several late-nineteenth-century First Commissioners.[61] Taylor's buildings were designed with an unpretentious competence which shows the continued influence of Pennethorne. In this respect Taylor was his main architectural heir.

---

60 *The Builder*, 8 Sept. 1877, 898.   61 *Ibid.*, 3 May 1912, 528.

5

PUBLIC OFFICES

PENNETHORNE designed his first official buildings at a time when government was being drawn into an ever closer involvement in the lives of the British people. Despite all the official protestations of devotion to the principles of *laissez-faire*, the civil service doubled in size during his lifetime.[1] Departments, sub-departments and Royal Commissions proliferated. Paper accumulated at a rate which far outstripped the capacity of the buildings in which it was housed. It was the responsibility of the Office of Works to satisfy both the civil servants' need for more space and the politicians' determination to organise government business more rationally and efficiently.

The organisation of government offices in the 1840s spoke not of rationality but of bureaucratic muddle. The heart of Victorian government was the site of the old Palace of Whitehall, close to the Houses of Parliament and the Law Courts at Westminster. But government buildings were also scattered haphazardly through other parts of central London. Several public departments and government-sponsored bodies occupied rooms in Somerset House, the first large-scale, purpose-built block of government offices in London. The General Post Office, the Royal Mint, the Custom House and the Excise Office were in the City. Some departments, like the Ordnance Office, were divided between several sites, leading inevitably, in a pre-telephone era, to wasted time. Several were accommodated in rented buildings, often houses on the Crown estate. As rental costs rose, so too did demands for concentrating the work of each department in a single place – a thoroughly utilitarian aim which, like some other utilitarian proposals, drew central government inexorably into spending large sums of money. Pennethorne began to work for the government at a time when administrative reform was in the air. The lax and easy-going methods of Dickens's Circumlocution Office were being replaced by a new ideal of administrative efficiency championed by serious

---

1 S. Checkland, *British Public Policy* (Cambridge, 1983), pp. 110–11.

144

and highly motivated civil servants. These ideals of rationalisation and 'concentration' were tangibly expressed in the architecture of Pennethorne's official buildings.

THE PUBLIC RECORD OFFICE

Pennethorne's first really large government building was designed to house the records of England's past. The history of European states could not be written without their government archives, and the care of these archives is tied up with the very principle of nationality. By the early nineteenth century England had accumulated a very rich collection of archives, ranging from Domesday Book and Magna Carta to the correspondence of kings and statesmen, and, as historical research increased, the care of these documents came under closer scrutiny. At the same time the quantity of records grew remorselessly.

The condition of the public records first began to cause concern in the early 1820s. There was no purpose-built repository for the English records to match Robert Adams's magnificent Register House for the Scottish papers in Edinburgh. The English papers were scattered among a number of different buildings, only one of which – Sir John Soane's State Paper Office overlooking St James's Park – was purpose-built. Some were housed in the Tower of London, others in the Chapter House of Westminster Abbey, yet more in the official residence of the Master of the Rolls in Chancery Lane. The awkwardness of this arrangement – or lack of it – not only caused inconvenience to historians and lawyers. It also offended the tidy-minded staff of the Record Commission, created in 1800 to catalogue and publish the papers. In an age when efficiency and the concentration of government offices appealed to reformers, a plea for a single building to house all the public records could not fail to attract influential support. It is no accident therefore that a proposal for a General Record Repository should have been published by the Record Commission in 1832, the very year in which Parliament itself was reformed.

The physical condition of the records gave the question added urgency. The destruction of the Palace of Westminster by fire in 1834 gave a graphic illustration of the vulnerability of public buildings. None of the older buildings in which records were stored was fire-proof. Some were susceptible to damp and theft. Under an Act of 1838 the last Record Commission was disbanded, and the records placed under the control of the Master of the Rolls, Lord Langdale, and a Deputy Keeper, Francis Palgrave, a barrister and mediaeval historian. Palgrave began consolidating the records by bringing many of those housed at Westminster to Carlton Ride, the former riding-house of the Prince Regent's Carlton House situated at the eastern end of Carlton House Terrace. Here they were arranged and classified by one of the Assistant Keepers, Henry Cole, a former clerk to Palgrave and later to become one of the most energetic of all Victorian civil servants. Conditions were far from ideal:

A small iron stove, with an iron pipe over a chimney about 50 feet long, was carried up through the roof. In frosty weather [the] aged guardian used to light the stove so vigorously that the iron chimney became red hot, and the old fellow used to sit shivering before it, rubbing his hands until he fell fast asleep.[2]

The older repositories were in many respects worse, prone to damp and a prey to mice. By the end of the 1830s the provision of a new building was seen as essential to the very survival of the records.

Few people disputed the need for a new purpose-built record office, but it took over a decade to find a suitable site and to arrange for adequate funding. The eventual site on the Rolls Estate, between Chancery Lane and Fetter Lane, was first suggested in 1831 by the then Master of the Rolls, Sir John Leach,[3] and in 1837 an Act of Parliament vested the estate in the Crown and gave the Office of Works powers to build a new record office there. The estate consisted of a row of early eighteenth-century brick houses fronting Chancery Lane, with an entrance to a narrow courtyard around which were arranged the early Georgian Rolls House, the mediaeval but much-altered Rolls Chapel (Plate 54) and other legal buildings. Behind was a garden stretching back to Fetter Lane. On either side of the estate were old and often run-down buildings, some of them dating from before the Great Fire, which did not penetrate this far west. The site had two main advantages: it already belonged to the government, and it was in the heart of London's legal quarter from which it was assumed that most of the searchers would emerge. Proposals to build new Law Courts in the area made the site even more attractive, and in 1840 Thomas Chawner was asked to prepare a block plan showing how an office could be built there in five stages.[4] This was the germ of the plan eventually adopted.

It was unfortunate that the Public Record Office was conceived at about the same time as the more glamorous Houses of Parliament. By 1840 work had already begun on the foundations of the larger building, and its vast and ever-increasing cost – well over twice the original estimate – cast a shadow over all proposals for government buildings for the next two decades. Since there was expected to be a surplus of space in Barry's building, the Treasury officials suggested placing the records in what was to become the Victoria Tower. Barry feared that the tower would be abandoned because of cuts in funding and stated optimistically that, given some pruning of the records, it would be 'likely to prove sufficient for several centuries'.[5] The record officials disagreed with him, but the scheme was not dropped until 1845.

It was at this stage that, in the significant words of Henry Cole, 'a public opinion

---

2 H. Cole, *Fifty Years of Public Work*, I (1844), p. 23; PRO, Work 2/3, p. 367.
3 PRO, Work 12/67/1, f. 4.
4 *Ibid.*, 12/64/1, ff. 37–41; Work 30/2600.
5 *Ibid.*, 12/64/1, ff. 21–4; 1st Rep. Deputy Keeper of Public Records, *PP* 1840, 28, p. 6; 2nd Rep. Deputy Keeper of Public Records, *PP* 1841 (2), I, pp. 8, 22.

54. The Rolls Chapel and Rolls House. The chapel was first built in the thirteenth century as part of an establishment for converted Jews. It later became annexed to the office of the Master of the Rolls, who was responsible for the papers of the Court of Chancery, and was remodelled on several occasions, leaving very little of the original fabric visible. The adjoining Rolls House was designed by Colen Campbell and built in 1717–24. The buildings in the picture were all demolished to make way for the west wing of the Public Record Office.

was created'. Extra-Parliamentary pressure contributed to many of the achievements of Victorian government, and while the question of housing the public records was hardly one to arouse great extremes of passion, it could appeal both to the nation's pride and to the growing belief in the need for efficiency in the management of its affairs. The condition of the records was brought up in Parliament in 1846, one MP

147

commenting that it was 'little less than a reproach to the state of civilization in this country that so little attention should be paid to this matter. No nation that had a history, and valued it, would be careless or negligent of such documents. They were, in fact its history.'[6]

Early in 1847 the Royal Commission on Metropolitan Improvements finally recommended placing the Record Office on the Rolls Estate and re-routing Pennethorne's 'Great Central Thoroughfare' along its northern flank. Pennethorne had already prepared designs for what was to become his largest public building (Plate 55). He met Cole for the first time in 1845, and towards the end of 1846 prepared a model of a room which incorporated his ideas on the proper storage of records. The dimensions of this room, which eventually served as a module for those of the whole building, were largely determined at the insistence of James Braidwood, Superintendent of the London Fire Brigade.[7] The weight of the documents made it essential to use iron in the structure, but Braidwood pointed out that 'of all building materials [iron] is the most rapidly and most seriously affected by fire'. He therefore insisted that the ironwork would have to be clad in brick or stone. The rooms were, as far as possible, to be completely isolated from each other, and Braidwood wanted to heat each of them by open fireplaces rather than by hot air or hot water pipes, so that ventilation would be improved and a central furnace rendered unnecessary. These considerations were the most important factors affecting the design of the building when work eventually began.

Pennethorne's plans were based on an estimate of shelf space provided by Cole, and prepared 'in great measure under his immediate supervision'. There would be 1,370,655 cubic feet (38,790 cubic metres) of space for records on two or three floors, together with search rooms and offices. The building would house not only all the present records in store, but also those which would accumulate over the next century. It would stretch from Chancery Lane across the Rolls Garden to Fetter Lane, from which point a long wing would extend south to Fleet Street and, to reduce the danger of fire, it would be completely isolated from neighbouring structures. Both the intended realignment of Fetter Lane and the building of the southern wing would involve extensive purchases of property, whose price Pennethorne estimated at £109,107, and the gross expenditure would amount to half a million pounds, about two thirds that of the Houses of Parliament as first estimated.

Pennethorne's original intention was to design a 'massive and splendid, but moderately decorated Building' in the Elizabethan style he had recently employed in New Oxford Street and at Victoria Park. Had these proposals been adopted, the Public Record Office would have been very different from the formidably

6 *Hansard*, 87 (23 June 1846), 906–8.
7 6th Rep. Commrs. for Improving the Metropolis, *PP* 1847, 16 [861], p. 28.

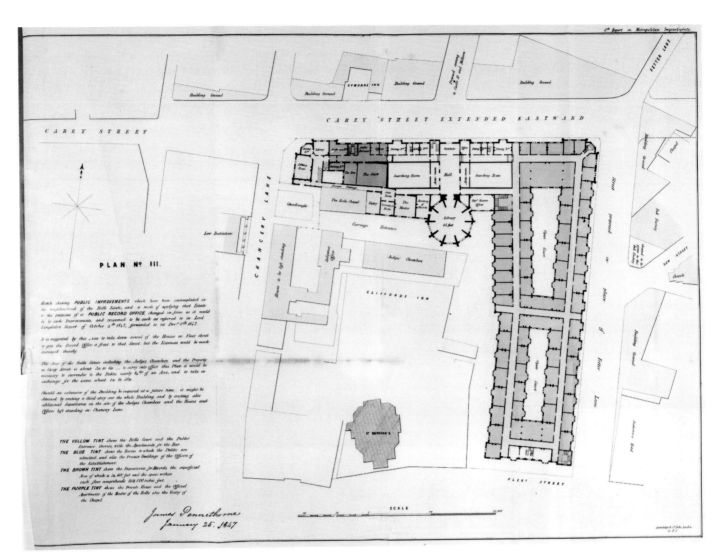

55. Ground plan of the Public Record Office as first proposed. The building would have been entered from the north from a new street which Pennethorne intended to form part of his 'Great Central Thoroughfare'. The records were to be kept in the eastern part, which was to stretch south to Fleet Street, and the Rolls Chapel, facing Chancery Lane, was to be preserved.

functional structure eventually constructed. To the north there would have been a symmetrical main block facing the new street – 'the greatest thoroughfare in London' – entered through a vestibule and two-storied hall, with two-storied search rooms on either side and an octagonal library straight ahead. The whole of the eastern wing, extending down to Fleet Street, would have been devoted to the depositories for storing the documents, each one lit by a tall window.[8] The

8 PRO, Work 12/64/2, ff. 31–4; 6th Rep. Metropolitan Improvement Commrs., pp. 11 and 26.

building would have been more spacious and, almost certainly, more aesthetically satisfying than the present one.

Fears about the cost caused the Russell government to postpone the project for two years. Finally Palgrave jettisoned Pennethorne's ambitious plans altogether and, together with Alexander Milne, the Second Commissioner of Woods and Forests, and Inman, the Surveyor of Buildings, produced a much simpler and cheaper scheme 'founded upon principles of the strictest economy'. The new proposals carried utilitarian starkness to a new pitch of refinement. Palgrave insisted that the building should be 'disengaged from all extraneous considerations whatsoever, the architect must take no thought concerning Metropolitan Improvements, or display of architectural grandeur, and he must turn all his intelligence to the purpose of raising the required building on the most reasonable terms'. There was to be 'nothing for display, nothing for the attraction of the public', and the building should contain only what was 'absolutely and not hypothetically needful for the transaction of work and business at the smallest possible expense'. It would be entered from Chancery Lane, and would contain only 250,000 cubic feet (7,075 cubic metres) of storage space, sufficient to cater for the accumulations of the next fifty years. The Office of Works would determine the style of architecture 'and other Minor details', but Palgrave's preference was for the simple Palladianism of the Rolls House, 'which though plain is handsome [and] might be adopted as being the cheapest, and yet sufficiently respectable'. The cost would be only £40,000, excluding fittings.[9]

In the course of long discussions with Palgrave and many visits to existing archives, Pennethorne modified this scheme into something very closely resembling the present building. His conclusions were presented in a lengthy report and a set of drawings which were finally approved in July 1850.[10] The proportions of the cell-like depositories still determined those of the whole building. They were twenty-five feet (five metres) high, divided by floors with gratings into two parts of equal height, and reached through iron doors so that 'nothing but wilful incendiarism committed by a person having access to the building could make a kindling, which would die out before any harm would ensue worth noticing'. Palgrave had wanted the building to be vaulted with brick or stone, but Pennethorne calculated that each room, including the records, would weigh ninety tons, and pointed out that such huge internal supports and external buttresses would be needed that both space and light would be lost. He therefore proposed resting the floors on wrought iron beams and girders, with rows of brick arches of five-foot (one and a half metres) span underneath to protect them from the heat of any fire that might break out (Plate 56)

9 PRO, Work 12/64/2, ff. 1–9; Work 2/8, p. 111; *PP* 1850, 34 [571], pp. 2–6; R. Ellis, 'The Building of the Public Record Office', in A. E. J. Hollander (ed.), *Essays in Memory of Sir Hilary Jenkinson* (1962), p. 14.
10 PRO, Work 12/64/2, ff. 15–27; MPD 177, ff. 31–40.

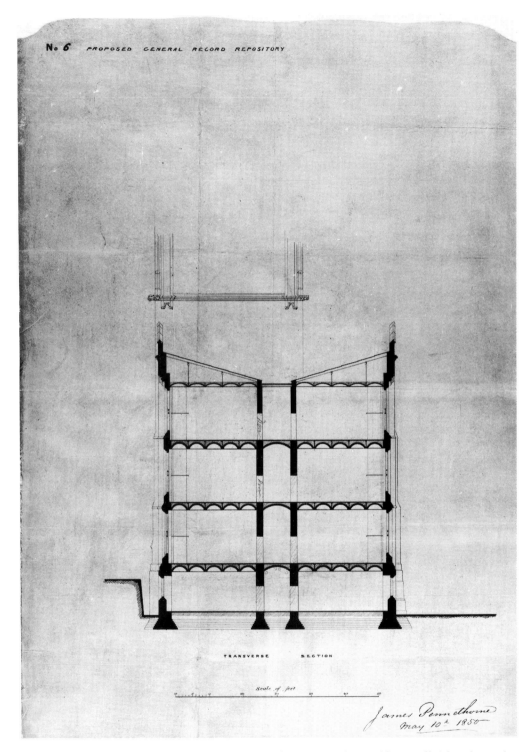

No. 6 PROPOSED GENERAL RECORD REPOSITORY

TRANSVERSE SECTION

Scale of feet

James Pennethorne
May 10th 1850

56. Cross section of the Public Record Office. The floors are made up of fireproof brick arches and are supported by massive walls of brick clad in stone. A corridor bisects the building.

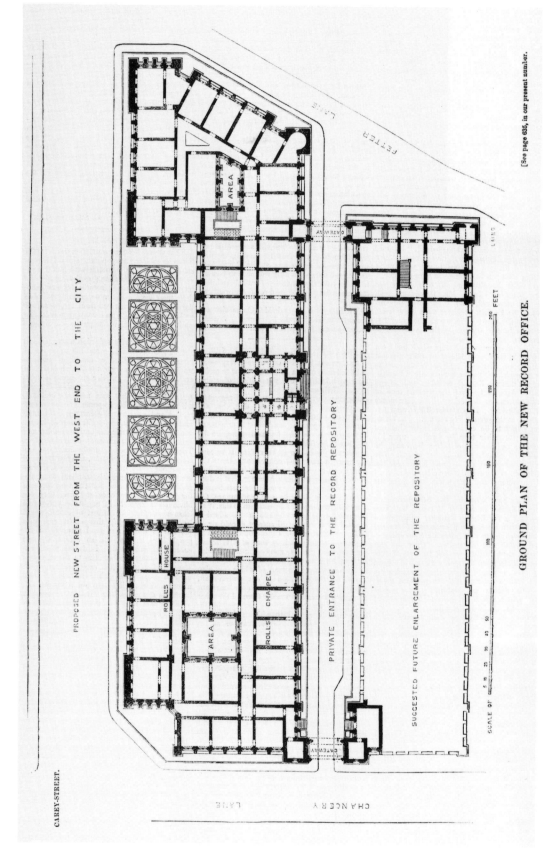

GROUND PLAN OF THE NEW RECORD OFFICE.

[See page 635, in our present number.]

57. Revised ground plan of the Public Record Office. The entrance has now been shifted to the south and the search rooms and eastern block severely curtailed. The central portion was built first.

– the normal nineteenth-century fireproof construction first evolved in mills, and later extended to complexes of warehouses like the noble Albert Docks at Liverpool, begun a few years before in 1841.[11] The record depositories took up most of the available space on the three main floors, with a semi-basement (contrary to Palgrave's original wishes) for workshops and the storage of 'papers of secondary importance' and a broad corridor running along the spine of the building (Plate 57). Little space was allotted to search rooms, and the only vestige surviving of the spacious planning of the 1847 scheme was the entrance hall, which was now to be approached from the south.

The building was designed so as to be erected in five stages, the first or central portion in the Rolls Garden, the second to the east with a frontage to Fetter lane, and the third on the site of the Rolls House and chapel facing Chancery Lane. Two more sections were to occupy the space to the south of the main building, but the long southern wing envisaged in the 1847 proposals was abandoned. Thirteen years later, after much of the building had been completed, Pennethorne still regretted the abandonment of the 1847 scheme, pointing out that 'in those days we foresaw the necessity for a large library, for large searching rooms . . . &c &c; all these things were washed away by economy, and will hereafter have to be provided at greater cost and with less convenience'.[12] This has indeed proved to be the case. Equally unfortunately, the Government's refusal to go ahead with Pennethorne's new east–west street meant that the building lost much of the monumental public character originally intended and, in the words of Sir William Molesworth, was 'almost unseen by the Public who (not knowing what had been contemplated) complain of so restricted a site having been chosen for so handsome an Edifice'. In 1853 Molesworth tried to build the part of the street running along the north front between Chancery Lane and Fetter Lane, but he failed to persuade the Treasury to release surplus funds from the other Metropolitan Improvements.[13] Today the north facade is hemmed in by other buildings and can only be seen in sharp perspective.

The architectural treatment of this vast warehouse of state documents was strictly determined by its function. Like many classically trained architects of the nineteenth century, both in England and on the Continent, Pennethorne was at heart a rationalist, believing that the requirements of modern buildings could be logically and lucidly expressed within the grammar of the orders, ornament being introduced where necessary to enhance the dignity of the building. But here the requirements were so unusual that a different approach was needed. The building consisted of a multitude of relatively small rooms with large windows, arranged on a grid-like plan. Had it been a commercial structure, a strictly functional brick facade would no

---

11 The fireproofing arrangements were also said to have been influenced by those at the Bedford Estate's muniment room in Montagu Street, Bloomsbury: *The Builder*, 11 Oct. 1851, 635.

12 PRO, PRO 8/4, f. 41; *RIBA Transactions*, 1st series, 22 (1871–2), 57.

13 PRO, Work 6/147/1, ff. 57–66; LRRO 1/2059.

doubt have sufficed, as in the warehouses of the London docks. But the Public Record Office was to be more than a warehouse; it was, as the foundation stone put it, the 'treasure house of the national records and archives', a building which would in some respects embody England's vision of her past. For such a purpose a purely utilitarian exterior would be inappropriate. Neither the classical vocabulary nor the Elizabethan style which Pennethorne had proposed two years earlier could be easily reconciled with the heavy buttresses and large, but thin and narrow, windows that necessity now dictated. Pennethorne therefore concluded that it was 'almost impossible satisfactorily to have recourse to any other than what are called Gothic forms, if an Ecclesiastical feeling can be at the same time avoided'.[14]

The Public Record Office was the first major government building after the new Houses of Parliament to be designed with a Gothic exterior. But the character of the two buildings could not be more different. Pennethorne's revised plans show a rigidly symmetrical building, with a tower, of vaguely north-European character, imparting a note of nightmarish fantasy. There is none of Nash's grace and charm, none of Barry's irregular massing and subtle use of decoration. The sheer heaviness of the unrelieved elevations, with the monotonous repetition of a single motif – three superimposed windows set within a pointed relieving arch resting on buttresses (a motif found in the fourteenth-century Papal palace at Avignon) is very intimidating, as it was presumably intended to be. There can be little doubt that the obsessive concern for security repeatedly expressed by Palgrave and Braidwood communicated itself to Pennethorne, and forced him to design a structure with very adequate 'commodity', almost excessive 'firmness' and very little 'delight'. Something of the same overpowering massiveness is found in the prisons, workhouses and hospitals which are so characteristic of a period in which ruthless obsession with organisation was combined with a deep underlying fear of social disorder. If Gothic architecture consists of no more than the use of the pointed arch in combination with a strictly functional system of construction and planning, then the Public Record Office is a triumph of the Gothic Revival; otherwise it is difficult to agree with Pevsner that it was 'Gothic of a kind true enough and yet functional enough to have pleased Pugin if he had seen it'.[15] In fact, far from echoing the glories of the Middle Ages, the building looks forward to the remorselessly utilitarian architecture of the twentieth century.

Funds for the first part of the building were voted in the summer of 1850. Lengthy discussion of materials followed. The original intention was to use a magnesian limestone from Anston (Nottinghamshire) for facing the walls, as in the Houses of Parliament. But it was soon found that the stone was not available in sufficient quantities, and that Kentish rag would have to be used instead, with

14 *Ibid.*, Work 12/64/2, ff. 25–6.
15 N. Pevsner, *The Buildings of England: London*, I (1973 edn), p. 102.

Anston only used for the dressings.[16] This decision increased the rugged appearance of the building, but in the long run it turned out to be fortunate; the Anston stone has now crumbled, but the Kentish rag has weathered well. For the internal construction Pennethorne proposed the relatively novel use of wrought iron 'in the manner now adopted for Railway Bridges [like the Britannia Bridge over the Menai Straits] the formulae for which are now satisfactorily established'. The girders were to be surrounded by fire bricks, with close-jointed brick arches and tension bars underneath. Pennethorne's early association with Nash had introduced him to the problems of iron construction, and here he must have chosen wrought over cast iron because of its potentially greater strength and lack of brittleness. Eventually, though, the higher cost forced him to resort to cast iron, and a tender from Messrs Grissell of the Regent's Canal Works to supply 289 girders for £1,698 was finally accepted in May 1851.[17]

A contract was signed in March 1851 with Messrs J. & H. Lee of Chiswell Street, the builders of the Houses of Parliament, and the foundation stone was laid on 24 April. In August Pennethorne came to an agreement for the carving around the main entrance with John Thomas, the sculptor at the Houses of Parliament, whose experience there made him 'a particularly proper person to be entrusted with the work'. And later in the year the strange crenellation originally proposed for the parapet was replaced by a lighter and more intricate design shown in the elevation published in *The Builder* (Plate 58), together with a somewhat more elegant but still embarrassingly awkward superstructure for the tower. Completion was held up by delays in supplying the stone, and the carcase of the building was finished in 1853.[18]

Further delays were caused by indecision about fitting up the rooms in which the records were to be stored. A strong room was fitted up in March 1853 to serve as a model for the rest, but a year later no more progress had been made, and the estimated costs had risen to nearly fifty per cent above those contemplated in 1850. Finally, in September 1854, a contract was signed for the provision of metal doors with ventilators, and after some controversy it was agreed to disregard Pennethorne's advice and use slate for the racks holding the records, pushing up the cost further. With a zeal for security that verged on the paranoid, the new Master of the Rolls, Lord Romilly, now insisted that the cases should be enclosed by wire doors, each of them having its own separate key. Pennethorne warned that the cost would be 'fearful', but Sir William Molesworth deferred to Romilly's advice, and so committed the Government to an expenditure of £4,100 for the shelves and no less than £24,905 for the doors. Strangely enough, this quite unnecessary expenditure not only escaped Parliamentary criticism, but was also sanctioned by a Treasury

16 PRO, Work 12/63/14, ff. 56–9.
17 *Ibid.*, 1/36, p. 295; Work 12/64/14, ff. 57–68; Work 30/214.
18 *Ibid.*, 12/64/4, ff. 2–8, 18–21, 26; Work 30/2585; MPI 172.

whose customary carefulness was already being severely strained by the demands of the Crimean War.[19] In the event the wire doors were never even used, and were finally consigned to Somerset House. As a result of these delays, the building was not finally opened until 1859.

Surrounded by old houses, with no facade onto any major or even minor street and its tower still unbuilt, the first part of the Public Record office did not present a very imposing appearance to the outside world. A writer in *The Saturday Review* in 1855 thought that 'the general effect combines the workhouse, the jail, and the Manchester mill. The style is meant to be Tudor, with every large feature and every detail of that style misapplied and distorted . . . [It is] profoundly contemptible'.[20] To another commentator it was

a strange monument of self-defeating ingenuity. It was built for fear of fire, by which the public records have never yet been destroyed, and in disregard of damp, the critical enemy of our public records. Dark and strong, with its slate shelves and iron presses, it has proved as little suitable for the purpose of keeping papers as the Peak of Peverel would be, and the building from which fire was to be excluded is now crowded with stoves and open grates, to which are to be added gas and other appliances for heating. Strong and dark, in a congerie of caves too confined for the purpose, documents are crowded in a building which looks spacious outside, but which proves not to be half big enough for the stores which are still in course of being carried to it.[21]

A few years later J. S. Brewer, professor of English and lecturer in History at King's College, London, was commissioned to prepare a Calendar of the State Papers of Henry VIII. He found the interior

even less attractive than the exterior. A square vestibule, badly lighted, conducts the visitor to a number of narrow passages flagged with brick; iron doors to the right and left, marked with cabalistic numerals, and furnished with small circular ventilators, divide these passages with geometrical exactness . . . No thought of beauty or general effect has entered the mind of the architect, or, rather has been permitted to enter it . . . One thought, that of security, has absorbed all other consideration.[22]

These words will strike a chord with historians who have followed the prison-like *via dolorosa* from the public entrance to the search rooms.

Long before the new building opened it had become obvious that it would not be large enough to house all the public records, which from 1852 included those of all the government departments. The second stage was to be the east wing, but it was repeatedly postponed because of what the Treasury described as 'more pressing needs', and meanwhile records continued to be crowded into the Westminster

---

19 PRO, Work 1/45, pp. 487, 565; Work 12/64/14, ff. 70–105; T 26/1, p. 235.
20 *The Saturday Review*, 17 Nov. 1855, 49.
21 *BN*, 6 Feb. 1857, 147.   22 J. S. Brewer, *English Studies* (1881), p. 2.

58. The north elevation of the Public Record Office as proposed in 1851. The central portion was built as Pennethorne intended, but the wings and the upper stages of the tower were later redesigned to give the building a slightly less grim appearance. The foreground is shown cleared for the new street which was never built.

Abbey Chapter House and the houses in Chancery Lane where the west wing was eventually to go.[23] The demolition of the State Paper Office in 1862 to make way for the new Foreign and India Offices made the extension even more necessary, but the Treasury insisted on building only the southern part of the east wing at first. Work began in 1864 and the building was ready by the early summer of 1866.[24] It was now possible to remove the remaining records from Carlton Ride, allowing Pennethorne to complete Carlton House Terrace to Nash's design. The Record Office staff could also give up the Chapter House of Westminster Abbey, enabling that magnificent late-thirteenth-century building to be restored by Gilbert Scott.

---

23 *21st Annual Rep. Deputy Keeper of Public Records*, 26 April 1860, p. xxi.
24 PRO, Work 12/65/9; Work 12/65/17, ff. 13–78; Work 30/2585–2654; *BN*, 20 Oct. 1865, 741.

The east wing of the Public Record office differs in several respects from Pennethorne's original intentions. Because of the final closure of the Anston quarries, he was obliged to use Mansfield stone for the north front and Portland for the walls to Fetter Lane. And he decided to enliven the skyline by adding ogee-shaped turrets to the roof, like those of the Tudor royal chapels – a happy decision which was repeated by John Taylor in his Chancery Lane facade. There were even greater changes internally. No special provision had been made for search rooms in the original plans, but two were now provided: a Legal Search Room (the present Long Room) on the ground floor facing Fetter Lane and Literary Search Room (now called the Round Room) in the middle of the new block. The absurd rule against central heating was abandoned, and both were heated by water pipes from an adjacent furnace. The Round Room (Colour Plate II) is the most impressive in the building. Two-storied, with a gallery and a domed roof of glass and iron, it makes the most of the awkward site and in its circular plan and its frank use of structural ironwork recalls the interior of J. B. Bunning's earlier Coal Exchange in the City (1847–9). With that superb building now demolished, the Round Room ranks as one of the finest remaining examples of Victorian cast-iron architecture in London.

The provision of adequate search-rooms at last gave the Public Record office some of the qualities of a major public building. The building of the tower in 1865–7 gave it its most distinctive external feature (Plate 59). The decision to proceed with the tower came about primarily because of the need for a water tank to quell any fire that might break out now that the taboo on central heating had been relaxed. Pennethorne took the opportunity to replace the strange super-structure originally intended with the present much more attractive upper storey, with its four corner turrets of English late-mediaeval character and parapets broken by lower turrets containing statues of queens (Matilda, Elizabeth, Anne and Victoria) by Joseph Durham, one of the most prolific of Victorian sculptors.[25] The last part of the building to be completed in Pennethorne's lifetime was the northern part of the east wing, built in 1869–70, with its two gaunt and impressive towers (Plate 60) enfolding the Round Room.

While the east wing was being completed, Pennethorne made detailed plans for the eventual completion of the rest of the building. In December 1868 he produced a plan showing the west wing, with two more search rooms and a tower like that originally proposed in 1850 over a new public entrance from Chancery Lane. Lord Romilly objected to this scheme because it involved the demolition of the Rolls Chapel, and Pennethorne therefore produced a second scheme preserving the Chapel, though altering its walls and incorporating it in the main building.[26] This

25 PRO, Work 12/65/8; MPI 169/4A.
26 Ibid., MPI 169/5, 169/9; RIBA Transactions (1871–2), 57.

59. The south front of the Public Record Office. The tower was added in 1865–7.

second scheme formed the basis of the present Chancery Lane block built to the designs of John Taylor in 1891–6, but in the end the walls of the Rolls Chapel proved to be unsafe and it was demolished.[27] Taylor's block (Plate 61) matches Pennethorne's building, but he wisely decided to abandon the tall tower, replacing it by a lower structure rising only one storey above the main block and adorned with the neo-Tudor turrets first introduced by Pennethorne in the east wing. In this form it fits in happily with the varied buildings in the relatively narrow street.

Pennethorne's plan for a south range between Chancery Lane and Fetter Lane remained unrealised. An attractive but undated watercolour,[28] probably by a later architect, shows a south wing enclosing a courtyard with two almost Bodley-esque lower blocks faced in smooth ashlar. The building of these blocks would have given the building an almost collegiate character and would, at a stroke, have given the design a coherence which it had lacked ever since the abandonment of Pennethorne's original designs. But there is no evidence that the quadrangular scheme was ever taken seriously, and the building is now L-shaped, the two wings enfolding an empty and featureless space surrounded by undistinguished twentieth-century offices. The decision not to build the extra depositories on the Rolls site not only gave the Public Record Office a somewhat truncated appearance. It also ensured that, with the huge growth in government activity which has characterised the twentieth century, it would rapidly become overcrowded. The idea of expanding the building was not finally abandoned until the 1960s when it was decided to build a new Office at Kew, which was eventually opened in 1977. In its adoption of practical considerations to the exclusion of virtually any others, this monument to the functionalism of the modern age may yet prove more than a match for Pennethorne's building.

The Public Record Office, for all its Gothic detailing, was one of the most forward-looking buildings of its age (which does not mean that it was one of the most beautiful). Writers on architecture have often talked about letting a building's function determine its form, but there are few nineteenth-century public buildings where this advice was put more determinedly into practice than Pennethorne's massive warehouse of state documents. Henry Cole thought that it had 'an architectural expression of truth, originality and of its purpose . . . It is wonderful for its completeness in Europe, or even perhaps in the world.'[29] In its method of design it also anticipated what has since become normal in architectural practice. Many of the most important decisions about its form and construction were made by outside experts, Pennethorne's task being to plan the building and style it so as to evoke its purpose and to fit it into its surroundings. Some nineteenth-century architects took full responsibility for both the practical and the aesthetic aspects of their buildings.

---

27 PRO, Work 12/66/11.   28 *Ibid.*, 30/2655.
29 Cole, *Fifty Years of Public Works*, p. 32.

60. The east range of the Public Record Office, from Fetter Lane. Neo-Tudor turrets replace the crenellation originally proposed for the roof-line.

But as society became more complex, buildings larger, and knowledge more copious, this omnipotence became more and more difficult to sustain. In this respect the Public Record Office, like the much better-known Houses of Parliament, broke new ground in government patronage of architecture.

THE ORDNANCE OFFICE

By the time work on the Public Record office got under way, Pennethorne had already completed his first building for a government department. Military administration in Britain before the mid nineteenth century presented such a chaotic appearance, that one wonders how the country ever won a war. Business was transacted through several departments and boards whose offices were scattered around the capital. Of these the most important was the Board of Ordnance which traced its origins back to the fifteenth century – two hundred years earlier than the standing army. The Ordnance officials controlled the supply of weapons, barracks and fortifications to the British army. For some time they were all housed in the Tower of London, but an increase in staff during the Napoleonic Wars led in 1806 to the purchase of the Crown lease of the eighteenth-century Cumberland House (86 Pall Mall), built to the designs of Matthew Brettingham in 1761–3. This housed the 'superior officers', and the wings (85 and 87 Pall Mall) were turned into official residences for the permanent civil servants. Three years later a pair of plain eighteenth-century houses next door (nos. 83–4) were occupied for use by the engineers' and barrack departments. But by the 1840s clerks were still working in the Tower – a division that could not fail to cause delays.[30]

The inefficiencies of the Ordnance department were seized upon by reforming politicians eager to reduce bureaucratic waste. The question became urgent early in 1846, when the condition of two of the Pall Mall buildings started to cause concern. The foundations were found to be 'much decayed', and the Board's secretary asked the Treasury about the possibility of pulling the houses down and replacing them by 'eligible offices' which could house the whole establishment. Further progress was delayed by the Corn Law crisis and the fall of Peel's government, but soon after taking office as First Commissioner, Lord Morpeth asked Pennethorne for a report. His view was that the concentration of the establishment could best be achieved by building a four-storied block of 'large and good offices' on the site of 83–4 Pall Mall. A cheaper alternative solution would be to add an extra storey to Cumberland House, leaving the older houses untouched, and Pennethorne supplied a drawing showing how this could be done. The Treasury opted for Pennethorne's first proposal, probably because it promised more space.

---

30 *Survey of London* 29 (1960), pp. 364–5, 369; PRO, MPD 134/1–3; T 1/5193/20425.

61. The Chancery Lane front of the Public Record Office (1891–6). John Taylor retained the main elements of Pennethorne's designs, but replaced his proposed tower over the public entrance by a more delicate neo-Tudor superstructure.

The construction of the new building was delayed for three years because of the government's reluctance to seek funds from a Parliament where there were many members only too eager to attack what they saw as excessive spending on the military departments. But in 1849 the inefficiency of the existing arrangements in the Ordnance Department came under severe scrutiny once more, and a Select Committee reported that the division of business between the Tower and Pall Mall 'renders it difficult to obtain information as to current transactions, delays business, and seriously interferes with the prompt discharge of official duties'.[31] Pennethorne estimated the total cost of the necessary alterations and additions at £17,000, together with £5,000 for fittings. In February 1850 the government finally agreed to ask Parliament for the money, having abandoned an earlier idea of financing the building out of the Land Revenues of the Crown.[32] Building began in September, and the new office was completed in the summer of 1851.

Pennethorne's building was a dignified three-storied Renaissance *palazzo* of brick, with a three-bay facade and a low-pitched roof of the Italian type (Plate 62). He had already used this style in the Museum of Practical Geology not far away in Jermyn Street, and the proximity of the great Pall Mall club houses made its choice almost inevitable here. The proportions were to some extent determined by the need to make the floor levels conform with those of Cumberland House next door, and as the building was entered through the existing Ordnance buildings there was no need for a doorway. The corners were emphasised with heavy quoins, the floor levels marked by prominent string-courses and the windows, with their deeply moulded stone architraves, gave the impression of being punched out of the wall surfaces. The Florentine quattrocento effect was further enhanced by the row of lamp-holders at ground-floor level.

With the new building completed, Pennethorne was asked in May 1852 to produce an estimate for alterations to the former Cumberland House made necessary by an increase in staff. Work on adapting the east wing was authorised in June and was 'advancing rapidly' in the following month. The work on the centre was carried out during the summer of 1853 and further minor alterations to the exterior were proposed at the suggestion of the Royal Engineers, though without Pennethorne's involvement, in 1854.[33] In the following year the Ordnance department was merged with the new War Office, and the future of its buildings became tied up with plans for the enlarged department in which Pennethorne was to become deeply involved.

---

31 2nd Rep. Sel. Cttee on Army and Ordnance Expenditure, *PP* 1849, 9 [499], p. xxiii.
32 PRO, Work 1/35, p. 5; Work 2/8, pp. 12–13, 52–5, 102–6.
33 PRO, MPH 99.

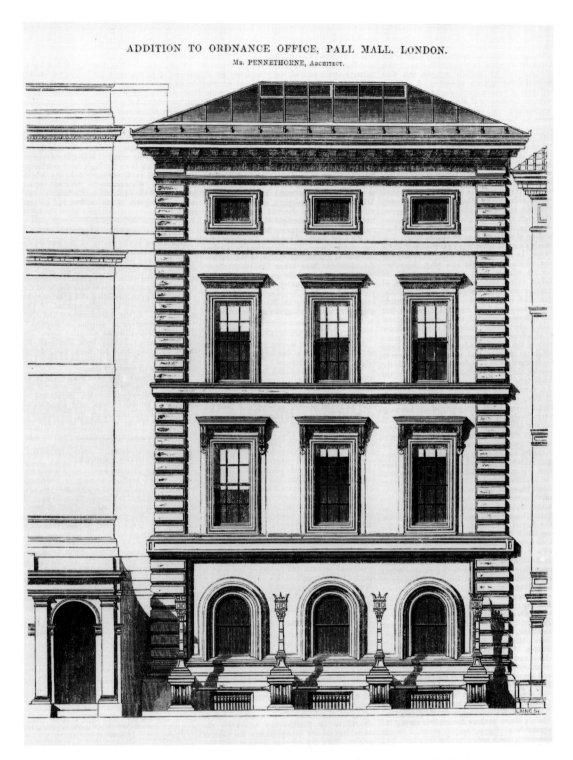

ADDITION TO ORDNANCE OFFICE, PALL MALL, LONDON.
Mr. PENNETHORNE, Architect.

62. The Ordnance Office extension. The building was attached to the former Cumberland House, part of which is shown on the right. It later became part of the War Office and was demolished in 1908–11.

63. The courtyard of Somerset House, by Sir William Chambers (1776–96).

THE INLAND REVENUE OFFICES AT SOMERSET HOUSE

Somerset House, one of the finest eighteenth-century buildings in England, was the first government office building in London to be conceived and executed on a monumental scale. Begun in 1776 to the designs of Sir William Chambers, its construction owed much to George III's wish to provide a suitable home for the newly-founded Royal Academy and for the learned societies which enjoyed royal support. But the main impetus came from the growing realisation that efficiency was promoted by the concentration of public offices in a single building. This was why advocates of 'economical reform' like Edmund Burke backed the project.

The accommodation was arranged around a quadrangle between the Strand and the Thames (Plate 63), with the finest rooms in the north range fronting the Strand. Here Chambers supplied a suite of superbly decorated rooms on the first floor (now occupied by the Courtauld Institute galleries). They were used by the Royal Academy until it moved to Trafalgar Square in 1837. They were then handed over to the government-financed School of Design – the ancestor of the Royal College of Art. Other rooms in the north range were occupied in the 1840s by various government departments and chartered institutions, among them the University of London which in its infant years required only minimal office space. The east wing contained, *inter alia*, the offices of the Audit Department, the Tax Office and the Duchy of Cornwall, while the south and west wings were given over to those Admiralty departments for which there was not adequate space in Thomas Ripley's eighteenth-century building in Whitehall.[34]

The first extension to Chambers's building occurred in 1829, when King's College was built on a site to the east to the designs of Sir Robert Smirke, its river front harmonising with that of the older building. To the west there was only a free-standing row of nine plain brick terraced houses originally intended for Admiralty officials, the backs of which were exposed to the public gaze when the roadway leading north from the new Waterloo Bridge was opened in 1813. In 1823 Smirke designed new offices for the Duchy of Lancaster on the opposite side of the road, but by the end of the 1840s the eastern side was still 'a rude, unsightly surface of brick wall, patched over with windows placed at random'.[35]

The development of this site was not seriously contemplated until the 1840s, when the officials of the newly created Inland Revenue Department began to ask for more space. The department itself was a monument to a series of important changes in the taxation system. The Whigs united the two departments responsible for direct taxation, the Stamp Office and the Tax Commission, into a single Department of Stamps and Taxes in 1834. When the Tories came to power in 1841, Sir

---

34 R. Needham and A. Webster, *Somerset House Past and Present* (1905), pp. 215–35; C. Knight, *London Pictorially Illustrated*, IV (1851), pp. 283–4.

35 *The Westminster Review*, 36 (1841), 411.

Robert Peel inaugurated an ambitious fiscal policy whose intention was to shift the burden from indirect to direct taxes, an object which was achieved by the lifting of a multitude of revenue duties and the revival of the income tax. Finally, in 1849, Russell's government merged the Excise Department with the now much more important Department of Stamps and Taxes to form the new Inland Revenue department, responsible for all revenue except that derived from external customs duties. The Stamp office already occupied a basement at the corner of the south and east wings of Chambers's building, and it was calculated that the cost of a new edifice to house the whole establishment could be defrayed from the sale of the old Excise Office buildings in Broad Street in the City. Administrative efficiency would thus be achieved without any strain on the public finances – a prospect to please any Benthamite.[36]

The offices were to fill the gaping space between the old Admiralty houses – the main structure of which would be preserved – and the road leading north from Waterloo Bridge. Thus one of the main approaches to central London would at last receive the monumental treatment it deserved (Plate 64). Work was delayed by difficulties in arranging accommodation for the various public departments occupying the former Admiralty houses. One of these bodies, the Poor Law Board, moved to the eighteenth-century Gwydir House in Whitehall in 1851, but most of the others had to be moved to the north wing of Somerset House where space was found by the removal of the School of Design to Marlborough House. These arrangements took some time to organise, and it was not until the end of 1850 that the government could begin to acquire the rest of the ground on which the new building was to go. The site was part of the Duchy of Lancaster's Savoy estate, and the Treasury agreed that it should be held by the Inland Revenue Board on a ninety-nine-year building lease, the Board paying the Duchy a lump sum out of the proceeds of the sale of the old Excise premises in the City. Formal approval for the new building was finally granted in April 1851.

The decision to build the new offices occurred in the last years of the combined offices of Woods and Works, when governments were still relatively immune from the virus of architectural competitions. Pennethorne was first asked to prepare a design by Lord Morpeth in 1849 and by August 1851, after much consultation with the Inland Revenue officials, it was said to be 'so far matured as to exhibit the general character and extent of the intended Building'.[37] Work was to start on the south wing, the rest of the building following as the various government departments vacated their old premises. First of all foundations had to be dug fourteen feet below river level and large quantities of concrete brought by barge. Work got under way in the autumn, and in December Pennethorne produced his final design which

36 *Hansard*, 122 (18 Jan. 1852), 936–7; PRO, T 1/5706B/25092; Needham and Webster, *Somerset House*, p. 241.
37 PRO, Work 12/99/6, ff. 1–6.

64. Lancaster Place from Waterloo Bridge. On the left is the Duchy of Lancaster Office (Sir Robert Smirke *c.* 1817–23: since demolished) and in the background the entrance to Wellington Street, which led north to Endell Street and Bloomsbury. The west wing of Somerset House is on the right.

incorporated certain changes suggested by the Chancellor of the Exchequer, Charles Wood, and was approved by the Treasury in January 1852.[38]

The Inland Revenue's requirements were relatively straightforward: ample office space above street level, including a Court of Appeal, and premises for the Stamping Department in the basements. There were not to be any elaborate rooms or grand internal spaces. The new building was created by extending the existing Admiralty houses forwards to the west, preserving their east-facing brick facades and

---

38 *Ibid.,* 1/38, p. 523; Work 12/99/6, ff. 19, 51; *The Builder,* 6 Dec. 1851, 763.

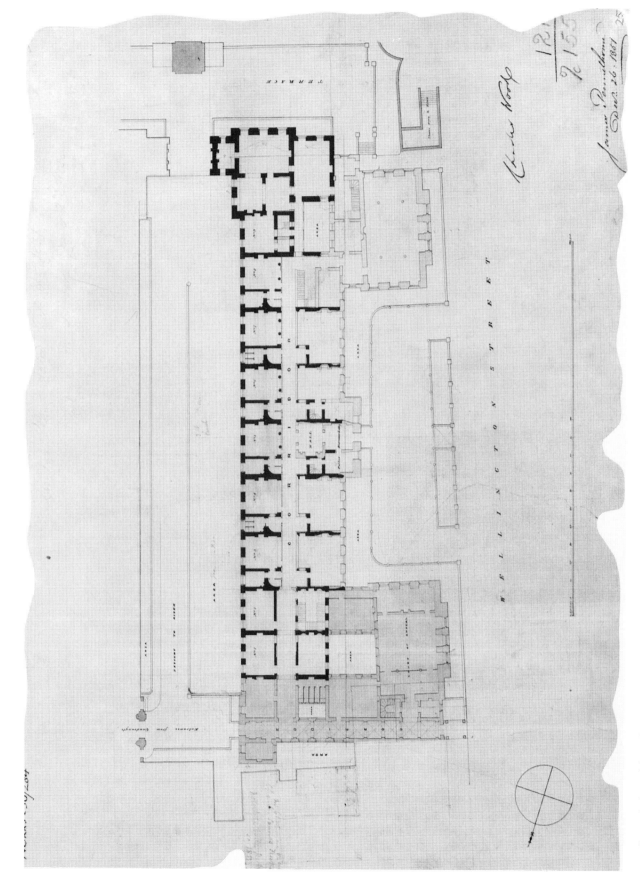

65. Ground plan of the Inland Revenue Offices in the west wing of Somerset House. The darker shading represents the older houses incorporated into the new structure.

front rooms and building an impressive new street frontage in the same style as the Chambers building – a necessity in view of the fact that the two buildings would adjoin each other on the river side. The ground sloped down steeply from the Strand to the river, and an ambitious substructure of vaults and basements had to be constructed in order to create a level forecourt. Construction proceeded by fits and starts over a period of four years. The main reason for the slow progress was the refusal of some of the government departments occupying the old Admiralty houses, notably that of the Registrar General of Births, Deaths and Marriages, to quit their premises until they had been adequately rehoused. As a result the builder, John Kelk, was forced at one point to stop work and remove his materials, and he later claimed a loss of over £4,500.[39]

The building consists of two ranges of rooms separated by a corridor, with projecting wings at each end (Plate 65). The 350 feet (107 metre) long Portland stone facade (Plate 66) was designed as a composition in its own right, with a pedimented central block and two wings which project, not strictly at right angles, from the main facade – a neo-Palladian arrangement which produces a dramatic effect when seen, as it always is, from an oblique angle.[40] Pennethorne followed Chambers by making his building three stories high, with the normal Palladian arrangement of a rusticated ground floor and a *piano nobile* upstairs. But by introducing an attic storey in the centre he improved the relationship between width and height, and there are other subtle differences, such as the introduction of oval medallions over the first floor windows on the street fronts of the wings and the placing of statuary over the projecting central frontispiece and the porch at the north end of the north wing. The composition is now more satisfying than that of the river front, from which Pennethorne took most of the details and the general principles of composition. That facade is now much longer than Chambers ever envisaged, and with the construction of the Victoria Embankment its dramatic power – deriving from the massive rusticated base rising straight from the river to support the palatial superstructure - was irreparably lost. Pennethorne's building, by contrast, has remained much as he left it, dignifying the approach to central London from Waterloo Bridge and paying tribute to the continuing validity of the tradition of monumental classical architecture of which both he and Chambers formed a part.

Sculpture plays an important part in the overall effect. Pennethorne originally wanted to entrust the sculpture to the younger Richard Westmacott who, he believed, would supply 'first rate works of Art like the Sculpture on the other fronts – which were executed by Bacon, Nollekens, and others of the first men of that day'. But the Treasury officials insisted on holding a limited competition, and this

---

39 PRO, Work 12/99/6, ff. 161, 215–24, 323–33.
40 The north wing projects seven feet further from the main block than the south wing.

was won by William Theed, a prolific sculptor who had lived for twenty years in Rome, where he had trained under Gibson and Thorwaldsen, returning in 1848 to build up a successful practice, including a considerable amount of work for the royal family.[41] The subjects are emblematic and patriotic. Britannia sits with her lion on top of the pediment, there are six female figures representing important towns and cities (London, Edinburgh, Dublin, Belfast, Manchester and Sheffield) in front of the attic storey, and two more figures representing History and Fame rest languidly on either side of the clock over the entrance door (Plate 67).

The interior of the building is less palatial than the outside might suggest. The government did not want to spend large sums of money on civil servants' offices, and the need to make as economical a use as possible of the available space meant that Pennethorne had little opportunity for grand effects. The main entrance leads into a vertiginous hall, lit from above by a glass roof. From here a spinal corridor leads to the main staircase in the south wing, from which the most important offices on the *piano nobile* are reached. There are similar corridors on each floor, and another, more impressive, one with a groin vault leads from the former public entrance in the north wing past the Tuscan-columned Court of Appeal – the most impressive room in the building – to the main courtyard. Structurally the main problem was to reconcile the floor levels at the back of the building with those at the front, where the heights of rooms had to conform to the Renaissance standards of proportion adopted by Chambers, and this was so successfully resolved that it is difficult to realise the building embodies work of two different dates. The floors are supported on iron girders, hidden by plaster mouldings, but the basement stories, containing the Stamping Department, were more of a structural *tour de force*, with two floors divided by iron columns, the upper one lit by a skylight in the courtyard in the entrance forecourt.[42]

Pennethorne's extension to Somerset House was one of his most successful designs. His cosmopolitan architectural philosophy was similar to that of Chambers and he found no difficulty in adapting his own style and method of composition to that of the older master. He later disclaimed any great artistic originality: '[My] own share in the work consisted chiefly in endeavouring to follow out as nearly as possible the feeling of the original designer . . . and I was not aware of any particular merit in the second part'.[43] In fact the similarity of style masks great skill in adding a new range to an eighty-year-old building with a very pronounced character of its own. The new building reminds us that there is virtue in 'propriety' – the appropriateness of a building to its purposes and surroundings – as well as in originality or in adherence to a spurious *Zeitgeist*. This is a lesson that is only now being painfully relearnt by today's architects after decades of neglect.

41 PRO, Work 12/99/6, ff. 84, 111–13, 132–42.
42 *BN*, 27 May 1857, 215.   43 *RIBA Trans.* (1864–5), 2.

66. The west wing of Somerset House from Lancaster Place.

THE STATIONERY OFFICE

Like Somerset House, the Stationery Office was a product of the widespread changes in administrative machinery which went by the name of 'Economical Reform'. Until 1785 government papers had been printed by private individuals on a contract basis, but now they were to be printed by the government itself under the strict control of the Treasury. The Office took over premises on Crown property in James Street, Pimlico in 1820,[44] but the rapid growth of government business and Parliamentary enquiries soon made them inadequate, and large sums were incurred in renting extra storage space. The Comptroller of the Office, John Ramsay McCulloch, a well-known writer on statistics and questions of political economy, told the Office of Works that the accommodation in the buildings was 'defective in various particulars, and more especially in the want of proper accommodation for Packing, and for the loading and unloading of Waggons'.[45] Demands therefore grew for a new building in which the various functions of the Office could be 'concentrated'.

The building in James Street was finally vacated in 1851 because of the growth of the adjacent Ordnance Barracks (now the Wellington Barracks). The new home was in an existing building, the Parliamentary Mews in Princes Street (now Storeys Gate), close to Westminster Abbey and next to Westminster Hospital, for which Pennethorne had competed unsuccessfully in 1831. The Mews were built on Crown property in 1825 to the designs of Decimus Burton, and provided stabling for MPs' horses arranged around a quadrangle. The building presented an impressive Greek Doric facade to the street, but it was not a financial success, and by 1851 it had become something of a white elephant, with much of the stabling empty and part of the rest in use as a police barracks.[46] Burton was still alive, but it was Pennethorne who was asked first to estimate the building's capacity, and then to send in a scheme for converting it into a Stationery Office at a cost of £20,000.

It took over three years to carry out the work. The Treasury approved Pennethorne's scheme in March 1852, but with Parliamentary 'blue books' being turned out at an ever-increasing rate McCulloch now had second thoughts and told Pennethorne to raise the floors of Burton's building, while transferring the proposed warehouse in the central courtyard to the east range. These changes made it necessary to rebuild the facades and to insert cast-iron columns to support the new floors and concrete foundations to bear the extra weight. The estimated cost now rose by £8,000, provoking an angry riposte from the Treasury officials who blamed Pennethorne for the extra expense. Pennethorne insisted that his estimates had 'scarcely ever been exceeded' and that the proposed alterations had been sanctioned by McCulloch. A compromise was finally reached under which he agreed to simplify the new facade to Princes Street, which was now to be 'of brick and of the plainest character'.[47] He sent in his working drawings in

---

44 P. Cunningham, *Handbook to London* (1850), p. 470.
45 PRO, Work 12/102/1, ff. 15–16.
46 J. M. Crook and M. H. Port, *The History of the King's Works*, VI (1973), pp. 536–7; W. Thornbury and E. Walford, *Old and New London*, 6 vols. (1873), IV, p. 34.
47 PRO, T 26/1, pp. 24, 73–5; Work 12/102/1, ff. 72–104.

67. The main entrance to the west wing of Somerset house. The figures on either side of the clock were carved by William Theed and represent History and Fame.

68. The Stationery Office shortly before demolition.

June 1853, and work got under way in the autumn. The building was finished by March 1855.[48]

Like the Public Record Office, the new Stationery Office was conceived as a utilitarian building, part factory, part warehouse. Decorative flourishes were kept to a minimum. There was no need for the building to 'tell a story', and Pennethorne was allowed to employ the restrained classical manner in which he was most at home. Burton's monumental Grecian facade was replaced by an understated but

---

48 *Ibid.*, Work 12/102/1, ff. 107, 157, 166–8, 186.

well-proportioned brick frontage of fifteen bays with conventional Italianate detailing (Plate 68), and the rest of the building was plain in the extreme. The inexorable growth of government ensured that its capacity was eventually outstripped, like that of its predecessor, and it was demolished in 1952. The site, having served for a long time as a car park, is now occupied by the Queen Elizabeth II Conference Centre.

6

MUSEUMS

STATE PATRONAGE of the arts and sciences has a long pedigree in England. But for a long time that patronage was exercised by, and on behalf of, the monarch. It was only with the foundation of the British Museum in 1753 that Parliament and government began to sponsor cultural activities independently of the king. And with the building of the north range of Somerset House the government provided the first purpose-built accommodation for cultural bodies under state patronage: the Royal Academy, the Royal Society and the Society of Antiquaries.

These institutions could justifiably claim to exist for the benefit of the public, but in practice only a tiny fraction of the population ever came into contact with them. In the nineteenth century there was a noticeable change of mood and scale. The state's collections of antiquities, books and works of art grew much larger, especially after the Napoleonic Wars. For those of an improving frame of mind it began to be seen as essential to transmit the cultural legacy of the past to the enquiring middle classes and to spread 'useful knowledge' to the as yet unregenerate masses. Hence the construction of the first purpose-built public museums in London: Sir John Soane's art gallery at Dulwich (1811–14), Sir Robert Smirke's new British Museum in Bloomsbury, begun in 1823 but not completed until the mid 1840s, and William Wilkins's National Gallery in Trafalgar Square (1834–8). The first of these galleries was paid for by a charitable foundation, but the British Museum and the National Gallery were funded by central government. Like the near-contemporary museums in Edinburgh and Manchester, and those in Berlin and Dresden in Germany, these solemn neo-classical buildings proclaimed a growing diffusion of interest in the arts. But by the 1840s governments were coming under pressure to provide even more space, not only for the display of antiquities and works of art but also for objects of scientific interest. Pennethorne could hardly avoid being drawn into the question of museum accommodation, and the solutions he and his contemporaries achieved helped shape the cultural map of London down to the present day.

1. James Pennethorne's final design for the restoration of the Roman Forum. It was this which gained him membership of the Accademia di San Luca in 1826.

II. The Round Room of the Public Record office.

III. Design by Alfred Stevens for decorating the main staircase of the Museum of Practical Geology, Jermyn Street, watercolour c. 1846. The scheme was never carried out.

IV. The Ballroom of Buckingham Palace soon after completion in 1856, watercolour by Louis Haghe. The painted decorations were all swept away in 1902, but the throne canopy designed by Pennethorne still survives.

v. James Pennethorne's final, unexecuted scheme for the government offices in Whitehall as seen from St James's Park, August–September 1855. The lower, colonnaded building stands on the site of 10–12 Downing Street, with William Kent's Treasury building to its left. To the right, on the site of the old Foreign Office, is the tower of a taller block which was intended to stretch south to Parliament Square.

vi. Design for the Piccadilly frontage to Burlington House 1862 (unexecuted). The building occupies the site of the present entrance block by Banks and Barry, and carries the names of famous British artists on panels on either side of the archway. To the left is the Burlington Arcade in its original form.

THE MUSEUM OF PRACTICAL GEOLOGY

The science of geology played a large part in shaping man's view of himself in the nineteenth century. By demonstrating the great antiquity of the rocks which made up the earth's surface, the geologists helped create a new view of the origins of the planet which threw into question earlier religious and mythic explanations. The new discoveries expounded in books like Lyell's *Principles of Geology* (1830) aroused great public interest. The growth of manufacturing industry led meanwhile to a more systematic exploration of the earth's resources, and the geologist's skills came to have a very immediate practical relevance. It was this realisation of the economic value of geological research which lay behind the building of London's first public scientific museum.

The museum was an offspring of the Geological Survey, set up by the Government in 1837 under the overall aegis of the Board of Ordnance. The Survey's function was to produce a series of accurate geological maps of Great Britain, but with the encouragement of its energetic director and founder Sir Henry de la Beche it soon began to accumulate a substantial collection of rocks to illustrate the application of geology to industry. These collections were substantially enlarged by the inclusion of stones acquired by the Royal Commission set up in 1839 to recommend suitable building materials for the new Palace of Westminster. A further extension of de la Beche's empire came from the setting up of a Mining Records office, where models of coalfields and pit machinery were kept and displayed.[1]

The Survey's first premises were in a house on the Crown estate, 5 Craig's Court, at the northern end of Whitehall. With the establishment of the Museum of Economic Geology, as it was known from 1836 to 1848, the Survey expanded into the adjoining house, but by 1844 de la Beche was complaining that 'we are becoming in a sad state now for want of the necessary space'. His plea for new premises was supported by the Prime Minister, Sir Robert Peel, who recognised the connection with the economic growth which his government was trying to promote. The site chosen for the new building in August 1844 was Darby's Court, a long and narrow plot of Crown land sloping down from Piccadilly to Jermyn Street, with the usual mixture of poor housing and noxious trades – in this case a distillery. The removal of this blot on the landscape would enhance the value of the Crown property, which would be further increased if the ground floor of the new building were let for shops.[2] The building was to house not only the museum but also the offices of the Geological Survey, the Mining Record Office, some laboratories and a lecture room for the School of Mines – one of the constituent parts

---

1 J. S. Flett, *The First Hundred Years of the Geological Survey* (1937), pp. 33–6
2 PRO, Work 17/7/1, ff. 6–7, 11; J. M. Crook and M. H. Port, *The History of the Kings Works*, VI (1973), p. 460.

of what later became Imperial College.[3] This combination of a government-funded educational and research establishment and a museum open to the public was an unprecedented one, and called for considerable ingenuity on the part of the architect.

The selection of Pennethorne came about in a casual way which recalls the easy-going methods of the eighteenth century. He was never given a written order to design the building, and later admitted: 'I was employed because I was there'.[4] His preliminary designs were enthusiastically received by de la Beche in September 1844: 'I like them much . . . Those great rooms with their galleries would hold great stores of things . . . Give us but the kind of place we have here sketched out, and I believe we should even surprise ourselves, and that is saying something.'[5] The arrangement of the rooms was to a large degree determined by the shape of the confined site. The shops were to be placed on the Piccadilly front, with the museum collections in a top-lit 'great room' behind them and the main entrance on the Jermyn Street side. The rest of the accommodation would have to go on the upper floors of the Piccadilly and Jermyn Street ranges.

Pennethorne was formally told to examine the site and prepare plans in October 1844, and a month later he estimated the cost of the building at £28,860 – a sum to be supplied out of the revenues of the Crown estate.[6] Detailed plans and elevations followed in 1845, but progress was delayed against a background of growing political crisis and 'haggling between different public offices' – a reference to Treasury obstruction. The autumn of 1845 saw the first catastrophic effects of the Irish potato blight and in January 1846 Peel declared his intention to move for a repeal of the Corn Laws. Peel's government fell in 1846, and not long afterwards de la Beche managed to persuade the new First Commissioner, Lord Morpeth, to provide more space by omitting the shops from the Piccadilly front. Pennethorne now sent in another set of elevations[7] showing the two facades treated in the style of the Renaissance *palazzi* which he had so admired when he was in Italy twenty years before. This style had become normal in the Pall Mall clubs, but was still a novelty in the architecture of museums. Pennethorne's drawings (Plate 69) show his ability to reinterpret the architectural language of the Italian quattrocento and cinquecento in a powerful and original way. Because of the sloping site the Piccadilly facade had to be lower than that to Jermyn Street, and because it fronted one of London's most important streets Pennethorne wanted it to be the more highly ornamented of the two, with an arcaded ground floor and elaborate moulded panels in the spandrels which were originally to contain specimens of English and

---

3 PRO, Work 3/6, p. 6; Geological Survey Library, GSM 1/13.
4 PRO, T 1/6693A/3774.
5 Geological Survey Library, GSM 1/13; PRO, Work 17/7/1, ff. 8–14.
6 PRO, Work 17/7/1, ff. 14–18, 26, 72–3.
7 *Ibid.*, Work 3/6, pp. 249–53; Work 17/7/1, ff. 76–80; PRO 8/5, p. 6.

69. The Museum of Practical Geology, facade to Piccadilly as proposed in 1846.

Irish stone[8] – an anticipation of the interior of the University Museum at Oxford, built less than ten years later. Two alternative treatments were suggested for the plainer Jermyn Street facade, one faced in stone with a massively rusticated ground floor, and the other, much plainer and £750 cheaper, of brick.

Work started in October 1846, and the basement was ready three months later. Lord Morpeth now called on Lord de Grey, first president of the Royal Institute of British Architects and an amateur architect of some distinction, to comment on Pennethorne's designs for the two facades, and they were also, according to one account, 'improved' by Charles Barry.[9] As a result of these interventions Pennethorne was told to hide the pitched roofs behind parapets and to simplify the elevations.[10] The five proposed openings on the Piccadilly front were increased to an un-classical six – a strange decision for which Pennethorne should probably not be held responsible – and the aedicules around the upper-floor windows on both facades were replaced by simple surrounds. The more elaborate Piccadilly front was faced with Anston stone chosen by de la Beche but, as an economy measure, stone was omitted from the entrance front to Jermyn Street in favour of pale gauged brick from Colchester, with Anston dressings. Work restarted in July 1847.

In their final form the elevations presented sophisticated but contrasted treatments of the Italianate idiom. The most striking feature of the Piccadilly front (Plate 70) was the ground-floor arcade – a reminder of the original intention to devote the ground floor to shops – with its deeply undercut piers and spandrels and curious roundels imparting a note of almost Mannerist complexity. The south-facing Jermyn Street facade (Plate 71) was an object lesson in astylar restraint, with its heavy cornice, pronounced quoins and strongly emphasised architraves around the windows and doorway, which cast deep shadows on the otherwise plain brick exterior. A writer in the *Civil Engineer and Architects' Journal* was especially impressed by the doorway, describing it as 'noble and even imposing for its amplitude, and though simple in its general composition, singularly rich in design . . . [We] would readily give half-a-dozen of our usual Doric or Ionic porticos for one such portal as that we are noticing'.[11]

If Pennethorne's original intentions had been carried out the entrance doors would have been adorned by the first major work of Alfred Stevens, one of the few nineteenth-century English sculptors who can bear comparison with the masters of the Renaissance. Stevens was assistant master at the government's School of Design and was appointed in 1846, apparently at the suggestion of Pennethorne and

---

8 *The Builder*, 27 March 1847, 141.

9 PRO, T 1/5556A/8614; information supplied by Dr David Blissett.

10 A note on the original design for the Jermyn Street facade, in a different hand from Pennethorne's, says that '[the] construction will be greatly improved and the cost lessened by a Parapet as shewn in blue': Geological Survey Library, MS GSI/210.

11 *Civil Engineer and Architects' Journal*, 10 (1847), 337.

70. Geological Museum, Piccadilly facade as built. The number of bays has been increased to six, the doorway proposed in 1846 left out and the architraves of the first-floor windows simplified. The building originally stood higher than its late-Georgian neighbours, but they had been replaced with taller buildings by the time this photograph was taken.

71. The Jermyn Street front of the Geological Museum.

Cockerell, to supply a design with bronze panels containing figures symbolising the museum's aims. He started working on the design by October of that year, and there was a model of the 'Coal Getter' in his studio in 1850.[12] An early photograph (Plate 72) indicates a composition of great nobility with powerful figurative groups in the eight main compartments.[13] But the commission was never completed owing to

12 K. R. Towndrow, *Alfred Stevens* (1930), pp. 78–9.
13 See also Victoria and Albert Museum, E. 2600–1911; E. 2727–1911.

72. The entrance doorway of the Geological Museum, showing proposed panels by Alfred Stevens. The panels, representing aspects of the science of geology, were never executed. The architectural frame is by Pennethorne.

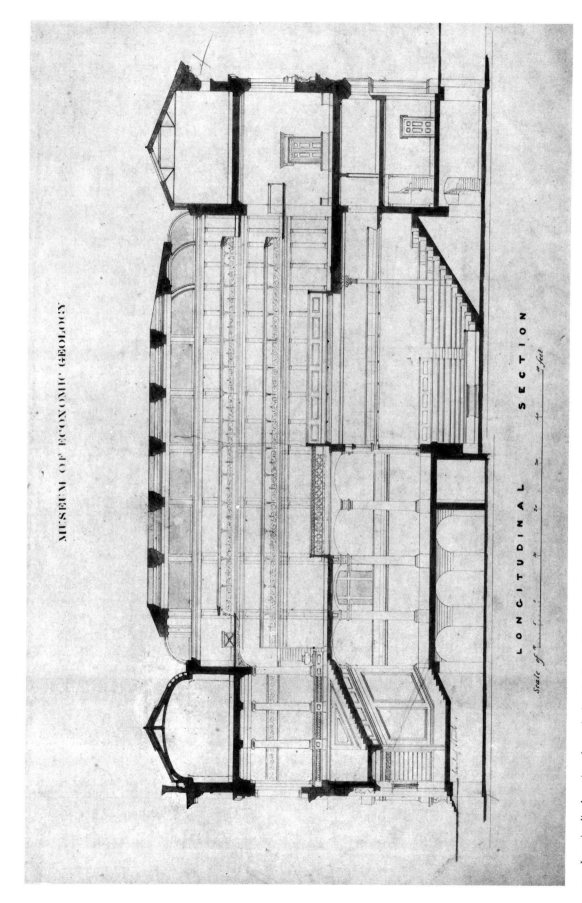

MUSEUM OF ECONOMIC GEOLOGY

LONGITUDINAL SECTION

Scale of

73. Longitudinal section through the Geological Museum. The main entrance, from Jermyn Street, is on the left, leading into the entrance hall and main staircase. The iron-and-glass-roofed main gallery is in the centre over the lecture room, and the offices are on the Piccadilly front to the right.

what one of his biographers has called Stevens's 'procrastinating love of perfection'.[14]

Stevens also prepared a scheme for the decoration of the entrance hall and staircase (Colour Plate III).[15] De la Beche wanted marble decoration to be introduced inside the building for didactic purposes, and Stevens's drawings show how painted decoration might have been used in conjunction with the marble to create an effect of great splendour, with arabesques and Michelangelesque figures against backgrounds of deep red and blue. But official economies combined with the difficulties of Stevens's temperament to ensure that the design was never carried out. Marble and mosaics for the entrance hall were being supplied in 1851, and the decoration was eventually entrusted to one of Pennethorne's former assistants, Charles Frederick Reeks.[16] It took some time to install the costly fittings, and the museum was not finally opened to the public until May 1851. The final cost exceeded the estimate by £4,406, but in a note to the Treasury, Morpeth exonerated Pennethorne from blame and called the building 'one of the most successful of our recent additions to the Public Buildings of the Metropolis'.[17]

The museum was the first building to demonstrate what Goodhart-Rendel called Pennethorne's 'peculiar powers of organised design' (Plates 73–4).[18] It was entered from Jermyn Street through a hall, divided by Tuscan columns supporting iron girders. The hall extended into the depths of the building and was 'devoted to the exhibition of all the building and ornamental stones of these islands', some of which – Derbyshire alabaster, Scottish granite and Irish serpentine, were used on the walls.[19] Two flights of stairs led upwards to a landing which gave access to the glass-roofed 'great room' or main gallery (Plate 75). Here the exhibits – fossils, minerals and specimens of glass and pottery – were arranged in three tiers of cases around the walls, with the uppermost tiers reached by cantilevered galleries, an idea which Pennethorne took from the Hunterian Museum of surgical specimens added by Charles Barry to the Royal College of Surgeons in Lincolns Inn Fields in 1835–7 (since demolished). The cramped nature of the site made it essential for Pennethorne to admit as much natural light as possible, and recent advances in iron construction enabled him to construct a glazed roof without encumbering the floor with troublesome supports. It was held up on a series of huge cast-iron hoops with a span of fifty-five feet (seventeen metres), their cross-section not unlike that of the four-centred late-mediaeval stone arch found in buildings like Oxford University's Divinity School. The uprights were placed six feet (two metres) away from the

14 W. Armstrong, *Alfred Stevens* (1881), p. 9.
15 There are two slightly different alternative designs: Geological Survey Library, MS IGS 1/684.
16 PRO, PRO 8/5, p. 21; Geological Survey Library, GSM 1/210.
17 PRO, PRO 8/5, pp. 7–23; T 1/5556A/8614.
18 H. S. Goodhart-Rendel, *English Architecture since the Regency* (1953), p. 118.
19 J. Weale, *London Exhibited in 1851*, p. 576.

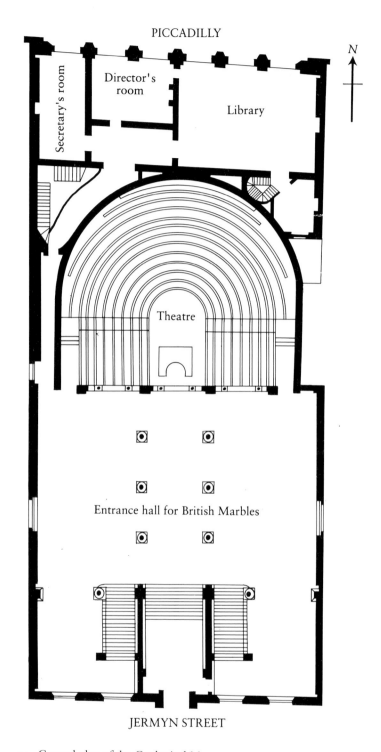

74. Ground plan of the Geological Museum.

75. The main gallery of the Geological Museum, looking south to the main staircase landing. Light enters through the glazed roof and penetrates down through the central light well to the ground floor. The galleries give access to display cases around the walls.

outer wall, allowing for the introduction of recesses to contain the display cases. So at a stroke Pennethorne managed to solve the crucial problems of lighting, access and display without which no museum can be counted successful.

At the centre of the 'great room' was an open well surrounded by a balustrade, through which some natural light penetrated into the tenebrous lecture room below. Offices, library and laboratories occupied the block facing Piccadilly, and there was a fire-proof assay furnace in the basement, together with furnaces for a sophisticated heating and ventilation system.[20] So, for all its Renaissance exteriors, the building was an up-to-date elaborately serviced structure making use of the best technology the nineteenth century could provide – a successful union of the old with the new.

The Museum of Practical Geology soon became an important centre for scientific education, as its founders had intended. Lectures were held there regularly, some of them attended by Prince Albert, and at one of the lectures, given in 1851 by Sir Lyon Playfair, Professor at the School of Mines, a reporter from *The Illustrated London News* noted approvingly that '[the] theatre was crowded by a most attentive audience; and we were much gratified to observe that many of the working men had brought with them pencils and paper, and were busy taking notes throughout the lecture'.[21] But there was no room for expanding the collections and the museum's educational activities, and in 1898 a Commons Select Committee recommended removal to South Kensington. Bomb damage to nearby buildings during the First World War weakened the iron roof structure, and in 1933–5 the present Geological Museum was built in Exhibition Road to the designs of the Office of Works architects Sir Richard Allison and J. H. Markham, who had already built the neighbouring Science Museum.[22] Their galleried interior bears some resemblance to that of Pennethorne's building, but the ponderously classical exterior is far less subtle in its effect. The old building in Piccadilly was demolished and replaced by Simpson's outfitters, as much a monument to the advanced taste of the 1930s as Pennethorne's building was to that of the 1840s.

With the demolition of the Geological Museum, London lost one of its most impressive early Victorian buildings. Pennethorne's choice of the Italian Renaissance style, coinciding with the completion of the British Museum, marked the end of the reign of the Greek Revival in London's museum architecture. The museum was also one of the first English public buildings to make an open use of the new glass and iron techniques. John Nash had used cast iron in the glazed roof of the picture gallery at Attingham Park (Shropshire) in 1805–7, but it was mainly in more utilitarian structures like market halls, shopping arcades and railway stations that a new architectural language of iron and glass was first developed.

20 *The Builder*, 25 Oct. 1848, 522. The heating and ventilation system was designed by a Mr Sylvester.
21 *ILN*, 21 Feb. 1852, 161.
22 PRO, Work 17/252–3.

Pennethorne's building vied with Labrouste's slightly earlier Bibliothèque Ste Geneviève (1843-50) in Paris in applying the new techniques to a major public building. There is no indication that he knew Labrouste or his buildings. But he shared the same cast of mind and, in the Geological Museum, he succeeded in showing that new technology could be combined with classically-derived elevations to produce an architecture that was geared to immediate needs, yet also timeless in its appeal both to the eye and to the mind.

THE NATIONAL GALLERY

The national collection of pictures grew out of a bequest of thirty-eight pictures by the merchant John Julius Angerstein in 1824. The pictures were shown at first in Angerstein's house in Pall Mall, but in 1832 the Whig government decided to build a new gallery on the site of the Royal Mews on the north side of the newly created Trafalgar Square – 'the finest site in Europe' in the words of Sir Robert Peel. Three architects, including John Nash, were asked to provide designs, but it was William Wilkins who gained the commission. He was a scholarly classicist whose works included Downing College, Cambridge and the new University College in Gower Street, Bloomsbury. He was also treasurer of the Royal Academy, which was to share the new building, and this, as well as the supposedly low cost, may have swayed the committee selected by the Prime Minister to choose a design.

The new building (Plate 76) began to be criticised before the first stone was even laid, and in one of his last recorded utterances William IV is supposed to have called it 'a nasty little pokey hole'. No sooner had it opened in 1838 than complaints began to be voiced about the excessive heat, the foul air, the lack of space, and the loose composition of the facade.[23] There is certainly a smallness of scale and lack of robustness in the design, especially in its absurd pimple of a dome and the notorious 'pepper pots' at the corners. But Wilkins had to work under severe constraints imposed both by the site and by the availability of funds. Stringent financial restrictions were imposed by a government eager for retrenchment and anxious to placate public opinion. The building had to be strung out along an unusually long and narrow strip of land, with a barracks and the parochial work-house of St Martin-in-the-Fields hemming it in at the back (Plate 77). Public passageways to these institutions had to be supplied, ensuring that the ground floor of the new building would be virtually useless for showing works of art. Wilkins also had to realign the facade so as to preserve the vista from Pall Mall to the portico of St Martin-in-the-Fields – itself not a bad idea, but fatal to any attempt to make the

---

23 S. C. Hutchison, *History of the Royal Academy 1768–1968* (1968), p. 103; C. Holmes and C. H. Baker, *The Making of the National Gallery* (1924), pp. 52–4.

76. The National Gallery from Trafalgar Square. Until the building of the Sainsbury Wing (opened in 1991), the expansion of the building has taken place behind William Wilkins's facade.

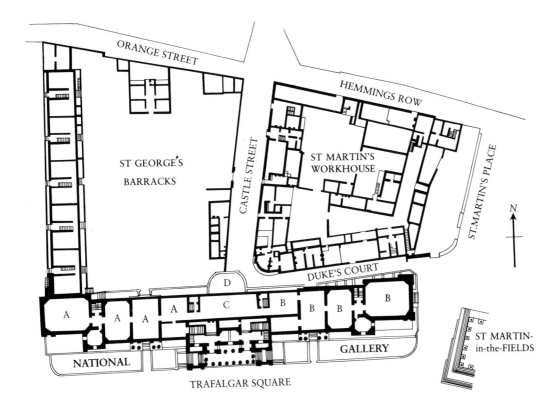

A Original galleries for National Gallery
B Original galleries for Royal Academy
C Gallery built by James Pennethorne
D Royal Academy Sculpture Room

77. Ground plan of the National Gallery, showing the layout of the building after the construction of Pennethorne's new gallery in 1860–1 and the removal of the Royal Academy to Burlington House. The workhouse of St Martin-in-the-Fields stands on the site of the present eastern galleries, and St George's Barracks on that of the western galleries, which were not built until the twentieth century.

new building dominate Trafalgar Square. Most irksome of all, the National Gallery had to share the premises with the Royal Academy, ejected from its original home in Somerset House to make way for the newly founded School of Design. Inside, there was only one room of real visual distinction, a two-storied Staircase Hall in the centre, from which staircases led up to the National Gallery's five picture galleries in the western part of the building and the Royal Academy's to the east. A one-storied apsidal projection behind the Hall housed the Royal Academy's sculpture collection, and the poorly lit space at ground level was used for storage, offices, and the display of casts.[24]

24 Crook and Port, *King's Works*, VI (1973), pp. 462–3; R. W. Liscombe, *William Wilkins* (1980), pp. 180–4; Rep. Sel. Cttee. on Arts and Manufactures, *PP* (1836), 9 [568], plan facing p. 98.

The mortar was scarcely dry before assorted architects and meddlers began preparing schemes for altering or extending the building. The most distinguished of these proposals came from Charles Barry, the architect responsible for the layout of Trafalgar Square in 1842–5.[25] He wanted to rebuild the facade in a richly detailed Renaissance manner, but nothing came of his plans and the first practical efforts to alter the building were much more modest in their intention. The initiative stemmed from the Prime Minister, Sir Robert Peel, an active trustee of the gallery and a major art collector in his own right. He became worried about the poor lighting in the picture galleries and the Royal Academy's sculpture gallery and, with Wilkins dead and Barry deeply involved in the new Houses of Parliament, Pennethorne was approached for architectural advice. He prepared designs for a new sculpture room and a 120-foot (37 metre) long picture gallery early in 1845,[26] but no sooner were they produced than Peel began exploring the possibility of moving the collection out of Trafalgar Square altogether. This followed the publication in May 1845 of an open letter from the Keeper of the National Gallery's pictures, Charles Eastlake, one of the most powerful figures in the Victorian art world. He pointed out that the pictures in the upstairs gallery were placed too close together and recommended the building of a completely new gallery like Klenze's Alte Pinakothek in Munich, arguing that '[if] you provide for really valuable pictures ample and suitable means of exhibiting them, the expense of constructing a magnificent gallery will at no distant period be repaid by presents and bequests'.[27] He suggested the centre of Hyde Park as a possible site, but Peel preferred building on the site of St James's Palace, which he thought was 'a great blemish on the best part of London', and Pennethorne prepared block plans to show how this could be done.[28] But the idea never got off the ground and Peel fell from power in 1846.

The shortage of space at Trafalgar Square was highlighted when Robert Vernon, a discriminating collector who had made his fortune as a contractor of horses to the government during the Napoleonic Wars, offered his collection of 157 paintings by recent British artists to the nation in 1847. Since the only space currently available was in the Staircase Hall and the Board Room, Pennethorne was asked to prepare plans for a new picture gallery built within the walls of the Hall at first-floor level. Together with a new sculpture gallery for the Royal Academy, this would cost a mere £8,000.[29] The proposal was held up by the politicians, and in 1850 the Vernon pictures were put on display at Marlborough House in Pall Mall, recently

25 A. Barry, *Life and Works of Sir Charles Barry* (1867), pp. 274–5; G. Martin, 'Wilkins and the National Gallery', *Burlington Magazine*, 113 (1971), 321; *The Builder*, 30 June 1860, 417.

26 PRO, Work 17/13/7, f. 2; Rep. Sel. Cttee. on National Gallery, *PP* (1850), 15 [612], p. 76.

27 C. S. Parker, *Sir Robert Peel*, III (1899), pp. 181–2; C. Eastlake, *The National Gallery: Observations on the unfitness of the present building for its purpose* (1845); Hansard, 81 (27 June 1845), 1338.

28 PRO, Work 34/888.

29 Minutes of National Gallery Trustees, i, pp. 352–3; PRO, Work 17/13/7, ff. 3–7; Rep. Sel. Cttee. on National Gallery (1850), pp. 76–7.

vacated by the death of Queen Adelaide. Here they remained until 1859, when they were taken to the South Kensington Museum – the forerunner of the Victoria and Albert Museum – where they can be seen today.[30]

The government meanwhile decided to refer the long-term question of housing the National Gallery's pictures to a Commons Select Committee, which met in 1848 and recommended that Pennethorne's designs should be shelved, the Royal Academy turned out, and the gallery rebuilt on the Trafalgar Square site, taking advantage of the possibility of expansion at the back of the building. In this way Eastlake could realise 'the great purpose for which the National Gallery is supposed to be established; that of forming a complete collection relating to the history of the art, and to exhibit the pictures that are collected so as to benefit those who are to study them'. This didactic aim involved arranging the pictures into schools – something taken for granted today, but then still a novel idea – and incorporating the British Museum's sculptures into the collection – a proposal also supported by James Fergusson in a pamphlet produced in 1849.[31] In March 1850 Lord John Russell announced that he would ask Parliament for money to enable the Royal Academy to find new accommodation at the earliest possible moment', and in the same month Pennethorne produced a new and more ambitious set of designs (Plate 78) for extending the Trafalgar Square building at a cost of £80,000.[32] Wilkins's frontage would remain intact and new galleries be built in a T-shaped block at right angles to the existing rooms, with the British Museum sculptures in side-lit galleries downstairs and the paintings, including the Mantegna Cartoons from the Royal Collection, in the rooms above. A new staircase would lead to a central gallery, fifty feet (fifteen metres) wide and fifty feet high, like that of Leo von Klenze's Alte Pinakothek in Munich – Pennethorne's 'ideal of a good National Gallery' – and there would be smaller galleries on either side. There would also be a library 'for books on art . . . which are usually most necessary for study and the reference of artists, but far too expensive for students, or even professors, to possess'.[33] Pennethorne believed that picture galleries should be high and lit from above through thick glass, making them 'a mass of light, and not lighted by only rays of light'.[34] He therefore proposed roofing the new galleries with glass pedentive domes – a Soaneian effect. But the opulent internal decoration would have been more reminiscent of the recently-completed staircase of the Fitzwilliam Museum at Cambridge than of anything by Soane or Wilkins, and anticipates the decorative character of the present central and eastern galleries.

---

30 PRO, T 1/5282/19832; Holmes and Baker, *Making of the National Gallery*, p. 55.

31 Rep. Sel. Cttee. on National Gallery (1850), pp. iii, 77–87; J. Fergusson, *Observations on the British Museum and National Record Office, with Suggestions for their Improvements* (1849). Fergusson proposed that the British Museum building should be turned into a national library and record office.

32 *Hansard*, 109 (25 March 1850), 1368–9.   33 RIBA Library, MS Pe J1/1.

34 Rep. Sel. Cttee. on National Gallery (1850), p. 3.

Had it been carried out, Pennethorne's scheme would have solved the National Gallery's overcrowding at a stroke and given the building an architectural coherence which it has never achieved. But Russell's government, always short of cash, does not seem to have ever seriously contemplated carrying it out. A major stumbling block was the Royal Academy's extreme reluctance to leave its central site. It had been clearly stated in 1838 that it would only be allowed to remain in Trafalgar Square for as long as the National Gallery did not need the rooms, but it did not have the funds to move out of its rent-free accommodation, and unless the government could supply it with equally convenient premises it had every incentive to stay where it was.[35] The removal of the Vernon pictures to Marlborough House in 1850 took away the immediate pressure on the Trafalgar Square building, and the government decided to refer its ultimate fate to another Select Committee.

By now a new anxiety had surfaced: air pollution. A waterworks and public baths had been built behind the Gallery in Orange Street, and smoke belched out from the steam engines powering the fountains in Trafalgar Square, only 300 feet (90 metres) away to the north. To make matters worse, the trustees now believed that the 'dust and impure vapours' exuded by the three thousand people who used the building each day were causing a film of dirt to be deposited on the pictures. The Gallery was, according to one MP, 'frequently crowded by idle persons, who brought children there with them, cracked nuts, and wore jackets which smelt of smoke and dirt. These persons stretched themselves luxuriously on the benches and seemed to have gone in there merely for the purpose of sheltering from the excessive heat of the sun'.[36] With evidence of this sort in mind – not to mention the cost of purchasing the barrack and workhouse sites, later estimated at £160,000 – the Select Committee dealt the final blow to Pennethorne's scheme by refusing to recommend any new buildings on the site.[37]

Both Russell and Eastlake were now in favour of moving the collection out of central London altogether. A Royal Commission appointed in 1851 recommended two sites in Kensington Gardens, one to the north of Kensington Palace, and the other adjoining Bayswater Road, slightly to the west of the Serpentine.[38] A few months later, in July 1852, Benjamin Disraeli announced in Parliament that the National Gallery question had 'engaged the attention of that illustrious Prince who had done so much towards elevating public taste in this country'. Prince Albert was one of the guiding spirits behind the hugely successful Great Exhibition of 1851, and he now gave his influential backing to a proposal to move the Gallery to the South Kensington estate which was in the process of being acquired by Commissioners out

---

35 W. Sandby, *History of the Royal Academy of Arts*, II (1862), pp. 125–7.
36 *Hansard*, 112 (1 July 1850), 814.
37 Rep. Sel. Cttee. on National Gallery (1850), p. iv.
38 Rep. Commrs. for Considering Site for new National Gallery, *PP* 1851, 22 [642], p. 1.

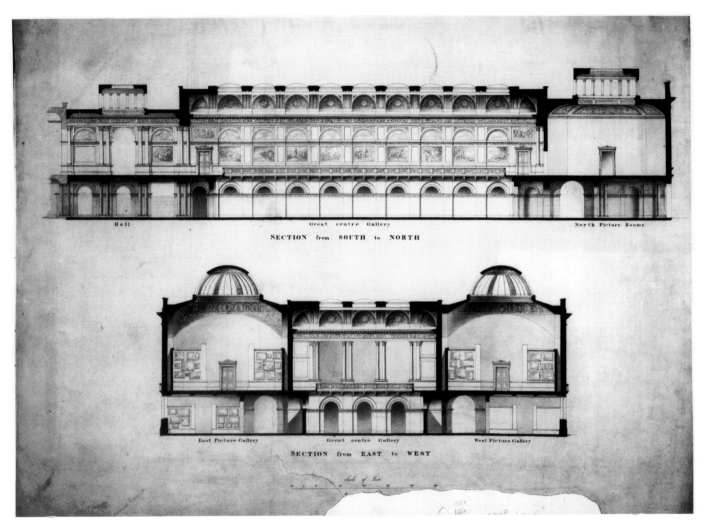

Hall   Great centre Gallery   North Picture Rooms

SECTION from SOUTH to NORTH

East Picture Gallery   Great centre Gallery   West Picture Gallery

SECTION from EAST to WEST

78. Design for an extension to the National Gallery, longitudinal section and cross-section 1850. The galleries would have stretched north from the centre of the existing building, with the central gallery flanked on either side by smaller top-lit galleries and another range on the Orange Street side.

of the profits.[39] A new Select Committee was appointed in 1853 to enquire into all aspects of the Gallery's management, including the currently contentious policy of cleaning the pictures. Having heard evidence from the leading members of the Victorian art establishment and from several architects including Klenze, who favoured a building in the 'Picturesque' style, it concluded that the Trafalgar Square building was inadequate and that expansion would be 'attended with unusual difficulty and expense'. In his evidence Pennethorne suggested two more possible

---

39 *Hansard*, 122 (4 June 1852), 10; H. Hobhouse, *Prince Albert: His Life and Works* (1983), p. 76.

sites for the gallery: one at Kensington Gore (where the Albert Memorial now stands) and the other on a raised site to the south of the Round Pond in Kensington Gardens. His proposal for the second site involved the construction of a 625-foot (191 metre)-long building with apsidal ends echoing the treatment of the east end of Elmes's recently completed St George's Hall, Liverpool, which would form 'an architectural feature with reference to the garden and palace, if at any time the latter should be enlarged and treated architecturally'. But this adventurous plan, like the more conventional scheme for the Albert Memorial site, was rejected because it would involve encroaching on public open space. The same objection applied to all the proposed sites in Hyde Park and Kensington Gardens, and, with a majority of just one vote, the Select Committee finally recommended the appointment of another Royal Commission to discuss the building of a new gallery on the South Kensington estate for which Pennethorne made yet more plans (Plate 83).[40]

The start of the Crimean War in 1854 put a temporary stop to discussion of the plans for South Kensington, and the government did not finally introduce a Bill to mark out a site for the new gallery there until June 1856. The announcement caused an outcry. The critics, backed by *The Times*, condemned the site for being too remote from central London.[41] Many people disliked the idea of creating a cultural ghetto and saw the backing of the Prince Consort as evidence of unhealthy and unconstitutional pressure from behind the Throne – a foretaste of more recent architectural controversies. After a long debate the government's proposals passed by a majority of nine, but the slimness of the majority persuaded the Prime Minister, Lord Palmerston, to drop the Bill, despite an angry letter from the Queen hoping that the government would not be deterred from acting by 'a knot of persons who delight in nothing but making mischief . . . Really nothing worthy of the Country can be ever produced if the repeated decisions of Royal Commissions, Committees of the H. of Commons, Govts &c &c are thus to be everlastingly set aside & all progress & preparation made to be lost labour'.[42] In July Lord Elcho, one of the leading malcontents, succeeded in persuading the government to appoint another Royal Commission which, after deliberating for a year, concluded that the British Museum's sculptures should stay at Bloomsbury and the National Gallery's pictures at Trafalgar Square, where they would be protected from air pollution by being placed behind glass. Wilkins's building would be demolished to make way for one 'worthy of the British people'.[43]

Meanwhile the Gallery's collections continued to grow. In 1854 the trustees bought the nucleus of the present collection of early German pictures, but they soon found that there was no space to display them. A hundred and thirty-nine more

---

40 Rep. Sel. Cttee. on National Gallery, *PP* 1852–3, 35 [867], pp. xv–xviii, 723–6 and *passim*.
41 *The Times*, 21, 27 and 28 June 1856.
42 *Hansard*, 142 (27 June 1856), 2097–2154; 143 (30 June 1856), 13; Royal Archives, Add F25/171.
43 Rep. Commrs. on National Gallery Site, *PP* 1857 (2), 24 [2261], pp. iii–vi.

pictures, many of them of the early Italian and Flemish schools, were bought by Eastlake during his Directorship, which lasted from 1855 to 1865, and the collection was further swelled towards the end of 1856 by the bequest of J. M. W. Turner's 283 oil paintings and 19,049 drawings.[44] This, together with the imminent removal of the Vernon pictures from Marlborough House, now earmarked as the official residence for the Prince of Wales, made it urgently necessary to provide more wall space. So Palmerston began once more to explore the possibility of creating more accommodation within the existing building. As a first step he asked Pennethorne to resurrect his plans for flooring over the central hall to form a gallery, and in August 1856 he submitted a revised set of drawings.[45]

It took five more years of vacillation to carry out even these modest proposals. The pressure on Trafalgar Square appeared to be removed in 1858, when Lord Derby, who had succeeded Palmerston as Prime Minister, came up with a proposal to move the Royal Academy to Burlington House in Piccadilly, acquired by the government in 1854. But it took ten years to persuade the Academy to move. Meanwhile a new gallery was built at the recently established South Kensington Museum in 1858–9 for the Vernon collection, the recently acquired Sheepshanks collection of early nineteenth-century paintings and, for a time, the Turner Bequest.[46] The architect of this modest structure was Francis Fowke, the Royal Engineer who had designed the nucleus of the museum buildings. He subsequently prepared a plan for remodelling the Trafalgar Square building, only to see it rejected by Palmerston when he returned to power later in 1859 on the grounds that 'its adoption would preclude the choice of a more thorough improvement, while it would not do enough to give us a Building worthy of the Site or the purpose to which it is destined'.[47] This left no alternative but to carry out Pennethorne's 1856 scheme for a new gallery, the cost of which had now risen to £15,000. The money was finally voted in August 1860, and work began to a slightly altered design in the following month, the whole gallery reopening on 11 May 1861.[48]

Visitors entered the remodelled building as they do now, through the portico, which gave access to a vestibule. From here new staircases led to the Royal Academy's rooms to the right, and the National Gallery's to the left, while another led down under the new gallery to a new sculpture room for the Royal Academy. The picture gallery (Plate 79) formed part of an *enfilade* with Wilkins's galleries to the west. It was less lavish than the rooms Pennethorne had proposed in 1850, but was nevertheless large and impressive, measuring seventy-five by thirty feet

---

44 D. Robertson, *Sir Charles Eastlake and the Victorian Art World* (Princeton, 1978), pp. 78–80, 134–8, etc.; A. J. Finberg, *The Life of J. M. W. Turner RA* (1961), pp. 441–5.

45 PRO, Work 17/10/2, f. 1.

46 Hutchison, *History of the Royal Academy*, p. 122; *Hansard*, 152 (8 Feb. 1859), 181–4; J. Physick, *The Victoria and Albert Museum* (Oxford, 1982), pp. 39–45.

47 *BN*, 1 Apr. 1859, 299–300; PRO, Work 1/66, p. 50.

48 Minutes of Trustees, iv, 239–42, 249–51; PRO, Work 17/10/2, ff. 15–46.

(twenty-three by nine metres) and roofed with a barrel vault held up on iron trusses. The skylight was of embossed plate glass, and the coves adorned with plasterwork representing palettes, olive branches and bay leaves, causing one commentator to remark: 'It has rarely, if ever, been our lot to see better work. The materials and workmanship are evidently the best that could be procured, and they contrast strongly with the majority of the buildings which competition has forced upon the public'.[49] The new gallery was hung at first with High Renaissance works, and the rest of the collection was rearranged into schools, fulfilling Eastlake's aim and making the gallery, in the words of the Prime Minister, 'instructive as well as pleasing to the eye of the connoisseur'.[50] The new sculpture room on the ground floor (Plate 80) was less warmly received, partly because of the awkward mode of access, but Palmerston nevertheless judged it to be 'vastly superior to the little black hole in which the statuary used to be exhibited'.

Pennethorne's effective but modest extension ameliorated the gallery's lack of space but did not solve it. There were already four hundred and four pictures at Trafalgar Square in 1860, and overcrowding increased in October 1861 with the transfer of the Turner paintings from South Kensington. The artist had insisted in his will that his pictures should be housed with the rest of the national collection, and a legal judgement stated that the bequest would become invalid if this condition were not adhered to within ten years of his death, a time now rapidly approaching. In July 1861 therefore a House of Lords Select Committee recommended their removal from South Kensington to a new gallery to be built to Pennethorne's designs on iron posts over the barrack yard at Trafalgar Square at a cost of not more than £25,000.[51] An undated picture (Plate 81), which seems to have been prepared in connection with this design, shows a long room divided into three bays and painted deep red, with lavish decoration in the form of Renaissance arabesques and 'grotesques' and light entering through a flat glazed roof supported by a clerestory – a different system from that employed in the earlier gallery. Pennethorne insisted that this new gallery could serve as the first stage of a much larger reconstruction which would double the available wall-space.

This was too much to hope for. With a manic restlessness which seems to have afflicted all mid-Victorian politicians involved with the National Gallery, the Palmerston government now began to explore a new scheme to remove the whole collection to Burlington House, leaving the Trafalgar Square building to the sole use of the Royal Academy. This was on the face of it an attractive idea. The government owned the land already, and so would avoid the huge costs involved in a major extension at Trafalgar Square, and the Academy would not lose its central site. In

---

49 *BN*, 8 March 1861, 211–12.
50 *Hansard*, 164 (16 July 1861), 1015; *BN*, 19 July 1861, 598.
51 Rep. Sel. Cttee. on Turner and Vernon Pictures, *House of Lords Session Papers* (1861), 5 [201], iv, 25–9; Finberg, *Turner*, pp. 448–9.

79. The new picture gallery at the National Gallery, Several of the pictures can be recognised, including Sebastiano del Piombo's 'Raising of Lazarus' on the far wall. This gallery was demolished to make way for the present staircase in 1885.

80. The Royal Academy's new sculpture room. The part of the room nearest the viewer was underneath the new picture gallery.

1861 therefore, with his extension at Trafalgar Square just completed, Pennethorne prepared two designs for a gallery on the Burlington House site (Plate 116). But once again the government's plans to move the pictures ran into fierce opposition in Parliament. The National Gallery was a genuinely popular institution and the Trafalgar Square building attracted crowds of visitors. The Royal Academy, on the other hand, was widely criticised as a secretive, self-perpetuating body which did little to further the cause of art. The critics argued that it was misusing its privileged position by holding on to its rent-free premises in Trafalgar Square while the National Gallery was being squeezed out, and in July 1862 the government agreed to appoint a Royal Commission to investigate the Academy's affairs. Its characteristically ambiguous findings, published a year later, gave little practical assistance, and the government pressed ahead with plans for moving the National Gallery to Burlington House.

81. Design for a gallery for the Turner collection at the National Gallery, *c.* 1861. This magnificent room with its red-painted walls and copious arabesque decoration would have been built over the eastern portion of the barrack yard.

The objectors found a champion in Lord John Manners, now on the opposition benches in the House of Commons. In populist vein he took exception to an earlier statement by Eastlake that 'a quiet preparation before approaching pictures by the Old Masters is desirable' and poured scorn on William Cowper's assertion that a gallery in Burlington Gardens would be less of a 'resort for idlers' than the present building:

. . . the right honourable Gentleman told them that the soldiers went in. Goodness gracious! Why should they not? You could do the people no greater kindness than by giving them access to anything that would educate their taste . . . [Above] all other considerations, they should have a site that was convenient to the great masses of people who had not leisure, and to whom every half hour was of importance.

He attracted the support of a number of Liberal backbenchers who were 'inimical to the Academy or its continuation in the present building' and the scheme was soundly defeated[52] – a minor victory for anti-academic movement which forms so important a part of the artistic history of the nineteenth century.

Since Parliament had killed the idea of moving the National Gallery to Burlington House, the government had no option but to return to the earlier plan of ejecting the Royal Academy and expanding the premises at Trafalgar Square, where the eighty-two Turners displayed in the West Gallery now made up a quarter of the whole collection. It seemed that Pennethorne would finally be allowed to build the galleries which had for so long been maturing in his mind, and in December 1864 he sent Cowper four sketches embodying new ideas for enlarging the Trafalgar Square building in four stages. He believed that he had been promised the commission as long ago as 1858, and Cowper must have given him some encouragement for in April 1865 he sent in an estimate for the extended buildings, and a month later submitted plans for a 185-foot (56 metre)-long room extending north over the eastern part of the barrack yard – an updating of the scheme for the Turner gallery. The scheme was officially approved in May, and soon afterwards he delivered more plans for a future extension over the workhouse site.[53]

The plans for building over the barrack yard now ran into opposition from the army, whose Commander in Chief, the Duke of Cambridge, made it clear that he was 'extremely averse' to any proposal which might involve giving up any of the site, which the generals believed would be of vital importance in the event of civil commotion.[54] Pennethorne therefore prepared another set of plans showing his new gallery extending north from the centre of the existing building over the guard

---

52 *The Times*, 23 July 1862; *Hansard*, 175 (6 June 1864), 1301–16; *The Builder*, 11 June 1864, 431.
53 PRO, Work 1/78, p. 116; Work 2/29, p. 90; 2/31, p. 8; Work 17/13/12, ff. 1–9.
54 Broadlands Papers WFC/A/2, 26 April 1865.

room of the barracks, so as not to interfere with the soldiers' yard.[55] It would be matched by a similar gallery running from north to south on the eastern part of the workhouse site, with the intervening space filled by another gallery stretching east and west, with six smaller galleries leading off it. The facade should not be rebuilt because it 'was designed purposely to harmonize with, and not to overpower, St Martin's Church . . . and to produce richness and picturesqueness of effect as seen from Pall Mall and the Strand'. A rebuilding in the style of the 1860s 'might change the character from that of a Classic Gallery, to that of an Italian Palace – and would not produce the picturesque effects of light and shade which the present building possesses'[56] – an interesting assessment of the building's value as a piece of townscape.

Pennethorne's plans would, like his 1850 scheme, have solved the National Gallery's space problems for the forseeable future and saved many more years of acrimonious discussion. But once again they fell victim to political expediency. Having forced the government to abandon its plans for moving the National Gallery to Burlington House, the malcontents now saw an opportunity to bring the Office of Works under closer Parliamentary control by demanding a competition. Cowper gave in to pressure, writing to the Treasury on 11 September 1865:

Under more ordinary circumstances I might be content to entrust the formation of the plan to the architect of this office, but in this instance there are such special difficulties to be met and overcome that I am unwilling to restrict myself to the aid of a single architect, however able he may be, and it will be expedient to involve the assistance of several of the most eminent and experienced architects in order to provide the materials for a careful consideration of the alterations that might be adopted, and to enable the government and Parliament to come to a deliberate and sound judgement on the subject.[57]

Pennethorne was not asked to compete, and his final direct involvement with the building was to estimate the costs of purchasing the property for the extension.[58] But as a 'consolation prize' he was asked to design the new premises for the University of London on the site behind Burlington House formerly allotted to the National Gallery, and this proved to be his architectural swansong.

The National Gallery competition was announced in 1866 and elicited highly original designs from G. E. Street, Matthew Digby Wyatt and others.[59] The prize went to Charles Barry's son E. M. Barry, but his ambitious scheme for a complete rebuilding in the 'Wrenaissance' manner was set aside and in the end he was asked

55 PRO, Work 17/13/12, f. 11; Work 33/1335.   56 *Ibid.*, 17/13/15, f. 13.
57 *Ibid.*, 17/13/15, f. 15.   58 *Ibid.*, 1/85, p. 264.
59 See H. Grubert, 'The 1866 Competition for a new National Gallery' (MA thesis, Courtauld Institute of Art, University of London, 1967).

to design only the present eastern galleries (1872–6), grouped around a central rotunda on the workhouse site. They remain the finest rooms in the building. There was now another rehanging of the collection, in which the Italian pictures were removed from Pennethorne's gallery and a selection of Turner's works put in their place.[60] Meanwhile purchases and donations of pictures continued. Despite the extra space provided by the new galleries and by the Royal Academy's removal to Burlington House, wall space remained severely limited, and in 1881 Eastlake wrote to the Treasury pointing out that the collection had now become one of the finest in Europe, and emphasising the need for more room. Rather than risking another competition, G. Shaw Lefevre, First Commissioner of Works in Gladstone's second government, asked John Taylor to provide more space by building new galleries on the eastern part of the barrack site recently vacated by the soldiers. They would be reached by a new staircase – the present main staircase (Plate 82) – constructed on the site of Pennethorne's gallery of 1860–1, which Eastlake and others had in any case criticised for its inadequate lighting.[61] The work was carried out in 1885–7, and now nothing remains of Pennethorne's contribution to the building. But Taylor was told to decorate the new galleries in a style harmonious with the existing work, and to that extent something of Pennethorne's careful and scholarly influence can be said to survive in the building we know today.

Pennethorne's long involvement with the National Gallery epitomises the difficulties which attended his career. The necessity for new accommodation was universally recognised, but changes of government, unstable Parliamentary majorities and, above all, the need to placate public opinion combined to smother all his most ambitious schemes and ensure that piecemeal solutions were adopted in their place. The subsequent history of the building has been no less fraught with vexations, changes of plans and mediocre compromises. With the exception of the new Sainsbury Wing (1991), none of the twentieth-century galleries approach the architectural quality of Barry's or Taylor's, let alone those which Pennethorne might have built. In many ways the building is a monument to the national talent for muddling through. Yet it undoubtedly enjoys the affections of most of its visitors. There is nothing intimidating about it, and to that extent it is perhaps an appropriate expression of a democratic, pluralist culture, as Robert Venturi seems to have grasped in his 1991 extension. The English have often preferred the homely and picturesque to the elevated and formal even at the expense of opting for the second-rate, and the National Gallery embodies both the virtues and the vices of this aspect of our public taste.

---

60 J. C. Horsley, *Recollections of a Royal Academician* (1903), pp. 285–6.
61 PRO, Work 17/14/15, ff. 3–37.

82. The main staircase of the National Gallery. The building of the staircase in 1885–7 entailed the demolition of Pennethorne's new gallery and sculpture room, but in its design and decorative character John Taylor followed the general character of Pennethorne's many proposals for the building.

SOUTH KENSINGTON

South Kensington – today London's main museum district – was an offshoot of the Great Exhibition of 1851. Backed by Prince Albert, the exhibition's promoters decided to use the profits to purchase a large tract of land to the south of Hyde Park which could be turned into a centre of cultural and scientific endeavour. The aim according to Edgar Bowring, one of the Commissioners, was to afford 'the means of education in art and science, and to concentrate it as much as possible, by bringing together all the different departments and bodies representing art and science'.[62] Accommodation could be provided for the National Gallery, a new Museum of Manufacturing and for the various government-supported learned and scientific societies which were in the process of being forced out of Somerset House. Lord Derby's ministry was sympathetic enough to the project to move in December 1852 for a vote of £150,000 to match the Exhibition Commissioners' funds, and the purchase was completed early in 1853.[63]

Pennethorne surveyed the estate on the government's behalf in 1851 and in the autumn of 1853, soon after delivering block plans for a new National Gallery in Kensington Gardens, he prepared some detailed schemes for the layout of the estate. Prince Albert had already produced his own plan for the site, and in the wake of the report of the Select Committee which recommended moving the National Gallery from Trafalgar Square to South Kensington it was sent to Gladstone, Chancellor of the Exchequer in the new Aberdeen administration. Gladstone thought that more buildings could be fitted into the site than Prince Albert had envisaged, and Pennethorne was one of the architects who prepared plans showing how this ideal could be achieved.[64]

His designs all envisaged the main buildings being placed on either side of an axis stretching from the site of the present Royal Albert Hall to that of the Natural History Museum.[65] In his first scheme, dating from October 1853, the National Gallery stands on a terrace on the site of the present Albert Hall with a large circular garden surrounded by formal plantations on the lower ground to the south and arranged around courtyards beyond, on either side of a large colonnaded open space. This scheme received Prince Albert's 'qualified approval', but since some of the property on the northern part of the site still remained in private hands Pennethorne was asked to prepare a revised plan with the National Gallery on a narrower site between the two blocks of private land and a thirty-foot (9 metre)-high terrace to the south; it was to overlook gardens flanked by oval-shaped buildings, one of them housing a 'College of Industrial Arts and Science', and the other 'Houses of Societies of Professional Men' and a 'Museum of Industrial Arts and Patented Inventions' – an early plan for what were eventually to become the Science Museum and Imperial College.

The most impressive of all the plans (Plate 83) shows the National Gallery placed slightly further south, with the two southern buildings aligned at right angles to

---

62 Rep. Sel. Cttee. on National Gallery (1852–3), 35, p. 609.

63 Physick, *Victoria and Albert Museum*, pp. 19–21.

64 *Survey of London*, 38 (1975), pp. 57–8. Other designs were prepared by C. R. Cockerell and T. L. Donaldson.

65 Imperial College, London, MSS of the Royal Commission on the Great Exhibition, memorandum from Pennethorne dated 22 October 1853 and letter dated 7 November. The original plans have been lost, but there are contemporary photographs in 'guard books' in the V & A Picture Library, 2506 and 2512–13.

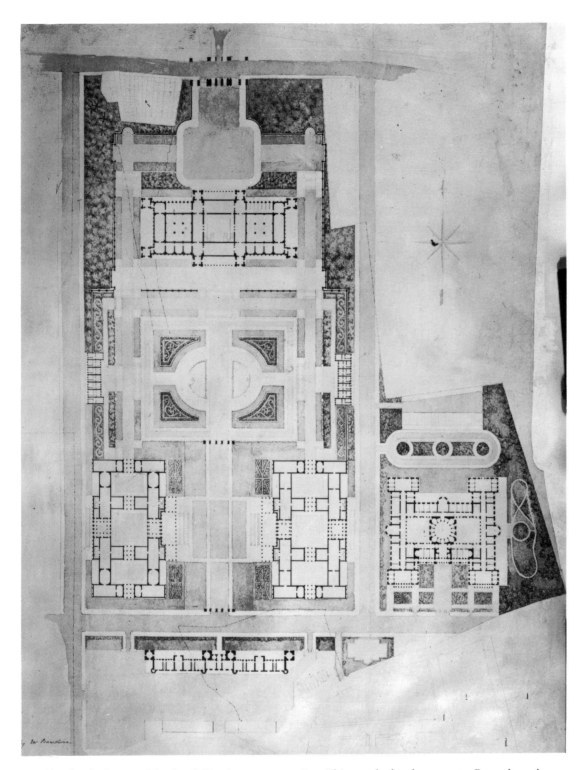

83. Plan for the layout of the South Kensington estate, 1853. This superb plan demonstrates Pennethorne's mastery of monumental classical town planning. The building at the top – a little to the south of the site of the Royal Albert Hall – was intended as a new National Gallery and the others to the south were presumably intended as scientific and cultural institutions of the sort promoted by the Prince Consort. They stand on the site of the present Natural History Museum, and the building on the right is on that of the Victoria and Albert Museum.

what is now Cromwell Road, and another large building with a circular central hall and two internal courtyards on the site of the present Victoria and Albert Museum. The National Gallery rooms would have been arranged around two courtyards which could be roofed over to create top-lit sculpture courts. There would be a 'lofty and rich architectural facade' in the 'Italian or Palladian style of architecture' with colonnades on the long sides to south and north and towers placed at the corners, which could be used for keepers' residences.[66] No elevations survive, but it is obvious from the overall planning that Pennethorne envisaged a treatment in the monumental classical manner which he was soon to elaborate in his schemes for the government offices in Whitehall.

The plans, taken together, represent Pennethorne's *beau idéal* of a setting for a national centre of art and culture. In his hands South Kensington would have consisted of a series of spacious, formal classical buildings lucidly arranged around ample open spaces. These ideals appealed more strongly to Continental than to English minds, and for that reason his schemes stood very little chance of ever being accepted by politicians and voters who, then, as now, were moved by pragmatism, a suspicion of the grand manner, and a dislike of spending large sums of public money on comprehensive schemes of planning. The proposals were dropped – if they were ever seriously considered – at the end of 1853, and the plans to move the National Gallery to South Kensington were finally abandoned in 1856.

The initiative now passed to the Department of Science and Art (formerly Practical Art), the sub-department of the Board of Trade which managed the government's School of Design. One of the aims of the School was to improve the quality of industrial design, and it was with this object in mind that a collection of decorative objects, books and plaster casts was gradually built up. The collection was greatly augmented by Henry Cole, who had moved on from his triumphs at the Public Record Office to become one of the promoters of the Great Exhibition and, in 1852, superintendent of the School. He and his ally Richard Redgrave moved the School and its growing collections from Somerset House to Marlborough House, but this was only intended as a temporary home and in 1854 they produced their own plans for the South Kensington estate, including new premises for the School on the site of the present Science Museum and other public buildings, including a Patent Office and a Senate House for the University of London on the rest of the site.[67] It soon became obvious that the government was not going to provide any money for these buildings, so in 1855 Cole decided, with Prince Albert's backing, to place the School in Brompton Park House, to the east of Exhibition Road – the site of the present Victoria and Albert Museum – and to build temporary galleries for the collections (the notorious 'Brompton Boilers')

---

66 Rep. Sel. Cttee. on National Gallery (1852–3), pp. 625–7.
67 V & A Picture Library, Guard Book, no. 2510.

close by. The site was adjacent to the main estate, but its development need not interfere with any grandiose plans which might be carried out there at some future date.[68]

Work on the temporary galleries of the South Kensington Museum began early in 1856, but it soon became clear that a further building would be needed to link them to Brompton Park House and at the same time to provide a lecture room, library and offices. The 'Boilers' had no sooner become visible than they attracted widespread abuse and ridicule and the museum officials, backed by Prince Albert, decided to ask the Office of Works for a design for the new 'junction building'. Pennethorne was therefore asked to provide designs for a functional structure (Plate 84) which could be executed within the £10,000 recently voted by Parliament.[69] The most important feature was a circular lecture theatre forty-two and a half feet (thirteen metres) in diameter, which stood on the site of the present Victoria and Albert Museum quadrangle. A temporary building constructed within such severe cost limits could hardly be expected to display any great felicity of design. Yet a correspondent in *The Builder* thought that the exterior had 'some degree of effect', and praised the construction of the lecture room roof, which was 'framed without ties, the principals meeting at the apex'.[70]

Pennethorne's role at South Kensington now became a purely advisory one. The Department of Science and Art took complete control of the Brompton House site in 1858 and, in the continued absence of an overall plan for the Commissioners' estate, began to construct permanent buildings to the designs of Cole's new *protégé*, Captain Francis Fowke. He now became the architectural guiding spirit of South Kensington, and his buildings form the nucleus of the present Victoria and Albert Museum. Pennethorne's lecture room was demolished in 1865 to make way for an extension of Fowke's galleries, and the rest of his block disappeared in 1878 when the splendidly polychromatic main quadrangle was finally completed.

The rest of the Commissioners' site was developed in a manner very different from that envisaged by Pennethorne in 1853. The central area remained undeveloped until 1858, when it was leased to the Royal Horticultural Society for their gardens which were surrounded by arcades and conservatories designed by Francis Fowke and Sydney Smirke and opened in 1861. They did not last for long, and the site was eventually covered with miscellaneous buildings of a cultural and scientific nature, including the now-demolished Imperial Institute, the Royal School of Mines, the Science Museum, and finally the new Geological Museum which replaced Pennethorne's building in Piccadilly. The area to the south,

---

68 H. Cole, *Fifty Years of Public Work*, I (1884), pp. 320–3; Physick, *Victoria and Albert Museum*, pp. 22–3. The 'Boilers' were designed by Charles Young for £15,000.

69 PRO, Work 1/50, p. 317; 1/51, pp. 155–6.

70 *The Builder*, 24 Jan. 1857, 45; Physick, *Victoria and Albert Museum*, pp. 28–9; *Survey of London*, 38 (1975), pp. 99–100.

84. Part of the South Kensington Museum in 1863, showing Pennethorne's temporary lecture room and office block. Francis Fowke's Sheepshanks Gallery can be seen in the background.

fronting Cromwell Road, was set aside for the International Exhibition of 1862 and subsequently for a new structure to house the Natural History collections of the British Museum. Fowke designed the temporary exhibition building and later won the Natural History Museum competition, for which Pennethorne was an assessor. But he died before work could begin, and the present splendid neo-Romanesque structure – one of the greatest of all Victorian museums – was built to the design of Alfred Waterhouse and opened in 1881.

The northern fringe of the estate remained in the hands of the Commissioners until after the death of Prince Albert in 1861. Pennethorne produced an impressive design for the Albert Memorial (see pp. 272–4), but it was set aside in favour of the present Gothic memorial by Gilbert Scott. Plans for the Commissioners' land on the opposite side of Kensington Gore, where Pennethorne had proposed to put the National Gallery, languished for want of funds until Cole seized the initiative in 1864 by asking Fowke to design an Albert Hall in the form of a Roman amphitheatre. When Fowke died in the following year Cole turned to another Royal Engineer, Lieutenant-Colonel Henry Scott, and it is his confident building, constructed with the aid of a public subscription in 1867–71, which now faces the Albert Memorial – an object-lesson in the stylistic pluralism which finally put paid to Pennethorne's plans for developing the area.

7

BUILDINGS FOR THE ROYAL FAMILY

THE ROYAL PALACES were the oldest of the responsibilities of the Office of Works. When Pennethorne began to work full-time for the Office, the main residences of the monarch were, as they are now, Windsor Castle and Buckingham Palace. Both had been extensively and expensively rebuilt by George IV, the latter on such a thorough scale that it was in effect a new building. The older royal palaces – St James's Palace, Kensington Palace (Queen Victoria's birthplace) and Hampton Court – were occupied by other members of the royal family or used for grace and favour residences. The sites of the palaces of Whitehall and Westminster had long been turned over to the needs of Parliament and government. Of the more recently constructed houses which had been built by, or come into the hands of, royalty, York House (now Lancaster House) was sold in 1841 to the Duke of Sutherland and the profits put towards Victoria Park. Marlborough House, on the other side of St James's Palace, was occupied by William IV's widow, Queen Adelaide, and the short-lived Carlton House had recently disappeared to make way for Carlton House Terrace. Frogmore House in Windsor Great Park was occupied by Queen Victoria's mother, the Duchess of Kent, and Claremont, at Esher (Surrey) by her uncle, King Leopold of the Belgians. The Brighton Pavilion lay empty, symbol of a departed era.

By the time Pennethorne began to work for the Office of Works, royal building was at a low ebb after the excitements of the George IV era. The taste of the young Queen and her consort ran more to villas than to spectacular palaces. Osborne and Balmoral, the best manifestations of this taste, were private commissions in which the Office of Works played no part. Most of the relatively little work undertaken in the older palaces in the 1830s was managed by Edward Blore, who succeeded Nash at Buckingham Palace, and by Sir Jeffery Wyatville at Windsor. Pennethorne, as Nash's architectural heir, suffered from the decline in the older architect's reputation after the death of George IV, and it was not until 1842–4 that he received his first employment from the Crown: the building of a block of stables at Claremont and the construction of some farmhouses on Crown land at Egham and

Englefield Green on the edge of Windsor Great Park, for all of which Thomas Chawner had provided the designs.[1] In 1846 he prepared plans for the widening of High Street and Thames Street, Windsor, and the demolition of the picturesque but ramshackle and insanitary old houses which 'encroached' on the castle moat. This project was not finally completed until 1857, and by this time Anthony Salvin had become architect to the castle and had begun to remodel the Curfew Tower and the walls overlooking the widened street with Carcasonne-like thoroughness.[2]

Pennethorne's contribution to the royal palaces was centred on Buckingham Palace and the immediate surroundings of St James's Palace, including Marlborough House. Critics had long lamented what a writer in the *Gentleman's Magazine* for 1826 called 'the disgraceful littleness of the Metropolitan palaces'. But while it was easy to ridicule their lack of grandeur it was harder to remedy it. Under a constitutional monarchy palaces had to be financed out of the public purse, and the constraints which affected government building also applied to the royal palaces. This must always be borne in mind when examining Pennethorne's work for the royal family.

BUCKINGHAM PALACE

The main royal residence in central London was the creation of an elderly and impetuous monarch and a protesting but necessarily compliant architect. It occupied the site of Buckingham House, rebuilt by William Winde at the beginning of the eighteenth century and extended by Sir William Chambers for George III and Queen Charlotte in 1762–80. Work started on transforming this externally modest building into the main London residence of the King in 1825, but the project was dogged by difficulties from the very beginning. George IV originally intended the palace as a mere *pied à terre*, or private residence, but at the end of his life he changed his mind and told Nash that he wanted to hold his Courts there rather than at the dilapidated St James's Palace, which had been damaged by fire in 1809. Buckingham Palace therefore grew to become one of the largest buildings in London. Costs mounted, and Nash bore much of the blame for what came to be seen as a misuse of public funds.

The change of plans also had an unfortunate architectural effect. In its completed form the palace consisted of a massive main block containing new state rooms built onto and into the former Buckingham House, with an open courtyard flanked by long wings stretching forward to the Mall and entered through the Marble Arch.

---

1 PRO, Cres 2/1201, 2/1219, 2/1229; T 1/6693A/3774.
2 R. R. Tighe and J. E. Davis, *Annals of Windsor*, II (1858), pp. 643–55; PRO, Work 19/30/4, ff. 1–5; Cres 19/34, p. 176. Pennethorne also prepared plans for developing some of the Crown land to the south of the town: see p. 318.

The conception was French in inspiration, but in the handling both of the masses of masonry and the detailing Nash was no match for the French. The composition looked disjointed and lacked that underlying unity and monumentality which characterises the French classical school. The lavishly decorated interiors were and are more successful. They also owe much to France, in this case the heavy richly ornamented style of the early nineteenth century, and it is possible that, as Nash's chief assistant at the time of their conception, Pennethorne may have played a subordinate part in their genesis.[3] But if he did, all documentary record has vanished.

For a time after George IV's death the palace seemed set to become a huge and costly anomaly. Despite the considerable size of the new building there was still not enough accommodation for the vast numbers of visitors who had to be invited to the ceremonial occasions inseparable from the duties of the head of state. William IV refused to live there, preferring the more modest comforts of his old home, Clarence House, in the grounds of St James's Palace, and the new palace was not fully occupied until Queen Victoria came to the throne in 1837. She soon discovered that there was not enough space for her expanding family and house-hold, so minor internal alterations were carried out in the early 1840s, and in 1843 Blore converted the iron-framed south west conservatory on the garden front into a chapel. He also modified – and improved – the appearance of the garden front by building an attic in the centre over Nash's small egg-like dome (Plate 85). But two years later, in 1845, the Queen, now the mother of five children, told Sir Robert Peel that further expansion was an 'urgent necessity':

Sir Robert is acquainted with the state of the Palace, and the total want of accommodation for our little family, which is fast growing up . . . Independent of this, most parts of the Palace are in a sad state, and will ere long require a further outlay to render them *decent* for the Royal Family or any visitors the Queen may have to receive. A room, capable of containing a larger number of those persons whom the Queen has to invite in the course of the season to balls, concerts, etc. than any of the present apartments can at once hold, is much wanted. Equally so, the improved offices and servants' rooms, the want of which puts the departments of the household to great expense yearly. It will be for Sir Robert to consider whether it would not be best to remedy all these deficiencies at once, and to make use of this opportunity to render the exterior of the Palace such as no longer to be a *disgrace* to the country, which it certainly now is.[4]

Peel agreed with the Queen and told the Cabinet that the enlargement of Buckingham Palace to accommodate Court functions could free the site of St James's Palace for a new National Gallery. In his view 'the present building at St James's [could not] long remain. It is a great blemish to the best part of London

---

3 J. Summerson, *The Life and Work of John Nash, Architect* (1980), pp. 165–6.
4 *The Letters of Queen Victoria 1837–1861*, ed. A. C. Benson and Viscount Esher, II (1908), pp. 33–4.

85. Buckingham Palace from the air. The main block, containing the state rooms, is in the foreground. The nearer of the two low buildings projecting towards the garden is the chapel, and to its right is Pennethorne's south wing, with Buckingham Gate in the bottom right-hand corner. Blore's east wing is on the further side of the palace courtyard and St James's Palace and Marlborough House can be seen in the distance. The layout in front of the palace dates from the early twentieth century.

. . . It would seem much more decorous that the Queen's subjects should wait on Her Majesty at the Palace which is her residence than that she should leave it for the purpose of waiting upon them'. Political considerations also intruded. The masses were often restless, the monarchy was by no means totally secure in the public's affections, and 'at times of excitement it would be much better that the Sovereign should hold her Levées &c. at the Palace, where she resides, than that she should

217

have to pass and return through an immense concourse of people'.[5] Pennethorne was therefore asked to draw up a block plan showing a new National Gallery on the fire-damaged northern and eastern sides of St James's Palace flanked by new roads, one of which would have led across St James's Park. There would also have been a new chapel on the south front, a new entrance hall and new private apartments to the north of Clarence House.[6]

These proposals did not come to anything, and towards the end of 1845 Peel's government agreed to add to Buckingham Palace instead. Blore was once again chosen as architect, and in 1846 he produced a scheme for a new domestic range linking the ends of the two wings which projected east from the main block. The building of this new wing involved moving the Marble Arch, which was taken to its present site at the north-east corner of Hyde Park in 1850. Prince Albert took an active interest in the interior design, and insisted that the builder should be Thomas Cubitt, with whom he had been collaborating in the design and construction of Osborne House on the Isle of Wight.[7] The east range was finished in 1850, but by this time Blore had quarrelled with the Commissioners appointed by the government to oversee the work and had resigned. The new building satisfied some of the Queen's requirements, but on other grounds it was not a great success. The new front to the Mall, supposedly modelled on the gargantuan palace of the Neopolitan Bourbons at Caserta, was blank and undistinguished. The design was widely criticised and neither the public nor, one may assume, the Queen herself, can have been amused when the Caen stone used as a facing material began to crumble and fall off in 1853.[8] The building was finally refronted in its present grandiloquent – and visually far more satisfactory – form by Sir Aston Webb in 1912.

Before his resignation Blore provided drawings for a large extension attached to the south-west corner of the palace.[9] This range was intended to contain a ballroom which would be easily accessible from Nash's state rooms, but the late 1840s were a time of financial stringency and the plans were not acted upon for fear of imposing too great a strain on the public purse and thus provoking unrest. The sale of the Brighton Pavilion in 1850 released funds which made it possible to contemplate building the new wing without having to ask Parliament for large sums of money. The original intention seems to have been that Cubitt would both design and construct the new wing, taking Blore's designs as a starting-point, and in the summer of 1851 he presented Lord Seymour, the First Commissioner of Works, with a series of plans (now lost) which met with the approval of the Queen.[10]

---

5 C. S. Parker, *Sir Robert Peel*, III (1899), p. 182, 1 July 1845.

6 PRO, Work 34/888.

7 W. Ames, *Prince Albert and Victorian Taste* (1967), pp. 61–2; H. Hobhouse, *Prince Albert: His Life and Work* (1983), p. 134; H. Hobhouse, *Thomas Cubitt, Master Builder* (1971), p. 396.

8 PRO, Work 19/9, f. 3371.

9 BL, Add MS 42047, pp. 20–31.   10 PRO, Work 19/9, ff. 3065–6.

86. The south wing of Buckingham Palace as projected in 1852. The Ballroom and Supper Room block rests on a rusticated podium containing kitchens and domestic offices. The south range of Nash's palace is on the right.

A few months later Cubitt was displaced as architect by Pennethorne. No reason was given, but presumably Lord John Manners, Seymour's successor as First Commissioner, felt uneasy about entrusting so important a structure to someone who, for all his close association with the Prince Consort, was technically a builder and not an architect.[11] Pennethorne had already diverted the Kings Scholars' Pond Sewer, which ran through the site, as part of the Pimlico improvement scheme and in April 1852 he submitted a set of designs for the new wing (Plate 86), which may have incorporated some of the ideas sketched out by Cubitt in his last plans.[12]

There were to be two very large reception rooms on the first floor, a Ballroom and a Supper Room, each of them forty-five feet (fourteen metres) high, linked by spacious galleries to the main building (Plate 87). One of the galleries would lead

11 Sir William Molesworth later said that Pennethorne's position at the Palace had never been clearly defined: PRO, Work 19/9, ff. 3342–8.
12 Royal Library, RL22076; PRO, Work 34/360, 34/363–4, 34/371; Hobhouse, *Cubitt*, p. 419.

from the main staircase at the southern end of Nash's building and the other would give access to the State Dining Room recently redecorated by Blore. A circuit would thus be formed, and the building finally transformed into a full-scale palace capable of accommodating large numbers of guests on formal occasions. The service accommodation on the ground floor was planned on an equally lavish scale. The new range was designed to provide more extensive kitchens and ancillary rooms. A new kitchen was to occupy the south-west corner, with a scullery and roasting kitchens between it and the chapel, flanked by larders. To the east were rooms for the cooks and their apprentices and for the comptroller and clerk of the kitchen. A new servants hall, and linen rooms occupied the remainder of the space.[13]

In his external elevations Pennethorne abandoned Blore's rather fussy Italianate manner and returned to the purer French-inspired style of Nash. The ground floor is faced with his characteristic bands of rusticated Bath stone, relieved only by severely plain round-arched windows and two massive doorways. In the elevations of the upper floors his main aim was not to overwhelm the existing building, and in this he was so successful that today it is difficult to tell where Nash's work ends and his own begins. The roof-line was deliberately left plain – a mere line of urns over a virtually non-existent cornice – and otherwise ornament is limited to pairs of Corinthian columns on the south front, an enriched frieze continued round from the main building, and Flaxmanesque relief panels.[14]

At Prince Albert's request Thomas Cubitt was kept on as builder, but did not have to tender competitively and he promised to limit any profit he might make to seven per cent.[15] His tender of £47,000 was accepted in June 1852, and by the beginning of 1853 he was 'urging the people on with the work, being anxious to get the scaffold [of the Ballroom] down before the Queen returns'.[16] Pennethorne submitted his first plans and cross-sections of the Ballroom and Supper Room in September 1852, and a month later he presented twenty-two more plans and drawings, which received the approval of the Prince Consort.[17] These drawings (Plate 88) are of superb quality, some of them tinted, others minutely detailed in black ink. They show that from the beginning Pennethorne envisaged a style of decoration loosely based on that of the early Renaissance, with a profusion of small-scale motifs covering the surfaces of walls and ceilings – something quite different from the style of Nash's state rooms or the fashionable neo-Rococo employed by Wyatville in the Grand Reception Room at Windsor.

The proceeds of the sale of the Brighton Pavilion were largely exhausted by the

---

13 PRO, Work 34/363.
14 A design for one of the panels is in the Royal Library, RL23235.
15 PRO, Work 19/9, f. 3508. In the event he made only one and a half per cent profit.
16 *Ibid.*, ff. 3254–8, 3262, 3325, 3508.
17 *Ibid.*, ff. 3257, 3536.

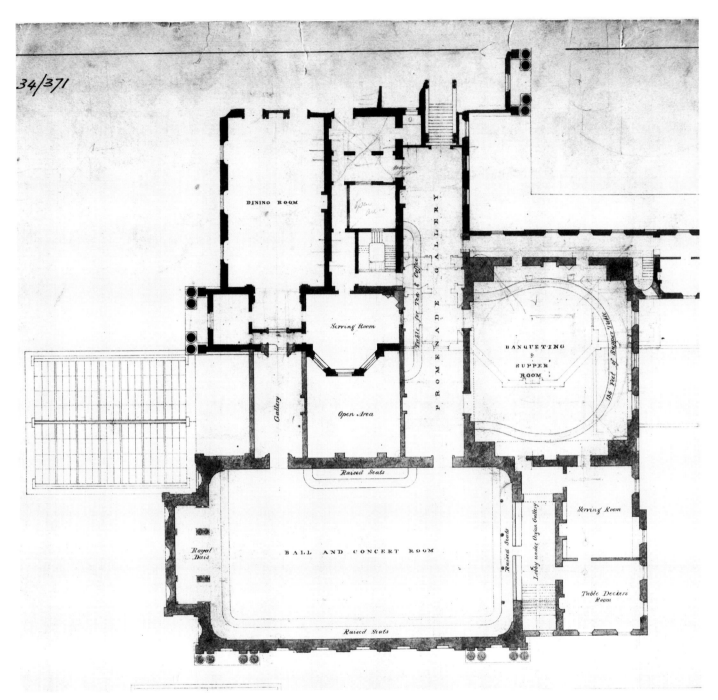

87. Ground plan of the main floor of the south wing, Buckingham Palace, as first projected in 1852. The Promenade Gallery leads from the main staircase to the Supper Room and Ballroom, and a second gallery (the Approach or West Gallery) leads back to the Dining Room in the main block. A second gallery (the Cross Gallery) was later added to link the other two galleries.

construction of the new wing, and work on decorating the interior could not start until September 1853, after the Treasury had promised to include an extra sum of £40,000 in the Parliamentary estimates for the ensuing year.[18] Pennethorne's designs were now subjected to a series of alterations, most of them suggested by Prince Albert, in the course of which the character of the interior was changed drastically, and probably for the better. First Pennethorne was told to enlarge and redesign the Ballroom doorways and to match them on the opposite side of the room with similar structures containing mirrors 'of extraordinary size', fifteen feet (five metres) high by ten feet (three metres) wide, which were judged to be 'very essential to the general effect of the Rooms, as they would stand opposite to very long vistas'.[19] Then William Theed, whose smooth, rather anaemic style made him a great favourite of the royal family, was brought in to design and carve the extensive sculptural enrichments to the Ballroom, Supper Room and galleries. And finally, for the all-important painted decoration which was to cover the wall surfaces, the Prince turned to the Dresden-born Ludwig Grüner, who had trained in Rome and had been responsible for the redecoration of Nash's main staircase at Buckingham Palace, as well as the internal painting at Osborne.

Grüner had encouraged Albert's enthusiasm for Raphael, and in his hands the interiors – especially that of the Ballroom – acquired a more authentically Raphaelesque character than Pennethorne had originally envisaged. This mode of design had become popular in Germany, the birthplace of the Nazarene painters, and had been employed by Klenze at the Hermitage in St. Petersburg, as well as by Albert and Grüner in the now-demolished circular pavilion in the garden at Buckingham Palace (1844–6). But it had made relatively little impact in England, and Albert, who saw the new rooms as his 'Creation and Child', seized the opportunity of employing it on the most sumptuous scale.[20] Grüner paid two visits to Rome to authenticate the details, and it was presumably on one of these forays that he secured the services of Nicola Consoni, a painter who had worked on the new church of San Paulo fuori le Mura. Consoni carried out the most important parts of the revised scheme, leaving the rest to be executed by Charles Moxon, who had worked under Grüner's direction on the decoration of the staircase in 1845. Work began in October 1854 and was finished early in the following year.[21]

The lighting and furnishing of the new rooms took up much of 1855. Pennethorne first wanted to light the Ballroom by chandeliers hung from brackets

18 PRO, Work 1/42, p. 125; Work 19/9, ff. 3379, 3491–3; Work 34/376–459.
19 *Ibid.*, 19/9, f. 3479; Royal Archives, Vic. Add /PP 62, 1 March 1854 and 9 May 1854.
20 D. Miller, 'Headquarters of Taste', *Country Life*, 4 Dec. 1986, 1764–6; W. Ames, *Prince Albert and Victorian Taste* (1967), p. 272.
21 PRO, Work 1/44, p. 606; Work 19/9, ff. 3497–503; Royal Archives, Vic. Add /PP 62, 16 Dec. 1854.

88. Pennethorne's first design for the Ballroom of Buckingham Palace, October 1852. The drawing was made before Prince Albert called in Ludwig Grüner to supervise the interior decoration.

projecting from the walls, but this plan was abandoned in favour of one which was to create an effect of unusual brilliance: gas burners were to be hung from the ceilings, and large free-standing chandeliers (designed by Grüner) placed at floor level. Gas ceiling lights had been used in the 'Great Music Hall' (presumably the Town Hall) at Birmingham, but the method employed by the contractors, Messrs Osler, was 'altogether so new, so experimental, and so subject to alterations and improvements as they proceeded that the cost could not have previously been estimated'.[22] The lighting was ready and the organ was being installed in September 1855, but by the end of the year the funds were exhausted. Pennethorne had already been told '*on no account* to sanction or commence any work at Buckingham Palace without the previous consent of the First Commissioner and the Treasury', but he could not argue with the Prince Consort, and had to look on powerlessly as the costs rose.[23] He now admitted that not enough money had been set aside in the original estimate either for the interior carvings which were 'different from those of almost every other Building upon which Builders are employed' or for 'the innumerable mouldings and small surfaces which, by multiplication of parts, have caused every small item to swell into an important sum'. Other changes, probably originating with Prince Albert, had pushed up the cost further; they included making the seats in the ballroom movable so that it could be turned into a banqueting room, and raising the roofs.[24] The First Commissioner, Sir Benjamin Hall, was predictably unimpressed by this explanation, claiming that, with the exception of the gas lighting, none of the alterations had been sanctioned by him or his predecessor. But he had no option but to ask the Treasury to pay the bills, and the new rooms were used for the first time on 8 May 1856.[25]

Most visitors approached the new wing from Nash's main staircase. This led into the spacious glass-roofed Promenade or East Gallery (Plate 89), the lower parts of which were painted an ochre colour, with large *trompe l'oeil* paintings by Moxon of vases of flowers arranged within semicircular-arched 'windows'. The paintings are now hidden behind textile wall coverings, but Consoni's grisaille panels of cupids can still be seen on the attic level above. From here a doorway, copied from doors in the older parts of the palace, led into the Supper Room (Plate 90). In its original form this well-proportioned room must have been stunningly colourful. The walls were painted by Moxon in imitation of marble and the shallow dome painted with cords in the manner of a canopy or *velarium* studded in a quasi-oriental manner with gold stars and painted birds. Further brilliance came from the huge gas burners and from plate-glass mirrors let up through the floor in front of the windows at night, and there was a frieze with classical bas-reliefs by Theed after designs by John Gibson based on Raphael's Cupid and Psyche.[26]

At the end of the East Gallery another doorway led into the Ballroom, the largest room in the palace and, in its original form, one of the most spectacular of all Victorian interiors. It is an uninterrupted space 110 feet (34 metres) long, 60 feet (18 metres) wide and 45 feet (14 metres) high (a ratio of approximately 8:4:3),

22 PRO, Work 19/9, f. 3605.
23 *Ibid.*, f. 3498v, 7 Sept. 1854.
24 PRO, Work 1/45, p. 371; Work 19/9, ff. 3516, 3606–8; Royal Archives, Vic. Add /PP 62, 8 Jan., 23 March, 25 Aug., 19 Nov. 1855.
25 PRO, Work 1/49, pp. 8–9; *Letters of Queen Victoria* III, p. 190.
26 *The Builder*, 31 May 1856, 256; *ILN*, 18 July 1857, 51. Plate-glass mirror shutters had also been used by Prince Albert in the Drawing Room at Osborne in 1846.

89. The Promenade Gallery, Buckingham Palace, in 1873. The vases of flowers on the walls were painted in cheerful colours by Charles Moxon. They have since been covered over, but Nicola Consoni's paintings of cherubs on the frieze level are still visible.

somewhat similar in its proportions to Inigo Jones's Banqueting House in Whitehall, with a two-storied elevation and a compartmented ceiling with elaborate mouldings hiding the cast-iron roof trusses. The generous proportions made it possible to accommodate very large numbers of crinolined guests dancing the waltz, then at the height of its popularity, but the room was also 'admirable for music', resonant but free from echo,[27] and it came to be used for concerts and state

---

27 *The Builder*, 29 Dec. 1860, 835.

225

90. The Supper Room, Buckingham Palace, in its original state. The colourful decorative painting all disappeared when the room was remodelled in 1902.

banquets as well as for dances. There was a recess at the east end containing an organ (Plate 91), with a case designed by Pennethorne which still retains its early Renaissance arabesque decoration, and at the opposite end there was a throne inside an arched aedicule supported on Corinthian columns, with a bas-relief medallion of Victoria and Albert by Theed at the apex of the arch. Theed was also responsible for the bas-reliefs of the triumphs of Flora and Bacchus over the doorways and their matching mirrors which were praised for giving 'boldness and vigour to the general design of the apartments, which no flat painting could effect'.[28]

As in the Supper Room, the total effect depended as much upon the lighting and

---

28 *Art Journal*, 18 (1856), 192.

91. The Ballroom, Buckingham Palace, in its original state. Grüner's elaborate wall decorations are clearly visible, as is Pennethorne's organ case at the east end of the room.

colouring as upon proportion and architectural detail. Colour was a subject of absorbing interest to the mid Victorians, and the new Ballroom was one of the finest of all expressions of their taste for deep, rich colouring applied to the decoration of an interior (Colour Plate IV). The lower part of the walls was originally hung with red silk decorated in a criss-cross fashion, and the spaces between the windows were occupied by paintings of loosely-draped female figures, representing the Hours, on a blue background, painted from 'sketches by Raphael' by Consoni. The frieze and ceiling were covered with arabesques, 'grotesques' and mythical beasts designed by

227

Grüner but derived from Raphael's influential decoration of the loggias of the Vatican and the Villa Madama at Rome, which in turn drew their inspiration from Roman antiquity. The windows were lit up at night by gas-burners,[29] and there were more burners, combined with ventilation apparatus, in the ceiling compartments. Sir Charles Eastlake's wife gave a vivid account of the effect at the opening ball in 1856:

I was full of anticipations about the new ball-room and other rooms, but they far exceeded my expectations. The decorations of the ball-room are exquisite, the lighting most original and beautiful and the raised crimson seats . . . all that can be desired to look at, when filled with gorgeously dressed figures, and to look from . . . We were enchanted with the taste of the room, but heard the most ignorant stuff about it. One gentleman of high standing . . . lamented to my husband that better artists had not been employed to design the twenty-four Hours . . . Sir Charles heard him out, and then said: Very true, it is a great pity; the designs are only Raphael's. Another abused the introduction of the ornamental frieze of griffins above the hours as being taken from Nineveh, when there is hardly a decorated hall in Italy in which the griffin does not occur: and so on, simply finding fault à la Ruskin.[30]

From the western end of the Ballroom the Approach or West Gallery (Plate 92) led to the Dining Room and thence to the other state rooms on the garden front of the palace; there was also a third gallery, the Cross Gallery, added by Pennethorne at the suggestion of the Lord Chamberlain to link the Approach and Promenade galleries. Pennethorne's original design for these galleries remained relatively unaltered by Grüner and Prince Albert, and both have been less affected than the Ballroom and Supper Room by subsequent changes in taste. The wall paintings have been hidden, but Theed's boldly modelled relief carvings over the doors, representing the birth of Venus and Venus descending with the armour of Achilles still survive, as does Pennethorne's barrel-vaulted roof with its elaborate Roman-inspired coffering. Here alone in the Palace is it still possible to gauge his talent for designing impressive and richly-decorated interiors.

With the new wing completed, Pennethorne was asked in 1858 to design a wall stretching from the palace to the Royal Mews along Buckingham Gate and to re-face the outside of Sir William Chambers's riding house of 1766 with an enriched cornice and a bas-relief in the pediment. He transmitted working drawings for the urn-topped wall and the associated works in October, together with a design by Theed for a bas-relief of Hercules taming the horses of Diomedes for the pediment of the refaced Riding House, and the work was carried out in 1860.[31]

His last work at the Palace was the remodelling of the chapel and chapel approaches. Blore's chapel of 1843 was neither an aesthetic triumph nor a practical

---

29 PRO, Work 19/10/1, ff. 3–5.
30 C. Eastlake Smith (ed.), *Journals and Correspondence of Lady Eastlake*, III (1895), p. 85.
31 PRO, Work 1/65, p. 192; Work 19/10/2, f. 8; Crook and Port, *King's Works* vi, pp. 303–7.

92. The Approach or West Gallery at Buckingham Palace, as seen from the Ballroom. The Bacchic carving over the doorway in the foreground, by William Theed, was replaced when the Ballroom was remodelled in 1902, but his 'Birth of Venus' over the further doorway leading into the Dining Room still survives.

success, proving, as might be expected of a former conservatory, too hot in the summer and too cold in the winter.[32] The gallery in which the royal family sat was approached from the Dining Room through a narrow corridor with two right-angled bends, and in February 1860 Pennethorne reported that the approaches were too narrow for ordinary purposes and totally useless for State occasions. In the chapel itself the windows were too large, the roof too thin, and the seating arrangements inconvenient. A thorough remodelling was needed, and not a 'trifling or temporary relief'. He first sent in plans for alterations to the approaches, so that the chapel could be conveniently entered from both floors of the building, with a new staircase leading to the royal gallery alongside the new Approach Gallery, and this work was completed early in 1861.[33] Plans for alterations to the chapel followed, but the Office of Works, anxious not to ask the Treasury for money which would have to be voted by Parliament, balked at the expense, which was estimated at £8,140. In February 1860 therefore, Pennethorne sent in a modified proposal costing only £3,500. This involved adding a pedimented clerestory or lantern supported on iron trusses and building a rusticated screen wall with an arched niche joining the west wall to the new south wing.[34] These modest alterations were finished by the end of the year. More ambitious schemes for improvements inside the chapel were prepared by Prince Albert but discarded after his death, and Pennethorne's creative involvement with the Palace came to an end with the making of a new alabaster pulpit in 1863.[35] The chapel was bombed in the Second World War, and the present Queen's Gallery built within the walls.

In its account of the south wing, the *Art Journal* exclaimed that 'the good taste of the Queen and her august consort cannot ever have been more fully displayed than in the additions to their home – so happy a guide to every other home in her dominions'.[36] Unfortunately the rooms enjoyed a very short heyday, and the early cinquecento manner of interior decoration so assiduously promoted by Prince Albert never really caught on. Gloom descended upon the Court when Albert died in 1861, and in 1864 it was suggested, not for the first time, that the palace should be sold and used to house the National Gallery.[37] When the Queen finally started holding formal State ceremonies there, the accommodation in the Ballroom was found to be inadequate, and in 1872 John Taylor was called in to carry out minor alterations before adding a glass-roofed conservatory onto the south side in 1878, which was replaced in 1902 by the present Annexe Gallery.[38]

32 PRO, Work 19/294, f. 2.
33 *Ibid.*, ff. 7–8, 21; Work 34/487–97.
34 Broadlands Papers, WFC /P/27, Jan. 1861; PRO, Work 34/471–80; *The Builder*, 16 March 1861, 184.
35 PRO, Work 2/28, p. 80; Royal Archives, PP 1339, 1358, 1380, 1411, 1515, 1520, 1526.
36 *Art Journal*, 18 (1856), 192.
37 *BN*, 12 June 1863, 441; *The Builder*, 25 June 1864, 478.
38 PRO, Work 19/10/1, f. 46; Work 34/460–4.

This alteration spoilt the plain, clean lines of Pennethorne's south elevation, but far worse followed in 1902 when, as part of a general revulsion against mid-Victorian taste in interior design, Edward VII ordered the total remodelling of the Ballroom and Supper Room, to the designs of Frank Verity and C. H. Bessant. The colourful intricacy imparted by Pennethorne and Grüner now gave way to a more monumental, though also a more bland and lifeless, effect. The walls were white-washed, the mouldings simplified, and profuse gilding introduced in an attempt to make the rooms conform to the French *dix-huitième* taste currently in vogue. Since then there have been few changes, and in their present form the rooms testify both to the Francophile enthusiasm of the age of the *entente cordiale* and to Edward VII's determination to remove all traces of his parents' taste from the interiors of the royal palaces.

THE DUCHY OF CORNWALL OFFICE

Pennethorne's second commission for the royal family was for a much smaller building facing the Palace on the opposite side of Buckingham Gate. The Duchy of Cornwall has formed an important part of the revenues of the Princes of Wales ever since it was granted by Edward III to the Black Prince in the fourteenth century. In the mid 1800s the Duchy estates were administered from offices next to the Tax Office in the east wing of Somerset House.[39] The expansion of the Inland Revenue and its concentration at Somerset House after 1849 caused the tax officers to cast jealous eyes on the Duchy's premises, and early in 1853 the Treasury, urged on by Gladstone, the Chancellor of the Exchequer, insisted that either the Duchy or the Admiralty, which occupied the south range, would have to move out. The Admiralty refused to move, and Sir William Molesworth failed to find a suitable existing building to house the Duchy offices. He therefore recommended the construction of a new office on the ground cleared for the 'Pimlico Improvement', and in August 1853 the Prince Consort, as trustee of his son's hereditary revenue, agreed, subject only to the proviso that the new building should be fireproof and that the design should be approved by the Duchy's council.[40]

Pennethorne was an obvious choice as architect. The site was a prominent one, and Molesworth was anxious that the houses to be built on the rest of the ground should be of 'a new and better class' than their unimpressive predecessors.[41] A well-designed building would help attract wealthy tenants and would in itself improve the approaches of the palace. Pennethorne prepared a revised design incorporating suggestions made by Prince Albert and the Duchy council in November 1853, and

39 R. Needham and A. Webster, *Somerset House Past and Present* (1905), pp. 215, 245.
40 BL, Add MS 44381, ff. 177–9; PRO, Work 12/101/2, ff. 3–4.
41 *Hansard*, 135 (31 July 1854), 1031.

this was eventually put into effect, the cost, including that of compensation to the Crown estate, being shared between the Duchy and the government.[42] Work began in the late summer of 1854, but delays over the fittings meant that it was not occupied until early in 1857.[43]

In its original form the Duchy office is an accomplished exercise in the Italian Renaissance manner (Plate 93). Less austere than Pennethorne's earlier Italianate buildings like the Ordnance Office extension, it stands out from the common run of buildings of its type because of its successful exploitation of the corner site and the refinement of the decoration, which, in the words of one commentator, avoided 'that heavy excess of details which detracts from the effect of some of our modern examples of Anglo-Italian houses'.[44] The office was built of brick and faced with stucco – an echo of the Nash era. In its original form it had three stories: a rusticated ground floor over a basement, a *piano nobile* with windows in aedicules made up of Corinthian columns and pediments, and a second floor surmounted by a highly enriched frieze with roundels containing the Prince of Wales's feathers and a cornice. The entrance, in the centre, was approached by a short flight of steps and was flanked by Roman Doric columns supporting a balcony. Some of the subtlety of the design was also lost when the facades were needlessly remodelled and an extra storey added after the Second World War.[45]

The interior is ingeniously arranged on a butterfly-shaped plan (Plate 94), with the rooms arranged on either side of a central spine stretching through the building. The ground floor, resting on fireproof brick arches, is made up of offices and muniment rooms placed on either side of a hall, flanked by garlanded Ionic columns. This leads to a curved staircase, from which access is gained to an oval vestibule on the first floor with entrances to the council room, library and Prince's room. Bedrooms for the Duchy officials originally occupied the top floor. The Prince's room and the council chamber were intended to have elaborate plaster ceilings, but subsequent changes in taste, together with wartime bombing, have removed most of the original decoration except for that of the hall and some of the doorcases and chimneypieces.

MARLBOROUGH HOUSE

Marlborough House stands to the north of St James's Park, just to the east of St James's Palace and largely hidden from public view behind the houses of Pall Mall.

---

42 Rep. Commrs. of Woods, Forests, *PP* 1854–5, 29, p. 15.
43 PRO, Work 12/101/1.
44 *BN*, 6 Feb. 1857, 144.
45 There is a picture of the building in its original state in A. E. Richardson, *Monumental Classic Architecture in Great Britain and Ireland* (1914), p. 101.

93. The Duchy of Cornwall Office in its original state. An extra storey has since been added and other alterations made to the facade.

It was built in 1709–11 by Sir Christopher Wren as the London home of the first Duke and Duchess of Marlborough, but by the middle of the nineteenth century it had undergone many alterations. Sir William Chambers added an attic storey to the wings in 1771–3, and in the later 1770s and 1780s he and his pupil John Yenn remodelled the main ground floor rooms and added an entrance porch on the north side (Plate 95). When the lease to the Dukes of Marlborough expired in 1817 the house reverted to the Crown, eventually becoming the home of William IV's widow, Queen Adelaide. Large sums of money were spent on refurbishing the interiors for her benefit in 1837–8,[46] and in 1850, a year after her death, the house

46 Information from Dr Michael Turner, Crown Buildings and Monuments Advisory Group, English Heritage. The 1837–8 alterations were carried out under the supervision of John Phipps.

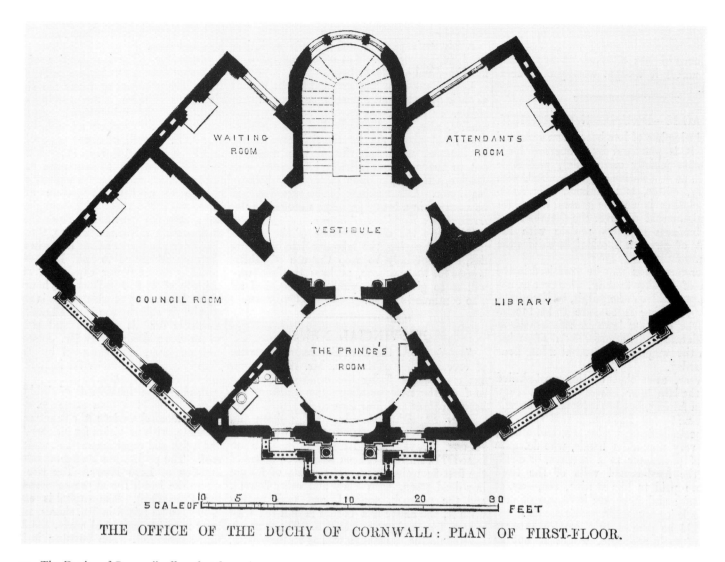

94. The Duchy of Cornwall office, first floor plan.

was earmarked as the future official residence of the Prince of Wales (later Edward VII). He was not allowed to occupy it until he reached the age of eighteen in 1859, and meanwhile it was used for various official purposes: as a temporary home for surplus pictures from the overcrowded National Gallery, as a museum for objects belonging to Henry Cole's Department of Practical Art and, for a short period, as offices for London University.

Pennethorne's involvement with the house began in July 1850 when he was asked to provide a design for a new stable block on ground to the east, behind the Ordnance Office in Pall Mall. Queen Adelaide had kept her horses in the old

234

95. The entrance front of Marlborough House in 1827, drawing by J. C. Buckler. A porch has been added and the attics of the wings raised since the house was first built, but otherwise the building is externally much as Sir Christopher Wren left it. Pennethorne's main contribution was to extend the ground floor forwards, adding the present carriage porch and a corridor linking the two wings.

Carlton House stables at the eastern end of Carlton House Terrace. Russell's government wanted to demolish the stables and the adjoining riding house so as to complete the terrace (a project not carried out until 1862), and as architect and surveyor to the Crown estate Pennethorne was the obvious choice as designer of what was never intended to be more than a modest, functional building.[47]

Nothing more was done until the house was taken over on behalf of the Prince of Wales at the beginning of 1859. After nine years in which the public had tramped through its rooms, the building was certainly in need of refurbishment. One writer

47 PRO, Work 19/18/1, ff. 172, 181–2.

thought that it was 'fitted neither for the display of princely state, nor domestic comfort . . . it is in every respect, both internally and externally, of the most prosaic and humdrum quality'.[48] The mid Victorians preferred elaborate Italianate mouldings to plain red brickwork and, given sufficient money, Pennethorne or some other architect would no doubt have been asked to build a new house, perhaps rivalling Stafford House or the magnificent new Dorchester House in Park Lane (1850–63). But in view of the recent overspending at Buckingham Palace, no government was prepared to face the wrath of the backbenchers by burdening the public funds with a brand new house for a youth of eighteen. So the Prince Consort decided to draw upon the Prince of Wales's own funds in order to bring the old-fashioned building up to date for the large-scale entertaining in which the Prince might be expected to indulge – and in which he did not disappoint expectations.

This object could not be achieved without a thorough internal remodelling and some structural alteration. Pennethorne was therefore asked for designs and submitted two alternative schemes to Prince Albert on 20 December 1859. The first and more expensive, costing some £46,000, would have moved the entrance to the west wing and provided a new ballroom beside the old main entrance which faced the backs of the houses in Pall Mall. The house would now be approached from a new gateway and lodge next to Inigo Jones's Queen's Chapel, where Pennethorne had recently driven his road linking St James's Street to the Mall. The second scheme, which Pennethorne claimed was 'not beyond such as is usually introduced into a first-class Residence for a Nobleman', kept the entrance on the north side, but added a new entrance hall and placed the new ballroom at the west end. It was estimated at £38,000. With certain revisions, including the omission of the ballroom, this scheme provided the basis of the alterations as they were eventually carried out. Work was conducted under the direction of the Prince's officials, with the Office of Works doing no more than paying a sum of £10,000 voted by Parliamentary grant.[49] The alterations began in the spring of 1860 and the house was handed over to the Prince of Wales at the end of 1862.[50]

Wren's house consisted of a 'double pile' main block with an entrance hall flanked by staircases and three smaller rooms on the south or garden front between slightly projecting wings containing 'apartments' with back stairs. Subsequent alterations removed nearly all the original interior decoration but, with the exception of the entrance hall, the rooms remained relatively small and not in any sense palatial. Most important of all, the house lacked a large dining room, drawing room and library which, taken together, were the *sine qua non* of mid-Victorian entertaining. Without making any major structural alterations,

---

48 *BN*, 21 Oct. 1859, 994.
49 PRO, Work 1/65, pp. 66–7; Work 19/18/1, ff. 179–83.
50 *Ibid.*, 19/18/1, f. 240; Royal Archives, Vic. Add /PP 1490.

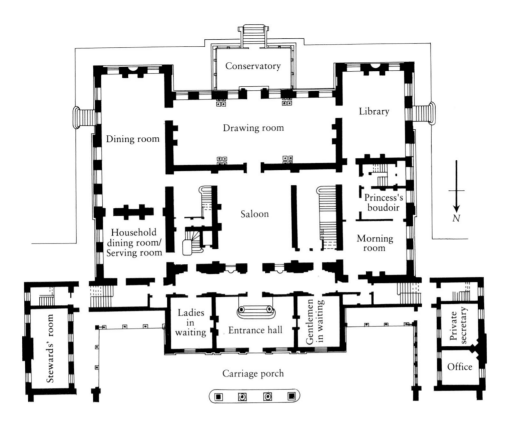

96. Ground floor plan of Marlborough House after remodelling by James Pennethorne. The main alterations were the creation of a new entrance and the formation of a new Dining Room and Drawing Room out of smaller rooms.

Pennethorne succeeded in supplying these needs, providing in the process a suitably lavish backdrop to the activities of the 'Marlborough House Set'.

Visitors now entered the house (Plate 96) through a carriage porch projecting far into the entrance courtyard, carried on Tuscan columns with bulbous urns on the balustrade. The porch led into an outer hall flanked by rooms for the ladies- and gentlemen-in-waiting, from which a flight of steps gave access to a transverse corridor lit by glazed saucer domes running along the front of the old house and linking the two already existing service wings. From here a doorway led into Wren's two-storied entrance hall (henceforth known as the Saloon), with a series of martial paintings by Louis Laguerre occupying the upper level; the main alterations here were the removal of a colonnade at the southern end and its replacement by a balcony at first-floor level supported on brackets, and the raising of the central panel of the ceiling into a skylight (since blocked in). The staircases on either side of the hall remain largely unaltered.

The most important of the new rooms was the Drawing Room (Plate 97), made out of the three small rooms (formerly the Small Drawing Room, Reception Room and Library) on the garden front. To compensate for the removal of the internal partitions Pennethorne inserted iron girders, but they were hidden by rich classical plasterwork. Painted Corinthian columns with 'fish-scale' decoration marked the divisions between the former rooms, and there was a highly enriched ceiling divided into panels. The doorway, and the mirrors set in intricately carved frames, were a development of the sumptuous manner of Buckingham Palace, as were the stencilled arabesque decorations on the walls; all this no doubt represented the taste of Prince Albert as well as that of Pennethorne. And, to add to the luxurious effect – so different from the *Biedermeier* neatness of the house in Queen Adelaide's time – a Conservatory was built out into the garden. The new Dining Room in the east wing was plainer. It was created by enlarging the existing drawing room to take in a small adjoining room and back stairs. A similar transformation took place in the west wing, where a new Library was created out of the former breakfast room with its adjoining bedroom and back stairs, remnants of one of Wren's apartments. A new back staircase was created to the north of the Library, beyond which was the Prince's Morning Room.

The house did not remain for long in the state in which Pennethorne had left it. A second floor was formed over the central block in 1870, just after his retirement, and in 1874 John Taylor built a new upstairs Study and Library for the Prince onto the north side of the central block.[51] Their neo-Jacobean internal decoration marked a major change in royal taste away from the Renaissance style espoused by Prince Albert. The addition of third floors to the wings in 1885 gave the house a disagreeably top-heavy appearance. Worse followed when a series of drastic internal alterations were carried out for the future George V and Queen Mary in 1902, and again by Queen Mary on behalf of her son, the future Edward VIII, in 1927–8. This new regime of bland neo-Georgian 'good taste' succeeded in draining the reception rooms of most of their character and vitality, and today the original effect can only be recaptured through old photographs.

Pennethorne's final contribution to Marlborough House was the building of the stables. Work had been delayed by the reluctance of successive governments to surrender the space in the old Carlton House stables and riding house. Eventually, though, in the summer of 1861, the Treasury allowed the demolition of the riding house to go ahead after the removal of the records stored there to the new Public Record office. Pennethorne was now instructed to work out detailed plans in consultation with Lieutenant-Colonel Maude, the Crown Equerry, and in December 1861 he produced four new plans 'in strict accordance with [Maude's] views and requirements'. The colonel had more lavish tastes than either Prince Albert or the government had envisaged, and the estimated cost now soared to

---

51 PRO, Work 19/18/1, ff. 241 *et seq.*; information from Dr Turner.

97. The Drawing Room of Marlborough House in the 1890s. The architectural framework is Pennethorne's, but Prince Albert had some influence on the decorative detailing.

£14,900. As with the house, the extra money came out of the Prince of Wales's own revenue, and work had begun by October 1862.[52]

In 1851 Pennethorne had proposed to build the stables in the form of a main block facing towards the Mall, with two wings projecting north. The horses were to be accommodated on two floors, with an inclined plane leading to the upper floor – an arrangement used by Nash in the old Carlton House stables. This scheme

---

52 *Ibid.*, ff. 213–27.

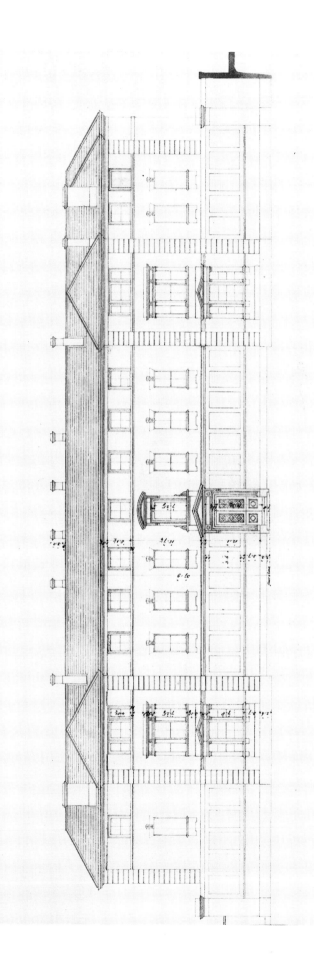

Elevation of South Front.

98. Marlborough House, the stable block, south front.

provided the basis for the stables as built, but there were some important modifications. The central block now contained the main coach-houses and was flanked by stables on either side, with harness rooms and offices in the wings. Most of the horses were accommodated on the first floor, and the stable-hands lived above them on the second floor. From the north or entrance side the building has the down-to-earth functional quality of many similar Victorian buildings, with its stock brick walls, glazed roof and frank exposure of iron columns. The red brick hipped-roofed garden front, by contrast, alludes to the late-seventeenth-century style of the house (Plate 98). Pennethorne was something of an architectural chameleon and, just as he had imitated Chambers at Somerset House and Nash at Buckingham Palace, he now showed himself capable of composing a facade in the manner of Wren and his contemporaries. He used some details borrowed from the main house like the 'aprons' under the first-floor windows, but in its overall effect the building is a creative reinterpretation rather than a copy. In this respect it is a little-known precursor of the 'Queen Anne' revival which was to have so considerable an effect on the architecture of late-nineteenth-century England.

8

THE REBUILDING OF WHITEHALL

THE IDEA OF rebuilding Whitehall as a centre of government can be traced back to Inigo Jones. His grandiose project for a new Palace of Whitehall fascinated later generations of architects, but nothing was done to realise it and in the mid nineteenth century the British Empire was still being governed from a disparate collection of buildings, some of which would have disgraced a town council. Overcrowding was increasing as the civil service grew, and the provision of extra office space in rented buildings offended the increasingly vocal apostles of administrative efficiency. They regretted the waste of public money and argued that the dispersal of offices led to delays in transacting business. Sir Charles Trevelyan, co-author of the celebrated Northcote–Trevelyan report on the Civil Service (1854), thought that 'to bring together all the Public Offices in the immediate neighbourhood of each other and of the Houses of Parliament is a national object of great permanent importance, and it is especially necessary in a financial point of view'.[1] The concentration of government offices was supported by the press and, with the inefficiencies of the Crimean War in mind, a writer in the *Building News* later asked: 'Who knows but if the heads of the War Department and Treasury had been accustomed to communicate personally more than once a year, that all the disasters of the Crimea would not have been avoided? . . . Non-concentration has jeopardised our honour and slain thousands.'[2]

The concentration of offices would finally enable Whitehall and its surroundings to be rebuilt in a manner befitting its role as the seat of government of the richest and most powerful nation in the world; Inigo Jones's vision could thus be realised. Most of the old Palace of Whitehall was destroyed by fire in 1697, but the area (Plate 99) was never laid out as a whole. By the beginning of the nineteenth century it boasted some impressive public buildings: Jones's Banqueting House – the only part of the palace to survive to modern times; the Admiralty of 1723–6; William Kent's

---

1 PRO, T 1/6094B/18482.   2 *BN*, 17 Sept. 1858, 928.

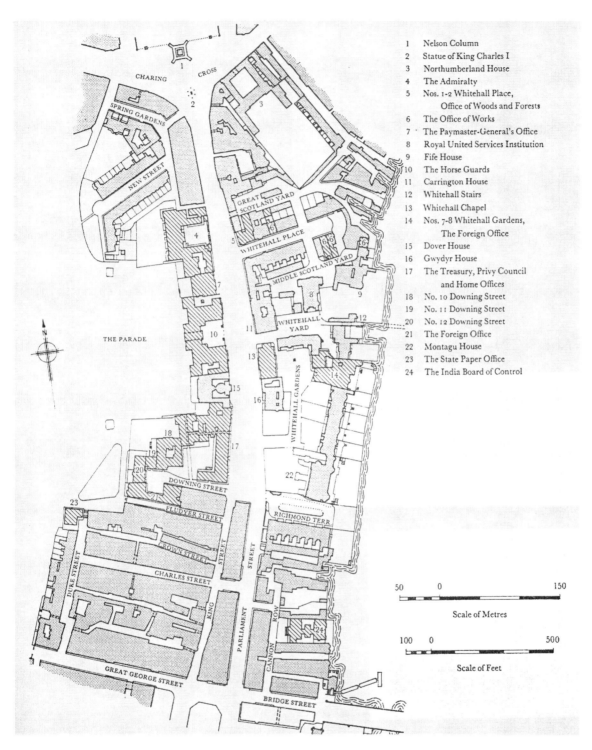

1	Nelson Column
2	Statue of King Charles I
3	Northumberland House
4	The Admiralty
5	Nos. 1-2 Whitehall Place, Office of Woods and Forests
6	The Office of Works
7	The Paymaster-General's Office
8	Royal United Services Institution
9	Fife House
10	The Horse Guards
11	Carrington House
12	Whitehall Stairs
13	Whitehall Chapel
14	Nos. 7-8 Whitehall Gardens, The Foreign Office
15	Dover House
16	Gwydyr House
17	The Treasury, Privy Council and Home Offices
18	No. 10 Downing Street
19	No. 11 Downing Street
20	No. 12 Downing Street
21	The Foreign Office
22	Montagu House
23	The State Paper Office
24	The India Board of Control

99. Whitehall in the mid nineteenth century, before the building of the Victoria Embankment and the Foreign and Colonial Offices; the cross-hatching represents public buildings.

Treasury, facing Horse Guards Parade, and the Horse Guards itself, built posthumously to his design as the headquarters of the Commander-in-Chief of the Army. There were also some aristocratic town houses, many of them now occupied by government departments, and streets of modest terraced housing – of which Downing Street is now the only survivor – leading off to St James's Park on one side and to the quays and muddy inlets of the unembanked River Thames on the other.

For all its undoubted charm, this was not the stuff of which imperial capitals should be made, and for much of the nineteenth century government officials, architects and assorted pundits toiled over projects for rebuilding the area – something which was not finally accomplished until the twentieth century. Pennethorne, whose office stood just to the north of the old Privy Garden of Whitehall Palace, was one of these architects and, starting in 1854, he produced a series of ever more ambitious plans for new government offices. These projects gave him the opportunity to design some of his most impressive buildings, but they fell victim, like so many of his designs, to political expediency and in the end none of his designs was carried out. They nevertheless occupy an important place both in the evolution of his own architectural style and in the never-ending saga of unbuilt London.

THE FOREIGN OFFICE

No story in the annals of Victorian architecture in England has been more often told than that of the building of the Foreign Office. A mismanaged competition, changes in government, and a controversy over style ensured that the choice of design took place against a background of publicity and fierce partisanship. In this drama Pennethorne is usually made to play Rosencrantz or Guildenstern to Gilbert Scott's Hamlet. In fact, his role is much more crucial than most writers have realised.

In the mid nineteenth century the Foreign Office occupied four former private houses at the western end of Downing Street (nos. 15–18) on the opposite side of Whitehall to the former Palace, and another two behind them in the now long-demolished Fludyer Street to the south (Plate 100).[3] The Colonial Office, whose importance naturally increased as the Empire expanded, occupied two adjoining houses (nos. 13–14) in Downing Street. It was always assumed that any new premises would go on or near the site of the existing buildings, situated as they were only a short walk from the Houses of Parliament. But expansion was bound to be

---

3 J. M. Crook and M. H. Port, *The History of the King's Works* VI (1973), pp. 551–62; I. L. Toplis, *The Foreign Office: an Architectural History* (1987), pp. 11–16.

100. The site of the new government offices in 1829, drawing by J. C. Buckler. William Kent's Treasury building is on the left, behind the Horse Guards and 10 Downing Street. The bow-windowed houses on the extreme right are part of the old Foreign Office which stood between Downing Street and Fludyer Street.

costly. Quite apart from the cost of the buildings themselves, much of the land in the adjacent streets was still in private ownership and would have to be compulsorily purchased.

As so often in government architecture in Britain, a succession of magnificent plans languished for want of the magnificent means with which to carry them out. Sir John Soane produced a plan for building new government offices on both sides of Downing Street in 1822, but only the northern part was carried out, in a modified form. This block of buildings, fronting Whitehall, housed the Home Office, the Privy Council and the Board of Trade. It was rebuilt in 1844–5 by Charles Barry with a more enriched facade, and Barry subsequently went on to

245

prepare elaborate – and abortive – plans for extending the building northwards and for rebuilding the Horse Guards as part of a 'Place d'Armes . . . second to none in Europe'.[4] The area south of Downing Street, to the east of the Foreign Office, was cleared of buildings in the 1830s, and between 1836 and 1838 Decimus Burton produced several designs for building new offices there. A Commons Select Committee found in 1839 that the existing Foreign Office was too dilapidated to warrant repairing, and recommended a plan which involved the building of a new Foreign and Colonial Office on the site of the existing buildings. Together with other offices on the south side of Downing Street, a new 'Downing Square' would thus be created. These plans were shelved because of the Melbourne government's lack of money. Later governments found Burton's designs too cramped, and objected to his proposed Foreign and Colonial Offices encroaching on St James's Park. His scheme was therefore abandoned.[5]

Meanwhile the Foreign Office was becoming ever more overcrowded and dilapidated. The eastern wall began to give way and had to be shored up in 1845, and in 1848 piles of documents had to be moved from one of the upper floors 'because the weight of them would hazard the stability of the building'. Even worse, in 1852 the Foreign Secretary was 'nearly overwhelmed . . . by the whole ceiling of the room coming down just after he had left the table at which he had been sitting'.[6] Reforms in office administration made the buildings appear all the more unsuitable. Pennethorne told a Commons Select Committee in 1855 that all the buildings around Downing Street were in a bad state of repair; their foundations rested on peat, and they had settled considerably. Some could be expected to stand for twenty or thirty years, but none was worth repairing: 'The Foreign Office is now propped or tied up in various parts . . . It is now quite impossible for anybody to go into the lower rooms . . . which are now occupied by bookbinders and printers, without seeing at once that they are improper places for workmen to be in; they are close and dark, badly ventilated, and improper in every respect'.[7]

It was the Foreign Office's misfortune that its own relatively modest plans for rebuilding were tangled up at a very early stage with the grandiose ideas of the administrative reformers. Soon after its formation in December 1853, the Aberdeen administration decided to include a new Foreign Office in a comprehensive plan for the remodelling of the whole Downing Street area. Administrative reform was in the air. The Northcote–Trevelyan committee had completed its investigations. The economy was reasonably buoyant, and a large-scale scheme for building

---

4 Crook and Port, *King's Works*, VI, pp. 551–62; A. Barry, *Life and Works of Sir Charles Barry* (1867), pp. 276–7.

5 BL, Add Ms 43200, f. 64; Rep. Sel. Cttee. on Downing Street Public Offices Extension Bill, *PP* 1854–5, 7 [382], pp. 7–8.

6 PRO, T 25/19, p. 254; *Hansard*, 101 (11 Aug. 1848), 100; 139 (15 June 1855), 2015.

7 Rep. Sel. Cttee. on Public Offices Bill (1854–5), pp. 1–4.

government offices could be contemplated without excessive qualms about the cost. Pennethorne, with his long experience as architectural adviser at the Office of Works, must have seemed an obvious person to draw up a general plan and to design the buildings cheaply and efficiently. He therefore sent in a plan intended to 'enunciate general principles' in April 1854, a month after the outbreak of the Crimean War, and in the following month Sir William Molesworth asked him to send in plans 'on a more expanded scale' showing buildings on each side of Downing Street, which was to be continued west into St James's Park.[8] Molesworth meanwhile told a Committee of Supply that he was prepared to order the redevelopment of Downing Street as soon as the Chancellor of the Exchequer sanctioned the expenditure.[9]

The money was not granted, probably because official minds were beginning to be attracted by yet more grandiose designs. Henry Tarring, better known for his nonconformist churches, published a plan for the layout of the whole area towards the end of 1854,[10] and in June Pennethorne was asked to prepare plans for offices which would spread south from Downing Street across Fludyer Street to Crown Street, including some vacant land belonging to the Crown on the edge of St James's Park. Accommodation would now be provided not only for the Foreign Office, but also for the Colonial Office, the War Office and the Board of Trade, and there would be official houses for the Prime Minister and Chancellor of the Exchequer (replacing nos. 10 and 11 Downing Street) and a suite of ministerial reception rooms. The offices would be built gradually as funds became available and the cost, including that of purchasing the land, was estimated at £502,000, subsequently revised upwards to £580,000. In September Molesworth asked Pennethorne to produce elevations of the Foreign Office buildings on the south side of Downing Street and plans of each floor. Plainness was the order of the day. The buildings were to be of brick, with stone dressings, but those to the north of Downing Street, for which Pennethorne had not yet prepared elevations, might be 'richer and more architectural'. This scheme was quashed when the Cabinet decided that Downing Street should not be continued into St James's Park because of the resulting traffic noise and lack of privacy.

Pennethorne now prepared another set of plans preserving the seclusion of Downing Street, and they were approved by the Treasury in November 1854. He prepared a detailed plan of the ground as a first step towards gaining Parliamentary approval and in January 1855 he submitted yet another set of plans and drawings, including two coloured perspective sketches. The new design differed substantially

---

8 The complex story of Pennethorne's plans can be pieced together from PRO, T 1/6693A/3774; Work 12/84/1; Rep. Sel. Cttee. on Public Offices Bill (1854–5) and Rep. Sel. Cttee. on Foreign Office Reconstruction, *PP* 1857–8, 11 [417].

9 *Hansard*, 133 (8 June 1854), 1278.

10 *The Builder*, 25 Nov. 1854, 601.

from the one which the Cabinet had rejected. The buildings were now to be laid out in an altogether more ambitious and architecturally satisfying manner around a quadrangle (Plate 101) bounded by Horse Guards Parade, Whitehall, Crown Street and St James's Park – an idea for which Molesworth took the credit. Downing Street and Fludyer Street were to disappear completely, and provision was to be made for a southern extension to take in the ground between Crown Street and Charles Street, although this was not included in the initial Bill for the compulsory purchase of the ground.[11] Pennethorne later claimed that his design was framed with reference to Soane's original views on the development of Whitehall; it was certainly intended to introduce an element of grandeur and coherence to the layout of an area in which these qualities had never been allowed to develop. The idea of the quadrangle may well have been influenced too by Somerset House, where his new western extension was nearing completion. It introduces a theme which was eventually taken up by Gilbert Scott and Matthew Digby Wyatt when they were finally commissioned to build the present Foreign Office/India Office complex.

The most important part of the project was a massive four-storied block of offices with a raised central section and corner pavilions facing St James's Park.[12] The wall-surfaces are more richly decorated than in Pennethorne's earlier government buildings, but the overall effect is still one of classical poise. The Foreign Office was to occupy the south-western corner of the proposed square and spill over into a plain three-storied building on the vacant ground next to Sir John Soane's *palazzo*-like State Paper Office on the edge of the site. On the Whitehall side he proposed to build a replica of the Board of Trade office and to demolish the houses at the southern end of the street which blocked the view of Westminster Abbey.

Lord Aberdeen resigned in January 1855 in the wake of criticism of his government's handling of the Crimean War. Pennethorne nevertheless continued to work on his designs under Molesworth, who stayed on as First Commissioner of Works under Palmerston. Molesworth wanted the undertaking to be carried out 'with the greatest possible expedition', starting with the Foreign Office, and in February Pennethorne reported that work could be begun in the spring. He supplied a modified version of the design in April 1855, allowing for more space in the Foreign Office to be provided by adding an extra storey to the building adjoining the State Paper Office and by replacing the parapet with a low-pitched hipped roof of Italianate character (Plate 102). The Colonial Office, on ground to the south belonging to Sir Samuel Fludyer and the Dean and Chapter of Westminster, was to be built in 1856, and both buildings would be ready by 1858. Work could then begin on the north range, containing new official houses for the Prime Minister and Chancellor of the Exchequer, and the much larger west range – for the War Office

---

11 PRO, Work 30/975, 30/977.
12 There is a faded contemporary photograph of a lost perspective drawing dating from early 1855 in the collection of Mr Peter Laing.

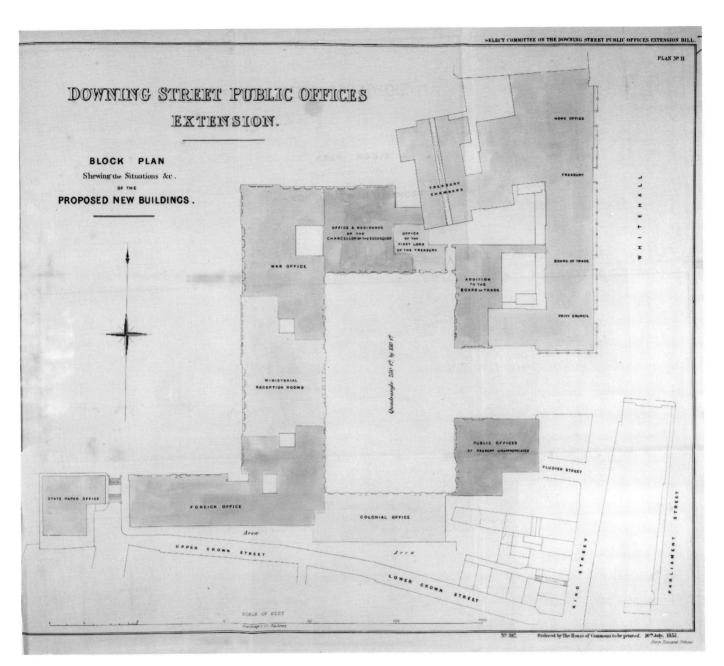

SELECT COMMITTEE ON THE DOWNING STREET PUBLIC OFFICES EXTENSION BILL.

PLAN Nº II

DOWNING STREET PUBLIC OFFICES EXTENSION.

BLOCK PLAN

Shewing the Situations &c.

OF THE

PROPOSED NEW BUILDINGS.

HOME OFFICE

TREASURY

TREASURY CHAMBERS

OFFICE & RESIDENCE
OF THE
CHANCELLOR OF THE EXCHEQUER

OFFICE
OF THE
FIRST LORD
OF THE TREASURY

WAR OFFICE

BOARD OF TRADE

ADDITION
TO THE
BOARD OF TRADE

PRIVY COUNCIL

WHITEHALL

MINISTERIAL
RECEPTION ROOMS

Quadrangle 250 ft. by 150 ft.

PUBLIC OFFICES
AT PRESENT UNAPPROPRIATED

FLUDYER STREET

STATE PAPER OFFICE

FOREIGN OFFICE

COLONIAL OFFICE

Area

Area

UPPER CROWN STREET

LOWER CROWN STREET

KING STREET

PARLIAMENT STREET

SCALE OF FEET

Nº 382.   Ordered by The House of Commons to be printed. 10ᵗʰ July, 1855.

101. Plan showing the layout of Pennethorne's proposed government offices. The scheme entailed the demolition of all the buildings to the right of the Treasury in Plate 100 and the disappearance of Downing Street and Fludyer Street.

102. Design for the new government offices on the Downing Street site, April 1855. The War Office, Foreign Office and a suite of ministerial reception rooms occupy the large block in the centre. The block to the right is for the Foreign Office and the lower block next to it is Sir John Soane's State Paper Office. The lake of St James's Park is in the foreground.

and ministerial reception rooms – facing St James's Park. This block was now to be given a low pediment absent from the earlier design. The new range fronting Whitehall would follow at an unspecified later date.

The Downing Street Public Offices Bill was introduced into Parliament on the day after Pennethorne submitted his drawings. Its prime object was to replace the Foreign and Colonial Offices, which Molesworth called 'perfect nuisances', and Parliament was asked to vote a sum of £90,000 to enable the extra property to be purchased.[13] For the next two months Pennethorne was involved in working out the planning of the interior with Edmund Hammond, a former diplomat who had become permanent under-secretary at the Foreign Office. The main entrance was to face east into the new quadrangle and would lead into a spacious hall and staircase leading up to the first floor apartments for the Foreign Secretary – a feature later incorporated into Gilbert Scott's building. Most of the staff accommodation was to go in a block next to the State Paper Office.[14] The plans were approved by the Foreign Secretary and, on the reasonable assumption that work was about to begin, Pennethorne sent in detailed elevations and some working drawings in August.

The first check to the scheme came from Parliament. The Public Offices Bill passed its third reading in the Commons unopposed, but in a Committee of Supply on 31 July 1855, Sir Francis Baring, MP for Portsmouth, expressed a fear that if work were to start on the Foreign Office the government would be committed to carry out the plans in full, at a far greater cost than the architect had anticipated. Molesworth now explained that a Select committee which had recently discussed the Bill had only recommended acquiring the land, and had not specifically advocated the adoption of Pennethorne's scheme at all. Palmerston, fearing a backbench revolt at a time when the Crimean War was still raging and party discipline slight, therefore proposed a vote of £10,000 for temporarily patching up the existing Foreign Office, and another of £30,000 for acquiring the land between Fludyer Street and Crown Street; another committee would be appointed in the next session to consider the plans for the new building in more detail.[15] This proposal won general assent.

The issue was further complicated when the Bill was read for the second time in the Lords. Lord Redesdale, the Chairman of Committees, urged the acquisition of the whole area between Downing Street and Great George Street (now Parliament Square), which was 'covered with as poor buildings as any part of the metropolis'. The present Bill, he said, did not go far enough, and would only have the effect of forcing up the price of the ground to the south, which would have to be bought

13 *Hansard*, 137 (26 April 1855), 1830–1.
14 PRO, Work 30/890–2. Pennethorne also made a model of the new building, but this has been lost.
15 *Hansard*, 139 (31 July 1855), 1575–5; M. H. Port, 'Pride and Parsimony: Influences affecting the development of the Whitehall quarter in the 1850s', *London Journal*, 2 (1976), 183.

103. Design for new government offices between Downing Street and Great George Street (Parliament Square), August–September 1855. The buildings face a Parliament Street widened by the demolition of the houses at the southern end. Most of the site is now occupied by Brydon's New Government Offices of 1898–1902.

sooner or later.[16] Molesworth's Bill, in its amended form, gained the royal assent, but the idea of building on a larger scale had now been implanted in official minds, notably that of Sir Benjamin Hall, who had just become First Commissioner. Hall shared Molesworth's belief in administrative reform, even if it involved going against the other Radical shibboleth of cutting government spending, and he was a great admirer of the *grands projets* with which Napoleon III was currently transforming Paris. Within a month of taking office he wrote that 'if there was to be any plan for alterations of Buildings, it should be a great plan for all the office – part to be executed annually'.[17] *The Builder* added its voice to the debate by lamenting that £25,000 a year was being spent on renting government offices, and calling on Hall to 'give the profession a fair chance' by holding a competition for the development of the site.[18]

Hall's first move was to ask Pennethorne to prepare sketches for building on an expanded site of ten acres (four hectares) stretching all the way from Downing Street to Great George Street. He produced four separate schemes at the end of August 1855, which he estimated would cost between £1,750,000 and £2,450,000, and three weeks later Hall asked him to produce more detailed plans based on 'Design no. 4', the estimated cost of which was two million pounds. Pennethorne later claimed that this final scheme was approved in October and that he was encouraged to begin work on more detailed drawings which he described as 'numerous, very complete and highly finished'; they were delivered to Hall after some revision in February 1856.[19] Only one of these drawings is now known to survive – a revised version of the building originally planned for the Downing Street site (Colour Plate v) – and there is also a faded contemporary photograph of another, showing the southern complex of buildings as seen from the present Parliament Street (Plate 103). They allow us to judge what London lost when Pennethorne was passed over as architect.

The Downing Street building in its revised form would have been lower and much more monumental than originally intended. The design owes more to the classical tradition as developed in France and Germany than to the Italian Renaissance, and it marks an important turning point in the evolution of Pennethorne's own architectural style. The low turrets in the earlier schemes are left out, and the massive structure is now enclosed within a giant Corinthian order supporting an enriched frieze with a severe Grecian attic – influenced surely by Schinkel's Schauspielhaus in Berlin (1818-21) – in the centre. A lower block links this very impressive building to a more elaborately detailed tower which stands in the place of the Foreign Office building originally intended for the site next to the State Paper Office. From here a four-storied block stretches south towards

16 *Hansard*, 139 (2 Aug. 1855), 1623.
17 PRO, Work 12/84/1, f. 137.   18 *The Builder*, 11 Aug. 1855, 382.
19 PRO, T 1/6693A/3774; *The Builder*, 25 Aug. 1877, 853.

Parliament Square. Pennethorne obviously hoped to treat the southern part of the expanded site as a single unit, with offices arranged around courtyards, but he breaks up the very long facades with towers placed at regular intervals. Unity is imposed by the discipline of the orders and the long continuous cornices, but a note of the sublime is introduced by pairs of taller towers facing Parliament Street and St James's Park. Against the leafy background of the park, with the Houses of Parliament and Westminster Abbey to the south, the effect would have been superb, even if a little overpowering.

In the end nothing came of any of Pennethorne's schemes. 'Benjamin the Magnificent' had already crossed swords with Pennethorne and, with the War Office also asking for new premises (see below, pp. 258–62), he decided in April 1856 to appoint a Select Committee to discuss plans for concentrating all the major public departments in Whitehall. Only two witnesses were called: Henry Hunt and Charles Trevelyan, both of whom shared Hall's ideas about the government offices. The designs for the new buildings were now to be chosen through competition 'in order', as Hall tartly remarked, 'that we might at last have some public building worthy of the metropolis'.[20] He also took steps to place the negotiations for purchasing the property on the Downing Street site in the hands of Henry Hunt, the new surveyor in the Office of Works. Pennethorne protested, but Hall told him that he could not 'accede to your request that you should be absolutely selected as the Architect of this great work merely because you are the Official Architect of the Department'.[21] Incensed, Pennethorne submitted a 'Memorial' to the Treasury in which he claimed that the abandonment of his designs for the Whitehall site was a breach of faith. In reply, Hall maintained that he had never wanted elaborate designs, and was 'much surprised' when presented with detailed drawings, which in any case he found objectionable.[22]

After more than a century, it is impossible to determine the precise rights and wrongs of the case. Clearly it was impossible to reconcile Hall's strongly held belief in the competitive principle with Pennethorne's equally strongly held wish to be granted a commission which would finally enable him to be placed with Barry and Cockerell as one of the leading classical architects of his age. Unfortunately Pennethorne's position in the Office of Works was not strong enough to prevent Hall from holding the competition on which he had set his heart and the official response to Pennethorne's complaint was that, while he deserved payment for the designs, he had 'misunderstood' his instructions in August 1855.[23]

The subsequent story is well known. In July 1856 the Select Committee endorsed Hall's proposal to hold three competitions: for the Foreign Office, for the War

---

20 *Hansard*, 141 (4 April 1856), 466–7; *BN*, 13 Aug. 1858, 807.
21 PRO, Work 1/50, pp. 195–6.
22 Rep. Sel. Cttee. on Foreign Office reconstruction (1857–8), pp. 129–30, 183–7.
23 *Hansard*, 175 (30 May 1864), 849.

Office on a much enlarged site, and for a block plan for the development of the whole area.[24] The competitions, announced in September, were doomed from the beginning because Hall – who was not a member of the Cabinet – failed to persuade Palmerston's government to pledge itself to abide by the results, or even to erect the buildings for which designs were invited. Income tax had doubled in the Crimean War, and a large budget deficit had been incurred. The Treasury was therefore less willing than ever to embark on what might turn out to be open-ended commitments to large public expenditure. Palmerston's own main concern was to rehouse the Foreign Office, where he had spent so many years himself, and in October, just after the competitions had been publicly advertised, he told Hall that the Cabinet had decided to abandon the plan to 'concentrate' the War Office in Whitehall. Instead, a new Foreign and Colonial Office would be built on the ground between Downing Street and Fludyer Street. The Prime Minister wondered, understandably, 'whether the Artists of Europe will not think that they have been trifled with in being asked to send in Plans for an undertaking which the Govt. had on consideration determined not to attempt'.[25] Palmerston has often been blamed for his role in the ensuing debacle, but at this stage at least it seems that his main fault was in failing to restrain Hall from holding the competition at all.

The competition entries were exhibited in Westminster Hall in May 1857, and the prizes were awarded in the following month.[26] The winning designs attracted little praise at Westminster, and the government refused to commit itself to carry any of them out. The Chancellor of the Exchequer, Sir George Cornewall Lewis, remarked to Palmerston that 'these schemes seem to assume that we are living in the Rome of Romulus, and are in a moment to convert it into the Rome of Augustus. The fact is that we are not lodged in straw huts, and that we cannot immediately provide marble palaces for all the public departments'.[27] MPs agreed in August to the government's request for a grant of £80,000 to complete the purchase of the site earmarked for the Foreign Office under the 1855 Act, and two days after Parliament rose Edmund Hammond was told that the Foreign Office would be built to Pennethorne's original design.[28]

The attempt to reinstate Pennethorne emanated from the Treasury, but it must presumably have been endorsed by Palmerston who later said that his designs 'had the merit of external simplicity combined with a sufficiency of ornament, and also harmonized with the other buildings in the locality' – something that was not true of the prizewinning designs.[29] In October the economist James Wilson, Financial

---

24 Rep. Sel. Cttee. on Public Offices, *PP* 1856, 14 [368], pp. iii–iv, 18–21, etc.
25 Broadlands Papers, GC/HA/55, 13 Oct. 1856.
26 The best recent accounts of the competition are in D. Brownlee, 'G. G. Scott's Design for the Government Offices', *Architectural History*, 28 (1985), 164–82 and Toplis, *Foreign Office*, pp. 20–65.
27 Broadlands Papers, GC/LE/74.
28 *Hansard*, 147 (24 July, 10–11 Aug. 1857), 364, 1295–311, 1459.
29 *The Saturday Review*, 24 July 1858, 83; *Hansard*, 152 (18 Feb. 1859), 523.

Secretary to the Treasury, asked Hall to re-examine Pennethorne's plans of 1855 and report on whether they would furnish the extra accommodation needed in view of a recent increase in the establishment. Decimus Burton had just been paid for his schemes of 1839, and the Treasury officials did not want to have to compensate Pennethorne too, let alone embark on the uncertain expense of carrying out the designs of one of the winning competitors. The decision not to go ahead with the purchase of the extra land intended by Hall had, in Wilson's opinion, invalidated the competition and restored matters to the status quo. This point of view was vociferously attacked by Hall, who claimed that 'the monopoly of erecting Government buildings by an officer of the Board, paid by the same amount of percentage on the outlay as other architects would claim, is by no means advisable, and is a source of discouragement to other architects'.[30]

The Foreign Office might nevertheless have been built to Pennethorne's designs had not William Tite, the only architect Member of Parliament, asked Hall to publish his recent correspondence with the Treasury.[31] Tite shared Pennethorne's classical bias and seems to have wanted him to be reinstated as architect, but he reckoned without the partisan zeal of the Gothic Revivalists. When the letters were printed Gilbert Scott, whose Gothic design in the Foreign Office competition had won him the third prize, felt, in his own words, 'at liberty to stir' on behalf of the competitors. He enlisted the support of the Royal Institute of British Architects, and in March 1858 sent a 'Memorial' to Lord John Manners, First Commissioner in the new Conservative administration which had recently replaced Palmerston's.[32] On the following day that other champion of secular Gothic, Beresford Hope, moved for a copy of this document to be placed before the House of Commons, claiming that:

all the promises which had been made to the [competing] architects had been thrown to the winds, and an attempt had been made by the Treasury to force on the Department of Works an old worn-out plan designed years ago by a gentleman who was very respectable in his private character, but who was atrociously unfit to execute any great national work.[33]

Now that the question had been thrown open to public opinion – at least that of the increasingly well-organised architectural profession – Lord Derby's minority government could hardly fail to pay attention. A new Select Committee was therefore appointed under Hope's chairmanship. The report, published after some internal disagreement in July 1858, virtually destroyed Pennethorne's revived hopes of designing the Foreign Office, and set the scene for the famous 'Battle of the

---

30 Copy of Correspondence . . . in relation to the erection of Public Offices in Downing Street, *PP* 1857–8, 48 [83], pp. 8–12.
31 *Hansard*, 148 (11 Feb. 1858), 1165–7.
32 G. G. Scott, *Personal and Professional Recollections* (1879), p. 180; *The Builder*, 6 Aug. 1859, 515.
33 *Hansard*, 149 (25 March 1858), 782.

Styles' in which Scott won his pyrrhic victory. While recognising that the competition did not bind the government to employ any of the competitors, a majority of the Committee succeeded in inserting a clause to the effect that it would be 'contrary to the public interest' not to do so.[34] One of the factors held against Pennethorne was that his designs of 1855 did not provide enough space for the enlarged requirements of the Foreign Office, although Edmund Hammond thought that if it could be expanded to the east and south it would still be more convenient than any of the prizewinning designs. More important, the practical advantages and aesthetic qualities of his design were submerged in a debate about style and about the rights and wrongs of architectural competitions. According to the writer of a series of articles in the *Building News*, the Committee's evidence showed that Pennethorne had been 'the victim of a most detestable system – a sufferer from routine and red-tape'. His scheme had never been properly considered by the public, and on practical grounds it was better than those of the prizewinners. If he did not receive the commission, it would probably go not to the first prizewinners Henry Coe and Henry Hofland, but to the second, Banks and Barry, or the third, Scott, all of whom had more powerful friends on the Committee.[35]

This prediction was soon proved true. The Tory Lord John Manners favoured Scott – son of an Anglican clergyman and an assiduous church builder – over both the unknown Coe and Hofland and the younger Charles Barry, whose father was the favourite architect of the Whig aristocracy. And as a former member of the 'Young England' group he was perhaps inclined to look on the Gothic Revival with more sympathy than other Victorian First Commissioners; he certainly claimed on a later occasion that a Gothic building would suit the *genius loci* of Westminster better than a classical one.[36] His biographer even claimed that the selection of Scott's Gothic design was 'the last occasion in which Young England found a practical expression in the House of Commons'.[37]

When Scott was finally confirmed as architect in November 1858 the 'Battle of the Styles' entered into the heart of the Palace of Westminster. The fall of Derby's government in May brought Palmerston back to power, but despite his earlier advocacy of Pennethorne he reluctantly conceded that Scott could not be abandoned.[38] Instead, he persuaded Scott to renounce his 'monastic' Gothic design and, after further changes of plan, to build the Foreign Office in its present form (Plate 104). This decision put paid to the machinations of the Goths and ensured that the rebuilding of Whitehall would continue in the classical style, with results which can be seen today. Pennethorne was finally paid for his own designs in

---

34 Rep. Sel. Cttee. on Foreign Office Reconstruction (1857–8), pp. iii–vii.
35 *BN*, 23 July 1858, 735; 6 Aug. 1858, 784–5; 10 Sept. 1858, 904.
36 *Hansard*, 152 (18 Feb. 1859), 519; D. Brownlee, *Architectural History*, 28 (1985), 168.
37 C. Whibley, *Lord John Manners and his Friends*, II (1925), pp. 77–8.
38 *The Builder*, 6 Aug. 1859, 515–16.

August 1864, after William Cowper, Manners's replacement as First Commissioner, had persuaded a sceptical House of Commons that 'it would not be honest of Parliament not to compensate an architect for work fairly done, and which had been of great use in forming a decision on the subject'.[39]

Discussion of the Foreign Office controversy has always suffered from the failure properly to assess Pennethorne's plans. It has been assumed, even in the most recent accounts, that these designs were mediocre and unimaginative, and that Hall's decision to call a competition opened the way to the selection of a better design. In fact Pennethorne's designs were not only preferred by the people who were going to use the building, the Foreign Office officials; they also had a coherence which the present building lacks, for all its scenic and picturesque qualities. This should be no cause for surprise; Pennethorne was at his weakest in his Gothic buildings, just as Scott was in his only major excursion into the classical manner. It is difficult therefore not to come to the conclusion that Pennethorne should have been allowed to design the Foreign Office.

THE WAR OFFICE

One of the aims of both Sir William Molesworth and Sir Benjamin Hall in planning new government offices in Whitehall was to concentrate the departments concerned with the army into a single building. The office of Secretary of State for War was created in 1854, and in the next two years it swallowed up the two-hundred-year-old department of the Secretary at War and the even more venerable Ordnance department. The new War Office was temporarily placed in Pembroke House, Whitehall, but the division between it and the Ordnance buildings in Pall Mall remained a drawback to efficiency. Pennethorne's successful completion of the Ordnance Office extension in 1851 made him a natural choice as architect for a new headquarters for the combined department, and in 1854 Molesworth asked him to include premises for the new War Office in his scheme for concentrating government offices in the Downing Street area. In his block plan (Plate 101), published in the following year, he showed the Office occupying space in the massive block he hoped to build overlooking Horse Guards Parade, close to the Horse Guards, the Foreign Office and the Admiralty.

Pressure for building a new War Office increased after the Ordnance department was merged with that of the Secretary of State for War in 1855. The Crimean War led to widespread criticisms of military administration, but its end did not lead, as some people had expected, to a significant reduction in staff. The need for more space became even more acute after the Indian army was brought under the aegis

---

39 PRO, Work 1/77, p. 185; *Hansard*, 175 (30 May 1864), 849.

104. The Foreign Office as built to the designs of Gilbert Scott in 1862–73. The composition is more picturesque but less coherent than Pennethorne had proposed.

of the Secretary of State for War after the Indian Mutiny in 1857. By 1858 there was a staff of five hundred, and between £5,000 and £6,000 a year was being spent on renting offices.[40] Given the difficulty of getting agreement to any plan for concentrating government offices in Whitehall, the simplest and cheapest course of action was obviously to extend the recently enlarged Ordnance Office in Pall Mall to accommodate all the civil servants, leaving the military officers in the Horse Guards. The Pall Mall premises could be extended by acquiring the Crown leases of the adjoining houses, the late-seventeenth-century Schomberg House to the west – then a fashionable textile retailing establishment – and the larger Buckingham

---

40 Rep. Sel. Cttee. on Foreign Office Reconstruction (1857–8), xi, p. 138; *BN*, 17 Sept. 1858, 927.

105. Design for a new War Office in Pall Mall, 1856. The building was to stand on the site of Buckingham House, between the Carlton Club, on the left, and the old Ordnance Office – the former Cumberland House – on the right. This is one of the first of Pennethorne's designs to exploit the new taste for decorative statuary, and it would, if built, have dominated the southern side of the street.

House to the east. Pennethorne surveyed both properties in 1855, but the government decided to acquire only Buckingham House, an eighteenth-century building remodelled by Soane in 1792–5.[41]

The Crimean War ended in the autumn of 1855. Soon afterwards, at the request of Lord Panmure, Palmerston's Secretary for War, an energetic reformer who had already made a study of French military administration, Pennethorne was asked to investigate the relative costs of repairing Buckingham House, adding to it, or building a new office on the site.[42] It soon became evident that Panmure entertained ambitious ideas about building a new War Office costing £80,000 to Pennethorne's designs on the site of Buckingham House and the adjoining 88–90 Pall Mall, which had yet to be acquired. Assuming that the backing of the War Office would secure him the commission, Pennethorne went ahead and produced detailed elevations and a plan early in 1856.[43]

His impressive but overpowering design (Plate 105) reflects the confidence of a nation which had just won a major war – however little the military administrators might have contributed to the victory. The new building was to consist of three ranges around a courtyard, with the old Ordnance building (Cumberland House) on the fourth side and the main frontage facing north onto Pall Mall. Here Pennethorne proposed to build a massive four-storied block with three-bay turrets at each end like those he had included in his first design for public offices in Downing Street. The facade was to be 'as enriched and as architectural as the other large buildings with which it must compare',[44] notably Sydney Smirke's recently built Carlton Club to the east (Plate 33), whose elaborate Renaissance elevations had brought a new note of extrovert Venetian splendour into the street. And in its profuse surface decoration the new office would indeed have out-Carltoned the Carlton and overwhelmed the old Ordnance buildings. Copious carvings of trophies and statues of military heroes would have left the spectator in no doubt as to the building's purpose, but there would also have been an underlying architectural discipline imparted by the heavily rusticated piers and string courses and the massive cornice. With features taken from French and German as well as Italian Renaissance architecture, the new War Office would, if built, have been one of the key monuments of high-Victorian classicism.

Pennethorne's design for the War office, like that for the Foreign Office, fell foul of Sir Benjamin Hall, who told him in February 1856 that he had decided to hold a limited competition, which he was invited to enter. By this time he had already produced detailed plans which met with Lord Panmure's approval. But Hall was

41 PRO, Cres 19/43, p. 59; Work 30/2501; *Survey of London*, 29 (1960), pp. 359–61.
42 *Hansard*, 139 (15 June 1855), 216; PRO, Work 2/13, pp. 333–4.
43 Rep. Sel. Cttee. on Foreign Office Reconstruction, pp. 38, 138; PRO, T 1/5997A/10002.
44 Rep. Sel. Cttee. on Foreign Office Reconstruction, p. 115.

determined to hold his competition and, as in the case of the Foreign Office, the views of the people who would have to use the building did not deflect him. With all the bravado of an amateur architect he declared that Pennethorne's plans had 'been drawn without any regard to two material requisites for a Public or other Building, viz. – light and air; and in the next place they have been drawn without reference to the Site which will actually be covered with Buildings. This fact, independently of the former consideration, renders new Plans necessary.' Without holding a competition it would be impossible to secure 'the very best talent of the Profession' and make the new building 'an ornament to the Metropolis'.[45]

Henry Hunt, the new Office of Works surveyor, had meanwhile come to the conclusion that the site was too cramped and that it would be better to sell the leases of all the houses and move the whole establishment to Whitehall. The result was the abandonment of the limited competition and its replacement by the widely publicised open competition for a new Foreign Office and War Office in Whitehall. Palmerston was not party to this decision, and on 13 October, just after the competition was announced, he told Hall that the Cabinet wanted the War Office to be housed in 'an unpretending but suitable manner in Pall Mall', a project which could proceed at the same time as the proposed Foreign Office between Downing and Fludyer Streets.[46] But the competition was still allowed to proceed, and in May 1857 the designs were exhibited in Westminster Hall.

There was an attempt to revive Pennethorne's scheme after the failure of the competition, but it came to nothing and in September 1857 the Cabinet decided to acquire Schomberg House, on the other side of the old Ordnance Office.[47] Here Pennethorne proposed to construct a more modest building, housing over two hundred people at a cost of £26,000. This project was also approved by the War Office, but it was blocked by the Treasury, which refused to sanction the expenditure on a building which would not bring all the establishment together onto a single site.[48] In the end nothing was done, and the civil servants continued to occupy Buckingham House, Cumberland House and Schomberg House until 1908–12, when they finally moved into the exuberantly neo-Baroque premises which now enliven the eastern side of Whitehall. In this way the aim of moving the office to Whitehall was finally achieved. The site of the former War Office buildings is now mostly occupied by Mewès and Davis's Royal Automobile Club of 1911, only Schomberg House surviving from among the older buildings.

---

45 PRO, Work 1/48, p. 365; 1/49, pp. 116–17, 124; Rep. Sel. Cttee. on Foreign Office Reconstruction, pp. 51–2, 117–19, 179–80.
46 Rep. Sel. Cttee. on Foreign Office Reconstruction, pp. 123–6; Broadlands Papers, GC/HA/55/1; M. H. Port, *London Journal*, 2 (1976), 193.
47 *PP* 1857–8, 47 [369], pp. 1–7.
48 PRO, Work 1/61, p. 34; Work 2/20, pp. 121–3.

THE ADMIRALTY

Until the 1870s the Admiralty was divided between two London buildings: the riverside range of Somerset House, and a block of offices and official residences on the western side of Whitehall built to the designs of Thomas Ripley in 1723–6 and subsequently screened from public gaze by Robert Adam in 1759–61. From these two premises, the one an undistinguished essay in the neo-Palladian manner, the other the masterpiece of the leading native academic architect of the eighteenth century, Britain exerted her naval supremacy over the whole surface of the globe.

With proposals in the air for centralising government offices, the Treasury authorised the Office of Works to prepare plans for an extension to the Whitehall building early in 1853, and later in the year Pennethorne was asked to investigate signs of structural settlement there.[49] Nothing was done, and in the next few years controversies over rebuilding the Foreign Office and War Office made the Admiralty's accommodation problems seem relatively insignificant. It was only after these questions were at least temporarily settled that the idea of bringing together the Admiralty's departments in one place was once again aired, and in the autumn of 1861 Pennethorne was asked to report on how the Whitehall building could be enlarged to include the branches at Somerset House. He suggested that any new building should go on Crown property behind the existing office and extend as far as New Street, a now vanished thoroughfare which ran from Spring Gardens to St James's Park. The Admiralty officials decided that planning and construction should be entrusted to the Office of Works rather than their own works department, and in December Pennethorne sent in a survey of the site, with estimates of £145,000 for constructing a plain, fireproof brick building and £30,000 for purchasing the Crown leases. His plans do not survive, and it is not known whether he ever proposed any elevations. In March 1862 the Treasury decided to enquire whether a less expensive solution could be adopted, possibly by building a southward extension of the existing building over the Admiralty Pay Office in Whitehall.[50]

The Treasury's committee on Admiralty accommodation recommended that Pennethorne should estimate the cost of moving the Somerset House departments into the existing Whitehall building by taking over the official residences there and rehousing the First Lord of the Admiralty in the new Inland Revenue wing at Somerset House. He was asked to prepare plans for acquiring the site at the corner of the Strand and Wellington Street for a northward extension of the recently completed wing to accommodate the displaced tax officers, and in November 1862

---

49 *Ibid.*, 2/10, p. 574; Work 1/46, p. 239.
50 PRO, T 1/6321B/16295; T 1/6380A/15699; T 26/3, pp. 245–6, 274; Work 2/25, pp. 188–9; 2/28, p. 190.

he reported that a new Stamping Department could be built on this site for £78,000.[51] Nothing came of these proposals either, and with other costly projects looming, all the schemes were temporarily dropped. The leases of the Spring Gardens houses were nevertheless finally acquired by the government and the remaining Admiralty departments moved there from Somerset House in 1873.[52]

Several schemes for building an extension over the newly acquired ground were made throughout the 1860s and 70s, starting in 1868 with the publication of three plans – by Lord John Manners, Sir Charles Trevelyan and Lieutenant-Colonel Clarke – for concentrating all the military departments in Whitehall.[53] But after a succession of changes of mind unusual even by Office of Works standards, and a widely publicised competition, nothing was actually built until 1890, when the present depressingly mediocre building by Messrs Leeming and Leeming of Halifax was begun. This was followed in 1910 by Aston Webb's Admiralty Arch, and with this theatrical structure the Admiralty at last acquired a building of real architectural distinction.[54]

THE EASTERN SIDE OF WHITEHALL

Pennethorne first became involved in plans for laying out the land to the east of Whitehall through his position as architect to the Crown estate. The Crown was landlord of the ground where the Palace of Whitehall had once stood, between Richmond Terrace to the south and Scotland Yard to the north (Plate 106). The embanking of the Thames meant that it would come into possession of a substantial tract of reclaimed land, and in 1850 Pennethorne prepared a plan for laying out the northern portion of this land with gardens overlooked by a terrace of houses reached by a new street leading along the line of Whitehall Yard from the Horse Guards to the river.[55] The plan was not intended to be implemented until the late 1860s, by which time the majority of the leases would have fallen in and – it was hoped – the Embankment finally built. The scheme was forgotten amid the publicity surrounding Sir Benjamin Hall's 'block plan' competition for the whole area, but the winning competition design, by the Frenchman A. Crepinet, was soon put on the shelf, as was a bold scheme prepared by Sir Charles Barry and his son E. M. Barry in 1857 for public buildings, gardens and a 'terrace promenade' along the river front

---

51 *Ibid.*, Work 1/72, pp. 224–5; Work 2/28, pp. 176–7.
52 R. Needham and A. Webster, *Somerset House Past and Present* (1905), p. 259.
53 Copy Rep. of Commrs. on the accommodation of Public Departments, *PP* 1867–8, 58 [281].
54 For the later history of the site, and of Whitehall generally, see N. Bingham, 'Victorian and Edwardian Whitehall: Architecture and Planning 1865–1918', University of London PhD thesis (1985).
55 PRO, Cres 35/2566; MPEE 51.

106. The eastern side of Whitehall, looking north in 1884. Inigo Jones's Banqueting House is the only important public building. Beyond it, on the other side of Whitehall Yard, is Carrington House, and the bow-windowed house in the middle distance is the Office of Woods and Forests (1–2 Whitehall Place). The houses between Whitehall Yard and Whitehall Place were all demolished to make way for the new War Office in 1895–8, and the Woods and Forests building was itself replaced in 1909.

and a new 'Charing Cross Bridge' on the site of that proposed by Pennethorne in 1847.[56]

The decision to build the long-awaited Embankment revived earlier plans for the eastern side of Whitehall. Pennethorne was not directly involved in planning either the Embankment itself, or the road which was to be built along the river front. But

---

56 Barry, *Life of Barry*, pp. 292–300; F. Barker and R. Hyde, *London as it might have been* (1982), pp. 112-13.

he was consulted over its effect on the Crown tenants in the privately occupied houses at the southern end of Whitehall, whose leases were not due to fall in for several years, and on the layout of the ground reclaimed from the river. Most of the tenants lived in a row of expensive houses built in the early nineteenth century on the site of the old Privy Garden. They were concerned about losing their private access to the river, and in 1861, when the precise line of the road was still being discussed, Pennethorne argued in favour of diverting the southern end away from the river bank and taking it into Whitehall just to the south of the Banqueting House; at the same time Parliament Street would be widened by the removal of the houses at the southern end of Whitehall.[57] This solution was favoured by a Commons Select Committee in 1862, but Pennethorne's support for the wealthy Crown tenants smacked of aristocratic influence, and the proposal was attacked both in *The Times* and on the floor of the House of Commons.[58] It was dropped in 1863, the roadway constructed along the river bank as far as Westminster Bridge, and Parliament Street widened at the end of the decade.

With the Embankment under way, Pennethorne revived his 1850 scheme for laying out the Crown's portion of the reclaimed ground, and in 1864 he investigated the possibility of housing the Patent Office in a new building on the site of Fife House at the end of Whitehall Yard; this would front the new street from the Horse Guards to the Embankment (now called Horse Guards Avenue) which he had suggested in 1850 but which was now to be built by the Metropolitan Board of Works.[59] Nothing came of this proposal, and in 1868 and 1869 he prepared more schemes for the layout of the area, the most ambitious of which envisaged all the ground between Whitehall Gardens and Trafalgar Square (Plate 107) being set aside for public offices in what he called 'a revival of Inigo Jones's design for Whitehall Palace'. Only the Banqueting House would be preserved among the older buildings, and a new street leading from Trafalgar Square to the river would run along the north side of the new buildings.[60] The shabby group of houses at the junction of Whitehall and Trafalgar Square would be replaced and the Jacobean Northumberland House – one of the greatest of London's aristocratic town houses – preserved. Pennethorne made no drawings of the elevations, and it is impossible to know what he wanted the new buildings to look like. But he talked approvingly both of Jones's Whitehall Palace designs and of Somerset House, and the new offices would no doubt have shared something of their restrained, controlled magnificence.

---

57 Rep. Commrs. . . . [for] Plans for Embanking the Thames, *PP* 1861, 31, pp. 126–30, and plan.

58 Rep. Sel. Cttee. on Thames Embankment Bill, *PP* 1862, 15 [334], pp. ix–x, 200–23; *Hansard*, 167 (3 July 1862), 1473.

59 PRO, Work 2/27, pp. 56–7; Rep. Sel. Cttee. on Patent Office Library and Museum, *PP* 1864, 12 [514], pp. 95–6.

60 Copy Rep. . . . for New Street between the Thames Embankment and the Horse Guards, *PP* 1867–8, 58 [399], pp. 1–3 and plans; 1st Rep. Sel. Cttee. on Hungerford Bridge and Wellington Street viaduct, *PP* 1868–9, 10 [200], pp. 88–97 and Appendix 2.

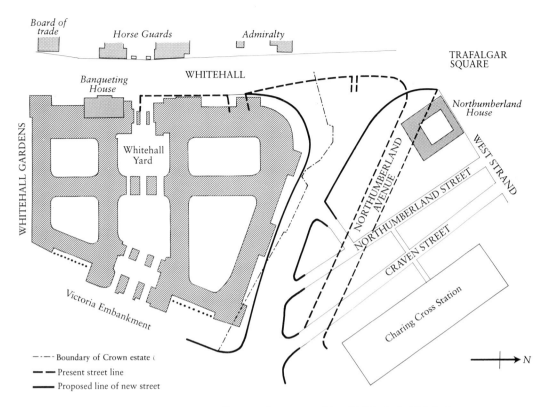

107. Outline plan for new government offices on the eastern side of Whitehall. This is the most ambitious of several plans prepared by Pennethorne for the area, none of which were implemented.

Not for the first time, Pennethorne's advice was rejected, and in 1870 he retired. In one of the worst instances of official vandalism in Victorian London, Northumberland House was demolished in order to make way for the gloomy Northumberland Avenue, projected by the Metropolitan Board of Works and built in 1876. Meanwhile, as politicians continued to argue vainly about the siting of new public offices, more plans were produced, only to gather dust on official shelves. Finally in 1884, at the prompting of Pennethorne's successor, Arthur Cates, a massive and exotically roofed block of flats, Whitehall Court, was built on the Crown land along the former river frontage next to the National Liberal Club. The reclaimed ground was laid out as public gardens by the Metropolitan Board of Works and the Crown compensated with land further south.[61] In 1892 the Liberal government decided to build the new War Office on the northern side of Horse Guards Avenue, and William Young's extravagantly Baroque pile was erected in

---

61 D. Owen, *The Government of Victorian London* (Cambridge, Mass., 1982), pp. 95–7; A. Saint, 'Whatever Happened to Jonathan Carr?', *London Journal*, 12 (1) (1986), 65–79.

1895–8. In the process Pennethorne's former office and the rest of the picturesque huddle of buildings in the former Whitehall Yard were demolished.[62] The transformation of the area was completed when the houses in Whitehall Gardens, further south, were replaced by the huge and ponderous Ministry of Defence, designed by E. Vincent Harris in 1913 but not completed until 1959.

The southern portion of Whitehall, between the new Foreign Office and Parliament Square, remained untouched for many years. By 1877 the cost of purchasing the ground had risen to £1,300,000, whereas in 1855 Pennethorne had estimated the cost of all the land south of the Treasury, including the site of the Foreign Office, at less than half that sum.[63] But with the building of the so-called New Government Offices overlooking Parliament Square by J. M. Brydon and the Office of Works architect Sir Henry Tanner in 1898–1912, his vision of a 'palace of administration' stretching from the Horse Guards to the southern end of Whitehall was finally realised. Thus, a generation after his death, the 'concentration' of the public offices was finally achieved in a dignified classical style of which Pennethorne might have approved.

---

62 M. H. Port, 'Public building in a Parliamentary State', *London Journal*, 11 (1) (1985), 8.
63 *The Builder*, 25 Aug. 1877, 853.

9

THE FINAL YEARS

THE ABANDONMENT of Pennethorne's designs for new government offices in Whitehall was the worst of the many disappointments in his career. They were produced when he was at the height of his creative powers. In the largest of his earlier government buildings – the Public Record Office and the Somerset House extension – he was constrained by the need to defer to the expertise of others and to the architectural manner of one of his greatest predecessors as government architect. In his designs for the government offices, he finally evolved a style which was timeless in its appeal yet well suited to the needs of the age. It is one of the architectural tragedies of the nineteenth century that these designs were pushed to one side by ministerial pigheadedness and architectural opportunism. It was only the departure of Sir Benjamin Hall from the Office of Works that allowed Pennethorne to resume his career as an architect, and when he did so he produced some of the finest English classical buildings of the 1860s.

THE STAFF COLLEGE

The first of these buildings was the Staff College at Camberley (Surrey). The College was founded in 1858 in the aftermath of the Crimean War. Parliamentary enquiries undertaken during the war had revealed that Britain was spending only £1,300 a year on military education, compared with £46,000 in France and £127,000 in Austria. Such a state of affairs was bound to pose a severe threat to the *Pax Britannica* in future, more technological, conflicts. Sidney Herbert, Lord Aberdeen's Secretary at War, urged that the Senior Department of the Royal Military Academy at Sandhurst should be turned into a separate staff college in 1854. His proposal was later taken up by Lord Panmure, who had already instigated reforms in the War Office, and in 1857, with the backing of the Prince Consort, he set up a Council for Military Education under the chairmanship of the

Commander-in-Chief, the Duke of Cambridge. The council established the college, drafted the syllabus, and decided that the new establishment should remain at or near Sandhurst, to protect the officers from the distractions of London. It was opened in temporary premises in the west wing of the Royal Military Academy in 1858.[1]

The question of providing new and permanent accommodation was first raised in April 1858, when the Office of Works was asked to investigate the possibility of building a college for at least thirty senior officers. Lord John Manners, the new First Commissioner, decided against holding a competition, and asked Pennethorne to prepare plans and estimates, possibly by way of consolation for the abandonment of his plans for a new War Office. The sum of £20,000 was voted in the Army estimates of 1858, and in June he was asked to prepare detailed designs.[2]

The site was about a mile to the south-east of the Sandhurst Academy, close to the London–Portsmouth road, from which it was screened by trees. It was to face west, overlooking woodlands and a lake, and was to house forty officers and their servants, each officer having two rooms. Pennethorne sent in a set of plans and a front elevation in July, but the estimated cost of £125,000 was dismissed as excessive by the Duke of Cambridge, and he was told to prepare new plans for a building costing less than half that sum. A new set of plans was therefore forwarded to the War Office in November, formulated with 'the greatest possible regard for economy' – a familiar refrain – with red brick facades, a plain eaves cornice and no stone dressings of any kind. The cost was now estimated at £70,000. For once in Pennethorne's career the demands of economy did not prevail, and this spartan scheme was superseded in the spring of 1859 by a much more splendid design which was carried into effect over the next three years. The occasion was the transfer of the buildings at Sandhurst from the care of the Office of Works to the direct management of the War Office.[3] With the straitjacket of Treasury control removed, the soldiers and civilian administrators decided to build a structure commensurate with the prestige of an army which had recently, for all its shortcomings, emerged on the winning side in a major European war. Pennethorne was therefore asked to prepare a new set of designs which were shown to Prince Albert and subsequently approved by the Queen. The foundation stone was laid on 14 December 1859, and the building finally completed in 1862 under the supervision of a Colonel Chapman of the Royal Engineers. The builders were Myers and Sons, contractors for the Royal Victoria Hospital at Netley (Hampshire) and other equally formidable mid-Victorian institutions, and they engaged 'a strange collection of master craftsmen,

1 E. M. Spiers, *The Army and Society 1815–1914* (1980), pp. 150–4; A. R. Godwin-Austin, *The Staff and the Staff College* (1927), p. 111.
2 PRO, Work 1/58, pp. 181–2; 1/59, p. 53; Work 6/186/6, ff. 56–63.
3 *Ibid.*, 6/186/6, ff. 66–83, 131–45.

108. The Staff College, Camberley in about 1900. An extra storey was added in 1912–14.

the best in Europe', whose temporary encampment – Cambridge Town – grew into the present Camberley.[4]

The Staff College (Plate 108) stands out from the usual run of mid-Victorian educational establishments. Most schools and colleges of the time looked back stylistically to the mediaeval collegiate tradition, but here both the plan and the elevations were conceived entirely within the framework of rationalistic classicism. The college is built of yellow brick, with Corsham limestone dressings. Decoration is sparsely applied and subordinated to the logic of the structure. The main front, 265 feet (eighty metres) long, is broken up by a central frontispiece with a raised pediment enclosing a sculptural representation of martial trophies. There are four-storied pavilions at each end like those which Pennethorne had introduced in

---

4 PRO, T 1/6693A/3774; Godwin-Austin, pp. 119–29.

his final scheme for the government offices in Whitehall. And, as in that scheme and at Buckingham Palace, the ground floor, the whole of the central three bays and the two pavilions are faced in stone applied in bands with deeply-cut incisions between each course. The rooms are arranged around two internal courtyards, with spacious corridors and a top-lit atrium-like hall (Plate 109) in the centre flanked by the main staircases. There is a pervasive feeling of dignity, space and lucidity, in sharp contrast to the restless straining after effect which characterises much English architecture of the 'high Victorian' era.

The Staff College is not only an impressive structure in its own right. It also gives an indication of what the western side of Whitehall might have looked like if it had been rebuilt to Pennethorne's designs. Though little known today, it shows that the classical tradition in public architecture was still alive in the 1860s. Inigo Jones, who implanted that tradition in England, said that buildings should be 'solid, proportional according to the rules, masculine and unaffected'. The Staff College is a building which possesses those qualities.

THE ALBERT MEMORIAL

Pennethorne first came into contact with the Prince Consort in the 1850s over the design of the ballroom wing of Buckingham Palace. The Prince's last public engagement was the opening of the Staff College, and when he died at the end of 1861 it is not surprising that Pennethorne should have taken an interest in the proposal to build a memorial in Hyde Park overlooking the South Kensington estate. In April 1862 therefore he sent a design for the memorial to Sir Charles Eastlake, one of a committee of four men selected to advise the Queen on the choice of a design.[5] In the following month the committee decided to seek the advice of six other architects – P. C. Hardwick, T. L. Donaldson, Matthew Digby Wyatt, E. M. Barry, Charles Barry junior, and Gilbert Scott – and in July they were asked to submit their own designs.[6] They were told that 'the design of the Architectural portion of the Memorial should be regarded chiefly as a means of ensuring the most effective arrangement of the sculpture which is to complete it; the object being to provide an Architectural base for groups of Sculpture surmounted by the Statue, which is required to be conspicuous'.

Classical architecture was for Pennethorne 'more suitable than Mediaeval or Romanesque, to commemorate the pure and Classic taste of the Prince Consort'[7] – a view shared by all the architects except Gilbert Scott. Pennethorne's design, submitted in December 1862, is an impressive exercise in classical abstraction

5 Royal Archives, Add H/1, ff.252–3.
6 *Survey of London*, 38 (1975), p. 150; S. Bayley, *The Albert Memorial* (1981), pp. 30 *et seq.*
7 Royal Archives, Add 1/17A.

109. The entrance hall of the Staff College in about 1900. The room remains largely unchanged today.

(Plate 110). The monument would have taken the form of a massive raised mausoleum sixty-five feet (twenty metres) square with a marble-clad circular chamber containing a statue of the Prince, 'of heroic, or colossal, size', lit by windows in an attic surmounted by a stepped pyramid taken from the Mausoleum of Halicarnassus. The details are Grecian, but, in contrast to most Greek Revival architecture of the early nineteenth century, there is a heavy voluptuousness about the design which derives largely from the copious use of statuary and relief carving. Pairs of bronze statues representing the Arts and Sciences flank the flights of steps leading up to each facade, there are bas-reliefs of events in Prince Albert's life at the corners, and groups representing parts of the British Empire over the entablature.

The memorial was intended to face a 'central institution for the promotion of scientific and artistic education' on the site of Gore House, to the south of the street now known as Kensington Gore. This was the site once earmarked for a new National Gallery, and when that proposal collapsed the Prince Consort suggested turning it into a 'central point of union' for men versed in the arts and sciences.[8] No elevation of Pennethorne's proposed 'Albert Hall' survives, but his plan[9] makes it clear that he envisaged a rectangular Grecian building aligned north and south, with a portico facing the memorial. On the south the building would have overlooked the recently-opened Horticultural Gardens.

Pennethorne's Albert Memorial proposals would, if carried out, have enabled him to make a permanent mark on South Kensington. But his scheme fell short of what the Queen and her advisers wanted. The statue of the Prince, far from being conspicuous, was to be enclosed within a mass of masonry, and the Queen objected to the gloomy associations of the mausoleum-like main structure. So, despite its formidable architectural qualities, Pennethorne's design was rejected in February 1863, and it is Gilbert Scott's splendidly romantic Gothic tabernacle which now overlooks the site whose development the Prince had done so much to promote.

THE PATENT OFFICE

Pennethorne's next commissions for the government grew out of the demands of the law. The Patent Office was a by-product of that remarkable flowering of ingenuity which helped transform nineteenth-century Britain into the world's first industrial nation. During the early heroic days of industrialisation, patents were granted only after a bewilderingly complex procedure involving applications to no fewer than nine different offices. Complaints about the inefficiency of this method led in 1851 to the setting-up of a Select Committee whose recommendations were embodied in the Patent Law Amendment Act of 1852. Under this legislation a single Patent Office was set up, with its own commissioners and staff.

The new office was opened in December 1852. Like the new Public Record Office, it occupied premises in London's legal quarter, in a building to the south of Staple Inn, Holborn at the back of 25 Southampton Buildings, a domestic-looking structure in the Palladian style built in 1792 for the Masters in Chancery and the Secretaries of Bankrupts and Lunatics (Plate 111). There followed a familiar process of overcrowding leading, after long delays, to piecemeal alterations and, eventually, total rebuilding. From the very beginning the Patent Office staff had to share the building with the Chancery lawyers, and matters were made more desperate in 1853 when a library – the nucleus of the present Science Reference service of the British

---

8 *Ibid.*, Add H/7, pp. 25–32.   9 PRO, Work 35/68.

110. Design for the Albert Memorial 1862. The building was to stand on the site of the present Memorial by Gilbert Scott, close to the site of the Great Exhibition of 1851 and overlooking the South Kensington estate purchased by the Exhibition commissioners.

Library – was set up by the former Manchester silk manufacturer Bennett Woodcroft, Superintendent of Patent Specifications and 'father of the Patent Office'. It soon became the only scientific library freely open to the public in England, and attracted the enthusiastic support of Prince Albert. At first it was housed in a dimly-lit seven-and-a-half foot (just over two metres) wide corridor on the ground floor of the building, which became known as 'the Drainpipe' or 'the Sewer'.[10] By 1864, books were being stored on floors, tables and passages, and the store rooms had become so overcrowded that the floors were sinking.

A call for extra accommodation was first made in 1853, and in 1857 the Attorney

10 H. Harding, *Patent Office Centenary* (1953), pp. 5–13, 34–5; *The Engineer*, 31 July 1857, 76; *The Builder*, 8 Sept. 1866, 663, 748.

General suggested building a new office on the site of the present Law Courts between Carey Street and the Strand. After seven more years of dithering – including the investigation of sites in Burlington House, Victoria Street and the eastern side of Whitehall[11] – the Palmerston administration finally agreed in 1864 to the appointment of a Select Committee to investigate the provision of suitable premises both for the Office and Library and for the technological collections amassed by Woodcroft, which were temporarily housed in the South Kensington Museum; they included models of patented machinery and such popular attractions as the pioneer steam locomotives 'Rocket' and 'Puffing Billy'. In his evidence Pennethorne suggested that the best site for a new Office and Library would be on the slum property to the north of the new street he still vainly hoped might be built between Chancery Lane and Fetter Lane, to the north of the Public Record Office. But the Committee recommended expansion on the existing site, using the surplus revenues derived from patent fees.[12] The museum was to stay at South Kensington, but no money was forthcoming for a new building there and the collections remained in the 'Boilers' until early in this century, when they were moved to the new Science Museum. The proposal to build a new Patent Office was also set aside, and early in 1865 Pennethorne was asked to estimate the cost of constructing a new library on top of the existing building at roof level; extra space for the office staff would be provided when the Chancery lawyers moved into the new Law Courts in the Strand – a move which did not take place until 1882. In July 1865 he was authorised to proceed with building a library with a fireproof floor, and it was finally opened in May 1867.[13]

The most interesting feature of the new library was its semicircular-arched iron roof (Plate 112). The arched central space contained the readers' desks, and on either side there were 'aisles' for the bookcases. The supports were articulated by Corinthian columns, and there were windows in the roof space over the frieze. Though plain, the room was 'inexpensively but tastefully decorated in delicate shades of colour relieved by a little gilding judiciously applied', with the names of eminent scientists painted onto the frieze evoking 'a humble but not inappropriate sort of Walhalla' – an idea which probably originated with Woodcroft.[14]

Pennethorne's library soon became as overcrowded as its predecessor. A small extension was made in 1885–6, but in 1895 John Taylor proposed building a new library.[15] A Select Committee of 1897 recommended demolishing all the existing Patent Office buildings – described as 'the dingiest, dirtiest and most ill-suited public building in London' – and replacing them by new premises on the same site. The new Patent Office, built to Taylor's designs in 1898–1901, has a bland enough

11 PRO, Work 2/10, p. 822; 2/19, pp. 209, 334–6; PRO, T 26/2, pp. 236–7.
12 Rep. Sel. Cttee. on Patent Office Library and Museum, *PP* 1864, 12 [504], pp. v–vi, 95–100.
13 PRO, Work 1/79, pp. 263, 331; Work 2/28, pp. 392–3, 429; 2/30, pp. 364–6.
14 *BN*, 5 July 1867, 457.   15 PRO, Work 12/195.

111. The entrance to the old Patent Office, Southampton Buildings, *c.* 1890. These buildings were all swept away shortly after the photograph was taken. The present Patent Office by John Taylor now stands on the site.

exterior, supposedly designed to match the adjoining neo-Jacobean structure built for the Taxing Masters in Chancery in 1851. But the library (Plate 113) is a triumph of iron construction, with a tall three-storied galleried interior which is clearly influenced by Pennethorne's earlier building both in its basilican plan and in the design of the roof. So Pennethorne's successor at the Office of Works paid him posthumous tribute, and in doing so gave London one of its finest late-Victorian interiors.

THE PROBATE OFFICE

Until the passing of the Court of Probate Act of 1857, testamentary matters came under the aegis of a bewildering variety of ecclesiastical courts. There were no fewer than 400 places for depositing wills in England and Wales, of which the most illustrious was the Prerogative Court of Canterbury. It occupied part of the College of Advocates, or Doctors' Commons, a collection of dilapidated late seventeenth-century buildings between Knightrider Street and Upper Thames Street in the city, to the south of St Paul's. This Dickensian institution contained several courts and lawyers' offices. It also housed many thousands of wills, including those of Shakespeare and Napoleon, which could be consulted in the Prerogative Office, a long narrow room from which a strong-room projected south.[16]

The Act of 1857 established some forty new provincial registries to replace the old ecclesiastical registries, but left the Principal Probate Registry in its new secular guise at Doctors' Commons. The premises here were already overcrowded; the increase of business which followed the concentration of the courts made the overcrowding chronic. The obvious solution was to expand into the remaining parts of Doctors' Commons, which were little used, but in 1859, after lengthy negotiations between Pennethorne and the lawyers, it was agreed to limit the purchase to the Prerogative Office itself, together with the adjacent houses. Pennethorne was now asked to enquire into the possibility of remodelling these buildings, and at the beginning of the following year he sent in proposals showing how the search room could be enlarged and the storage accommodation doubled at a cost of £30,000.[17] His plan was only partially carried out. A new strong room was built to his design in 1860, other minor alterations following in 1861, but over-crowding still remained a serious problem, and in 1864 the staff of 150 were said to be 'paralysed' by the lack of room.[18]

---

16 C. Knight, *London Pictorially Illustrated* v (1851), pp. 1–16; PRO, Work 30/1262.

17 Sel. Cttee. on Court of Probate (Acquisition of Site) Bill, *PP* 1859, 3 [220], pp. 23–7; PRO, Work 2/22, pp. 304–9; 2/24, pp. 375–6; Work 30/2850.

18 PRO, Work 1/65, pp. 299–300, 306; Work 2/28, pp. 134–7.

112. The new Patent Office library by James Pennethorne in 1886. The library was on the top floor of a building behind those shown in Plate 111, and was invisible from the street.

113. The present Patent Office library soon after completion. John Taylor did not depart from the layout, style and constructional methods of Pennethorne's library, but his building is much larger and more impressive.

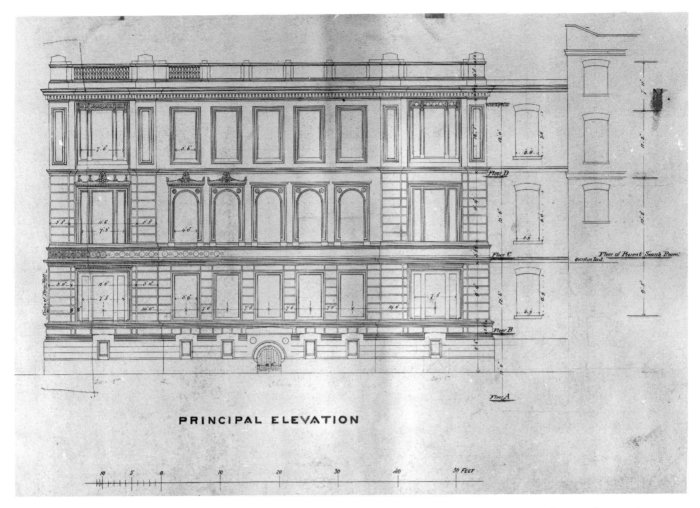

114. Design for an extension to the principal Probate Registry, 1866. The building was intended to stand on the site of Doctors' Commons, facing Queen Victoria Street.

By now the plans for the construction of the Victoria Embankment had been unveiled. As part of the related improvements, a new street (Queen Victoria Street) was to be built by the Metropolitan Board of Works from the eastern end of the Embankment at Blackfriars Bridge to the Bank of England, passing through the new strong-room. In November 1864, therefore, Pennethorne proposed constructing a completely new office, together with a new strong room one and a half times the size of the existing one, at a total cost of £34,000. Negotiations for the site dragged on for over a year, but in June 1866 he sent in working drawings (Plate 114) showing an enriched facade of three stories to Queen Victoria Street, with an impressively forbidding round-arched entrance on the heavily rusticated ground floor.[19] The design is evidence of the powerful monumentality of Pennethorne's later manner, but in the event the only part of the scheme to be carried out was the strong room, begun in 1868 and completed by the middle of 1869. Gladstone's first administration overturned the rest of the plans after deciding to build an extension to the Admiralty at Spring Gardens, thus allowing the wills to be moved to the river block of Somerset House. So in 1874 the Probate department moved there[20] and the remains of Doctors' Commons were demolished to make way for James Williams's Post Office Savings Bank, a restrained and well-proportioned classical building of which Pennethorne might have been proud. Today much of the site is occupied by the massive Faraday Building of 1932.

THE LAW COURTS

England's antiquated legal system was a target for reformers from Bentham to Dickens. As in so many cases the haphazard, *ad hoc*, nature of the system was reflected in the buildings. As more and more demands were placed on the law in the mid nineteenth century these buildings came to seem correspondingly inadequate. Ever since mediaeval times the main civil cases had been heard at Westminster Hall and adjoining buildings. Lesser courts were scattered around the capital, especially near Lincolns Inn, adding extra costs and frustration to the many vexations which have always attended litigation. Starting in 1820, Sir John Soane designed a characteristically ingenious series of new courts and offices alongside Westminster Hall, but they soon became full to capacity, and in 1841–2 Charles Barry prepared plans for concentrating the courts in a new Grecian building in the centre of Lincolns Inn Fields, close to the Inns of Court and the main haunts of the lawyers. The scheme was discussed by a Commons Select Committee, but it was shelved and in 1845 Barry prepared another proposal for a Gothic building on the site a little to the south, between Carey Street and Fleet Street.[21]

The new site, just to the west of the Public Record Office, not only had the advantages of saving a valuable open space in the heart of a very crowded area; it also promised to remove one of London's worst slums, so fulfilling one of the main objectives of Metropolitan Improvement. Pennethorne, a connoisseur of low neighbourhoods, later told another Select Committee: 'I have known most of the bad properties in London, and I do not know that I have met with any worse than

---

19 *Ibid.*, 2/28, pp. 134–7, 334–5; 2/29, pp. 433–5; Work 12/52/7.
20 R. Needham and A. Webster, *Somerset House Past and Present* (1905), p. 259.
21 D. Brownlee, *The Law Courts: the Architecture of George Edmund Street* (Cambridge, Mass., 1984), pp. 53–62; Rep. Sel. Cttee. on Courts of Law and Equity, *PP* 1842, 10 [476], p. 101.

in some parts of this'.[22] Demolitions for the new streets of the 1840s made overcrowding worse, and by 1865 an average of fifteen people, many of them unemployed, lodged in each of the rickety, badly maintained, mostly timber-framed buildings.[23]

The idea of building new courts at Carey Street languished until 1860, the year of Barry's death. A Bill to acquire the seven-and-a-half acre (three hectare) site was passed in 1861, but in the following years the Commons refused to vote the money. A new money bill was introduced in 1864 after the Palmerston government had established that some of the very considerable costs could be met by the use of the Suitor's Fund made up of accumulated legal expenses. Pennethorne was not involved in the detailed discussions about the Bills of 1861 and 1862, but he was asked by Cowper to prepare a new plan of the site and to estimate the cost of purchase and of constructing suitable buildings.[24] In February 1865 therefore he submitted a block plan of the site, together with estimates and two detailed sets of plans for what was to be the largest and most expensive Government structure since the Houses of Parliament. They were intended, like his plans for the Admiralty a few years earlier, to be 'a ground work for discussion hereafter', and any recurring doubt was removed when Cowper announced in March 1865 that the architect would be chosen by competition.[25]

Pennethorne's plans showed the building on a four- to five-acre (one-and-a-half to two-hectare) rectangular site between Fleet Street and Carey Street, along the line of which he had hoped to cut his 'Great Central Thoroughfare'; a new Probate Office could go further west. The main building, costing an estimated one and a half million pounds, would house eighteen courts, which could be placed in top-lit rooms on the first floor and reached through a central hall as large as Westminster Hall; the numerous ancillary rooms could go underneath and around the courts. The arrangement is similar to that proposed by Barry in his Lincolns Inn Fields scheme, as well as by most of the entrants in the competition which was eventually held in 1866.[26] It would be interesting to compare Pennethorne's plans with those of the competitors, but unfortunately they have disappeared. It is therefore impossible to say how far they influenced Cowper's successors when they came to choose the final design by G. E. Street, one of the last and greatest monuments of the heroic phase of the Gothic Revival.

22 Rep. Sel. Cttee. on Courts of Justice Construction (Site) Bill, *PP* 1865, 12 [124], p. 1.
23 PRO, Work 12/1, f. 153.
24 *Ibid.*, 1/77, p. 336; 1/78, p. 92; Work 12/1, f. 119.
25 *Ibid.*, 12/1, f. 119; Brownlee, *Law Courts*, pp. 67–74.
26 PRO, Work 12/1, ff. 143, 148; Rep. Sel. Cttee. on Courts of Justice Bill (1865), pp. 1–5.

BURLINGTON HOUSE AND THE UNIVERSITY OF LONDON

Pennethorne's last building was a new headquarters for the University of London in Burlington Gardens, behind Burlington House. Burlington House was one of London's great aristocratic town houses. First built in 1664–5, it was completely remodelled in 1717–20 by Colen Campbell for the third Earl of Burlington, apostle of the Palladian style, and it subsequently passed to his son-in-law the fifth Duke of Devonshire, before being sold in 1815 to his grandson Lord George Cavendish. Externally it remained in the 1860s much as it had been in the days of the great arbiter of eighteenth-century architectural taste (Plate 115). It stood on the northern side of a forecourt, with lower wings to the east and west and a curved colonnade by James Gibbs to the south behind a high blank wall which shut the whole complex off from Piccadilly. Behind the house there was a garden stretching back to Cork Street and Savile Row.[27]

The purchase of Burlington House by Lord Aberdeen's administration of 1854 enabled the government to solve the question of housing the nation's growing number of cultural organisations and learned societies which looked to it for accommodation. There was space both in the house and in the forecourt buildings, and there was also potential for providing more accommodation in the garden behind. It only remained to decide which institutions should go to Burlington House, and who should design and pay for any new buildings. Pennethorne, who had recommended the purchase in 1854, was involved in these decisions from the beginning. In July 1858 he prepared a plan showing how the whole site could be redeveloped as an academic and cultural centre, though the First Commissioner of Works, Lord John Manners, made it clear that he would not have any claim to design the buildings.[28] Accommodation would be provided for the University of London, some of the learned societies which had formerly been in Somerset House, the Patent Office and its museum, and the Royal Academy. This idea was welcomed by the *Building News* on the grounds that it promised an end to proposals encouraged by 'the officious meddling vanity of an illustrious personage' (the Prince Consort) to develop South Kensington as the main centre of London's cultural activities.[29]

In April 1859 the government finally unveiled a scheme, based presumably on Pennethorne's ideas, under which the Burlington House site would be covered with buildings arranged around two quadrangles, with the Royal Academy occupying a range of new buildings fronting Piccadilly. The Academy would be housed in a building designed by Sir Charles Barry, leaving the rest of the buildings

---

27 *Survey of London*, 31 (1963), pp. 390–429.
28 PRO, T 1/6223A/19527; T 1/6251A/9793; Work 1/59, pp. 155–6; Bodleian Library, Oxford, Disraeli Papers B/XX/M/106.
29 *BN*, 18 Feb. 1859, p. 159.

115. Burlington House before rebuilding, looking from Piccadilly. The house and gateway were built by Colen Campbell in 1717–20, but the wings, and probably also the curved colonnade, were by James Gibbs.

to be designed by his son Charles and his partner Robert Banks who, it was felt, deserved a major government commission after being pushed to one side by Gilbert Scott in the choice of design for the new Foreign Office.[30] But these plans were scotched by the fall of the Derby government in mid 1859.

The removal of the Royal Academy to Burlington House would have left the National Gallery in full possession of the present building in Trafalgar Square, but the second Palmerston administration complicated matters by its plans to move it to Burlington House (see pp. 200–4). Pennethorne was in good odour with the new government, and in August 1861 he produced a plan showing a new National Gallery on the vacant ground to the north of the house, with an entrance in Burlington Gardens (Plate 116). Three months later he prepared a second plan in which the National Gallery would be approached through a 'public hall' in Burlington House itself, with the upstairs galleries arranged around a courtyard and lit by skylights and glass domes. The front courtyard would be rebuilt to contain apartments and lecture halls for the learned societies, and there would be a new facade to Piccadilly.[31] Two designs for the Piccadilly frontage survive. They show a monumental building articulated by a range of giant free-standing Corinthian columns, with a row of statues above the entablature, larger sculptured groups at the heavily emphasised corners and a Grecian temple-like structure breaking through the roofline in the centre. In the first design (Colour Plate IV) the courtyard would have been entered through a plainly moulded, almost Soaneian, arch, flanked by openings with caryatids; in the later, dated 1863 (Plate 117), more enrichment is added and the attic storey is reduced in height to give a less ponderous appearance. Like his final, and equally abortive, scheme for the government offices overlooking Horse Guards Parade, the design has something of the flavour of the architecture of mid-nineteenth-century Germany. It also recalls the work of Pennethorne's Scottish contemporary, Alexander ('Greek') Thomson, perhaps the most gifted classical architect at work in Britain in the 1860s.

Plans to move the National Gallery to Burlington House were quashed in June 1864, leaving the future of the site more uncertain than ever. Two years of complicated negotiations followed before Sir Francis Grant, Sir Charles Eastlake's successor as President of the Royal Academy, finally managed to persuade the new government of Lord Derby to let the Royal Academy take over Burlington House, leaving the front courtyard and Piccadilly front to the learned societies (Plate 118).[32] The Royal Academicians chose their Treasurer, Sydney Smirke, to build their new galleries behind Burlington House in 1867–9 and to add the extra storey in 1872 which drastically altered the proportions of the original building. The new blocks facing the courtyard and Piccadilly were entrusted to Banks and Barry, and it is their

---

30 A. Barry, *Life and Works of Sir Charles Barry* (1867), pp. 282–3.
31 PRO, Work 30/529.
32 J. Steegman, 'The Royal Academy's Second Founder', *Country Life*, 7 June 1962, 1372–3.

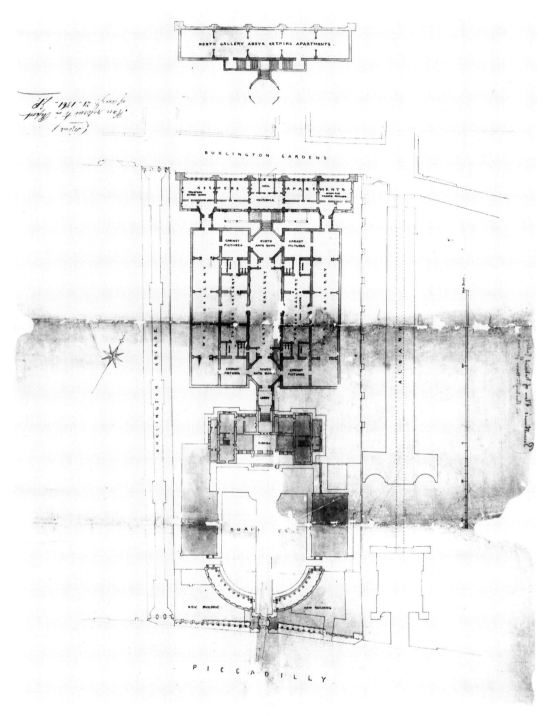

116. Plan showing Pennethorne's proposed new National Gallery on the garden behind Burlington House and a new building on the Piccadilly front, 1861. The central gallery, running north and south, would have housed the Mantegna Cartoons, and it would have been flanked on either side by galleries for the Vernon and Turner pictures. Another plan produced at about the same time shows the galleries arranged around a quadrangle.

117. Design for a new Piccadilly frontage to Burlington House, 1863. This is a variant of the scheme shown in colour Plate VI. The word 'PINACOTHECA' over the entrance is a reminder that the final decision to keep the National Gallery in Trafalgar Square was not made until 1864.

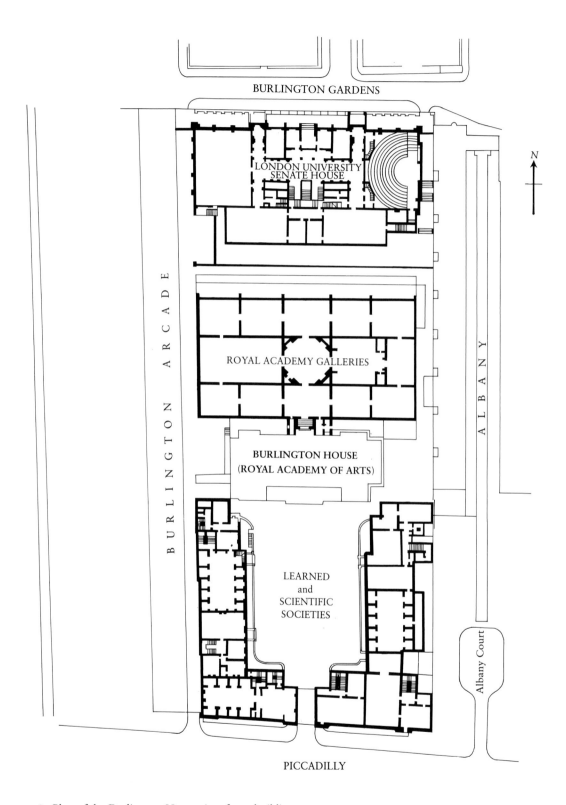

118. Plan of the Burlington House site after rebuilding.

ponderous and heavily ornamented pile of 1868–74 (Plate 119) which still dominates this part of the street today – a poor substitute for the noble temple-like building which Pennethorne had proposed.

Pennethorne's 'consolation prize' was the commission for the long-promised new buildings for the University of London on the Burlington Gardens site. The university grew out of the quest for 'useful knowledge' which helped to transform the intellectual and cultural climate of nineteenth-century England. Distressed by what they saw as the torpid obscurantism of the older universities, a group of Whigs, Radicals, utilitarians and nonconformists founded 'the London University' in 1827 to provide 'literary and scientific education at a moderate expense'. The new institution was housed in the stolid Grecian structure now known as University College in Gower Street, Bloomsbury, designed by William Wilkins and opened in 1828. In the same year a rival institution, King's College, was opened under Anglican auspices in premises adjoining Somerset House. In the early years neither King's nor the 'university' in Gower Street had the power to award degrees. But, as part of their reforming policy, the Whigs agreed in 1836 to grant a charter to a new University of London whose main function was to set examinations and grant degrees. It was to be equal in status to Oxford and Cambridge but 'freed from those exclusions and religious distinctions which abridge [their] usefulness'.[33] Teaching was to be the responsibility of the two new colleges, the London medical schools, and various other approved institutions, of which there were fifty-one by 1850, including some in the Colonies.

The University, like many of the Boards and Commissions established by the Whigs, was in effect a semi-autonomous government department. It had no endowments, three quarters of its Senate was nominated by the Crown, and it was dependent on the Treasury both for its day-to-day expenses and for its accommodation. Reliance on government funding led to a predictable and grow-ing shortage of space. For the first thirty years of its life, the administrators occupied temporary premises, first in the north range of Somerset House, then from 1853–5 in Marlborough House, and finally in Burlington House. For two years the administrators occupied rooms in the house itself, but in 1857 they moved into the block on the east of the forecourt, where they shared a newly constructed meeting and examination room at the back of the west block with the Royal Society.[34]

The University's increasing prestige was reflected in the grant of a new Charter in 1858 which allowed for the establishment of a convocation of graduates. As it expanded its scope and became better-known, it became more and more conscious of its corporate identity and began to press its paymaster, the Treasury, to provide it with a purpose-built senate house and examination rooms. Early in 1859, a

33 P. Dunsheath and M. Miller, *Convocation in the University of London* (1958), pp. 1–2; N. Harte, *The University of London, 1836–1956* (1986), pp. 61–80.
34 *Survey of London*, 31 (1963), p. 441.

119. The Piccadilly front of Burlington House as rebuilt by Banks and Barry. The design has some points in common with Pennethorne's, but the effect is altogether less impressive.

senate committee wrote to Lord John Manners, emphasising 'the importance of giving to the University that place in public estimation which it can never obtain until it shall be provided with an appropriate Edifice belonging exclusively to itself'.[35] It seems to have been assumed from the beginning that the new building would be on the Burlington House site, and Pennethorne included space for new premises in his first block plan of July 1858. Nothing more happened until the

35 University of London, *Minutes of Senate*, 9 March 1859, pp. 20–2.

summer of 1864, when an 'influential delegation' told Lord Palmerston that lack of examination space was jeopardising the University's efficiency, especially in science and medicine, where much of its reputation lay. New examination halls were desperately needed, together with a library, offices and meeting places for Convocation and the Senate. The dons suggested building on the Burlington Gardens site, and in December Pennethorne estimated the cost of the new building at £65,000.[36] He was finally confirmed as architect early in 1866.[37]

Pennethorne's first design was submitted in March 1866 (Plate 120), and the foundations were laid not long afterwards.[38] The building was to be free-standing, with only one important frontage, facing north. It would be very different in character from the structures usually conjured up in the English mind by the word university, with their dining halls, chapels and residential accommodation arranged around quadrangles. The University of London was and is run by administrators, and the centre of the building was to consist of a two-storied block containing offices, with pride of place given to a room for the governing body or Senate. Halls for examinations and lectures would flank this central block, with more examination rooms occupying the space behind and laboratories on the upper floors.

Pennethorne's original intention was that the facade would be in the 'plain classic' style he had proposed for the Piccadilly frontage, with a massive Corinthian portico at the centre. But the severity of this manner did not conform to the taste of the mid 1860s, one commentator remarking that 'in his endeavour to keep the style pure, the architect has made more sacrifice than the ideas of the day will tolerate'.[39] Three years earlier Lord Elcho had told his fellow MPs that:

. . . [a] great change was taking place in the spirit of British architecture. An earnest, truthful school was springing up, which abhorred pretences and used only bricks, stone, marble and such materials as looked what they really were. Although the rays of the *Lamp of Truth* had not yet penetrated the gloom of Downing Street, they were shed on buildings of all kinds, from churches down to warehouses and shops; and he did not despair of seeing a new London, at once truthful and picturesque in its architecture, rise on the ruins of the dead conventionalities and stucco shams of the present period.[40]

This view was shared by the University's registrar, Dr W. B. Carpenter, and in August 1866 he encouraged Pennethorne to prepare an alternative design in the 'Italian Gothic' idiom. With the Chancellor and Vice-Chancellor of the University both away on holiday, this design was shown to Lord John Manners who had become First Commissioner of Works for the third and last time. According to

---

36 *Ibid.*, 4 Nov. 1863, 6 July 1864, 20 July 1870; PRO, Work 2/28, p. 381.
37 *Minutes of Senate*, 19 April 1865, p. 28; 22 Oct. 1865; PRO, T 1/6611A/1902; T 1/6583C/17698; *Hansard*, 183 (30 April 1866), 192.
38 The history of the design is related in *Minutes of Senate*, 20 July 1870.
39 *BN*, 17 May 1867, 347. No elevation of this design survives.
40 *Hansard*, 172 (2 July 1863), 99–100.

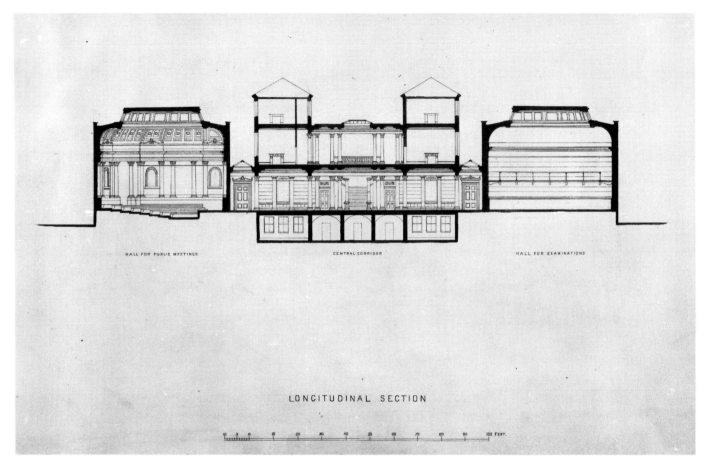

120. 'Plain classic' design for the Senate House of London University, longitudinal section, March 1866.

Pennethorne, he supported Carpenter's move to replace the original design with one of 'a character more Mediaeval or Renaissance'. Manners later said that, far from pressing for the use of Gothic, he 'had never directed Mr Pennethorne to form a design in Palladian, Gothic, Italian-Gothic, Byzantine, or any other style'.[41] But it does not seem very likely that Pennethorne would voluntarily choose to relinquish the classical manner, in which he excelled, in favour of the Gothic, in which he had only designed one important building, the Public Record Office. The most probable explanation is that the Registrar persuaded Manners to choose a Gothic design and that Pennethorne agreed to prepare one rather than lose the commission, rather as Gilbert Scott had agreed to design the Foreign Office in the classical manner a few years earlier.

Pennethorne's Gothic design (Plate 121) is a surprisingly attractive essay in the

---

41 *Ibid.*, 186 (2 April 1867), 1237–8.

293

121. The Gothic design for the London University building.

eclectic Franco-Italian manner popularised by Gilbert Scott. There is ample 'constructional polychromy', and sculptural enrichments abound. Symmetry was unavoidable because the foundations had already been built, and the front recalls Pugin's celebrated comment on the Houses of Parliament: 'All Grecian, sir! Gothic details on a classic body'. In place of the facade of giant Corinthian columns indicated in the first design, the central block now had a two-storied elevation, with 100-ft (30 metre) 'campaniles' at each end. The roof bristles with turrets, gables and ironwork, and the flanking wings are encrusted with ornament like mediaeval jewel-caskets. Without showing the new design either to the University Senate or to his fellow MPs, Manners called upon Pennethorne to prepare working drawings for the ground floor according to this design, and work began in February 1867.

When the 'Italian-Gothic' design was shown to the University Senate for the first time it caused an uproar, and in the following month a resolution was passed to the effect that 'a Building of which the style should be in harmony with that of Burlington House would be preferable to that represented in the proposed Elevation'.[42] This gave the cue for a minor skirmish in the 'Battle of the Styles' which enlivened the architectural life of Victorian England. The issue was raised in the House of Commons by A. H. Layard, soon to become First Commissioner of Works but still at the time a back-bencher. Eager to harry the minority Tory government and to publicise his own views on the beautifying of the capital, the excavator of Nineveh persuaded a reluctant Manners to exhibit Pennethorne's design in the Commons library, together with an alternative classic elevation. By departing from the plans approved by Cowper, Manners had adopted 'the extra-ordinary doctrine that the head of a department was not bound by any pledges made by his predecessors in office. That was a most mischievous and dangerous doctrine'. Layard's accusation led to a Parliamentary discussion in which Pennethorne found himself in the unusual position of being defended by his former detractor, Beresford Hope. For Hope, a Gothic University building might be 'a new starting point for metropolitan architecture . . . The time had come when the revolt was sounded against the monotonous repetition of Italian architecture in stucco and compo which had too long defaced our streets. Men were beginning to appreciate the picturesque forms of the Middle Ages, so well adapted to the purposes of our present life'. But his views attracted little support, and a suggestion by the MP for Oxford, Edward Cardwell, that both the existing designs should be scrapped in favour of a third, pointed the way to the eventual solution.[43]

With the walls now risen to a height of nineteen feet (six metres), Manners ordered work on the building to be suspended until MPs had had the opportunity to examine Pennethorne's designs. The drawings were placed in the Commons

---

42 *BN*, 7 June 1867, 397; *Minutes of Senate*, 27 March 1867.
43 *Hansard*, 186 (2 April 1867), 982–3, 1232–44.

library on 30 April, but Manners told the House that time was too pressing to allow for the appointment of the Select Committee that some had demanded; instead he would 'follow that course which had been taken with regard to the new Foreign Office'.[44] With public interest aroused, a writer in the *Building News* questioned how 'an accomplished designer in the Classical style should have been selected to carry out a building of the Italian Gothic type . . . [There] appears in this instance to have been an unusual want of discretion on the part of those in authority.'[45] This view of Manners's actions was upheld by MPs who voted on 31 May by fifty-two to forty-six in favour of an amendment by Layard that the £15,000 requested by the government to continue the building operations at Burlington Gardens should not be used to carry out the 'Italian Gothic' design – an early indication of what was soon to become a universal shift in public taste away from secular Gothic. According to Robert Lowe, soon to be Chancellor of the Exchequer under Gladstone, the Gothic design had been criticised 'with an unanimity which he had rarely witnessed . . . Ideas as to the character of University teaching associated themselves with the outlines of the building in which they were lodged . . . [The Department of Science and Art] had suffered much in public estimation from the simple fact that the public eye connected it with the Brompton Boilers.'[46] Having tried unsuccessfully to persuade MPs to let him seek a revised Gothic design which would allow the parts of the facade already constructed to remain as they were, Manners bowed to their will and agreed to ask Pennethorne for a completely new design.

The university officials now insisted on having their own say. They had joined in the chorus of disapproval of the Gothic design promoted by their own Registrar, but took fright at what they saw as Layard's attempt to force Pennethorne to build them a reproduction of Campbell's Burlington House. According to Dr John Storrar, chairman of Convocation, the University should insist on 'its right to be heard in the matter of the elevation and also that the Building should be so designed as to present the features of a separate and individual edifice – that it should be an University building and not an University in apartments, situated in the rear of a structure called Burlington House'.[47] This intervention was successful, and in its completed form the building turned out to be very different in character from the others on the Burlington House site. Pennethorne began work on the new elevation at the beginning of June 1867, 'taking the front of Burlington House as a foundation', and placed it in the Commons library on 30 June. A few days later Manners announced that he had not heard any hostile criticism of the new design, either in public or in private, and that he would instruct Pennethorne to carry it out. In October the views of the University were once again solicited, this time on the

---

44 *Ibid.*, 187 (31 May 1867), 265–6. 45 *BN*, 7 June 1867, 397.
46 *Hansard*, 187 (7 May 1867), 1468–9.
47 University of London Archives, RC 28/9, 11 June 1867.

122. The final design for the London University building (now the Museum of Mankind). The elements in the Gothic design in Plate 121 have all been classicised. The artist has made it look as if the building faces south onto a spacious square and not north onto a narrow street, as is in fact the case.

statuary with which the facade was to be liberally encrusted. Proposals were put forward in March 1868 and were accepted by Manners, after some minor haggling, a month later. Pennethorne sent in his final set of working drawings in March 1868, and by the middle of April building was proceeding fast. Detailed designs for the interiors were settled in the summer of 1869, and the building was finally opened by Queen Victoria on 11 May 1870.

By a skilful sleight of hand, Pennethorne succeeded in converting the Gothic facade of his second design into a thoughtful and highly original essay in the cosmopolitan classic manner he had been developing since the 1850s (Plate 122). From the time of his Foreign Office designs he had developed two main vehicles of expression, the one severe and monumental, and the other more exuberant and richly adorned. The 'plain classic' design was of the first type, the final design is the best surviving example of the second. The appreciation of this carefully controlled facade is made difficult by the fact that it faces north and therefore lacks much of the interplay of light and shadow which is so essential if classical architecture is to look its best. More importantly, it fronts a narrow street, and, like Street's slightly later Law Courts, can only be seen in sharp perspective. It was no doubt this consideration which encouraged Pennethorne to give it its pronounced sculptural quality, to introduce stonework of different colours, to adorn the roof-line with statuary, and to introduce the projecting porch.

The central block containing the main university offices and the meeting room for the Senate is more elaborately detailed than the rest of the building, with the first floor treated as a *piano nobile* articulated in an almost Sansovinesque way by engaged Composite columns supporting a richly carved entablature. Further variety is introduced by the projecting entrance colonnade, and by the low, flat-topped towers dividing the central block from the wings. They make less visual sense than those in the rejected Gothic design, but they nevertheless make an important contribution to the total effect. The wings are simpler in character. They are lit by rows of large first-floor windows divided by engaged Corinthian columns, while the plain rusticated ground floor is relieved by niches containing statues. Slightly projecting buttresses continue up between the windows to the balustraded roof-line – another reminder of the Gothic origins of the design.

The character of the facade owes much to the choice of materials. The walls are of stock brick, which can be seen exposed on the sides and back of the building, where the polychromatic bands of the Gothic design and the semi-Gothic window-arches were allowed to remain. But the main facade is faced in stone, and here Pennethorne chose to employ a classical version of 'constructional polychromy', with courses of grey Hopton Wood stone interrupting the white Portland ashlar and the first-floor columns of red Mansfield sandstone.

The external effect is further enlivened by profuse sculpture. Architectural sculpture has suffered so total a decline in the twentieth century that it is difficult for us now to 'read' a building like the university Senate House. The members of the Senate wanted their headquarters to present an image to the world of a humanistic, liberal-minded institution which transmitted a culture firmly rooted in a tradition stretching back to the ancient world. So there are four seated figures over the entrance – Bentham (Plate 123), Milton, Newton and Harvey – representing Englishmen famous in the four faculties of the University (Law, Literature, Science and Medicine) but freed from any taint of clerical obscurantism. Manners objected to the choice of Bentham, but was told by the Senate that 'no man can be selected to be as suitable as Bentham to represent the Faculty of Law'. Six standing figures on the roofline of the central block represent 'men of ancient times eminent in various departments of study included in the University Courses' (Cicero, Galen, Aristotle, Plato, Archimedes and Justinian). Six more recent worthies stand on the roofline of the two wings (Hume, Hunter, Dalton, Galileo, Laplace and Goethe), and the niches on the ground floor of the wings hold 'portrait statues' of other

123. Statue of Jeremy Bentham over the entrance to the London University building. The prophet of utilitarianism is here commemorated in stone at the University's first Senate House, only a mile or so away from University College where his mummified remains are preserved in a glass case. The statue is by Joseph Durham.

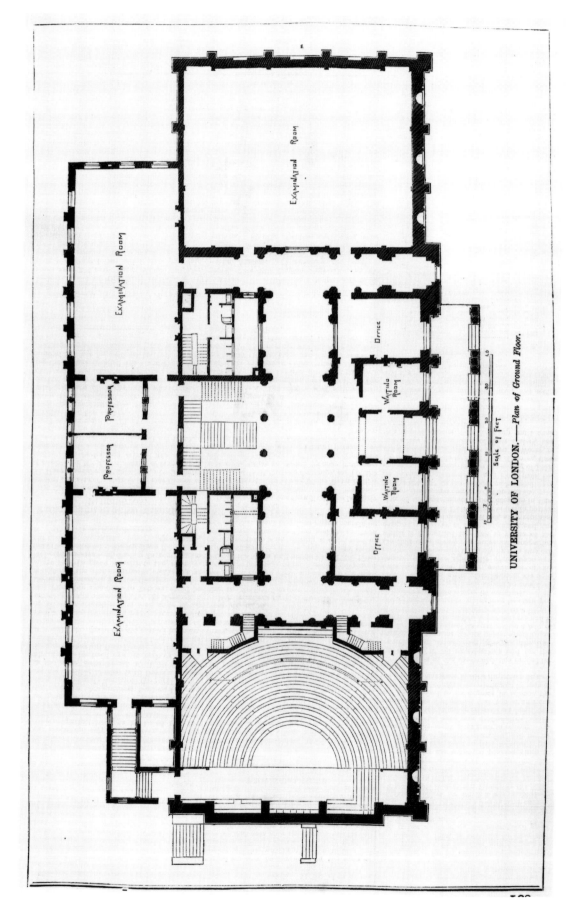

UNIVERSITY OF LONDON.—*Plan of Ground Floor.*

124. Ground floor plan of the London University building.

thinkers (Locke, Bacon, Adam Smith, Cuvinier, Leibniz and Linnaeus). Manners pleaded for the inclusion of Shakespeare, but was told that he did not represent any of the faculties of the University and would have to go inside the building. Pennethorne was responsible for the choice of sculptors: Joseph Durham for the seated figures over the porch, and the younger J. S. Westmacott and W. F. Woodington (the Curator of Sculpture at the Royal Academy) for the ancient philosophers on the roof. The modern *savants* in the niches were by William Theed and Patrick McDowell and the other figures on the roofline by Matthew Noble and E. W. Wyon.[48]

The interior is a masterly exercise in classical planning of the kind more usually associated with the French *Beaux Arts* tradition (Plate 124). The building was not 'one of those too numerous public institutions on entering which the visitor is puzzled as to which way to go, or where to discover what he wants'.[49] The ground floor is arranged around two intersecting axes, one stretching east to west between the lecture hall and the main examination room, which also served as a library, and the other from the entrance to the staircase leading up to the main rooms on the first floor. Because of the need to cater for large numbers of examination candidates, the cross-axis is a wide corridor with segment-headed arches supporting the iron beams of the first floor. Later changes have removed the original purpose of this corridor, and the entrance to the former lecture room is, at the time of writing, closed by an enigmatic stone figure from the British Museum's ethnographic collection. At each end transverse corridors led originally to smaller examination rooms at the back of the building. The staircase – Pennethorne's most impressive – follows the 'imperial' pattern with a single flight of stairs rising to a landing and splitting into two. Light comes from large windows set in circular relieving arches in a clerestory whose roof is supported on an elaborate arrangement of iron girders hidden by plasterwork. A large niche on the landing originally sheltered a statue of Shakespeare, but it now contains a fetishistic cult figure from the South Sea Islands which grins malevolently across to the Senate room (Plate 125), once the hub of the University's activities and elaborately embellished in the sumptuous manner already used by Pennethorne at Buckingham Palace and Marlborough House.

Like the earlier Geological Museum, the building was elaborately serviced. On the first floor there was a top-lit anatomical dissecting room with a roof supported on iron trusses, and a laboratory which was '[fitted] up with great completeness, each student having presses, basin, and water to his hand . . . A 'stink closet' in various divisions, is provided for dealing with offensive fumes; and there is a large air-shaft over the top of the room controllable with dampers.'[50] The two largest rooms in the building were the lecture hall and the examination hall in the wings.

---

48 PRO, Work 1/86, pp. 215–16.   49 *The Builder*, 14 April 1870, 377–8.
50 *Ibid.*, 14 May 1870, 377.

125. Lobby at the top of the main staircase of the London University building. The Senate met in the room to the left.

126. The main examination room of the London University building *c.* 1900. At the time of writing the room was divided up and the detailing hidden behind partitions and false ceilings erected when the building was turned into the Museum of Mankind.

The former had banked seating for 900 people arranged in a semicircle, with galleries supported on iron columns, and the latter (Plate 126) was a plain rectangle unimpeded by internal supports. Both rooms were divided up after the university vacated the building, in 1900, and with this subdivision the rationale of Pennethorne's plan has to a large extent been obscured.

The University Senate House was Pennethorne's last building, and also one of the most distinguished English buildings in the architectural tradition of which he formed a part. James Fergusson thought it was one of the few Victorian public buildings to reconcile successfully the language of the orders with modern needs:

The details are severely classical, and the form sufficiently monumental for the situation or the purposes to which the building is dedicated, that there is nothing about the building which can be called a sham or anything that can even be reproached as suggesting a falsehood. The two great halls in the wings . . . enabled [Pennethorne] to get repose and dignity from an unpierced basement, and the requisite support to the centre containing the council-room and other state apartments of the building. All this is expressed in the exterior as tastefully as in any mediaeval building, and with an elegance that satisfies the most refined taste.[51]

Another writer compared the new building favourably to Wilkins's University College:

What a ghastly edifice is that last-named seat of learning! With the remembrance of its long monotonous front, with the inevitable portico and cupola of the period still fresh in one's mind, it is quite a wonderful sensation to stand before the bright and highly ornate structure in which the University has taken up its abode.[52]

Pennethorne's University of London building demonstrated that ornament could be combined with structural logic and clear planning to create a sense of controlled dignity which would express the prestige of a major academic institution. It is in this reassertion of classical values in an unsympathetic age that its historical interest lies.

---

51 J. Fergusson, *History of the Modern Styles of Architecture* (2nd edn, 1873), p. 347.
52 *All the Year Round*, NS 4 (1870), 182.

10

EPILOGUE

IN 1868 THERE occurred one of those incidents which epitomises the passing of an age. The occasion was the design of a house for George James Howard, the art-loving nephew of the Earl of Carlisle (the former Lord Morpeth) on Palace Green, an open space in front of Kensington Palace to the south of Kensington Palace Gardens. Howard's architect was Philip Webb, friend of William Morris and one of the most original and uncompromising of the younger generation of architects. The house was to stand on the Crown estate and so the elevation had to be approved by Pennethorne. He found Webb's design 'almost unintelligible'. The house would be '*far inferior* to any one on the Estate – it would look most common place – and in my opinion [would] be perfectly hideous – it is probably intended for dutch or german but is unsuitable for London'. Webb expressed some surprise that Pennethorne should try to 'hinder the erection of a building which . . . possesses character and originality, tempered most certainly with reverential attention to the works of acknowledged masters of the art of architecture'. And when Pennethorne insisted on the addition of a heavy stone cornice he refused to conform and threatened to resign as architect. Pennethorne agreed in the end to a suggestion by T. H. Wyatt that a brick cornice should be substituted for a stone one, and the house was completed to this revised design in 1869 (Plate 127).[1]

The denouement shows how difficult it was for one man to act as architectural dictator for even a limited area of London in the second half of the nineteenth century. The architectural philosophies of Webb and Pennethorne were diametrically opposed, but by the 1860s Pennethorne's attempt to enforce his ideas of architectural propriety on the Crown estate was doomed. William Makepeace Thackeray, the occupier of the adjoining house in Palace Green, expressed a growing feeling when he said in 1860 that he 'should die from a surfeit of stucco'.

---

1 PRO Cres 35/2127; *Survey of London*, 37 (1973), pp. 185–7.

The way lay open for the seductive charms of 'Queen Anne' and the wild extravagance of the Edwardian 'free style'.

Pennethorne retired on 30 June 1870. As a long-standing civil servant he was given a pension, which amounted to £1,766 a year. With his London University building just completed, *The Builder* suggested that a knighthood would be 'highly esteemed by the profession', and in November that honour was conferred – something which, for political reasons, had eluded Nash. Five years earlier he had bought Worcester Park, near Malden (Surrey), a stuccoed villa first built in 1797 but subsequently enlarged by Nash and standing in spacious grounds which had once formed part of the park of Nonsuch Palace.[2] And it was in this comfortable gentleman's residence that he died suddenly, of a heart attack, on 1 September 1871.[3] He was buried in Highgate Cemetery and his property placed in the hands of his brother John and his two eldest sons, his wife having died before him.[4] None of his family followed him into the architectural profession. Worcester Park House was sold and has long since disappeared under the suburban sprawl of south-west London.

When Pennethorne died the country lost one of its most senior and respected architects. But what of the man? Here the historian must confess almost total ignorance. Speaking to the Royal Institute of British Architects in December 1871, just after Pennethorne's death, his former assistant Arthur Cates said that he was '[a] man of retired and studious habits, engrossed in the duties of his office, and mixing but little with society'.[5] Another obituarist called him 'a man of kindness, spotless integrity, and universal courtesy'.[6] But apart from these posthumous tributes there are no indications of his real character. No diaries survive, and there are hardly any letters to give a sense of a living human beneath the facade of the dedicated public servant. His only testament is his work.

In his lifetime Pennethorne was one of the most admired and respected of English architects.[7] For Robert Kerr he was 'the last of our government architects', representative of a tradition which went back to Jones and Wren, victim in the end of the Gladstone administration's determination to dispense with 'proper architectural advice'.[8] But since he died he has been largely forgotten and ignored. In an age of mammoth practices, when Gilbert Scott could design or restore a church in every county in England and Wales except Cardiganshire, he designed relatively few buildings, and some of those buildings have been demolished or drastically altered. Through no fault of his own, the street improvement schemes on which he spent so much time do not form a coherent picture. He published no books, had no

---

2 G. F. Prosser, *Select Illustrations of the County of Surrey* (1829).
3 *The Builder*, 16 Sept. 1871, 717.   4 Somerset House wills xiii (1871) 621, no. 14.
5 *RIBA Transactions*, 22 (1871–2), 60.   6 *The Architect*, 6 (1871), 13.
7 *Mechanics' Magazine*, 26 (1871), 286.   8 *RIBA Transactions*, 22 (1871–2), 63.

127. 1 Palace Green, Kensington, built by Philip Webb for the art-loving George James Howard in 1868–9. Webb's architecture was the antithesis of Pennethorne's, and Pennethorne's failure to significantly modify the design of this house on the Crown estate symbolises the passing of an era.

famous pupils, and generally shunned the limelight. His buildings make few concessions to those who judge the merit of architecture by its novelty or its decorative charm. Perhaps because of this, his most perceptive twentieth-century critics have been architects who have shared his classical training.[9]

Pennethorne's career, as the architectural writer Edward Hall pointed out in an obituary, spanned 'the entire course of modern architecture from the first revulsion against effete Palladianism to the parti-coloured epoch at which we have arrived'.[10] His earliest buildings, dating from the 1830s, are recognisable products of the Nash office, and in his parks and ornamental buildings he remained true to the Nash inheritance. But in time he developed a manner more monumental than that of Nash, yet less frigidly Grecian than that of Smirke, Wilkins and their generation. This style drew on the dignified style of the Italian Renaissance, but during the 1850s he moved beyond it to create a powerful and richly detailed synthesis of the antique and the modern. His mature style was closer to that of Cockerell, Elmes and his main Continental contemporaries – men like Labrouste, Hittorff, Stüler and Semper – than it was to the more ornate later manner of Barry and his many English disciples. He would have agreed with Vaudoyer that:

in order to satisfy the needs of our time, one must by preference study the rudimentary architecture of the ancients . . . So this architecture, that one calls Romantic, I don't know very well why, is an architecture which seeks to discover true principles, which demands that each form be determined by reason and necessity, which seeks to submit itself to the nature of materials, which tries, finally, to set this art in harmony with its century.[11]

To understand why Pennethorne was admired by so many of his contemporaries one has only to look closely at the Geological Museum and the London University building. In each he adapted the language of the orders to the exigencies of a modern public building, appealing both to our sense of tradition and, through the doctrine of 'apparent utility', to reason. Internally he overcame the limitations of site and budget to create sequences of public spaces which, at least in the case of the Geological Museum, made open use of the new materials of the age. In doing so he created structures which solved immediate needs and at the same time raised the spirits of their users – no easy task in a public building. If more of his later designs, like those for the Foreign Office and War Office, had been carried out, the history of Victorian architecture might have been different.

Pennethorne's architectural style almost died with him. By the 1860s the classical

---

9 A. E. Richardson, *Monumental Classic Architecture in Great Britain and Ireland* (1914), pp. 9, 98–9; H. S. Goodhart-Rendel, 'Piccadilly', *RIBA Journal*, 3rd series, 40 (1933), 365 and *English Architecture since the Regency* (1953), p. 189.

10 *Mechanics' Magazine*, 26 (1871), 272.

11 Quoted in D. van Zanten, *Designing Paris* (1987), p. 8.

tradition was being edged to the periphery of the architectural world in England, though not on the Continent or in Scotland. There was no École des Beaux Arts to maintain classical standards. Cockerell and Barry were dead and their pupils, with the exception perhaps of E. M. Barry, lacked their creative talents and never enjoyed their prestige within the profession. In the 1870s the individualism and sentimental attachment to the past which were such noticeable features of English life and culture came to the fore in architecture; in the very year of Pennethorne's death, Norman Shaw exhibited his perspective drawing of Leyswood (Sussex) at the Royal Academy, harbinger of the wave of picturesque eclecticism which swept the country in the last three decades of the nineteenth century.

But Pennethorne's architectural principles lived on in the Office of Works and in the private practices of a handful of architects who kept the flickering torch of classicism alight. Though not trained by Pennethorne, John Taylor clearly learnt a great deal from him, and his extensions to Pennethorne's buildings, notably the Public Record Office, are hard to distinguish from the original work. And in commissions like the Bow Street Magistrates Court (1879–80), the Patent Office library and the new staircase and galleries at the National Gallery he showed himself capable of imitating Pennethorne's style as effectively as Pennethorne himself had imitated that of earlier architects. The splendid Post Offices erected by James Williams, including the General Post Office extension in St Martins-le-Grand in the City, are also products of a continuing tradition stretching back through Pennethorne to Chambers and ultimately even to Inigo Jones. Williams died in 1892 and Taylor retired in 1898, but Office of Works classicism lasted well into the twentieth century, only to fall victim to the onslaughts of International Modernism after the Second World War.

Pennethorne's architectural principles were vindicated to some extent in the revival of classical architecture at the end of the nineteenth century. The free spirits of the 'Edwardian Baroque' – men like Mountford and Rickards – looked for inspiration to Wren and the European architecture of the seventeenth century rather than to the restrained classicism of which Pennethorne had been an exponent. Their inspiration was essentially pictorial. But the Beaux Arts–inspired manner of buildings like Sir John Burnet's north facade to the British Museum, the Royal Automobile Club by Mewès and Davis, and some of the buildings of Sir Reginald Blomfield and Sir Albert Richardson clearly forms part of the tradition to which Pennethorne belonged. It is only relatively recently that the merits of these buildings have come to be widely appreciated.

Pennethorne's achievement extended beyond the design of buildings to the planning of London as a whole. Speaking to the Royal Institute of British Architects in 1871, Arthur Cates wrote that 'any memoir of Sir James Pennethorne which would pretend to do justice to his labours would in fact be a history of almost all that has been done or projected for the improvement of London' within the previous thirty years.[12] Few major architects have been so single-mindedly involved with the design and architectural embellishment of London over so long a period of time. If his plans for a 'Great Central Thoroughfare' and for 'ring roads' on the northern side of the City and on the South Bank had been carried out, Pennethorne would have made as great a mark on the city as Nash. Like Nash, he understood the implications of London's rapid growth. He realised that some degree of bold overall planning was needed if good communications were to be maintained and the city made into an artefact commensurate with its political and economic importance. He was one of the first people to grasp the value of well-planned and generously planted parks for the inhabitants of the poorer suburbs, and by creating Victoria and Battersea Parks he made an indelible mark on the urban landscape of north-east and south-west London. His street improvements hastened a process under which the social geography of central London was transformed by rooting out the worst slums. Better sanitation was provided, schools and churches built and a degree of 'social control' imposed on the remaining inhabitants. To this extent Pennethorne played a part in the creation of London's modern infrastructure and in so doing he helped change the material lives of its people.

Yet his achievement remained incomplete. The reason lies partly in the fragmentation of London's local government before 1855, partly in the parsimony of the central authorities and partly in the provinces' distrust of the capital. But it also reflects the choices of ordinary Londoners. There was no tradition of elegant street life as there was on the Continent.[13] Streets were to be hurried through, not lingered in. The leisured classes spent their time in their houses, their clubs or the parks, and the middle classes increasingly escaped at the end of their working day to the suburbs. Suburban life represented for them an opportunity to realise a rural, arcadian vision which meant more than the attractions of the city. This compulsion even extended to the workers, if we can believe one of the witnesses to the Select Committee on Metropolitan Communications in 1855: 'The passion for country residence is increasing to an extent that it is almost impossible for persons who do not mix with the poor to know. You cannot find a broken teapot in which to stuff, as soon as spring comes, some flower or something, to give them an idea of green fields and the country'.[14] The coming of the railways made suburban residence a possibility for ever-growing numbers of people, and it is in the suburbs, not the central districts, that the most important contribution of Victorian London to city planning must be found.

The fascination with suburban life went hand in hand with an anti-urban prejudice which has never been eradicated. If Londoners had been less drawn to the

---

12 *RIBA Trans.*, 22 (1871–2), 53.
13 See, for instance, F. Bedarida and A. R. Sutcliffe, 'The street in the structure and life of the city', in B. M. Stave (ed.), *Modern Industrial Cities* (Beverley Hills and London, 1981), pp. 28-35.
14 Rep. Sel. Cttee. on Metropolitan Communications, *PP* 1854–5, 10, p. 158.

suburbs it would have been easier to fund new streets in the centre. If popular taste had been less averse to grand gestures there would have been more support for ambitious plans like those which Pennethorne drew up for the South Kensington estate. As Edwin Lutyens lamented in 1904:

Our new streets, oh the vapour of it all!! Look at Paris, how well they lay out there, the courage, sense and big obvious simplicity of it all . . . Our LCC is appalling compared with French authority. So there it rests, and will, until someone can awake the ignorant torpidity and guinea-pig waste of national energy. This saving of ha'pence and confusion of accounts, philanthropics and trade, does waste and mislead woefully. It is a long story, and is bred in the bone of the nation.[15]

Henry James called London 'a tremendous chapter of accidents'. In Paris, as the English have been reminded *ad nauseam* since the time of Napoleon III, 'the whole air of the place is architectural . . . Everything reminds you that the idea of beautiful and stately arrangement has never been out of fashion, that the art of composition has always been at work or at play'. In London, on the other hand, 'the absence of style, or rather of the *intention* of style, is certainly the most general characteristic'. What attracted Henry James about London was not its beauty but its variety and its immensity: 'A small London would be an abomination, as it fortunately is an impossibility'.[16] Throughout its history London has developed in a scattered, inchoate way. It has always been a monument to the energy of individuals, not the organising power of the state. Pennethorne, the greatest Victorian architect to devote himself to the service of central government, could not avoid the consequences of London's history or ignore the wishes of its people. His career not only throws light on the physical appearance of England's greatest city; it also helps explain its underlying and strangely persistent human character.

---

15 C. Hussey, *The Life of Sir Edwin Lutyens* (1950), p. 123.
16 *English Hours* (1905 edn), pp. 8, 15.

CATALOGUE OF EXECUTED WORKS

THESE TWO LISTS include all the buildings which James Pennethorne is known to have designed and all the Metropolitan Improvement schemes he carried out. They do not include unexecuted projects, many of which are discussed at length in the text, or questionable attributions. All the places are in London, except where otherwise stated, and, unless otherwise stated, the work was commissioned by the Office of Woods and Forests or (after 1851) the Office of Works. The commissions are arranged in chronological order of work starting, and the subsequent history of each is outlined. The cost is that of the completed work, excluding fittings or, if that is unknown, the sum mentioned in the tender. The references in brackets are to sources of factual information about dates, costs, and so on; some fuller bibliographical references have also been given under Lit (Literature) where appropriate, along with references to the architect's drawings where they are known to exist.

(a) *Buildings*

ST JAMES'S STREET BAZAAR, 10 St James's Street, for William Crockford 1831–2. Internal alterations 1847 (architect: Ambrose Poynter); more alterations for Junior Army and Navy Club 1881–2, including bay window to St James's Street (architect: Wyatt Papworth); further alterations 1897 (architect: Walter Emden); third floor and attics added for Motor Union Insurance Co. 1914–15.

Lit: *Survey of London*, 30 (1960), pp. 438–9.

10 CARLTON HOUSE TERRACE. Minor internal alterations, including bathroom, for Sir Matthew White Ridley 1831.

(Letters, Northumberland Record Office ZRI 33/3).

HOUSE AT NEWMARKET (SUFFOLK) for William Crockford *c.* 1832–40.

(*RIBA Transactions* (1856–7), 10). Pennethorne may also have been involved in work for other patrons at Newmarket: see p. 27).

SWITHLAND HALL (LEICESTERSHIRE), for George John Danvers 1834. Wings added 1852 (rainwater heads).

(*RIBA Transactions* (1856–7), 10).

HOUSE for MR WARD 1835.

(Letter in Kent Record Office, U543/E7. It is possible that this house is Northwood House, Cowes, Isle of Wight: see p. 28).

ST JULIENS, SEVENOAKS (KENT), enlargement and internal alterations for J. C. Herries 1836–7. Now divided into flats.

(Letters, Kent Record Office, U543/E7).

LAMORBEY PARK, SIDCUP (KENT), alterations for John Malcolm c. 1836–7. Now an adult education centre.

(*RIBA Transactions* (1856–7), 10).

CHAPEL at HALFWAY STREET, SIDCUP, for John Malcolm c. 1836–7. Demolished 1873 and replaced by Holy Trinity, Lamorbey.

(*RIBA Transactions* (1856–7), 10).

DILLINGTON HOUSE, ILMINSTER (SOMERSET), extensive rebuilding and expansion for John Lee Lee c. 1837. Now an adult education centre.

(*RIBA Transactions* (1856–7), 10; R. Dunning, *Some Somerset Country Houses* (1991), 40–1.

CHRIST CHURCH, ALBANY STREET, 1836–7. Altered internally 1843 and 1849 (architect: R. C. Carpenter); further alterations, including choirstalls (1853), new seating, wall paintings, etc. (1866–8) and pulpit (1884) (architect: William Butterfield). Now St George's Cathedral of the Patriarchate of Antioch.

Cost: £6,000, raised by public subscription (C. E. Lee, *St Pancras Church and Parish* (1955), p. 50).

Lit: *Survey of London*, 21 (1949), pp. 150–2.

NATIONAL SCHOOLS, ALBANY STREET, Demolished.

(PRO Cres 19/20).

HOLY TRINITY, GRAY'S INN ROAD, 1837–8. Internal alterations 1880–1. Demolished 1931.

Builders: Messrs Pearce and Guerrier.

Cost: £7,200 (*Civil Engineer & Architects' Journal*, 1 (1837–8), 14).

Lit: *Survey of London*, 24 (1952), p. 59.

CLAREMONT (SURREY). Rebuilding of stable block 1842–4 (with Thomas Chawner).

Cost: £8,605.

Lit: J. M. Crook and M. H. Port, *The History of the King's Works*, vi (1973), p. 322.

BLOCK of SHOPS AND CHAMBERS at junction of Bloomsbury Street and Broad Street, St Giles 1845–6. Demolished 1885.

Cost: £3,100.

Builders: Messrs H. and J. Lee (PRO, Work 6/94, p. 183).

Drawings: RIBA x20/19.

VICTORIA PARK, lodge, gates and bridge, 1845; arcade 1861. The lodge was destroyed by bombing in 1941 and the arcade after the Second World War.

Costs: £2,482 (lodge); £2,200 (bridge).

Builders (lodge and bridge): Messrs Lee (GLRO, Victoria Park Papers, vol. 2).

Drawings: GLRO, Victoria Park Plans

MUSEUM OF PRACTICAL GEOLOGY, Jermyn Street, 1846–51. Demolished 1935.

Cost: £29,572.

Builder: John Kelk.

Drawings: Geological Survey GSI/210; GLRO Metropolitan Board of Works plans 148–56.

Lit: *The Builder*, 27 March 1847, 18 Nov. 1848; *Survey of London*, 30 (1960), pp. 272-4; Crook and Port, *King's Works*, VI, pp. 460–1.

INSOLVENT DEBTORS' COURT, 33–4 Lincolns Inn Fields, conversion of no. 34 into three courts and offices 1847–8. Demolished *c.* 1911 to make way for Land Registry.

(Crook and Port, *King's Works*, VI, pp. 439–40).

THE QUADRANT, Regent Street, remodelled street frontage 1848. Demolished 1924 and replaced by present blocks by Reginald Blomfield.

Cost: £5,616.

Builder: John Kelk (PRO, Cres 19/35, p. 205).

ORDNANCE OFFICE, new wing on site of 83–4 Pall Mall 1850–1; minor alterations to main block (85–7 Pall Mall) 1852–3. Demolished 1908–11 to make way for Royal Automobile Club.

Cost: £20,165.

Builders: Messrs Winsland and Holland.

Lit: *Survey of London*, 29 (1960), pp. 359–68; Crook and Port, *King's Works*, VI, p. 471.

CENTRAL POST OFFICE, LIVERPOOL, internal alterations 1851–3. Destroyed by bombing 1941.

Cost: £13,120 (*RIBA Transactions* (1856–7), 10).

Drawings: PRO, Work 30/827–8.

PUBLIC RECORD OFFICE, Chancery Lane, central block 1851–9, south part of east wing 1864–6, tower 1865–7, north part of east wing 1869–70. West wing and Chancery Lane front added by John Taylor 1891–6.

Cost: central block £78,606, including fittings (*RIBA Transactions* (1856–7), 10); S. part of E. wing £29,355; tower £14,820; N. part of E. wing £44,000.

Builders: Messrs Lee (central block); Messrs Piper and Wheeler (S. part of E. wing); Messrs Jackson and Shaw (tower and N. part of E. wing).

Drawings: PRO, MPD 177; MPI 169; MPI 172; MPI 299; Work 30/197–224 (working drawings, central range), 30/2585–2665 (S. part of E. wing and tower), 30/2727–2737 (N. part of E. wing).

Lit: *The Builder*, 11 Oct. 1851, 635–6; R. Ellis, 'The Building of the Public Record Office' in A. Hollander (ed.), *Essays in Memory of Sir Hilary Jenkinson* (1962), pp. 9–24; E. Hallam and M. Roper, 'The Capital and the Records of the Nation', *London Journal*, 4 (1978), 74–90; Crook and Port, *King's Works*, VI, pp. 471–6.

BUCKINGHAM PALACE, south range, including Ballroom and Supper Room 1852–6; wall to Buckingham Gate and external alterations to Riding House, 1859–60; alterations to chapel and approaches 1860–2. Interiors of south range remodelled by Frank Verity and C. H. Bessant 1902; chapel destroyed by bombing 1940.

Cost: £77,655 (south range: *RIBA Transactions* (1865–7), 10); £4,300 (boundary wall and riding house); chapel alterations £5,900.

Builders: Thomas Cubitt (south wing); Messrs Piper (wall and chapel).

Drawings: Royal Library, Windsor RL 22076–22092 (first designs for south wing); PRO, Work 34/360–464 (working drawings, S. wing), 34/470–99 (chapel alterations), 34/530–48 (boundary wall).

Lit: *The Builder*, 31 May 1856, 297–9; 'The Ball and Supper Room of Buckingham Palace', *RIBA Journal*, 24 Nov. 1934; J. Harris, G. de Bellaigue and O. Miller, *Buckingham Palace* (1968).

SOMERSET HOUSE, INLAND REVENUE OFFICES, Lancaster Place 1852–6. South wing adapted for Stamping Department and subterranean floors under entrance courtyard altered 1857–8.

Cost: £81,123.

Builder: John Kelk.

Drawings: PRO, Work 30/284–307, 30/2756–2793.

Lit: *The Builder*, 27 March 1852, 193; *BN*, 27 May 1857, 215; R. Needham and Webster, *Somerset House Past and Present* (1905).

STATIONERY OFFICE, Princes Street, Westminster, converted out of former Parliamentary Mews 1853–5. Demolished 1952.

Cost: £25,792 (*RIBA Transactions* (1856–7), 10).

Builders: Messrs Piper.

DUCHY OF CORNWALL OFFICE, Buckingham Gate, with lodge and gates at entrance to Birdcage Walk (since removed), 1854–7. Extra storey added to Office and interiors altered after Second World War.

Cost: £9,609 (*RIBA Transactions* (1856–7), 10).

Builders: Messrs Haward and Nixon.

Drawings: PRO, Work 833–88.

Lit: *The Builder*, 3 Nov. 1855, 526–7; *BN*, 6 Feb. 1857, 144.

LODGE to MARLBOROUGH HOUSE, Marlborough Road, 1856–7.

Builders: Messrs Holland.

Drawings: PRO, Work 34/825–30.

OFFICE OF WOODS AND FORESTS, 1–2 Whitehall Place, minor additions and alterations 1856, 1861. Demolished to make way for Crown Estate Office 1909.

(PRO, Cres 19/44, p. 245; 19/48, p. 120; 19/49, pp. 136, 352; LRRO 1/2177)

SOUTH KENSINGTON MUSEUM, temporary buildings, including lecture room 1856. Demolished 1865–78 to make way for present Lecture Theatre and courtyard.

Cost: £5,500.

Builders: Messrs Kelk.

Lit: *The Builder*, 24 Jan. 1857, 45–6; J. Physick, *The Victoria and Albert Museum* (1982).

DISTRICT POST OFFICE, Buckingham Gate, 1859–61. Demolished.

Cost: £11,500 (PRO, T 1/6693A/3774).

(PRO, Work 1/63, p. 333; 1/68, p. 113)

STAFF COLLEGE, CAMBERLEY (SURREY), 1859–61. Pennethorne supplied the design, but the building was carried out under Colonel Chapman of the Royal Engineers. Attic storey added 1912–14.

Cost: £40,000–£50,000.

Builder: Myers and Sons.

Drawings: Some working drawings are preserved at the College.

Lit: A. R. Godwin-Austin, *The Staff and the Staff College* (1927).

PRINCIPAL PROBATE OFFICE, Doctors' Commons, Knightrider Street, new strong rooms and offices 1860–1, 1868–9. Demolished after transference of Probate Office to Somerset House 1874; site occupied by Post Office Savings Bank, Queen Victoria Street, and since 1932 by Faraday Building.

Cost: £7,000 (1860–1); £14,235 (1868–9).

Builders: J. and C. I'Anson.

Drawings: PRO, Work 30/2828–2846.

(PRO, Work 1/65, pp. 299–306; Work 2/24, pp. 251–2; Work 12/52/7)

NATIONAL GALLERY, Trafalgar Square, new picture gallery, sculpture gallery for Royal Academy and staircases 1860–1. Demolished 1885 and present main staircase built on site by John Taylor.

Cost: £16,704.

Builder: William Cubitt.

Drawings: PRO, Work 33/1333–1385.

Lit: *BN*, 8 March 1861, 211–12; *The Builder*, 6 April 1861, 233; G. Tyack, 'A Gallery Worthy of the British People', *Architectural History*, 30 (1990), 120–34.

MARLBOROUGH HOUSE, internal remodelling and carriage porch for the Prince of Wales 1860–2; stables 1862–3. Extra floors added to central block 1870, new Study and Library 1874, new storey to wings 1885 (architect: John Taylor); interior remodelled again 1902 and 1927–8.

Cost: £14,000 (house, excluding cost of interior decoration which was financed out of the Prince's own revenues); £17,000 (stables).

Builders: Messrs Kelk (house); Smith and Taylor (stables).

Drawings: PRO, Work 34/745–802 (house), 34/836–858 (stables).

Lit: *The Builder*, 7 March 1863, 169 (house); 12 Dec. 1863, 879–80 (stables).

CARLTON HOUSE TERRACE, completion of east block to designs of John Nash after demolition of riding house, 1862–4. Interiors planned by lessees' own architects.

(PRO, Cres 35/1963–4)

PATENT OFFICE, 25 Southampton Buildings, Chancery Lane, new library and offices 1865–7. Replaced by present library designed by John Taylor 1898–1901.

Cost: £13,300.

Builder: G. Mansfield and Son.

Drawings: PRO, Work 30/2513–2523.

Lit: *BN*, 5 July 1867, 457; H. Harding, *Patent Office Centenary* (1953).

STANHOPE GATE, HYDE PARK, addition of extra storey to Lodge designed by Decimus Burton, 1867. Demolished as a result of widening Park Lane 1960–3.

(PRO, Work 1/84, pp. 68, 414; Work 16/437)

UNIVERSITY OF LONDON SENATE HOUSE, Burlington Gardens 1867–70. Taken over by Civil Service Commission 1902 and in 1970 by Ethnographic Department of British Museum as the Museum of Mankind. East wing divided up to create premises for British Academy 1928 (architect: Arnold Mitchell).

Cost: £94,548.
Builders: Messrs Jackson and Shaw.
Drawings: RIBA x16/38 (rejected Gothic design); PRO Work 33/1745–1812.
Lit: *The Builder*, 23 Nov. 1867, 853–5; 14 May 1870, 377–8; *Survey of London*, 31 (1963), pp. 435–41.

(b) *Metropolitan Improvements and plans for the Crown estate*

PARK VILLAGE WEST, layout for Crown estate, under general supervision of John Nash, 1832–4. Pennethorne may also have designed some of the houses (see p. 27).

(MS diary for 1832, now lost).
Lit: *Survey of London*, 21 (1949), pp. 153–5.

KENSINGTON PALACE GARDENS, for Crown estate (with Thomas Chawner). Designed 1841, carried out 1842–5. The houses were all designed by other architects.

Plans: PRO, MPE 758; MPE 874; MR 55.
Lit: M. Girouard, 'Town Houses for the Wealthy', *Country Life*, 11 and 18 Nov. 1971; *Survey of London*, 37 (1973), pp. 152–83.

PRIMROSE HILL, layout designed 1841, carried out in part under Act of Parliament (5 and 6 Vict. c. 78) 1842.

Plan: PRO, MPE 1608.

CRANBOURN STREET, linking Coventry Street and Long Acre and widening of Upper St Martin's Lane under Act of Parliament (4 Vict. c. 12, 1841). Plans 1839–40 (with Thomas Chawner), carried out 1843–5.

Cost: £207,093.
Plans: PRO, MR 1082; Work 30/436–7.
Lit: *Survey of London*, 34 (1966), pp. 339–55.

NEW OXFORD STREET, linking Oxford Street and High Holborn under Act of Parliament (3 and 4 Vict. c. 87, 1840). Plans 1839–40 (with Thomas Chawner), carried out 1843–7.

Cost (to 1847): £287,155.
Plans: PRO, MPEE 50; MR 1082; Work 30/431–3.

ENDELL STREET, linking Bow Street and Gower Street under Act of Parliament (3 and 4 Vict. c. 87). Plans 1839–40 (with Thomas Chawner), carried out 1843–6.

Cost (to 1847): £96,408.
Plans: 1st Rep. Sel. Cttee. on Metropolitan Improvements, *PP* 1840, 12.

COMMERCIAL STREET, linking Whitechapel High Street and Christ Church, Spitalfields, and widening of Red Lion Street and Dock Street further south, under Act of Parliament (3 and 4 Vict. c. 87). Plans 1839–40 (with Thomas Chawner), carried out 1843–6. Northern extension from Christ Church to Shoreditch under new Act (9 and 10 Vict. c. 39, 1846) carried out 1849–57.

> Cost: (first part, to 1847) £136,241; (extension) £211,689.
>
> Plans: *PP* 1840, 12; PRO, MPI 261; Work 30/426 (extension).
>
> Lit: *Survey of London*, 27 (1957), pp. 256–61.

VICTORIA PARK, formed under Act of Parliament 1842 (4 and 5 Vict. c. 27). Designs 1841 (with Thomas Chawner), revised 1845–6 by Pennethorne alone. Carried out 1845–7.

> Cost: £115,000 (*RIBA Transactions* (1856–7), 10).
>
> Plans: PRO, LRRO 1/2029, 2036–7, 2041, 2046; MPE 837; MR 55; GLRO, Victoria Park plans.
>
> Lit: A. Fein, 'Victoria Park: its Origins and History', *East London Papers*, 5 (1962); G. F. Chadwick, *The Park and the Town* (1966); C. Poulsen, *Victoria Park* (1976).

WINDSOR IMPROVEMENT SCHEME (Castle approaches, widening of High Street and Thames Street). Designed 1846, completed 1852.

> Cost: £52,159 (PRO, Work 19/30/4).
>
> Plans: PRO, MR 442.

VICTORIA PARK, layout of surrounding streets for Crown estate. Designs 1846, revised 1854. Carried out 1853–8.

> Drawings: PRO, LRRO 1/ 2068, 2083, 2111, 2115, 2128, 2142, 2199; MR 55.

CROWN LAND AT WINDSOR. Design for new street on site of old stables of Windsor Castle 1844. Design for layout of the Keppel estate 1852. Both of these projects were delayed for several years.

> Plans: PRO, MPE 592 and MPE 613.

BUCKINGHAM GATE (the Pimlico Improvement scheme), linking Birdcage Walk and Buckingham Palace Road under Act of Parliament (15 and 16 Vict. c. 78). Designs 1851, revised 1853. Carried out 1853–8.

> Cost: £62,478.
>
> Plans: PRO, Work 34/12; Work 38/77–80, 38/149; *PP* 1856, 52.

BATTERSEA PARK, formed under Act of 1846 (9 and 10 Vict. c. 30). Designs 1845, revised 1853–4. Carried out, including river embankment and surrounding roads, 1854–63 (from 1857 under supervision of John Gibson).

> Cost (to 1857): £310,643 (*PP* 1856–7, 41).
>
> Drawings: PRO, Work 32/660–75.
>
> Lit: Chadwick, *The Park and the Town*.

MARLBOROUGH ROAD, linking Pall Mall and the Mall through the eastern part of St James's Palace. Designed 1855 as part of new route across St James's Park (unexecuted) and carried out on reduced scale 1856.

> Cost: £4,500.
>
> Plans: PRO, Work 32/225; Work 34/825.

CHELSEA BRIDGE ROAD, linking Chelsea Bridge and Sloane Street under Act of Parliament (9 and 10 Vict. c. 39). Carried out in 1857–8 after completion of Chelsea Bridge.
   (PRO, Work 6/139/1; 138/16).

LIST OF POLITICIANS CONCERNED WITH GOVERNMENT BUILDING 1839–70

Prime Ministers

−1841	Lord Melbourne
1841	Sir Robert Peel
1846	Lord John Russell
1852	Lord Derby
1852	Lord Aberdeen
1855	Lord Palmerston
1858	Lord Derby
1859	Lord Palmerston
1866	Lord Derby
1868	William Ewart Gladstone

Chancellors of the Exchequer

−1841	Francis Baring
1841	Henry Goulburn
1846	Sir Charles Wood
1852	Benjamin Disraeli
1852	William Ewart Gladstone
1855	Sir George Cornewall Lewis
1858	Benjamin Disraeli
1859	William Ewart Gladstone
1866	Benjamin Disraeli
1868	G. W. Hunt
1868	Robert Lowe

First (Chief) Commissioners of Woods, Forests (to 1851) and of Works (from 1851)

−1841	Lord Duncannon
1841	Lord Lincoln
1846	Lord Canning

1846   Lord Morpeth (Earl of Carlisle from 1848).
1850   Lord Seymour
1852   Lord John Manners
1852   Sir William Molesworth
1855   Sir Benjamin Hall
1858   Lord John Manners
1859   Lord Henry Fitzroy
1860   William Cowper
1866   Lord John Manners
1868   Alfred Henry Layard
1869   Acton Ayrton

BIBLIOGRAPHY

NOTE ON SOURCES

The main sources for a study of James Pennethorne's works are in the Public Record Office. They include the records of the Crown estates, especially the letters and reports on individual properties in Cres 2, the letter books in Cres 19 and the Crown estate registered files in Cres 35. Among the Treasury papers, those in T 1 (miscellaneous papers) include information about government building projects which is often not available elsewhere, and T 1/6041A/20465 and, especially, T 1/6693A/3774 supply the most detailed documentation concerning Pennethorne's position in the Office of Works, including a Treasury report on this subject compiled in 1859. There is more on Pennethorne's official status in T 1/6936A/ 20938. See also the letters to the Office of Woods and Forests in T 25 and to the Office of Works in T 26.

The copious correspondence between successive First Commissioners and Pennethorne can be found in Work 1, and further information on government projects is in the letters to the Treasury in Work 2. There is material on the Metropolitan Improvements in Work 6/92–103 (reports and letters), as well as papers on individual improvements in other categories in Work 6. Work 12 contains papers on government offices, Work 16 on parks, Work 17 on museums and galleries, and Work 19 on the royal palaces; precise references can be found in the notes to the text. Drawings for government offices are preserved in Work 30, for parks in Work 32, for museums and educational buildings in Work 33 and for the royal palaces in Work 34; other drawings can be found in the categories LRRO 1, MPD, MPE, MPEE, MPI and MR.

Most of the original papers relating to Pennethorne's parks are kept in the Greater London Record Office. For the National Gallery the Trustees' minute books preserved in the Gallery itself are invaluable, and for the London University building in Burlington Gardens the minutes of the University senate and committees preserved in the library of the present Senate House in Malet Street are equally useful. The library of the British Geological Survey contains papers and drawings relating to the Geological Museum in Jermyn Street. Other relevant manuscript sources and drawings in public collections are referred to in the notes to the text and the list of executed works in Appendix 1. For Pennethorne's work for the royal family the Royal Archives at Windsor are an important source. The main sources of information in private hands are the notebooks and miscellaneous papers belonging to Mr Peter Laing.

Among official publications the most valuable by far are Hansard's *Parliamentary Debates* and the voluminous *Parliamentary Papers*, details of which are given in the notes to the text. Other important printed primary sources are the volumes of *The Builder* and *Building News*, the *Companion to the Almanac* (1831–51), *The Illustrated London News* and the *Transactions* of the Royal Institute of British Architects, especially for 1 July 1856, 9 Feb. 1857, 21 Feb. 1859, 29 May 1865 and 18 Dec. 1871.

Most of the working drawings for Pennethorne's buildings are kept in the Public Record Office. Preliminary designs and drawings of unexecuted projects are scattered around several public and private collections; locations, where applicable, are indicated in the List of illustrations and in Appendix 1. The most comprehensive collections of photographs are in the Greater London Record Office and Photographic Library and in the National Monuments Record (currently at Fortress House, Savile Row). I have also gained great benefit, and pleasure, from working through that most fascinating of visual sources for the London topographer, the Crace Collection in the British Museum Print Room.

SELECT BIBLIOGRAPHY

This list contains the books and articles which are most valuable for understanding Pennethorne's work and its historical context. The place of publication is London, except where otherwise stated. For books referring more specifically to individual works the reader is directed to the notes to the text and to the references in Appendix 1.

Ames, W., *Prince Albert and Victorian Taste* (1967).

Barker, F. and Hyde, R., *London as it might have been* (1982).

Barker, T. C. and Robbins, R. M., *A History of London Transport* (1963).

Chadwick, G. F., *The Park and the Town* (1966).

Colvin, H. M., *A Biographical Dictionary of British Architects 1600–1840* (1978).

Crook, J. M. and Port, M. H., *The History of the King's Works*, VI (1973).

Dyos, H. J. and Woolf, M., *The Victorian City, Image and Reality* (1973).

Dyos, H. J., 'The objects of street improvements in Regency and Early Victorian London', in D. Cannadine and D. Reeder (eds.), *Exploring the Urban Past* (1982).

Girouard, M., *Cities and People* (New Haven and London, 1985).

Goodhart-Rendel, H. S., *English Architecture since the Regency* (1953).

[Hall, E.], 'Pennethorne and public improvements', *Mechanics' Magazine*, 7 and 14 October 1871.

Hitchcock, H.-R., *Early Victorian Architecture in Britain* (New Haven, 1954).

  Architecture: Nineteenth and Twentieth Centuries (3rd edn, Harmondsworth, 1971).

Hobhouse, H., *Prince Albert: His Life and Work* (1983).

Hyde, R. and Hoole, J., *Getting London into Perspective* (Barbican Art Gallery exhibition catalogue, 1984).

Middleton, R. and Watkins, D., *Neoclassical and 19th Century Architecture* (New York, 1980).

Olsen, D., *The Growth of Victorian London* (1976).

  The City as a Work of Art (New Haven and London, 1986).

Owen, D., *The Government of Victorian London* (Cambridge, Mass., 1982).

Parris, H., *Constitutional Bureaucracy* (1969).

Physick, J. and Darby, M., *Marble Halls* (V & A exhibition catalogue, 1973).

Port, M. H., 'A contrast in styles at the Office of Works', *Historical Journal*, 27 (1984).

    'A regime for public buildings: experiments in the Office of Works, 1869–75', *Architectural History*, 27 (1984).

    'Public building in a Parliamentary State', *London Journal*, 11 (1) (1985).

Pugh, R. B., *The Crown Estate* (1960).

Richardson, A. E., *Monumental Classic Architecture in Great Britain and Ireland* (1914).

Roseveare, H., *The Treasury: the Evolution of a British Institution* (1969).

Sheppard, F., *London 1808–1870: the Infernal Wen* (1971).

Summerson, J., *The Life and Works of John Nash, Architect* (1980).

    Georgian London (1978 edn).

    The London Building World in the 1860s (1973).

The Survey of London:

    16, *Charing Cross* (1935).

    20, *Trafalgar Square and Neighbourhood* (1940).

    21, *Tottenham Court Road and Neighbourhood* (1949).

    27, *Spitalfields and Mile End New Town* (1957).

    29–30, *St James, Westminster*, part 1 (1960).

    31, *St James, Westminster*, part 2 (1963).

    34, *St Anne, Soho* (1966).

    36, *St Paul, Covent Garden* (1970).

    37, *Northern Kensington* (1973).

    38, *The Museums Area of South Kensington* (1975).

Thornbury, W. and Walford, E., *Old and New London*, 6 vols. (1873).

Tyack, G., 'Sir James Pennethorne and London street improvements', *London Journal*, 15 (1) (1990).

Weinreb, B. and Hibbert, C. (eds.), *The London Encyclopedia* (1983).

Wheatley, H. B. and Cunningham, P., *London Past and Present*, 3 vols. (1891).

INDEX

Figures in italics refer to pages on which there are illustrations. All places referred to are in London unless otherwise stated.